Canon Lenses: From Snapshots to Great Shots

Canon Lenses: From Snapshots to Great Shots

Jerod Foster

Peachpit Press

Canon Lenses: From Snapshots to Great Shots
Jerod Foster

Peachpit Press
www.peachpit.com

To report errors, please send a note to errata@peachpit.com
Peachpit Press is a division of Pearson Education

Acquisitions Editor: Ted Waitt
Senior Editor: Susan Rimerman
Senior Production Editor: Lisa Brazieal
Development/Copyeditor: Suki Gear
Proofreader: Elaine Merrill
Composition: WolfsonDesign
Indexer: James Minkin
Cover Image: Jerod Foster
Cover Design: Aren Straiger
Interior Design: Mimi Heft

ISBN-13: 978-0-133-90407-9
ISBN-10: 0-133-90407-5

9 8 7 6 5 4 3 2 1
Printed and bound in the United States of America

Dedication

To my daughter Lola Mae, I love you.

Acknowledgments

It takes a team of great individuals to put together a project like this one, and I'm lucky to have worked with the wonderful folks at Peachpit for several of these books! Specifically, I would like to thank Susan Rimerman, Suki Gear, Lisa Brazieal, Elaine Merrill, James Minkin, Ted Waitt, and Sara Todd. I couldn't ask for a better team, and their patience with my travels and assignment work was invaluable in making sure the book stayed on the rails. Thank you, all.

Thanks also to my friends at Armadillo Camera for their generous support in lending me some lenses that I don't actually own. Steve, Larry, Wayne, and Raymond are the kind of fellows you want in your own local camera shop, and they were a great resource along the way.

Many thanks to the College of Media and Communication at Texas Tech University. I've been lucky the past few years to serve as a professor in the Department of Journalism and Electronic Media, teaching students photography all over the world and getting to share my passion for storytelling with thousands. Thanks especially to Dean David Perlmutter, PhD, and Todd Chambers, PhD, for affording me the opportunity to both work and teach in a great industry.

A large amount of gratitude goes to my wife, Amanda, and my two daughters, Eva and Lola Mae. Your support means the world to me, and your patience is infinite. Thanks for not only being a part of this project, but also for the continual love and encouragement you give me in every endeavor. Thank you will never be enough for you three. I love you very much!

Finally, thanks to anyone else who had a role in making this project come together—LIGHT Creative Co-Studio, Mike, Seth, Naomi, Alan, and countless others. Thank you.

Contents

Introduction

Photography just wouldn't be the same without the glass. Sure, we could make images without lenses, but then we'd be stuck with simple blobs of light and color. Lenses help us focus that light into discernable imagery. This book is all about how to make the most of the lenses we have in order to create art and tell the story of our environment and the people we encounter.

When executive editor Ted Waitt and I first sat down to discuss this project, it was clear that within the Snapshots to Great Shots series there was a need for a book on Canon lenses to complement the great texts on various Canon camera-body models. Those books discuss lenses, but they are more about helping the reader become acquainted with the camera and photography in general.

What's Covered in This Book?

Chapter 1 highlights the top factors to consider when using and shopping for Canon lenses, serving as a quick guide to the technology. Chapter 2 gets more technical and defines important terminology related to lenses and their use, such as depth of field, plane of critical focus, and perspective.

The next four chapters highlight different categories of Canon lenses based on their focal lengths (Chapters 3 through 5) and specialty purpose (Chapter 6). These chapters are where the rubber meets road, so to speak. They identify why certain lenses work well for specific types of photography, address key issues to consider when using lenses, and ultimately (my goal) help the reader start to produce great images using different focal lengths.

Lastly, Chapters 7 and 8 are resources. Chapter 7 highlights useful and even essential accessories to have when shooting, such as teleconverters, extension tubes, and several types of popular filters. Chapter 8 is a practical extension of Chapter 1 in that it covers in detail several best practices photographers can employ when using and maintaining their lenses.

Make sure to download bonus Chapter 9, "Postprocessing," which identifies several strong functions of Adobe Lightroom that can be used to correct lens issues and/or creatively apply lens effects to your images. First log in or create an account on Peachpit.com (it's free), then enter the book ISBN (9780133904079) on this page: peachpit.com/store/register.aspx. After you register the book, a link to access bonus content will appear next to the book on your Account page in the Registered Products tab. NOTE: If you purchased an ebook, you're covered—the chapter is already included.

Not a Technical Manual

This book serves as a great companion to other books centered around particular Canon camera models, but it also stands alone as a resource for getting the most out of your lenses. The book is chock-full of techniques and visual examples of lens use. Like all Snapshots to Great Shots books, this book is fairly anecdotal and refrains from being too technical, instead opting to show you how you can creatively employ your gear to achieve the images you want. The majority of images you see in the book were made on assignment or for stock image use, and I relate the text to the focal length and/or technique used for each.

This book is not a lens catalog, either. I provide tips on shopping for Canon lenses, and I offer up my preferred selection in each category (in sidebars titled "If I Had to Choose"), but if you're looking for a discussion on every lens manufactured, head to Canon's website.

Have Fun and Experiment

Remember, this book is just a guide. Don't get stuck only using one technique or compositional rule in only one setting. Experimenting is a vital part of developing your own style and photographic vision. My hope is for you to become so comfortable using your lenses that they almost become an extension of your mind. At the end of each chapter, you will find a link to the book's Flickr page, where you can show the rest of the world the fruits of your creative labor! I look forward to seeing your work soon.

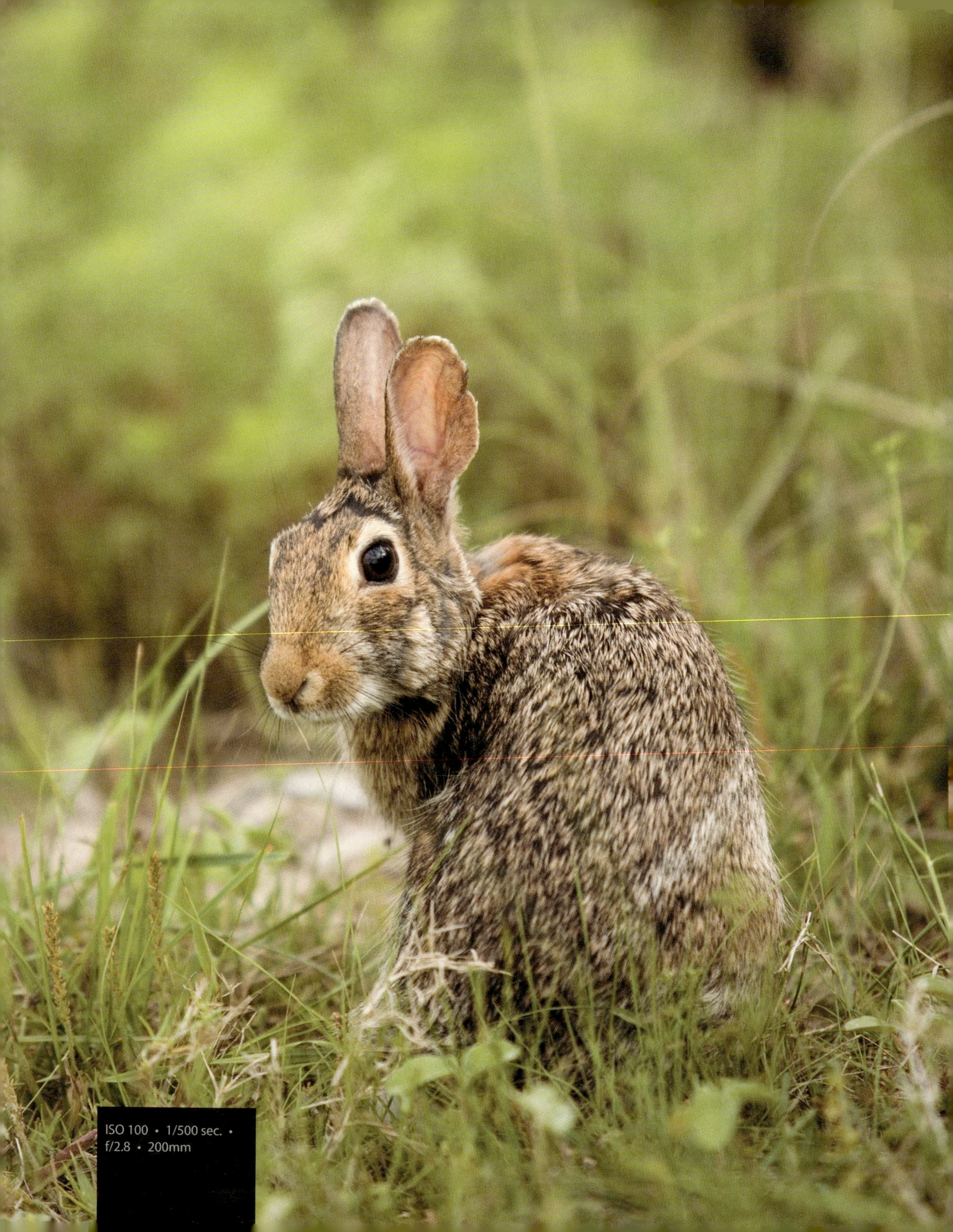

ISO 100 • 1/500 sec. •
f/2.8 • 200mm

1

The Canon Lenses

Top seven considerations

Photography wouldn't be much without lenses. Sure, you can make images without them, but if you want something more than just a blob of light and color, lenses come in quite handy. All you really need to make images is light, a way to focus the light, and something to capture or fixate the light. A lens's basic function is to channel a reflection of light through a number of pieces of glass (referred to as elements) and project it on the sensor or film. But lenses do so much more than just focus light.

Used well, they help bring our creative vision to some sort of reality. Lenses are an essential part of the photography equation. Each lens has its special use, and when pushing the limits of that use, all lenses offer creative routes to making great images!

Consider the following seven issues not only for researching and purchasing a new lens for your camera body, but also for learning about and using lenses in a way that resembles how a skilled artisan uses her tools.

Poring Over the Lens

Lens Front

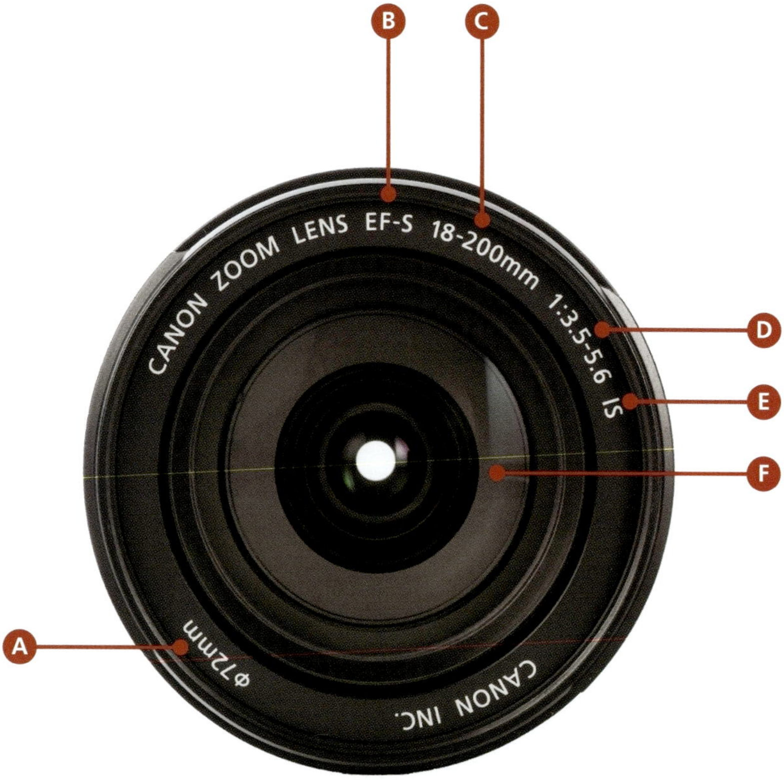

A Filter size

B Lens type (EF or EF-S)

C Focal length

D Maximum aperture value

E Indicator of Image Stabilization–equipped lens

F Front lens element

Lens Side

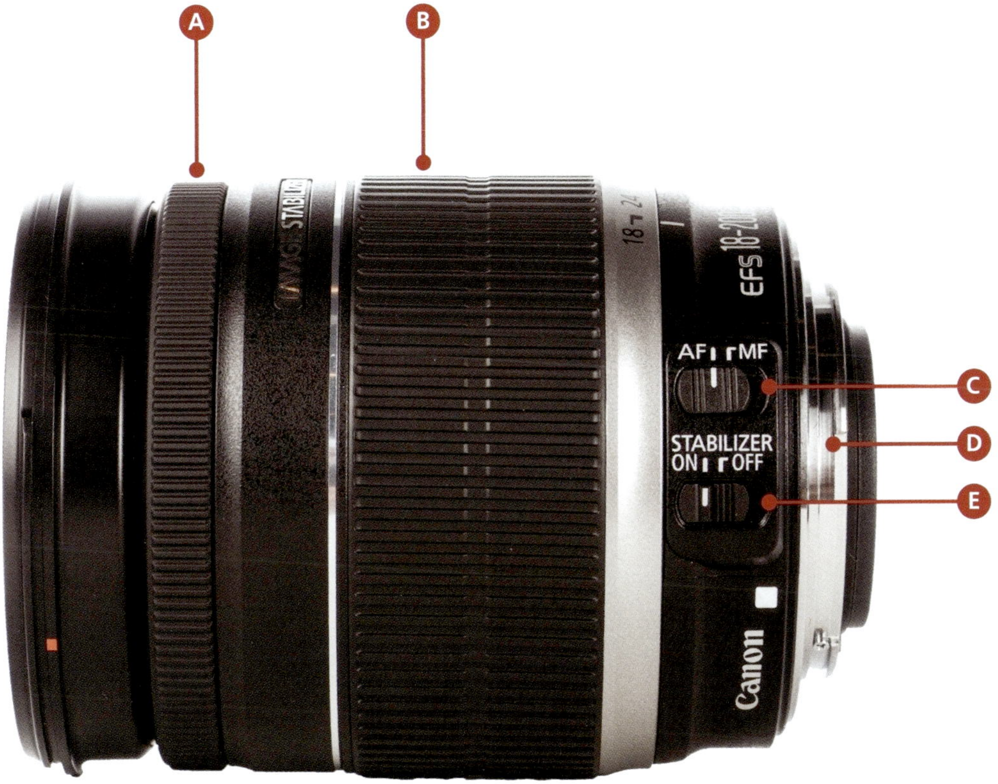

A Focus ring
B Zoom ring
C Auto/Manual Focus switch
D Lens mount
E Image Stabilization switch (only on IS-equipped lenses)

Lens Rear

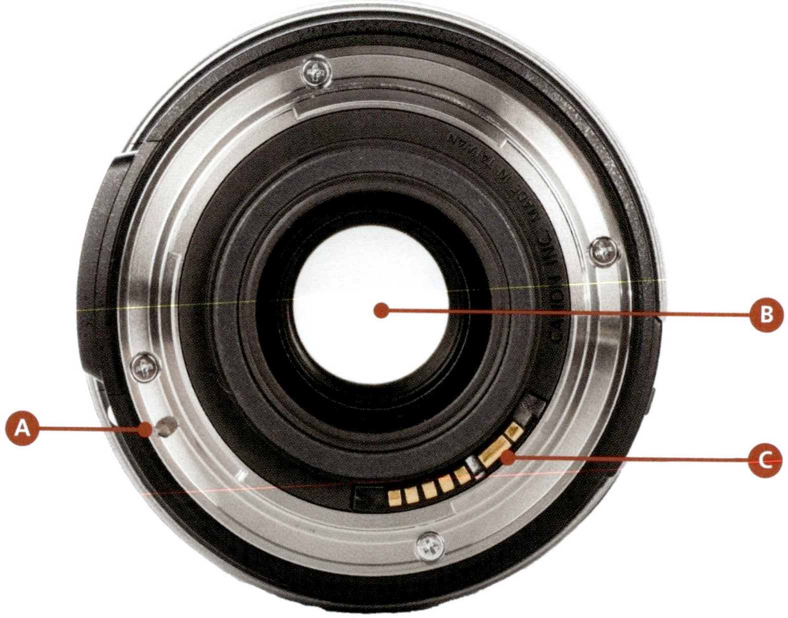

A Lens mount lock

B Rear lens element

A Lens contact points (transmits information between the lens and camera body)

1. Fast vs. Slow Lenses

Within all Canon lenses, there is something called the aperture. More specifically, the mechanism that makes up the aperture is the diaphragm, a ring of overlapping, thin metal plates that either close down or remain open during exposure. For the sake of clarity, we refer to this mechanism as the aperture.

The aperture controls two things: how much light is let in through the lens and exposed on the sensor (or film), and depth of field, or how much of the shot is in focus. We'll discuss these two points in the next chapter.

Lenses are often described as either fast or slow, based on their maximum aperture openings. When making an exposure in any given light condition, the larger, or more open, the aperture is, the *faster* the shutter speed needs to be. When you allow a large amount of light to pass through the lens, you need to cut it off more quickly for a proper exposure. Conversely, an aperture that is closed, or stopped down in that same light condition requires a *slower* shutter speed to create the exact same exposure (**Figures 1.1** and **1.2**). Essentially, faster lenses are those with large maximum apertures, and those that cannot open up as much are referred to as slower lenses.

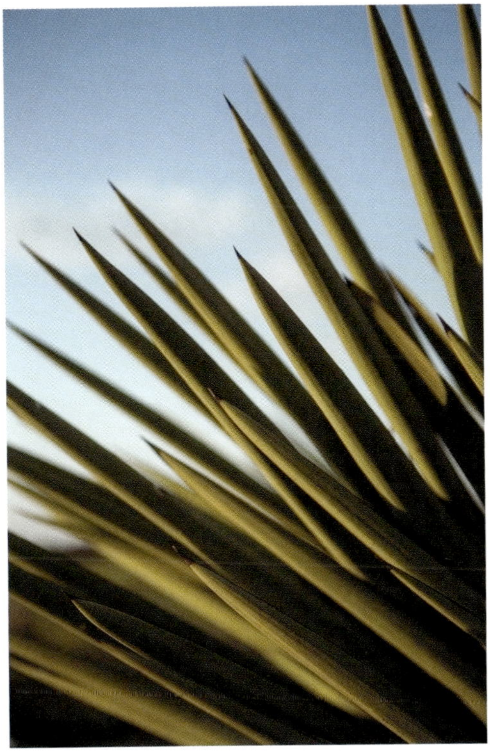

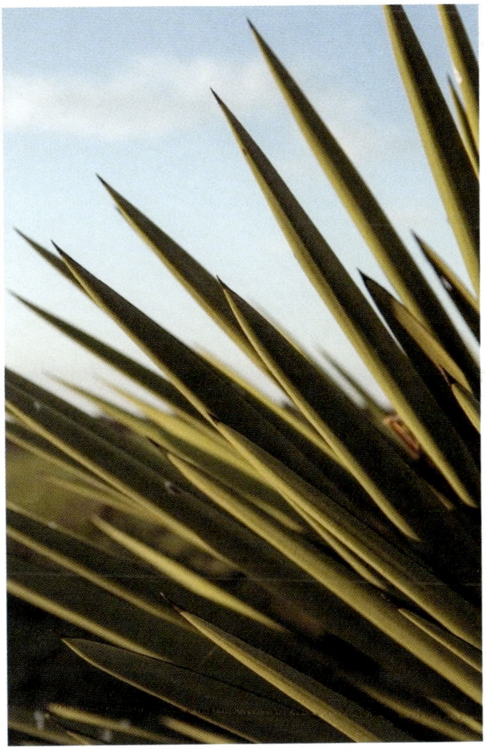

Figure 1.1 (left)
At f/2.8, the lens's aperture is considered fast since it allows much more light in at one time than a slower aperture value, such as f/5.6 (see Figure 1.2).

ISO 200 • 1/1000 sec. • f/2.8 • 46mm

Figure 1.2 (right)
An aperture value of f/5.6 is two stops slower than f/2.8, meaning the shutter speed used in this shot is two stops slower than the speed used in Figure 1.1.

ISO 200 • 1/250 sec. • f/5.6 • 46mm

Canon makes several variations on many of their lenses, and much of the variance between them is aperture based. For example, there are three different 50mm lenses in the Canon lineup: the flagship 50mm f/1.2L, the 50mm f/1.4, and the 50mm f/1.8 (also known as the "nifty fifty"). The number following the f-stop is used to identify the maximum aperture opening—the lower the number, the larger the opening.

The 50mm f/1.2L is the fastest of the 50s, and the 50 f/1.8 is the slowest. Practically speaking, the 50mm f/1.2L—at its maximum aperture—lets in more light and allows the shooter to use faster shutter speeds than the other two 50s allow. This comes in handy when shooting in low-light conditions (**Figure 1.3**). As we'll discuss later, faster lenses are also valuable on the sports field.

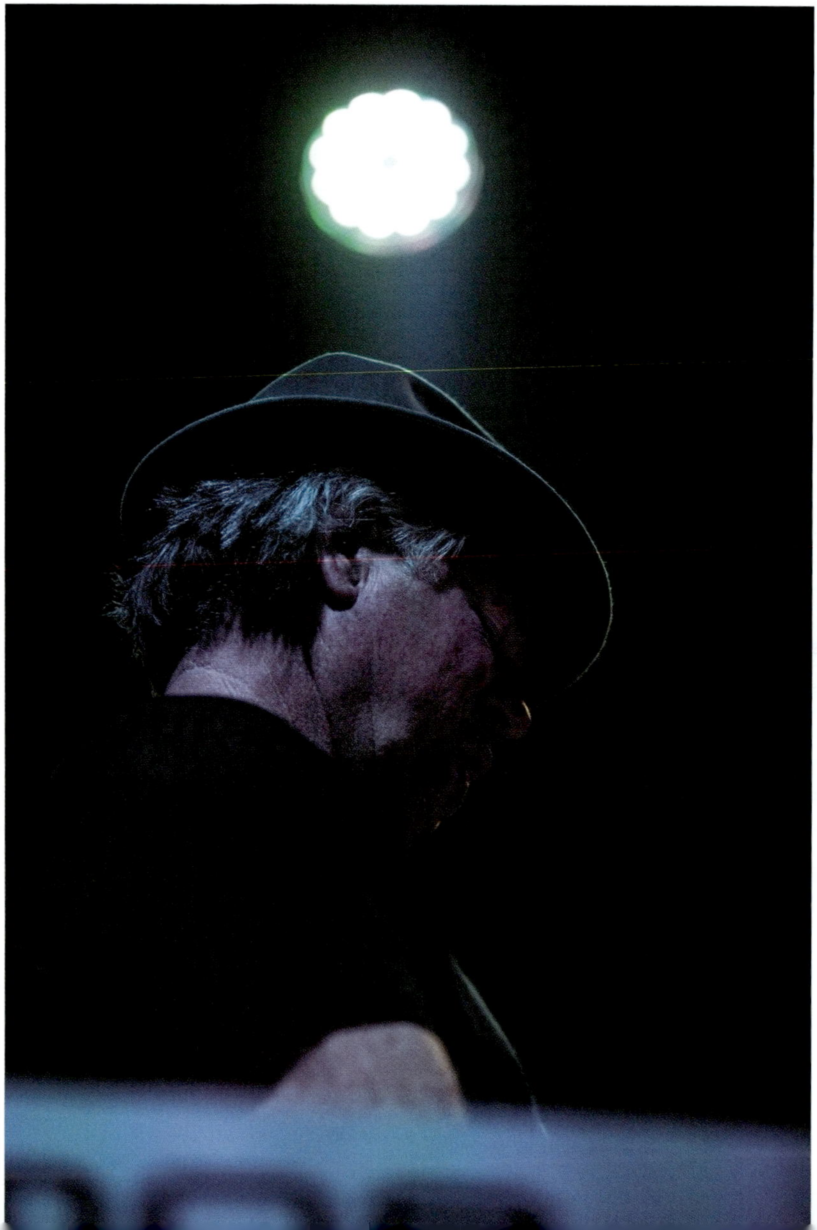

Figure 1.3
Shooting live music requires a fast aperture to freeze the action and handhold longer lenses, even if the shot is a tight headshot of a keyboard player.

ISO 2000 • 1/320 sec. • f/2.8 • 93mm

These three lenses are non-zoom lenses (also known as prime lenses, covered later in this chapter). Canon also manufactures many great zoom lenses, and in doing so, introduces another issue—lens speed. Some lenses, such as the 24–70mm L and the 70–200mm L have a fixed f/2.8 maximum aperture opening. However, other lenses, such as the 18–55mm f/3.5–5.6 and the 70–300mm f/4–5.6, have what is commonly known as *variable maximum apertures.* Simply put, lenses with variable maximum apertures will close down their maximum aperture as they are zoomed in to the scene. For example, when shooting with an 18–55mm f/3.5–5.6 lens at 18mm—the widest focal length on that lens—the maximum aperture is f/3.5. When zoomed in to 55mm, though, the maximum aperture changes to f/5.6. Along the zoom range, as the focal length increases, the maximum aperture changes to a slower aperture.

These types of lenses are fairly common, and the variable maximum aperture is a result of using smaller-diameter lens elements in the lens, which subsequently keeps costs down. It's worth noting here that the faster the lens, the more expensive it is. It takes more materials to manufacture faster lenses—more glass, more housing for that glass—since the diameter of the lenses are larger. Oftentimes, the fastest lenses are reserved for the L series. These lenses are made with premium materials, glass being just one of them (more on this subject later in this chapter as well).

Lens speed also refers to how a lens handles depth of field, so keep in mind that the faster the lens, the more one can theoretically throw the background (and foreground for that matter) out of focus. Consider again the 50mm example above. The 50mm f/1.2L, while set at f/1.2, will produce a softer *bokeh* (the area of the image that goes out of focus when using a faster aperture) than the 50mm f/1.4 and f/1.8 (**Figure 1.4**). It might be a stretch to see the difference between f/1.2 and f/1.4, but it is there. A more extreme example is the difference between the iconic sports lens, the 400mm f/2.8L, and the nimble-yet-razor-sharp 400mm f/5.6L. There is a considerable difference between the lowest amounts of depth of field each produces when set to maximum aperture.

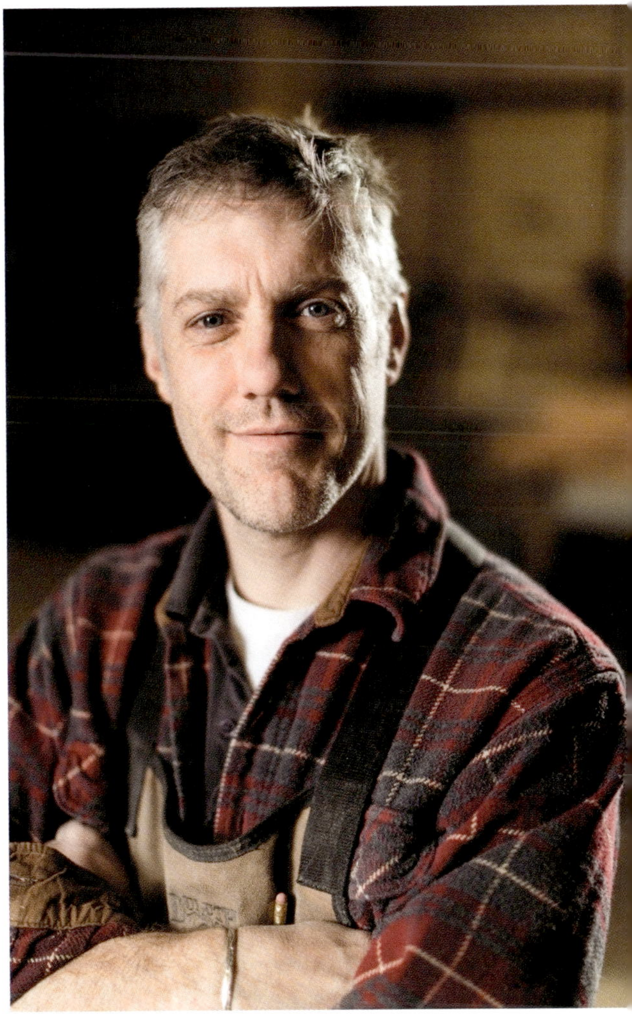

Figure 1.4 **An aperture lower than f/2.8 offers a unique way of isolating portrait subjects from otherwise distracting backgrounds. At f/1.2, there is only a sliver of carpenter Jason Duby in focus, while the rest of the foreground and background soften drastically.**

ISO 50 • 1/200 sec. • f/1.2 • 50mm

2. Full-Frame vs. Crop Sensors

Even if you're new to the world of digital single-lens reflex (DSLR) photography, you've probably heard a comparison between full-frame and crop sensors. It might not have meant much to you when purchasing your first camera, but it certainly means a lot in regard to the use of lenses and your future lens purchases.

Full-Frame Sensors

A full-frame sensor is the same size as a 35mm film frame—just think of the film shot in many pre-digital cameras. You can find full-frame sensors in Canon camera models such as the 6D, the 5D (all versions), the 1D-X, and all of the older 1D-S models. For those photographers moving from film SLR cameras (and many other types of cameras) to a DSLR, a full-frame sensor does not affect how you use your lenses and see your images, and you can more than likely use the same lenses, as long as they are designated as EF glass. For many, a full-frame sensor is much desired for many reasons beyond how it correlates with the use of our lenses, particularly among portrait and landscape photographers and photojournalists.

Crop Sensors

A crop sensor shares the same rectangular perspective (often referred to as the 3:2 ratio) but is considerably smaller. How much smaller? For Canon crop-sensor cameras, a bit more than 50 percent smaller. At the time of writing, Canon makes only one size of crop sensor, known as an APS-C sensor (**Figure 1.5**). These sensors can be found in anything "below" the 5D lineup, such as the Rebel series, the 70D (and its previous iterations), and the 7D. Up until a few years ago, Canon also manufactured another, larger crop sensor known as an APS-H sensor. It was exclusively reserved for the 1D lineup until Canon introduced the 1D-X, at which point the APS-H sensor disappeared from production.

The size difference for crop sensors is determined by the sensor's *crop factor*. This is where the sensor matters when it comes to lenses. A Canon APS-C crop sensor has a crop factor of 1.6x (the now-discontinued APS-H has a 1.3x crop factor). The larger the crop factor, the smaller the sensor. For the crop factor to become relevant in this case, you must multiply the focal length of the lens by 1.6 to determine the actual focal perspective in which you are shooting. Sounds confusing, and it is unless you see it for yourself!

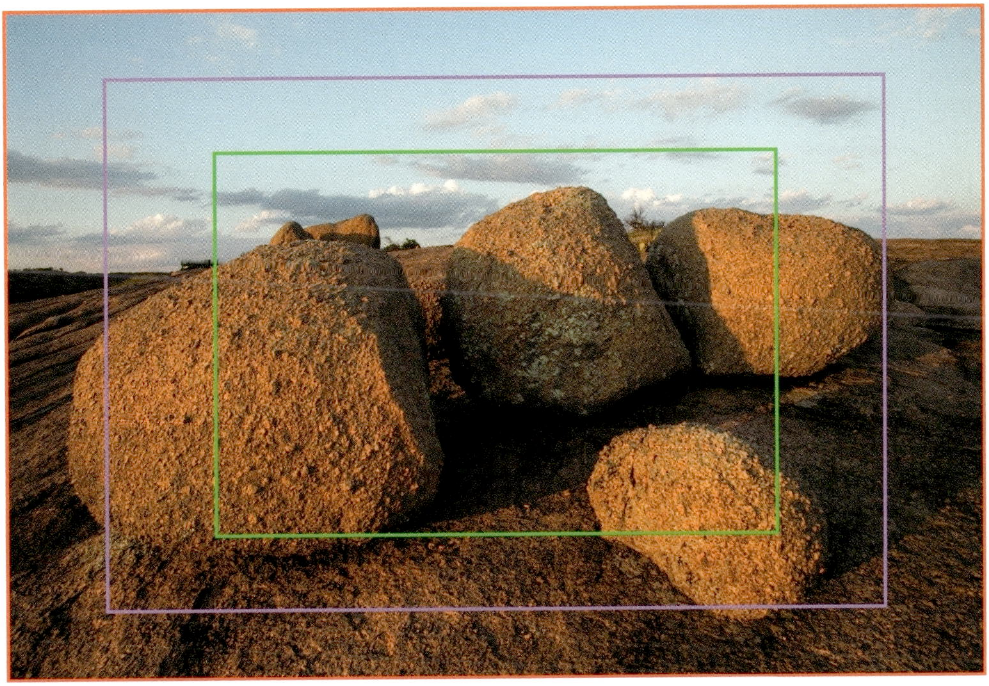

Figure 1.5 **This image represents what you would capture using the three different-sized Canon sensors. The red stroke represents a full-frame shot made at 17mm. When using the same lens, and APS-H sensor (purple stroke) captures a bit-tighter shot because of its 1.3x crop. Even tighter is the APS-C sensor's crop (green stroke), offering a roughly 32mm perspective.**

Let's say you are using a 50mm focal length on both a full-frame camera, such as the Canon 6D, and on an APS-C crop-sensor camera, such as the Canon 70D. For the full-frame camera, which has a crop factor of 1x, the perspective provided when looking through and shooting with the 50mm focal length is actually 50mm. However, for the 70D, we must multiply the focal length, 50mm, by the crop factor, 1.6, to determine the visual perspective with which we're shooting: 80mm. Since the crop sensor chops a considerable amount of sensor away from a full-frame chip's perimeter, the area of the lens now used can be equated to an 80mm lens on a full-frame sensor. If you are using a crop-sensor camera, multiply any focal length by 1.6 (or 1.3 if you have an APS-H camera), and you'll find out what the equivalent perspective is on a full-frame camera.

A crop sensor does not actually magnify the focal length of any lens. It simply crops the sides, top, and bottom of the lens's angle of view. However, crop-sensor cameras are a big hit with folks in the sports and wildlife photography arenas, because compared to a full-frame camera that packs the same resolution (megapixels) as a crop-sensor camera, the crop sensor provides a bit further "reach" when looking at two images of the same size. This is not magnification, just simply the result of two different-sized sensors of the same resolution being combined with the same focal length.

Putting Them in Perspective

So, practically speaking, how does this affect you? It really all depends on which camera you are using. If you are shooting with a full-frame Canon camera, the focal length of the lens with which you are shooting is going to result in that true perspective. However, on a crop-sensor camera, the perspective you get when putting any lens on the camera is simply not as "wide" as it would be on the former type of camera. There is nothing wrong with a crop-sensor camera. They are more affordable because of manufacturing costs, and many are built with the same structural quality as their full-frame versions. However, the next time you read online that an ultra-wide image was shot with a Canon EF 16–35mm f/2.8L on a Canon 5D Mark III, you might consider looking into a Canon EF-S 10–22mm f/3.5–4.5 for your Canon Rebel T5i. At 10mm with this latter combo, you are actually achieving the 16mm perspective of the former's image.

Wait, we're not done with this subject yet! To make it even more complicated, Canon makes a set of lenses that work exclusively with their APS-C crop-sensor cameras. Whereas all EF-marked lenses work on both full-frame and crop-sensor cameras, EF-S lenses only work on crop-sensor cameras. The EF-S lenses are fewer in number, but Canon tries to accommodate crop-sensor camera owners by offering equivalents to some of the most popular EF lenses (such as the previous example). Typically, EF-S lenses are more affordable than their EF counterparts, but if you are thinking about upgrading your camera body from a crop-sensor to full-frame sensor unit, you might hold out for EF glass instead of purchasing a lens that might be useless in the near future. This is one of the deficiencies of moving to a full-frame sensor camera system: Some, if not all, lenses might also need to be updated (or upgraded) to fit the new camera. Usually, photographers see this as a valuable transition from one system to the other, but it does come at a premium.

3. Autofocus vs. Manual Focus

The majority of lenses being manufactured today are capable of being used in either autofocus or manual focus mode. Canon does not make a single lens for their DSLR cameras that isn't capable of both. This wasn't always the case. Before Canon helped pioneer autofocus systems, it produced all-manual-focus FD lenses. FD lenses are antiques these days, some of which—if kept in good condition—still work well with older all-manual cameras, as well as newer cameras with the help of a mount conversion adapter.

After the development of autofocus, Canon began producing its current line of lenses, known as EF lenses. EF lenses, aside from having a new mount that fits on Canon's EOS system cameras (just think of pretty much any camera Canon makes these days that allows the interchangeability of lenses), can be put into autofocus mode or manual focus mode with the flick of a switch on the lens barrel.

Now, if you are a purist, you might be thinking, "Why would I ever want to shoot in autofocus mode?" To which my reply would be, "Why would you ever want to shoot solely in manual focus mode?" There is value in shooting in both modes, and knowing when to move to one or the other will help capture the image you want without undue frustration with your technology.

Autofocus is a fantastic innovation for camera technology—a paradigm shifter. It allows us to be efficient in shooting and more accurate in many cases. When subject matter is in motion, such as a running horse (**Figure 1.6**) or football player, autofocus is an innovation I do not like to go without. My "good" shot rate increases in circumstances where autofocus can be used, as opposed to manually focusing on such subject matter.

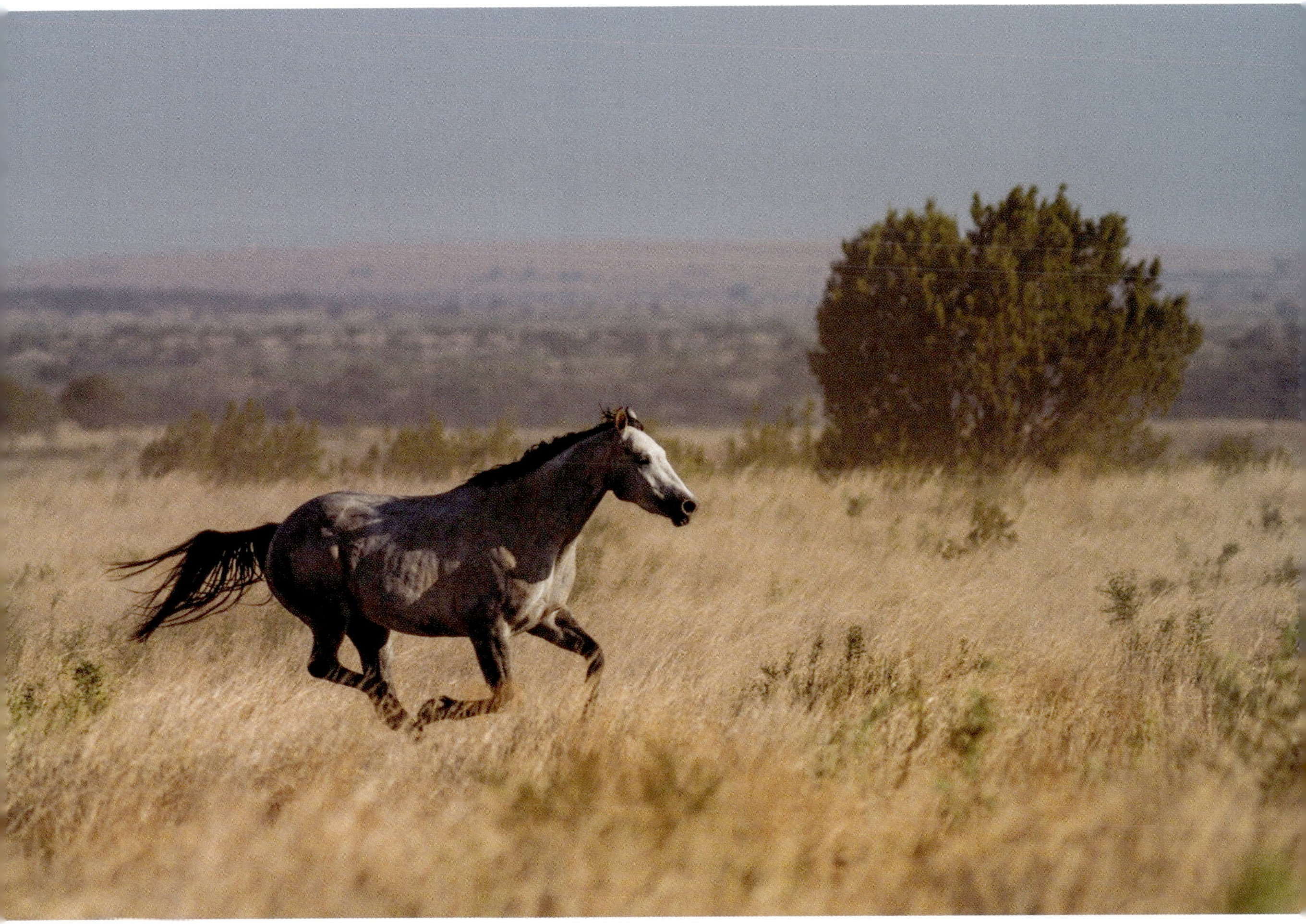

Figure 1.6 Continuous autofocus was necessary for me to capture this horse running fast and at an angle that closed the distance between us. Although possible, manually focusing this event would have presented a few more challenges and a lot more missed shots.

ISO 100 • 1/800 sec. • f/5.6 • 400mm

However, there are times when manual focus is indeed your best option. Autofocus in Canon DSLRs works well when there is enough contrast (the difference between light tones) on or between subject matter that the *camera* is able to detect. There are times when subject matter lacks enough contrast for the autofocus to work properly, leaving you with a lens—and really a camera—searching for focus. Low-light situations, such as dimly lit concerts or nighttime landscapes, come to mind (**Figure 1.7**). In these instances, flicking the switch on the lens to manual focus puts you in full control of the lens's focal plane.

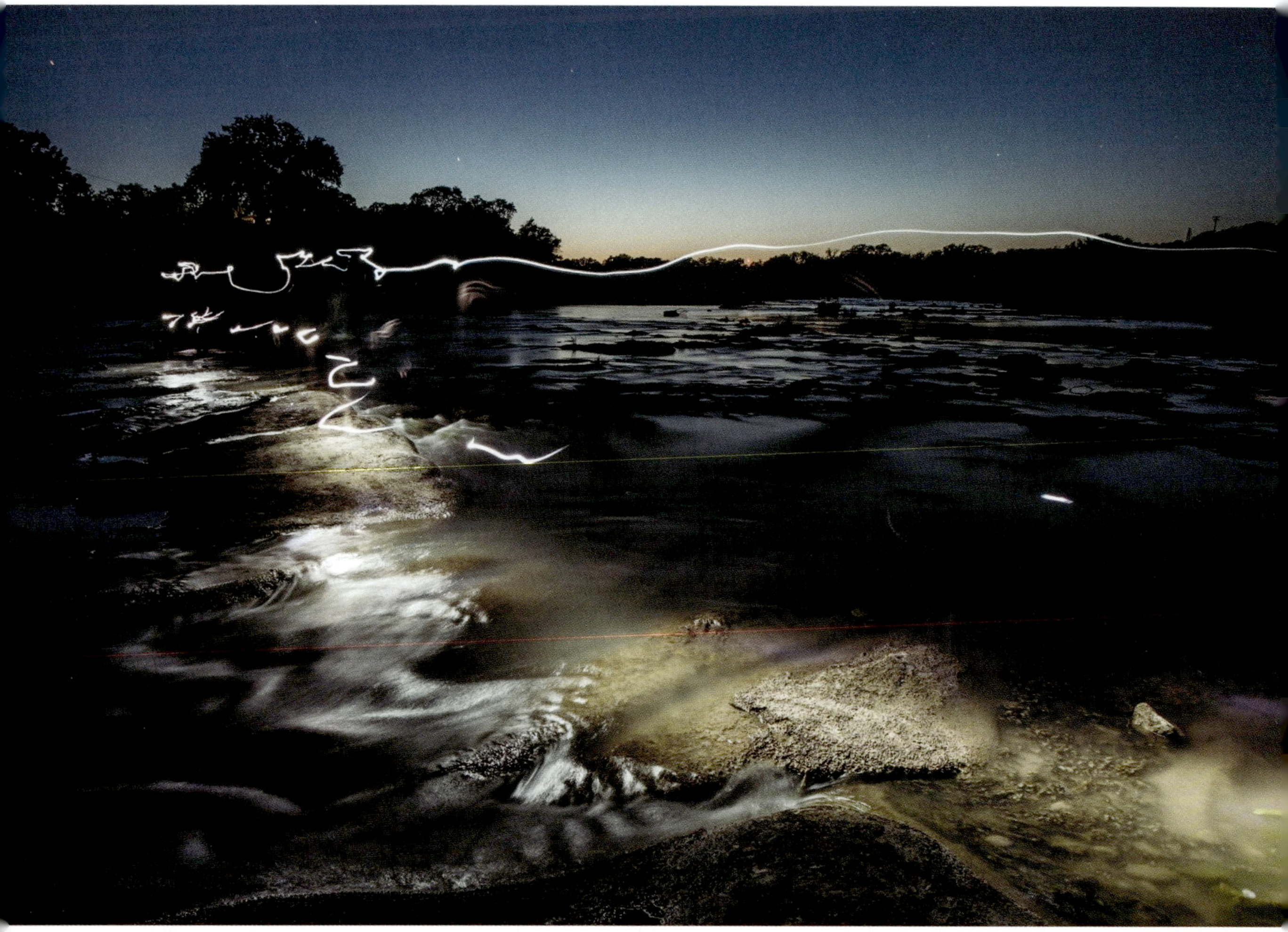

Figure 1.7 For a timed exposure of some adventurous photography students crossing the Llano River, I set my camera on a tripod and switched my lens to manual focus to maintain a steady shot and to keep the lens from "hunting" focus.

ISO 800 • 30 secs. • f/11 • 17mm

Shooting macro (extreme close-up) photography also benefits greatly from manual focus mode. There is nothing more frustrating to this nature photographer than trying to autofocus on the petals of a flower that is occasionally bumped by a soft breeze. Autofocus will continually search for something to focus on, even if the autofocus mode is turned to One Shot in the camera. This isn't easy on the eyes.

You can also use autofocus and manual focus together to achieve a single image. When shooting landscapes for which you want maximum depth of field, it is often helpful to use autofocus to focus exactly one-third into the scene (more on *hyperfocal distance* in the next chapter) and then switch to manual to keep the same focal plane when recomposing the frame. I do this when I intend to set up for a while—such as capturing a really large thunderstorm or light painting a structure—and want to make multiple exposures without refocusing for each shot.

In the end, using autofocus or manual focus is based largely on user preference. I am in autofocus 90 percent of the time. Over time, I've become used to the different autofocus modes Canon cameras allow the shooter to use, and I'm extremely comfortable in "AF." However, if manual focus is the wheelhouse in which you find yourself, then use it!

4. Prime vs. Zoom

Speaking of things purists and non-purists alike are passionate about, discussing the difference and overall value of prime lenses versus zoom lenses can cause some photographers to have a conniption. Many times, this argument is focused on which is sharper, lighter, or more true to the roots of photography. Nevertheless, photographers prefer to shoot with one or the other, or a combination of the two.

Prime Lenses

Prime lenses are those that are limited to only one focal length (**Figure 1.8**). The first camera lenses ever were prime lenses, and they are still very popular, especially among those wanting lighter loads and incredibly shallow depth of field. Prime lenses have fewer moving parts than zoom lenses, making them easy to carry around (aside from the super telephoto lenses), smaller (again, aside from the big glass), and less intrusive to subject matter (super telephotos might as well have red flags flying atop). Since they have fewer moving parts, and fewer pieces of glass or lens elements that might be moving otherwise, prime lens are arguably sharper than zoom lenses.

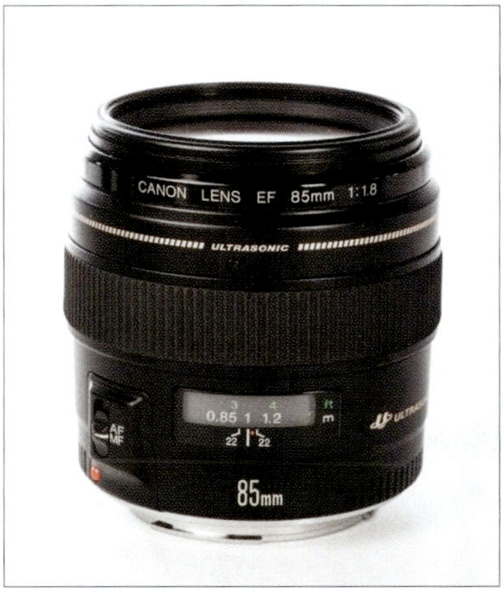

Figure 1.8 **Prime lenses, like this EF 85mm f/1.8 L, are appealing to many photographers for their size and quality.**

There are plenty of focus charts online and research on the subject. When you nail focus with prime lenses, especially at very large apertures, they *are* sharp. Perhaps the sharpness is heightened by the extreme bokeh. And when it comes to bokeh, prime lenses cannot be beat. At only one focal length, manufacturing is capable of building lenses that have very wide maximum apertures. Whereas the maximum aperture opening of any zoom lens Canon makes is f/2.8, some prime lenses open up all the way to f/1.2, a whole two-and-a-third stops more open. Talk about great lenses for low-light conditions and isolating subject matter from an environment!

Prime lenses are not without their issues. Some prime lenses do not allow stopping their aperture down more than f/8 (such as the EF 50mm f/1.2L and the EF 85mm f/1.2L). This might pose problems for the photographer looking to achieve hyperfocal distance depth of field, albeit the lenses that stop at f/8 are not ideal for landscapes and other types of photography that maximize depth of field. Prime lenses, as their name indicates, are also limited to just the one focal length. This isn't necessarily a negative, unless you are the type of shooter who requires a range of focal lengths but doesn't have room in the camera bag—nor the budget—for every prime lens available. Prime-lens advocates encourage those wanting the flexibility and convenience of zoom lenses to "zoom with their feet" and move around in the landscape. However, there are times when the prime lens comes up too short or too long, without the ability to change on the fly. This usually happens to me when I'm using telephotos such as the EF 300mm f/4L or EF 400mm f/2.8L. While shooting football games, these focal lengths are great, until the action comes real close, real fast!

Zoom Lenses

Zoom lenses, on the other hand, offer a range of focal lengths and are many folks' go-to lenses. Consider Canon's EF-S 18–200mm f/3.5–5.6. For crop-sensor camera users, this lens offers enough range for 90 percent of their work. On top of that, it's fairly light and much smaller than the EF 70–200mm f/2.8L and the popular EF 24–105mm f/4L.

Zoom lenses come in all shapes and sizes, and if you just bought a Canon Rebel or another crop-sensor camera, you more than likely combined it with Canon's standard EF-S zoom, the 18–55mm f/3.5–5.6. Many folks also purchase an EF-S 55–250mm f/4–5.6 IS or the affordable telephoto zoom, the EF 75–300mm f/4–5.6. With just two of these lenses, a shooter has an entire bag full of prime focal lengths—and more—at her disposal. Personally, I carry an EF 24–70mm f/2.8L the majority of the time, and when I'm on assignment where I expect a variety of shots and perspectives, I carry an EF 70–200mm f/2.8L attached to an additional camera body.

However, zoom lenses are anything but invisible. If your goal is to be inconspicuous in a crowd, a long telephoto zoom is probably not the best choice. Higher-end L-series lenses are also much heavier than their prime counterparts, as well as non-L-series zooms. Canon has done a great job in previous years of manufacturing lighter lenses, but big zooms are still heavy (part of which helps stabilize some to be handheld). Lastly, zoom lenses cannot reach the maximum aperture openings of many prime lenses. More expensive, higher-end zooms, such as those mentioned in the previous paragraph, can open up to f/2.8, the largest opening of any zoom lens Canon makes. But this doesn't compare to lower-end, less-expensive primes that open up to f/1.8 or f/1.4.

Which One?

Like shooting in manual focus or autofocus, shooting with prime or zoom lenses is a choice based on preference and shooting style. Ultimately, you might have the best luck working with a combination of the two types, if you have room in your camera bag. If I need a lens that offers as much flexibility as I can possibly squeeze out of it, I'll go with a zoom, particularly if I foresee shots made at multiple focal lengths. If I'm needing a lens that does not get in the way, is easy to carry—and more important, doesn't seem aggressive to my subjects—then a prime lens or two is what I will throw in a small bag. The majority of the time, though, I have a bag with a few zoom lenses and a couple of prime lenses.

5. Minimum Sustaining Shutter Speed

This is a simple issue, and more of a tip, when it comes to working with and even purchasing lenses. *Minimum sustaining shutter speed* refers to the slowest shutter speed one can handhold a lens and maintain focus. Any shutter speed slower may incur camera shake and potentially ruin an otherwise great shot (**Figure 1.9**). When shooting with shutter speeds slower than the minimum sustaining shutter speed, it is best to stabilize the camera by placing it on a monopod, tripod, or anything solid. So, how do you determine minimum sustaining shutter speed? The two determining factors are focal length and your own personal stability.

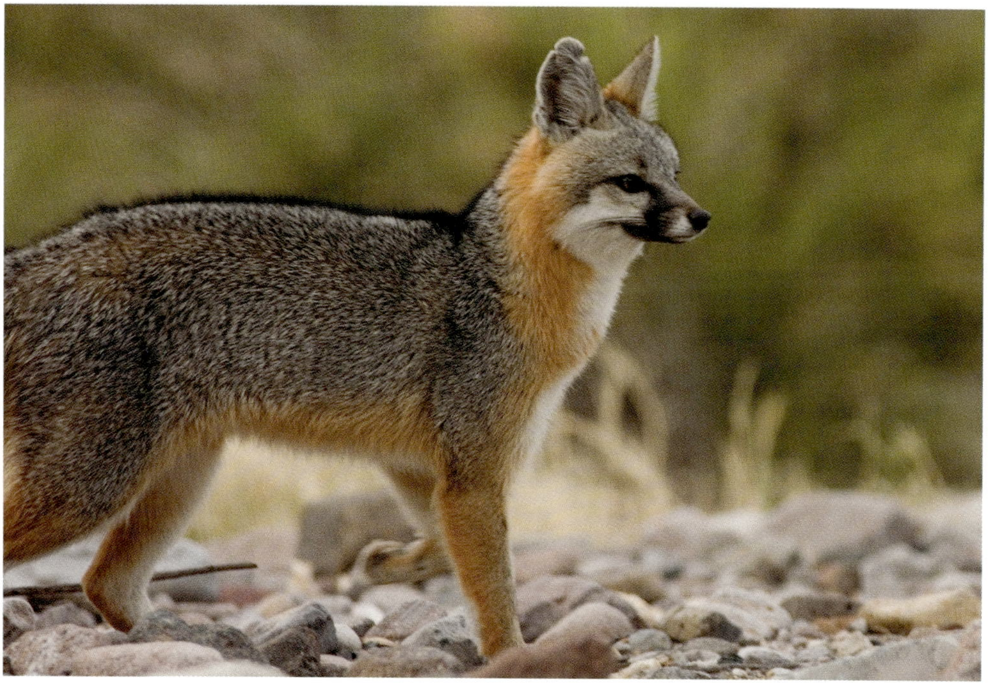

Figure 1.9
This shot of a gray fox is out of focus due to my inability to handhold the 300mm lens I was using at 1/250 of a second shutter speed, just a bit slower than the lens's minimum sustaining shutter speed.

ISO 160 • 1/250 sec. • f/4 • 300mm

Focal Length

The first factor is the most technical and worth keeping in the back of your mind. The minimum sustaining shutter speed is the shutter speed that has a denominator (since shutter speeds are measured in fractions of a second) that is closest to the focal length in which you are shooting. For example, let's say you are shooting at 100mm. Theoretically, a shutter speed of 1/100 of a second is your minimum shutter speed—the slowest you could shoot before your own body shake forces the image out of focus. For a 24mm focal length, 1/30 of a second might work best. For a much longer focal length, such as 400mm, 1/500 of a second might sustain focus.

Personal Stability

A minimum sustaining shutter speed also has a lot to do with your own stability. With experience and technique, and a better sense of balance, some folks can shoot with much slower shutter speeds than those suggested above. When I'm locked in a stable stance, I feel fairly comfortable shooting a 24mm lens, and especially a 16mm lens, at 1/15 of a second. Test your stability while practicing at different focal lengths, slowing your shutter speed down for any given focal length until you notice a big difference. Sometimes you can feel it, but it is best to run through a range of shutter speeds while focusing on the same subject and then review the files on a computer screen. Keep practicing, and your minimum sustaining shutter speed will lower.

Image Stabilization (IS) is a feature of many lenses in the Canon lineup (**Figure 1.10**), allowing photographers to shoot with slower and slower shutter speeds. Lenses with IS—such as the EF 70–200mm f/2.8L IS and the EF 70–300mm f/4–5.6 IS—contain a mechanism that shifts the optics in a way that stabilizes the unsteady hands of the shooter, especially for precarious shutter speeds. In some cases, Canon Image Stabilization claims four stops worth of IS, an amazing amount of stabilizing when you're in a pinch (**Figure 1.11**).

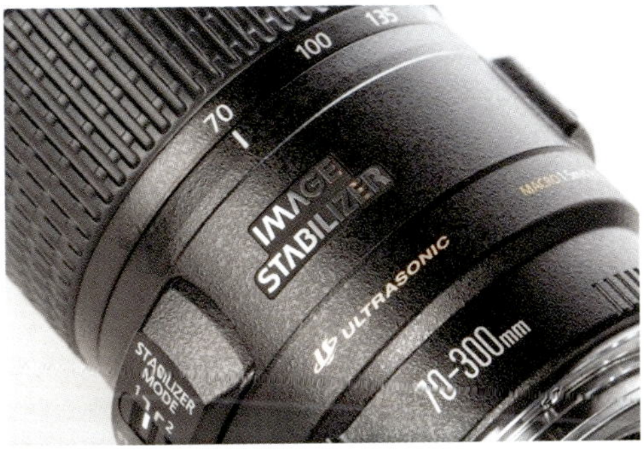

Figure 1.10 Image Stabilization logo on an EF 70–300mm f/4–5.6 IS

There is no rule stating you must shoot at the minimum sustaining shutter speed. In fact, you should shoot with as fast a shutter speed possible given your aperture and ISO. However, some moments call for shooting with slower shutter speeds, and when they do, it is worth knowing where your minimum sustaining shutter speed exists for the focal length in use.

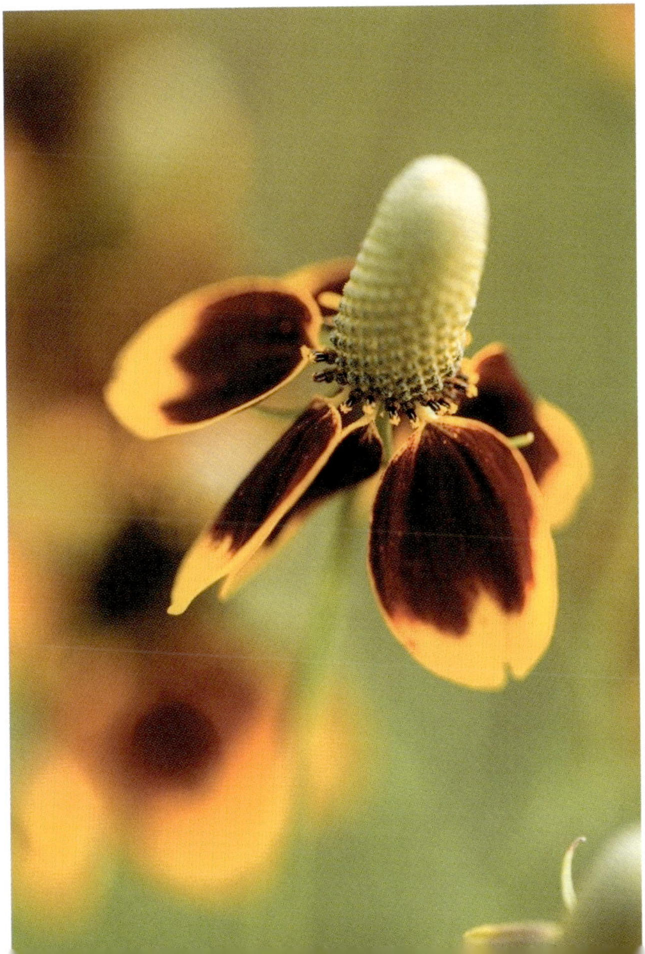

Figure 1.11 It is fairly common to place a camera and lens on a tripod to shoot macro work. Macro lenses with Image Stabilization help alleviate camera movement, allowing many to handhold these tight shots.

ISO 100 • 1/80 sec. • f/2.8 • 100mm macro

6. The Lens Trinity

Many photographers who have been at it a while develop an affinity to three lenses: a wide, a standard, and a medium telephoto. In an effort to accomplish as much range with as few lenses as possible, photographers are attracted to this "holy trinity" of glass (**Figure 1.12**). In all practicality, three lenses capable of covering focal lengths from the ultra-wide (less than 24mm) to the medium telephoto (approximately 200mm to 300mm) can make a lifetime of images.

Traditionally, the lens trinity is composed of a lens capable of going extremely wide, such as the EF 16–35mm f/2.8L, a standard zoom lens that moves from wide to just over normal (50mm), like the EF 24–70mm f/2.8L, and one that continues moving toward a longer focal length capable of handling portraiture, sports, and wildlife, such as the EF 70–200mm f/2.8L. These lenses—and really the focal lengths covered—are considered to be the trinity for full-frame cameras, such as the Canon 6D, 5D series, 1DX, and the 1DS models. These focal lengths are also what many of the EF-S lenses—made for the APS-C crop-sensor camera bodies like the Rebel series—are designed around when taking into consideration the cameras' crop factors.

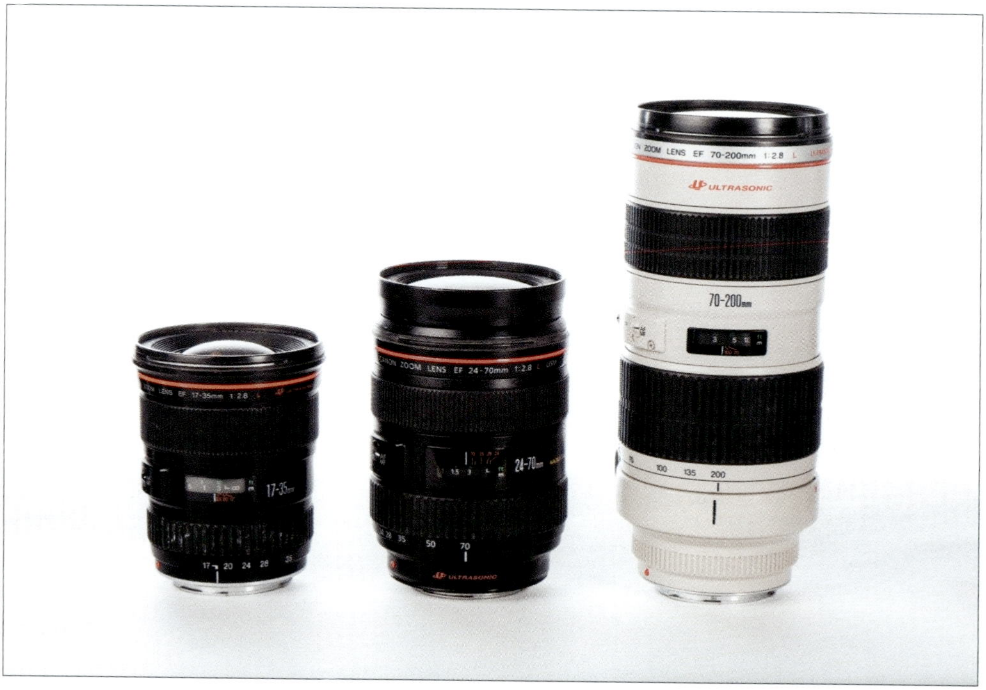

Figure 1.12
My own personal lens trinity: an EF 17–35mm f/2.8L, an EF 24–70 f/2.8L, and an EF 70–200mm f/2.8L. The majority of images I make are shot with these three.

A lens trinity for a Canon APS-C camera may look more like the EF-S 10–18mm f/4.5–5.6 IS for the ultra-wide zoom, an EF-S 18–55mm f/3.5–5.6 IS for the standard zoom, and the EF-S 55–250mm f/4–5.6 IS for the telephoto zoom (**Figure 1.13**). This doesn't mean the so-called full-frame trinity does not work on your crop-sensor camera bodies; you just wouldn't be able to take advantage of the visual perspective the wider EF-S lenses offer—which when factoring in the crop factor of APS-C bodies equates to trinity-esque focal lengths for a full-frame system.

The lens trinity is arguably the most popular set of lenses for those starting out in photography as well. Read online gear forums anywhere (using caution about some of the information on them) and you'll see many experienced folks encourage new photographers to seek out focal lengths resembling what the trinity offers.

I suggest starting with a standard zoom (which many of you just starting out probably have in an EF-S 18–55mm if you purchased an APS-C camera, or an EF 24–105mm f/4L if you purchased an entry-level full-frame camera). From there, I advise getting the medium telephoto zoom before the wide zoom, simply because it offers a bit more versatility to your shooting and comes in handy when you need the reach—which in my case happens more often than needing to go more wide.

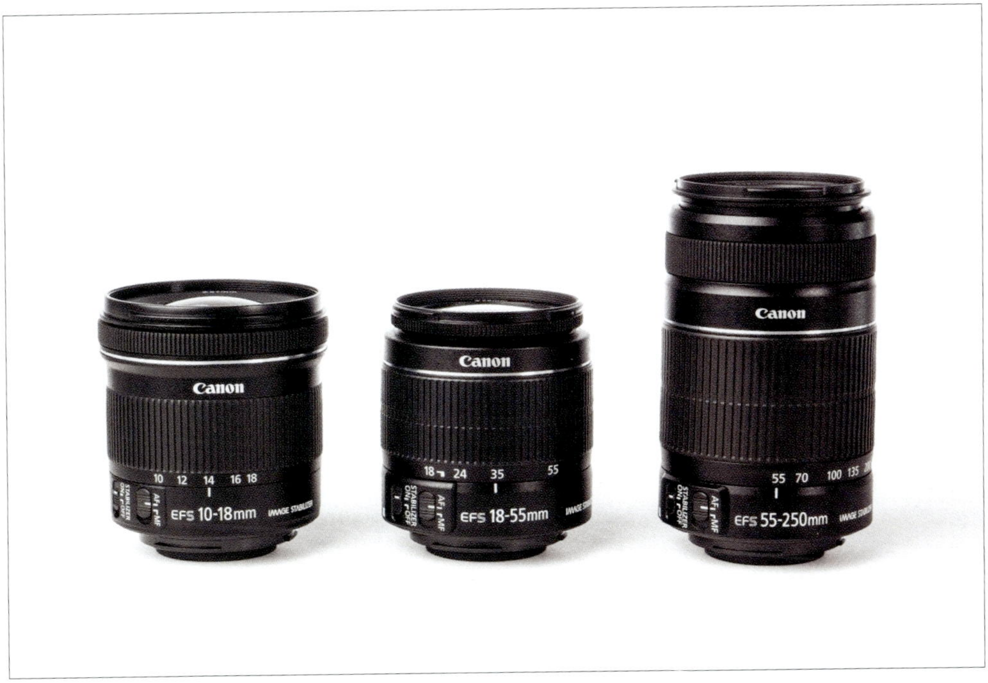

Figure 1.13
A lens trinity built for the APS-C crop-sensor camera: an EF-S 10–18mm f/4.5–5.6 IS, an EF-S 18–55mm f/3.5–5.6 IS, and an EF-S 55–250mm f/4–5.6 IS

Round out your trinity with an ultra-wide zoom lens. These lenses are usually operated at their maximum widths. There is something really special about shooting at 16mm on a full-frame sensor camera, or 10mm on an APS-C sensor. However, as visually interesting and attractive that focal length is, these types of lenses usually offer the least amount of range and focal lengths. I would lean toward the standard zoom and medium telephoto zoom before plunking down cash for an ultra-wide zoom, based on the sheer amount of images that can be produced with the former two.

7. Investment

By now, you're a few pages into this book, you have read about several different types of Canon lenses, and learned some essential information about them. And you understand the issues that position certain lenses at different price points. Lenses vary greatly in price, and they are generally split among three groups: 1) the EF-S crop-sensor body-only lenses, 2) non-L-series EF lenses, and 3) L-series EF lenses.

The EF-S lenses, discussed earlier, are generally crop-sensor equivalents to EF lenses and follow similar pricing as non-L-series EF lenses. Both EF-S and non-L-series EF lenses are considerably more affordable than L-series lenses. The iconic red ring encircling the end of Canon's L-series lens barrels is the visual indicator of premium lenses. (The L in L series is rumored to stand for several things, like low dispersion. However, Canon and others claim it stands for "luxury.") L-series lenses are among some of the best lenses in the world, and they demand a higher price.

To understand why some lenses are more affordable than others, let's look at the factors that determine price: quality of glass, construction quality, maximum aperture, and Image Stabilization.

Quality of Glass

All Canon lenses are made with a level of precision that results from many performance-testing, designing, and engineering hours. However, some lenses are less expensive than their L-series counterparts, based partly on the glass used and the manufacturing process. To quote Canon's highly technical but informative *EF Lens Work III, The Eye of EOS*, "The Canon EF lens L series possesses a level of quality sufficiently high to be called professional.... This name is reserved only for those few lenses that can meet stringent standards of performance, using fluorite (an artificial crystal), a ground and polished aspherical surface, UD, super UD lenses, and other special optical materials." Fluorite and UD (ultra-low dispersion) glass are extremely high-quality materials for lens construction and command a premium in combination with other superior construction materials used in L-series glass (**Figure 1.14**). Glass in higher-end lenses tends to flare or ghost less, as well as provide optimal contrast and lower levels of distortion and vignetting (but not in all cases).

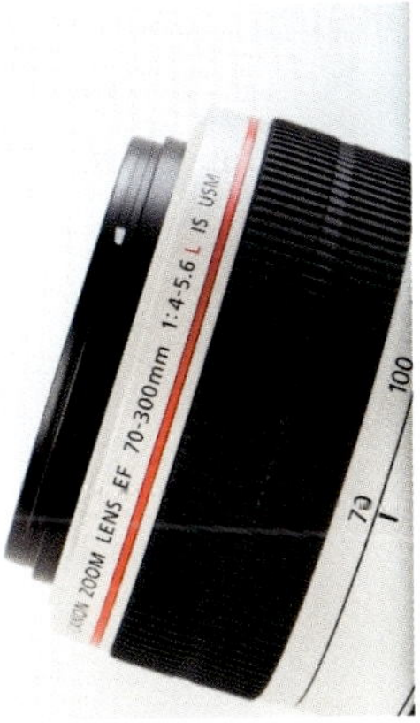

Figure 1.14 The iconic red ring around the end of the lens barrel paired with the red L symbolizes Canon's highest-quality glass and lens construction.

This doesn't mean that non-L-series lenses are poor performers. In fact, the glass quality in lenses like the EF-S 10–22mm f/3.5–4.5 and the EF 70–300mm f/4–5.6 IS is noted for being just as sharp. Canon glass is engineered, at each level, to perform with the highest quality possible. In the end (and at the end of this chapter, also), the choice between L-series quality glass and non-L-series quality glass is a budget issue and depends on your practical and professional use of the gear.

Construction Quality

When it comes to overall construction quality, L-series lenses are made to take a bigger beating than non-L-series lenses. Most are contained within relatively thicker metal barrels and mounts that are weather-sealed to protect the expensive internals from the elements (**Figure 1.15**). Many non-L-series lenses (and some L-series) are constructed with mostly plastic lens barrels or a combination of plastic and metal. Consider that trio of 50mm lenses highlighted earlier. The EF 50mm f/1.8's lens barrel is plastic, as is the EF 50mm f/1.4. However, the EF 50mm f/1.2L is a solid chunk of metal, increasing its weight (along with other factors such as the amount of glass it contains) and ability to take abuse under extreme conditions.

As for the weather sealing on many lenses, take it from someone who has field tested the weather sealing—it works. I once dropped and fully submersed a 24–105mm f/4L attached to a Canon 5D in a river for several seconds. After pulling it out, frantically wiping everything down with my shirt, rushing it all back to camp and setting it out to dry for several hours, the lens was fully functional with only a few water spots noticeable at aperture values higher than f/11. The camera did not fair so well since it was a pre-weather-sealed version of the 5D.

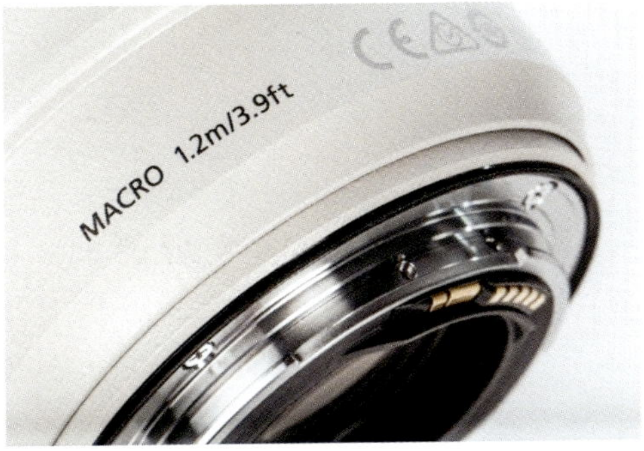

Figure 1.15 The small rubber flange on many of Canon's L-series lens mounts helps seal the lens to the body of the camera, preventing dust and moisture from entering both pieces of gear.

Maximum Aperture

The L-series lenses are also more likely to be those that have the widest apertures available. Aside from the super telephotos longer than 400mm, there are not many L-series lenses that do not open up to f/2.8 or wider. The widest aperture available on any Canon lens exists in the 50mm f/1.2L and the 85mm f/1.2L. Extremely wide apertures mean larger lens diameters, which mean lots of glass. And when it is extremely high-quality glass, those wide apertures play a part in the higher price.

The maximum aperture opening is a point on which many people base lens purchases, but it is important to consider your own applications for different lenses. For example, Canon makes an EF 16–35mm f/2.8L, which is considered to be a fantastic ultra-wide zoom, great for everything from landscape to editorial photography. However, if you are primarily a landscape photographer, where f/2.8 might not be used as much as more closed-down apertures, you might consider the EF 17–40mm f/4L. It is still a higher-quality lens, but with f/4 as its maximum aperture opening, it contains less glass and comes in nearly a thousand dollars under the price of the former.

Canon has many alternate versions of lenses, with their biggest difference in features being their maximum aperture openings. This is especially noticeable in their telephoto range. Personally, I am a fan of the EF 300mm f/4L IS and the EF 400mm f/5.6L lenses when it comes to longer glass. They are constructed with very-high-quality glass, but they are literally pounds lighter and several inches shorter than their counterparts sporting f/2.8 aperture openings (**Figure 1.16**). For an outdoors shooter, these lenses are easier to carry long distances and take up less space in the camera bag, leaving room for other lenses and accessories.

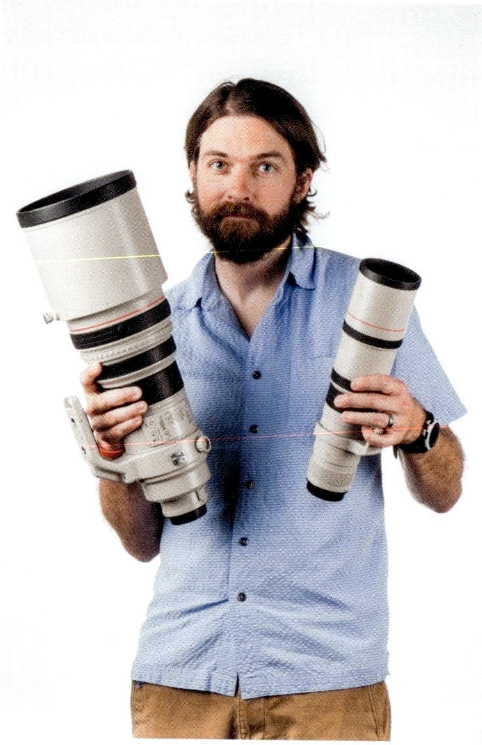

Photo by Sam Norman

Figure 1.16 Photographers choose lenses based on style, quality, and often size and weight. On the left, an EF 400mm f/2.8L IS (the most previous version) weighs nearly 12 pounds, and on the right, an EF 400mm f/5.6L is nearly three pounds.

I still use an EF 400mm f/2.8L IS for shooting college football each fall, though. Having the two extra f-stops of light (correlating with two stops of faster shutter speeds) comes in handy when stopping the action—not because I enjoy hefting a 10-plus-pound lens around for several hours every Saturday. If all games were day games, when the light was bright and I could afford to lose a couple of stops of light to the lighter f/5.6 lens, I would be tempted to cart it to the field instead.

Stouter lens construction and wider apertures make for physically larger lenses. Therefore L-series lenses are the largest Canon makes, no matter the focal length. Place an EF 70–300mm f/4–5.6 IS and an EF 70–300mm f/4–5.6L IS side by side, and compare the difference (**Figure 1.17**). They are the exact same focal length, but the L-series lens is considerably larger in circumference and weight due to its hardier construction. The heavier weight of L-series lenses is a turn-off for some. However, weight is simply the result of the higher build quality. Some folks enjoy the way the heavier lenses help them stabilize handheld shots (I even know some photographers who add more weight to their long lenses to make them "seat" heavier in their hands).

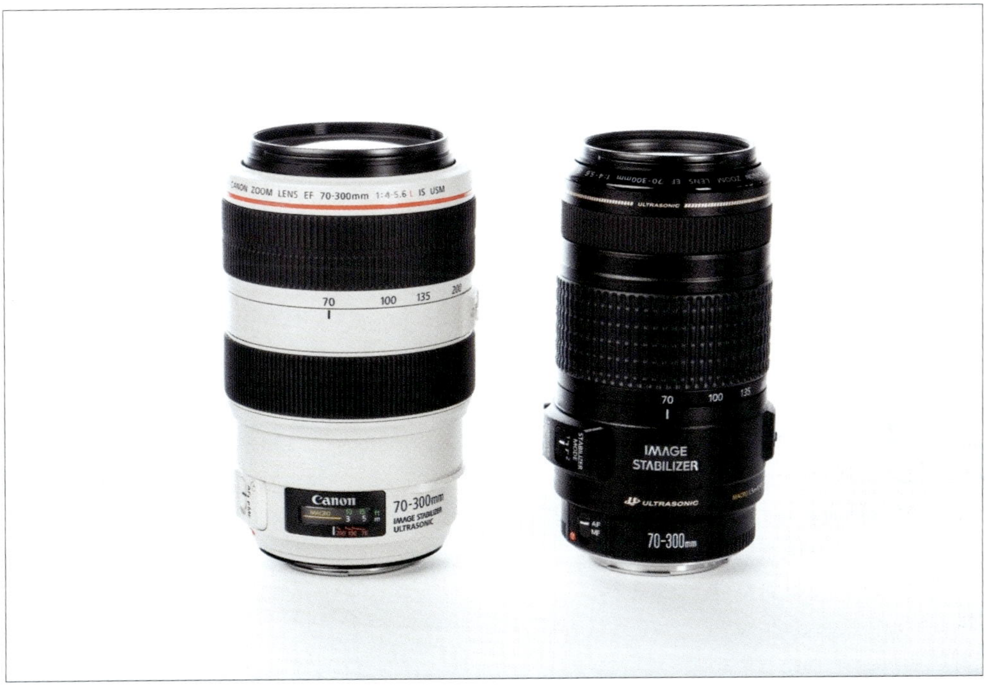

Figure 1.17
The L-series version of the EF 70–300mm is larger and much heavier than its non-L-series IS relative.

Image Stabilization

Another technology that increases the price of certain lenses is Image Stabilization, discussed later in the book. For those with unsteady hands or who work in low-light environments, this price difference may be worth it. It is technology that only gets better as it advances, and the Image Stabilization available on some lenses currently offers up to four stops of stability. IS increases the size and weight of the lens due to the internal mechanism that controls the technology, so take that into consideration when adding to your lens kit.

As with most tech products, today's innovations in professional-grade equipment tend to transfer to consumer-level gear over time. Image Stabilization is a great example of trickle-down technology. It can be commonly found in non-L-series lenses—albeit not all of them. Fortunately, no matter what your budget, you are more than likely able to enjoy some of the largest innovations in lens construction and operation of all time in Canon lenses, at all price points.

Buying New, Buying Used

Lenses are long-term investments when it comes to acquiring photography gear. Therefore, many folks (including myself) deliberate quite a bit over purchasing glass. One of the burning questions is whether one should purchase new or used.

There are several advantages that come along with buying new, all of which are similar to purchasing any new technology. New lenses offer up the latest and greatest technology to aid the photographer in the image-making process. Buying new from a reputable retailer usually means you get a warranty for the gear (go ahead and register your newly purchased gear at www.usa.canon.com/cusa/registration/professional/professional_cameras).

Like insurance, the warranty is for those "you never know" moments. However, unlike extensive insurance, warranties typically do not cover all types of damage to newly purchased lenses, so be sure to read the fine print. Buying new also means you can assume you are obtaining a pristine copy of the lens, free of defects, and if it isn't, the warranty comes in handy.

Finally, new and recent versions of lenses also come with support from Canon and Canon Professional Services (CPS). For the most part, Canon Professional Services is available for those who obtain professional-grade equipment, such as L-series lenses. However, several non-L-series lenses are supported as well.

The drawback to buying new glass, however, is the expense. The primary reason to buy used is simply to save money. I have nothing against buying used glass. In fact, half the lenses in my kit were purchased used. However, there are a few things to consider before plunking down money for used glass. First, make sure you are shopping from a reputable vendor (some of which might even offer a warranty for used gear). I am a fan of B&H

Photo (www.bhphotovideo.com) and Adorama (www.adorama.com), both of which have great used departments with many options from which to shop. In the business for many years, KEH (www.keh.com) is another resource. Also consider photography rental businesses, such as LensRentals.com. I have purchased used lenses from them and would not think twice about doing it again. They have great customer service, and both lenses I purchased were in exquisite shape when shipped to me.

This brings me to the second point to consider when buying used: lens condition. All of the above vendors thoroughly check the equipment they intend to sell before it is put on the market, and each of them has a very similar condition rating for their products. When shopping for used gear online, be sure to consult the descriptions for each value used to rate lens conditions, and if you have any questions, contact the seller.

I prefer to buy used lenses that have no scratches on the front or rear elements and show little to no sign of wear on the barrel. Scratches on the lens elements may not show up when the aperture is set to wide open, but they may begin to appear the more you stop down the aperture to achieve greater depth of field. Although wear on the lens barrels—especially for L-series lenses—may not matter too much to some, it might indicate some internal wear as well, as a result of being knocked around or dropped. I also want lenses on which all of the rings (zoom and focus) operate appropriately and the autofocus and Image Stabilization (if included) work well.

If you are purchasing from a local colleague or a friend, check for those issues mentioned above, but also spend some time with the lens(es). Ask to handle and possibly field test the glass before making a purchasing decision. Used lenses (and used camera gear in general) are much like used cars. Some have more mileage than others, some do not have as many or the newest features as others, and normal wear and tear needs to be taken into consideration. Overall, though, doing your research and smart shopping will most likely land you great versions of the lenses you want without paying for new.

Renting

Renting camera gear, especially lenses, is a relatively new opportunity for folks to get their hands on all types of equipment. Two reasons for which you might consider renting a lens: needing it for a one-time-only shoot or photographic experience and testing a lens you are considering purchasing. I do not have much need for an EF 85mm f/1.2L, but occasionally I will rent one for a few days for a fraction of the price it costs to purchase a new *or* used version.

If you are comfortable with the lens kit you have for your Canon DSLR, but occasionally want to shoot with another perspective, renting is a great alternative. It is even a smart alternative to borrowing a friend or colleague's lens because most rental services offer insurance in case of an accident. If you scratch the front lens element of your buddy's new

EF-S 18–200mm f/3.5–5.6 IS, you might be obligated to replace it for much more than the nominal insurance fee.

If you are thinking about buying a new or used lens, especially any pricey L-series lens, consider renting it first for a few days. Use it extensively during the time you have it, putting it through its paces with your shooting style. This trial period will hopefully inform your purchasing decision. Remember that 85mm I was just talking about? After renting one, I didn't buy it. However, after trialing an EF 50mm f/1.2L, I was convinced that it belonged in my bag, resulting in a visit to my local camera store.

So, where do you go to rent lenses? Check locally for any camera shops that rent. Many smaller shops are adding rentals to diversify their business, and with renting locally comes a level of support that few non-local entities can achieve. There are also several great online rental services, such as LensRentals.com, LensProToGo (www.lensprotogo.com), and BorrowLenses (www.borrowlenses.com). I have been a LensRentals.com user for years (several of the images in this book were made with gear I rented specifically for it). Online rental services usually offer more gear and also make it easy for the renter to return lenses back to headquarters.

Conclusion

Lenses, as opposed to many camera bodies, are long-term investments in your photography kit. Since 2004, I have owned six camera bodies as my primary workhorses (probably not many by some professionals' standards, but enough), and a few more as backups. In that time, I have owned only one version of every lens I have purchased. I bought my first L-series lens in 2005 (a five-year-old EF 17–35mm f/2.8L), and I don't see myself selling it or trading it in anytime soon. It's still sharp, functions like new, and I think it flares less than newer ultra-wide lenses. It is easily the oldest lens I own, and the rest of my "trinity" isn't too much younger.

The point is that lenses can offer you many more years of photography than a digital body. Depending on the model, a newer version of a camera body can be released what seems like every year. Lenses, because the technology does not change as frequently, have much longer shelf lives than cameras. Even though camera bodies cost more than lenses in some cases, the glass is where you see your kit really develop due to its longevity.

Lens investments are informed by our own personal, professional, and stylistic needs. Want to upgrade that kit lens immediately after purchasing your first DSLR combo kit? Spend a bit more time with it to see if the investment is necessary. I'm not one to encourage going into debt over photography; instead, consider your purchase options and your own style/needs to make an informed decision about the lenses you acquire.

Chapter 1 Assignments

Let's start the book's assignments by doing some homework and getting in some practice.

Get the manual out

There are many different Canon lenses, and all share the same basic functions. However, many have unique differences. Pore over the technical manual, familiarizing yourself with the features of a lens (many of which we cover in this book). At the same time, have the lens near you and handle it as you read about it. Getting accustomed to the size and form of the gear you use is essential to working with it efficiently, effectively, and more important, creatively.

How slow can you go?

Test out the minimum sustaining shutter speed you are capable of shooting with for various focal lengths. Choose any lens to which you have access. Perhaps it's the kit lens that came with your camera. Shoot at set focal lengths, such as 18mm, 24mm, 35mm, and 50mm (you can use any focal length you want). For each, test how slow you can shoot before the image becomes out of focus due to camera shake. Be sure to turn Image Stabilization off, and handhold the camera and lens. To be sure of focus, download the images later on the computer, and zoom in to see if and how blur occurs at slow shutter speeds.

Share your results with the book's Flickr group!
Join the group here: www.flickr.com/groups/canonlenses_fromsnapshotstogreatshots

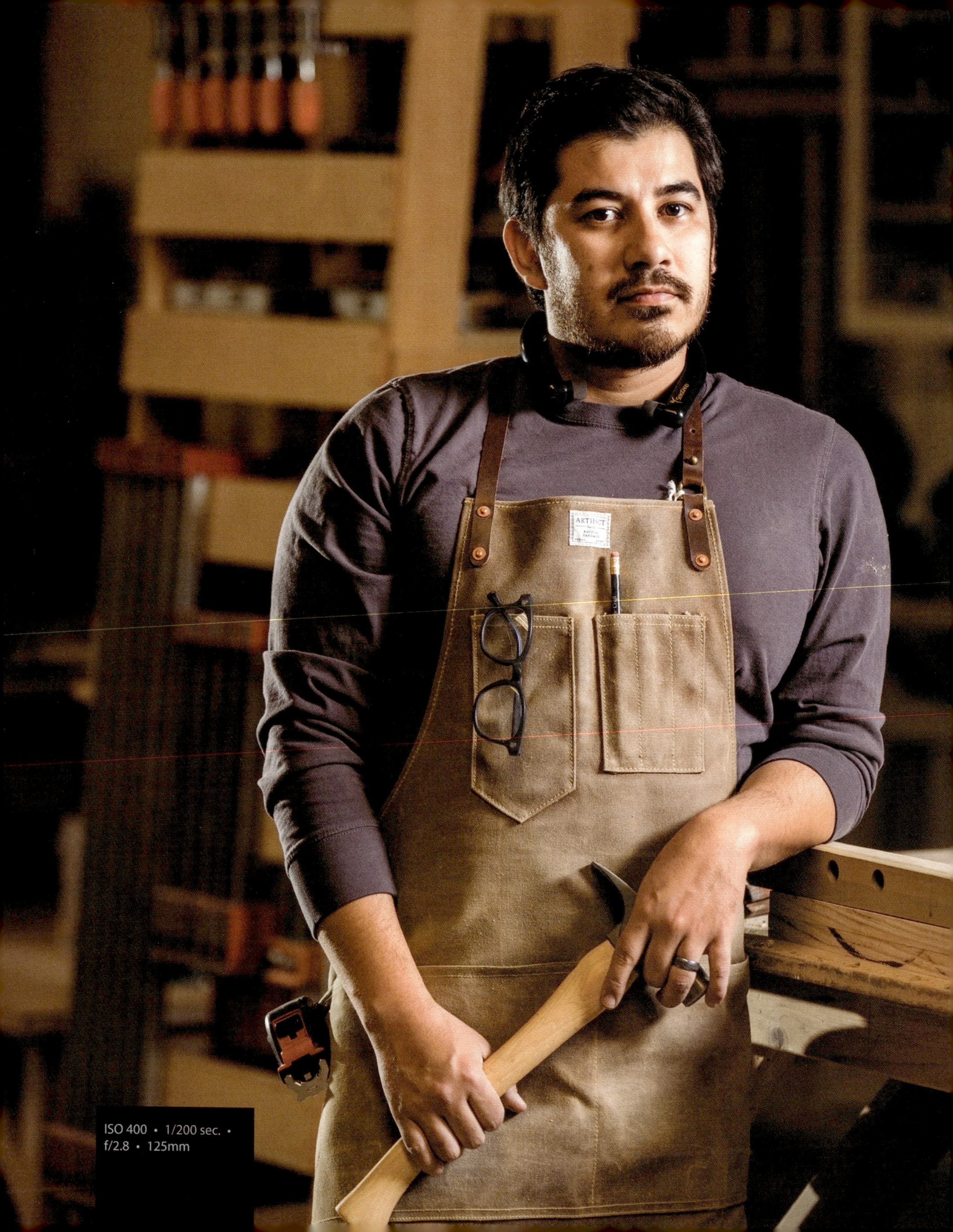

ISO 400 • 1/200 sec. • f/2.8 • 125mm

2

Depth of Field and Perspective

Using the visual controls of the lens

My favorite exposure mode is Aperture Priority (AV). I'm in this mode 80 percent of the time, moving to Manual (M) when I'm shooting in the studio and at times when exposure is a bit tricky for the camera's metering. However, I'm not in Aperture Priority because it's an automatic mode that does most of the heavy lifting with metering. Instead, I like Aperture Priority because I *think* and *see* in terms of the aperture and depth of field when sizing up potential shots. The ability to affect an image's depth of field with the flick of a switch and take advantage of one of photography's most important aesthetic controls is exciting—you'll benefit from becoming more comfortable working the aperture. This chapter covers the relationship between aperture and depth of field, hyperfocal distance, and how to make your photos more interesting using different perspectives.

Poring Over the Picture

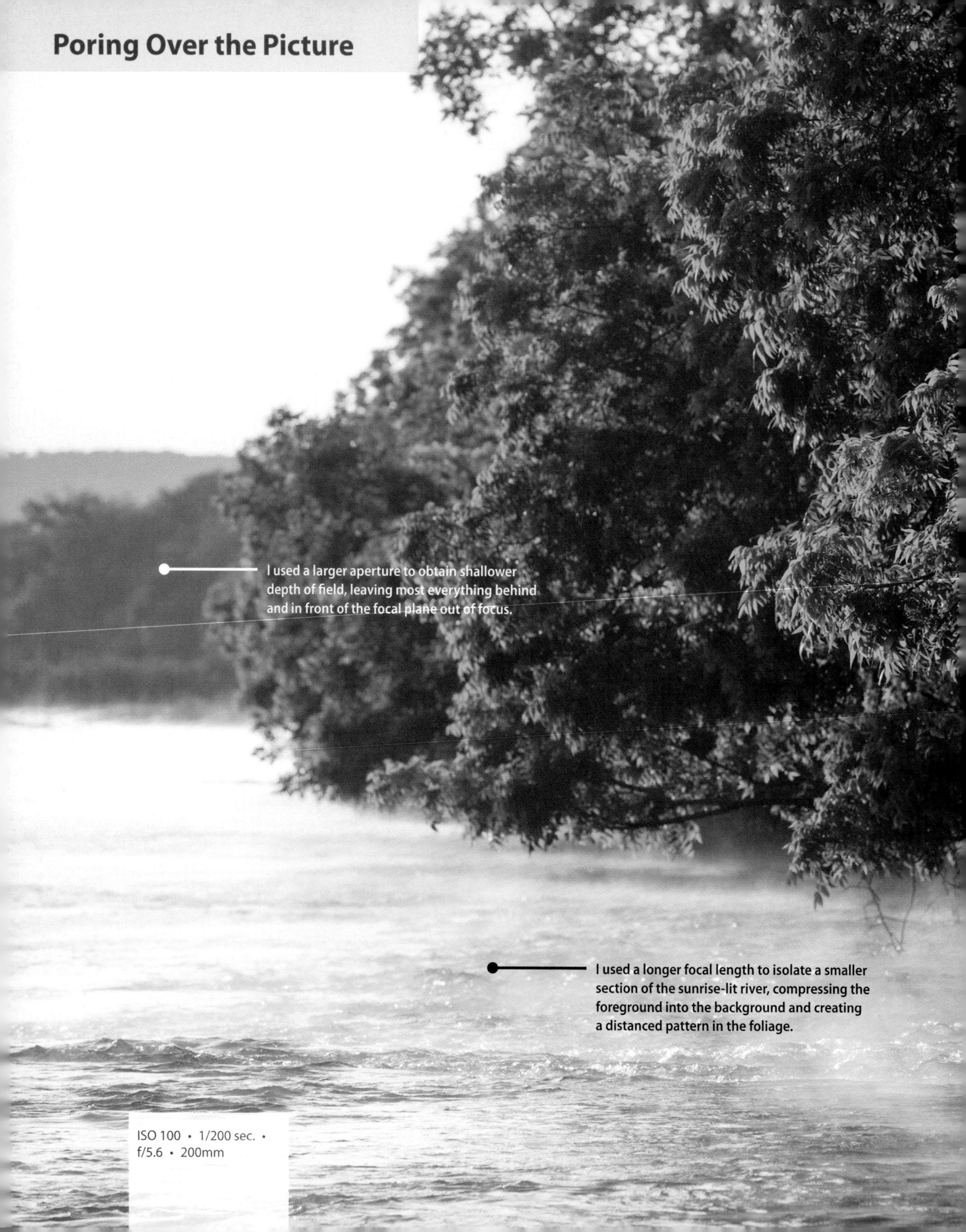

I used a larger aperture to obtain shallower depth of field, leaving most everything behind and in front of the focal plane out of focus.

I used a longer focal length to isolate a smaller section of the sunrise-lit river, compressing the foreground into the background and creating a distanced pattern in the foliage.

ISO 100 • 1/200 sec. • f/5.6 • 200mm

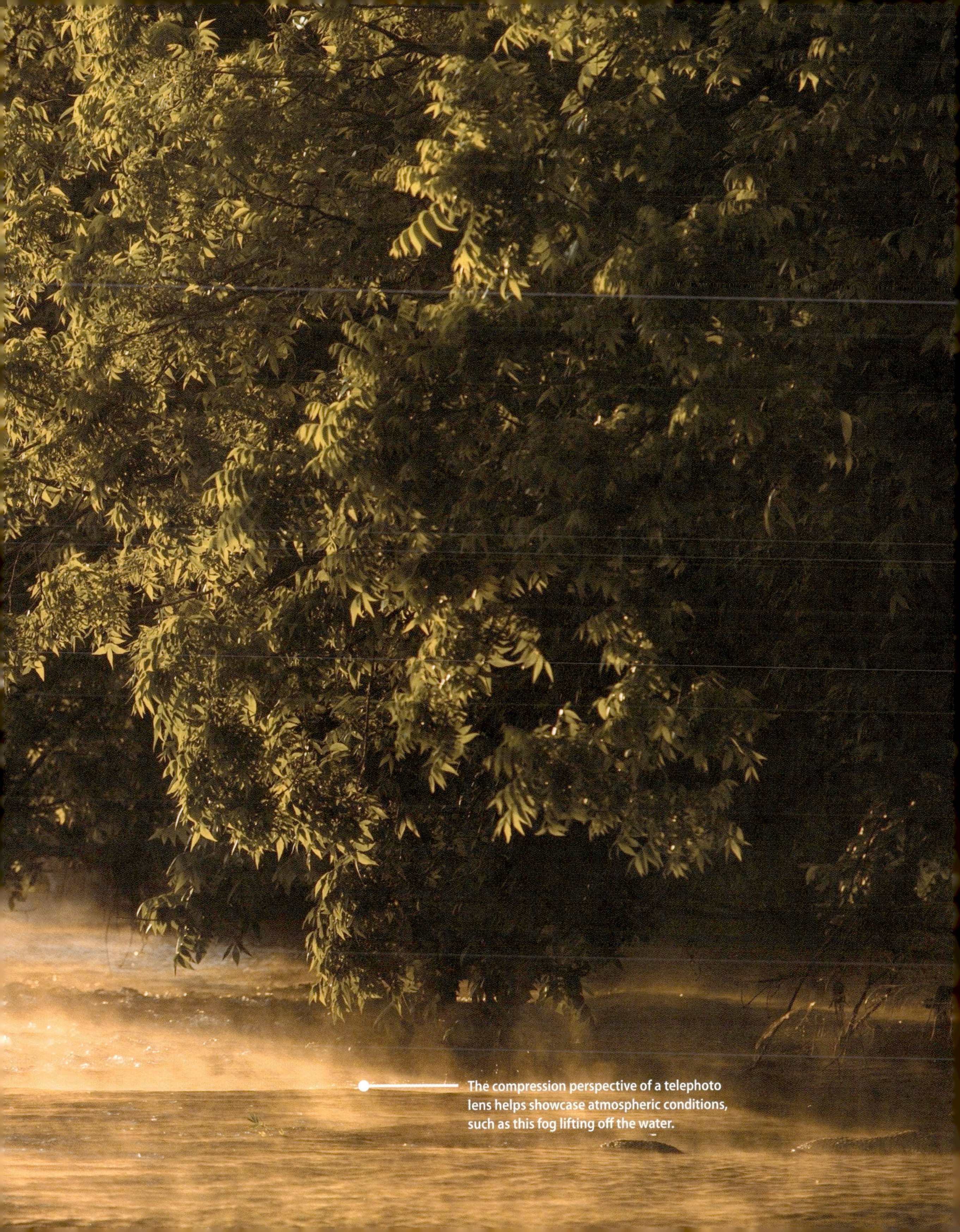

The compression perspective of a telephoto lens helps showcase atmospheric conditions, such as this fog lifting off the water.

Plane of Critical Focus and Aperture

The aperture, aside from the optical-grade glass and the barrel containing a lens's internals, is probably the most important mechanism of any lens. To be specific, the aperture is a set of overlapping metal leaves forming a ring within the lens, closing or opening depending on the user's or camera's determined settings. We colloquially call this opening and closing of the aperture "stopping" up or down. The aperture controls two things: depth of field and how much light is allowed through the lens to expose on the camera's sensor (or film). The aperture is just one of a few items that make up the formula for exposure; many folks use the aperture and shutter speed together for a desirable exposure. For the purposes of this chapter, we will look at aperture as it relates to depth of field (**Figure 2.1**).

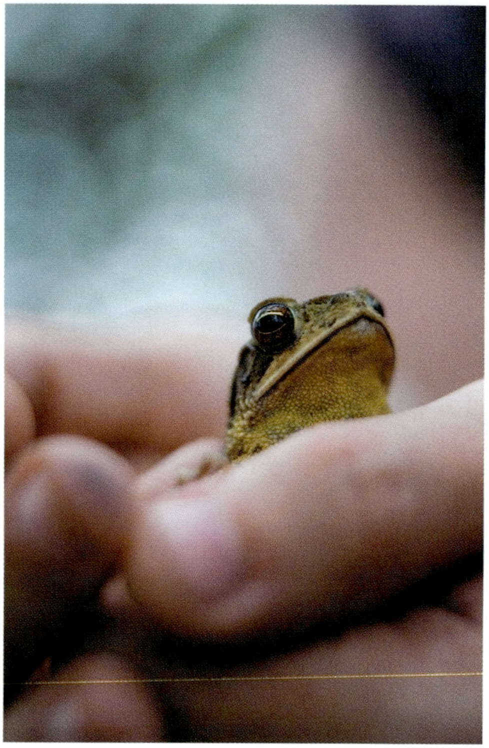

Figure 2.1 **The aperture is the direct control of depth of field, which allowed me to place the frog in tack-sharp focus and everything else out of focus.**

ISO 100 • 1/60 sec. • f/2.8 • 60mm

Aperture and Depth of Field

Before we delve into depth of field, we need to cover the *plane of critical focus*. Remember planes? Not the flying variety but rather the theoretical mathematic concepts you learned about in geometry? They are invisible, yet infinite, having no thickness but encompassing theoretical real estate that sprawls forever in space. The plane of critical focus is no different, and it is highly relevant when talking about focus and depth of field. Often referred to as the focal plane, the plane of critical focus is simply where focus is placed into an image. When you focus—manually or by using auto-focus—on a subject, this invisible plane exists at the very point at which you focused.

The plane exists parallel to the optics in the lens, and therefore the sensor in the camera, and it is positioned exactly perpendicular to the direction in which the lens is pointed. Anything existing on the plane of critical focus in an image (and theoretically everything on it outside the frame) is in focus (**Figure 2.2**). If you move exactly sideways in either direction, the plane stays at the same position, and everything that exists on the plane remains in focus. Not so if you move forward or backward. The plane then shifts accordingly, and what was once in focus—that which existed on the plane previously—is now out of it.

Unlike theoretical planes in geometry, though, we can manipulate the "thickness" of the plane of critical focus to adjust how much is actually in focus. This is where depth of field comes into play, as well as the aperture.

Depth of field is the amount of a shot that is noticeably in focus. It is called *depth* of field because it exists around the plane of critical focus. Technically, you do not adjust the thickness of the focal plane, but when depth of field is increased, areas in front of and behind the plane itself come more into focus. When depth of field is decreased, less of these areas is in focus. We commonly describe large amounts of depth of field as wide and small amounts as shallow (note: you probably hear "shallow" used more often than "wide").

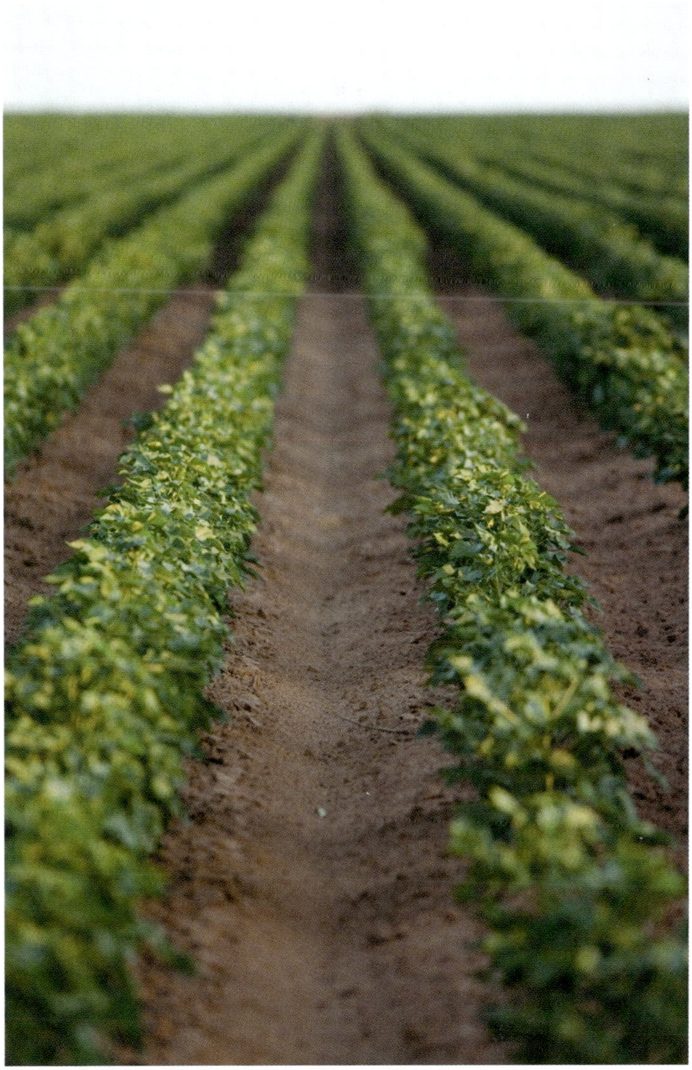

Figure 2.2 **At f/4 and at 300mm, only a few feet of these two rows of cotton are in focus, the area that surrounds where I placed the plane of critical focus.**

ISO 200 • 1/80 sec. • f/4 • 300mm

Landscape photography (**Figure 2.3**), where it is typical to have everything in sharp focus, regularly employs large amounts of depth of field. Conversely, shallow depth of field is used extensively in portrait photography (**Figure 2.4**), where the person or animal in the shot is in focus, but the background—and foreground, if you can see it—is thrown out of focus to help isolate and draw attention to the subject.

The mechanism used to adjust depth of field is the aperture. To increase—or widen—the depth of field in a shot, a photographer can decrease the physical size of the aperture. To produce shallower depth of field, a photographer can open up the aperture. What does this look like to the operator? Aperture values are represented by the number in the viewfinder or on the LCD screen containing a decimal. Aperture values are technically denoted as f-stops, which are ratios between the lens's focal length and the physical size of the aperture opening within the lens.

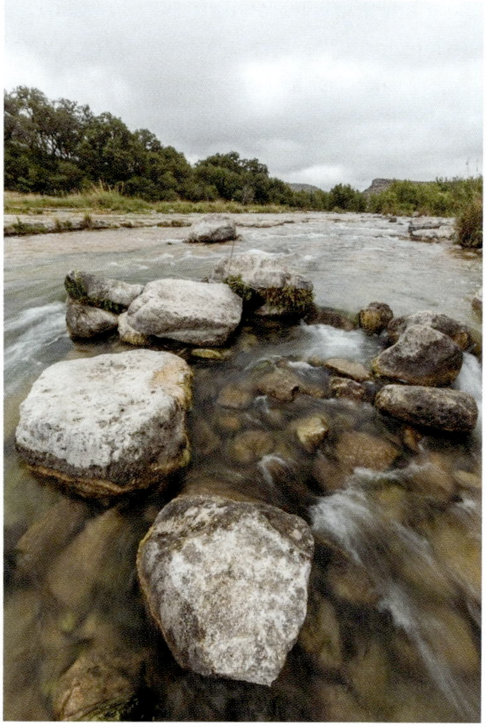

Figure 2.3 **Landscape shots like this one regularly employ a closed-down aperture, resulting in maximum depth of field, where everything from the foreground to the background is sharp.**

ISO 100 • 1/4 sec. • f/22 • 14mm

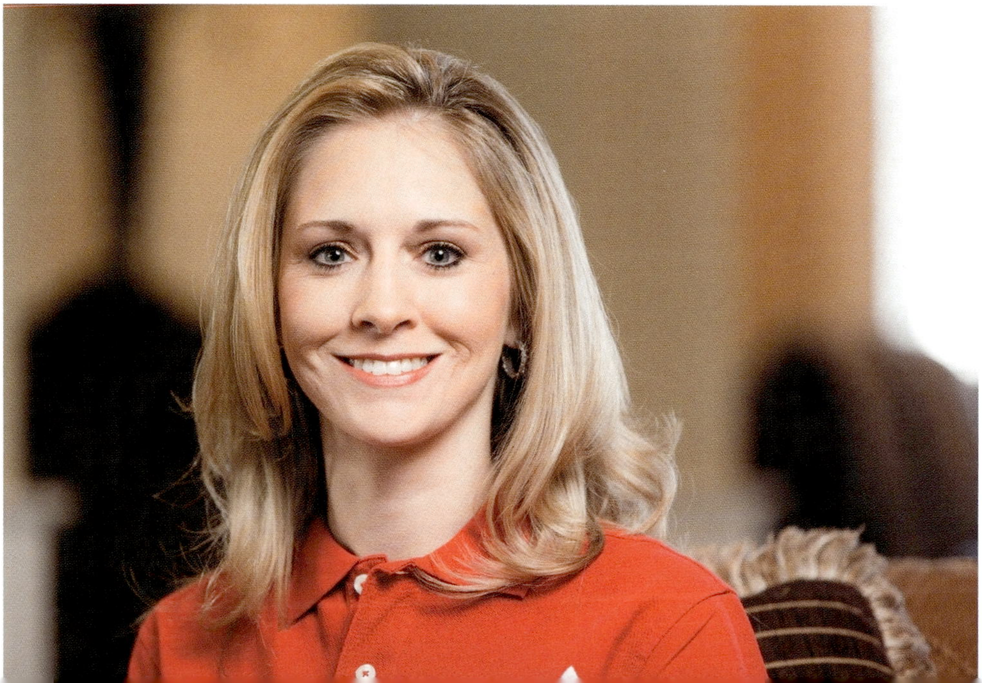

Figure 2.4 **With an aperture value of f/2.8 at 185mm, there isn't very much in focus except the subject's left eye, where the focal plane is placed.**

ISO 400 • 1/100 sec. • f/2.8 • 185mm

Meaning that even though the same aperture values exist for other lenses, the numbers are specific to each lens. Typical aperture values range from f/3.5 (or f/2.8 or f/1.2, depending on the lens) to f/22 or f/32.

Practically speaking, the lower the aperture value is, the shallower the depth of field (**Figure 2.5**). Inversely, the more closed, or stopped down, the aperture, the more depth of field one gets in a shot (**Figure 2.6**). Here's the counter-intuitive part: Shallower depth of field (meaning a larger aperture opening) is achieved with lower aperture values, and wider depth of field (a smaller aperture opening) is achieved with higher aperture values.

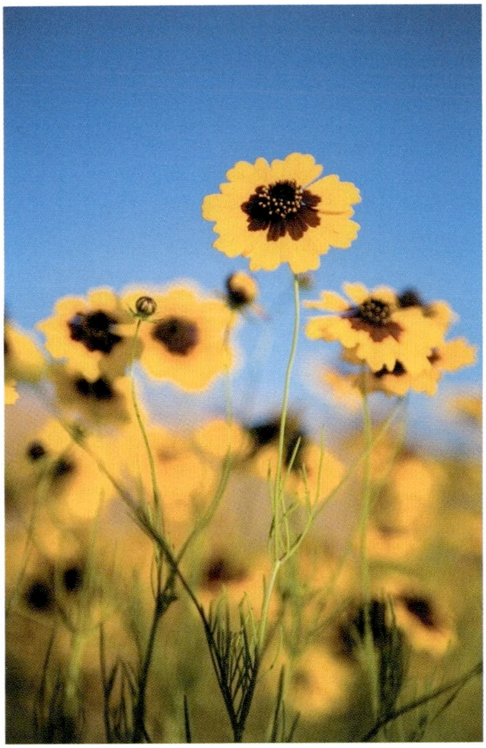

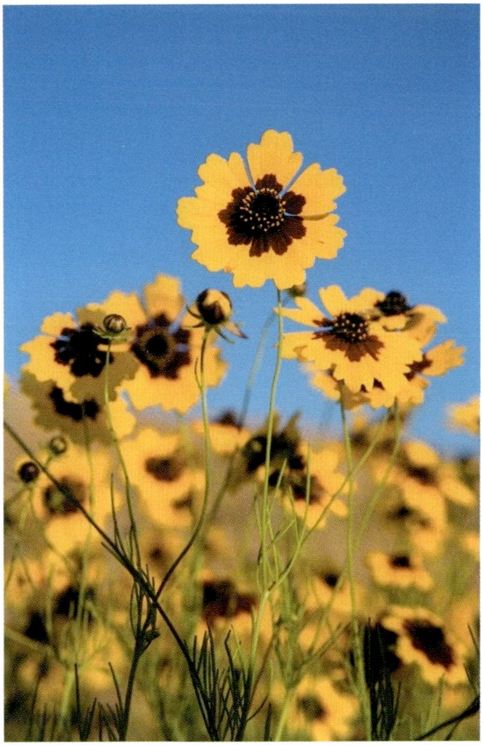

Figure 2.5 (left)
Shallow depth of field (aperture value of f/2.8) throws everything beyond the tallest flower in the shot pleasingly out of focus.

ISO 100 • 1/1600 sec. • f/2.8 • 64mm

Figure 2.6 (right)
At f/8, the flowers in the background come more into focus as a result of greater depth of field.

ISO 200 • 1/400 sec. • f/8 • 64mm

For the landscape example above, an aperture value of f/22 closes the physical aperture down so much that the depth of field is nearly infinite. A typical portrait, however, might employ an aperture value of f/5.6, f/4, or f/2.8 to create very shallow depth of field. Many lenses—and cameras—allow you to adjust aperture values by 1/3-stop increments, offering you finer controls for both exposure and depth of field than did older all-manual film cameras. It is worth running through the range of aperture values your lens has and getting a sense of how each affects the shot (**Figures 2.7** through **2.10**).

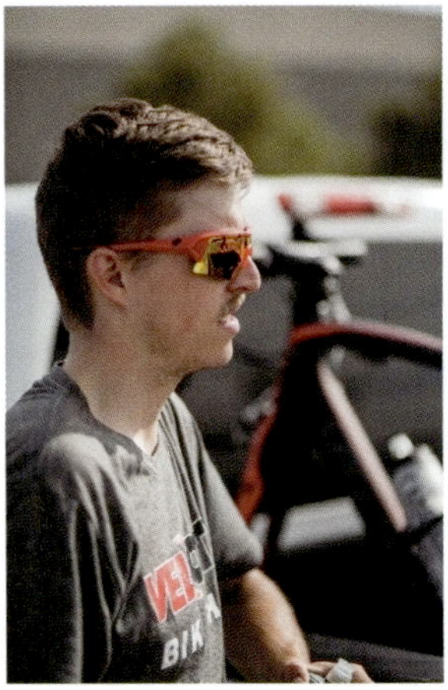

Figure 2.7 Compare aperture values for Figures 2.7 through 2.10, and notice how the bicycle and pickup truck come more into focus behind cyclist Cody Hale as they close down.

ISO 100 • 1/6400 sec. • f/1.8 • 85mm

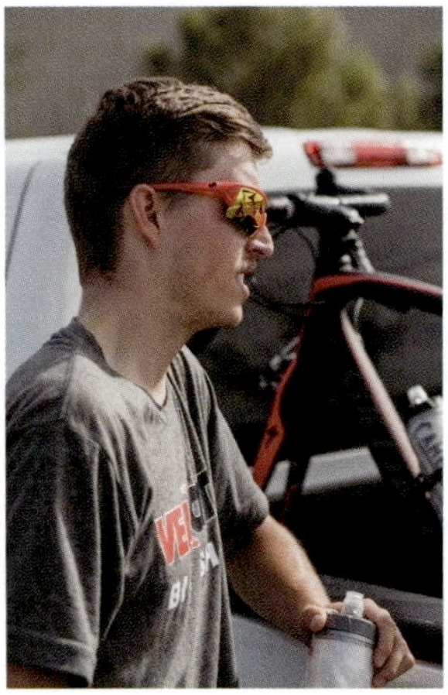

Figure 2.8 At f/4, the depth of field grows beyond just the camera side of Cody's face, and the background is more discernible.

ISO 100 • 1/1250 sec. • f/4 • 85mm

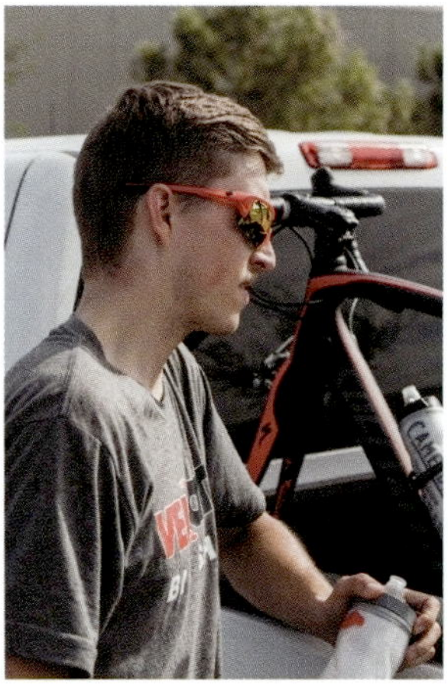

Figure 2.9 The depth of field is wide enough now to see that the background is the back of a pickup truck and the front of a bicycle.

ISO 100 • 1/320 sec. • f/8 • 85mm

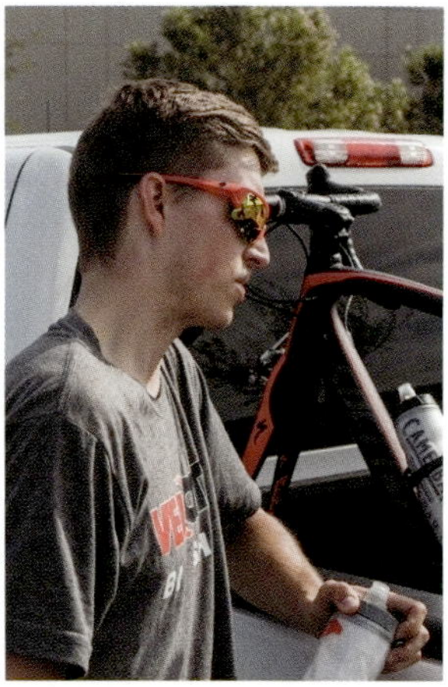

Figure 2.10 At f/16, the depth of field has grown so much it has become a distraction in the shot.

ISO 100 • 1/80 sec. • f/16 • 85mm

To run this experiment, simply frame up a shot for which you can focus on a stationary subject and make several exposures, adjusting your aperture value higher each time you shoot a new frame (you might benefit from placing your camera on a tripod and switching the focus over to Manual). Look at the change in the background for each shot, noticing that it comes more into focus the more closed, or stopped down, the aperture becomes. Keep in mind that for every adjustment you make to the aperture, you will likely have to adjust your shutter speed (if shooting in Manual exposure mode).

Distance and Depth of Field

The aperture is not the only thing that can visually affect depth of field. Although aperture is the only mechanism we can manipulate in-camera to control depth of field, physical distance between the subject and shooter also impacts how much of a shot is in focus.

At any given aperture and focal length, the closer you are to the primary subject (for example, a portrait subject), the more the depth of field drops off as long as you maintain your plane of critical focus on the subject (**Figures 2.11** and **2.12**). The opposite is true the more you move away from the subject, when you gain depth of field. Technically, it has nothing to do with the distance of the subject from the shooter but rather the distance of the focal plane from the lens. When the focal plane is closer to the lens, there is less depth of field, even if the lens is stopped down all the way to f/22 or f/32. However, the farther away the focal plane is from the lens, the more relative depth of field is gained, or at least visually apparent, even when the aperture is wide open. This has much to do with the relative size of the subject in the frame as well, which will be discussed later.

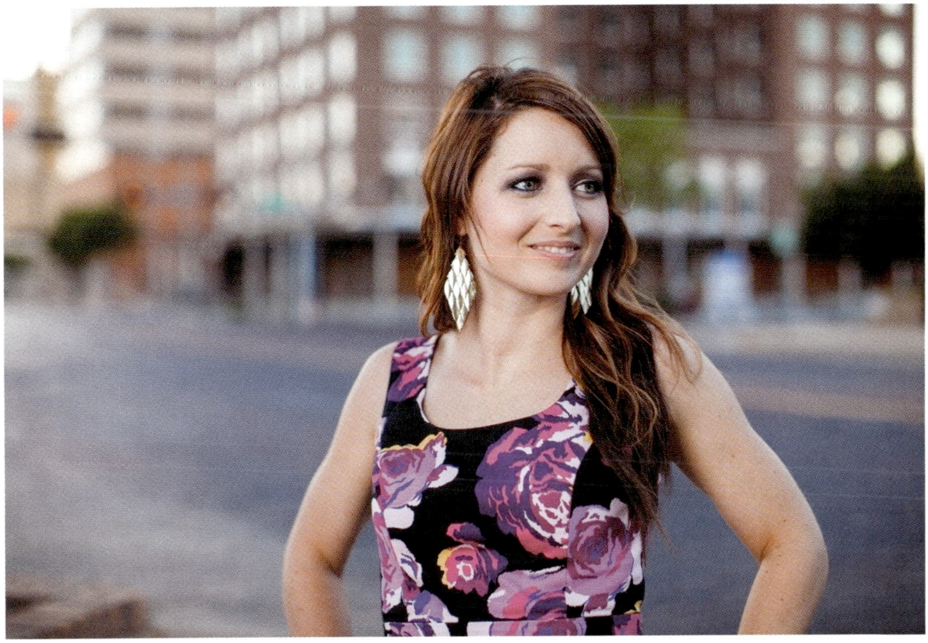

Figure 2.11
Compare the backgrounds of Figures 2.11 and 2.12. The closer the lens is to the subject at 50mm and a constant aperture, the more out of focus the background becomes.

ISO 100 • 1/80 sec. • f/2 • 50mm

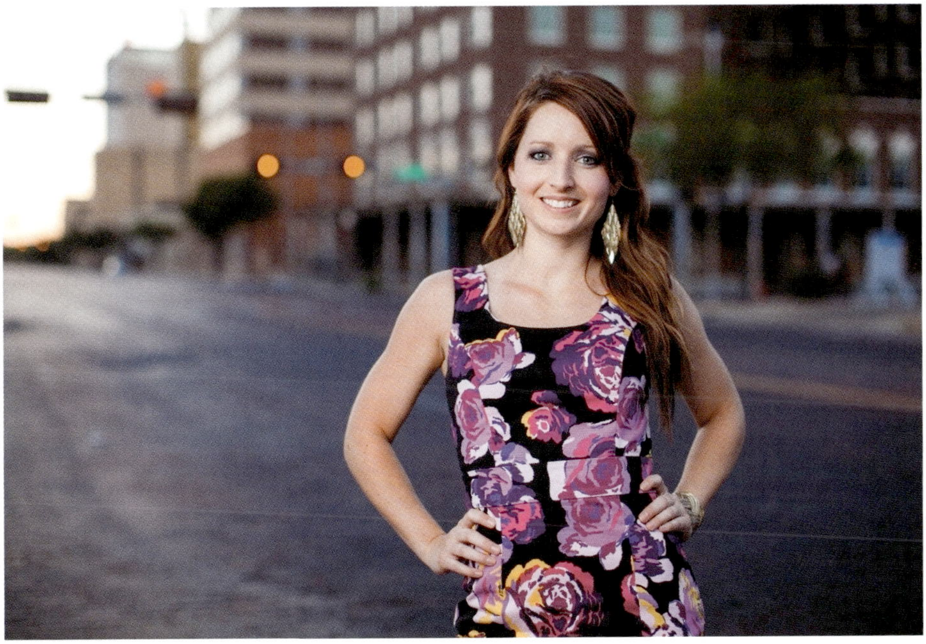

Figure 2.12
When the lens is farther away from the subject, the background comes more into focus, even at f/2. Compare the windows of the building.

ISO 100 • 1/80 sec. • f/2 • 50mm

An additional factor that affects the *appearance* of depth of field is the subject's distance from a background. Portrait photographers like to place their subjects against interesting backgrounds, like colorful walls or cascading plants in a garden (**Figure 2.13**). The closer the background is to the subject, the more it will appear in focus, even if the photographer is using an aperture of f/2.8 or lower. Even at large apertures such as f/2.8, f/2, f/1.4, and f/1.2, depth of field does not fall off immediately, albeit more drastically than at more closed-down apertures. In some cases, that nice background you wanted for ambience can instead be a distraction, unless you pull your subject off of the background more. Increase the distance between the subject and the background, and then see what you get (**Figure 2.14**).

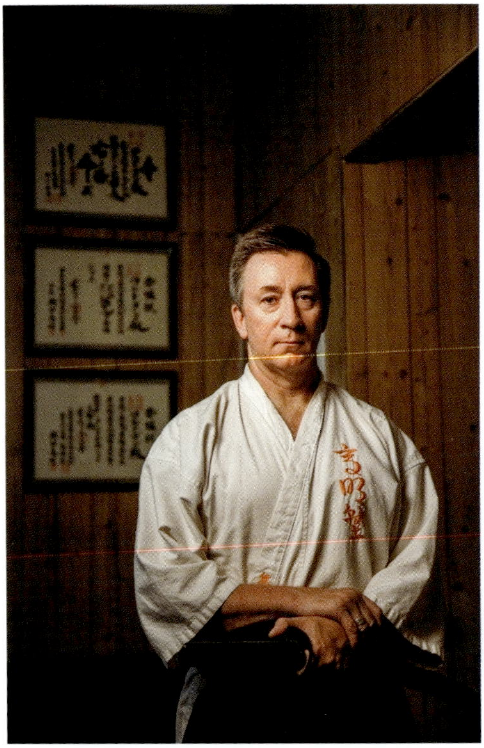

Figure 2.13 A martial arts instructor poses approximately 7 feet away from a wall containing his certifications, which appear slightly out of focus due to a large aperture setting.

ISO 400 • 1/160 sec. • f/4 • 65mm

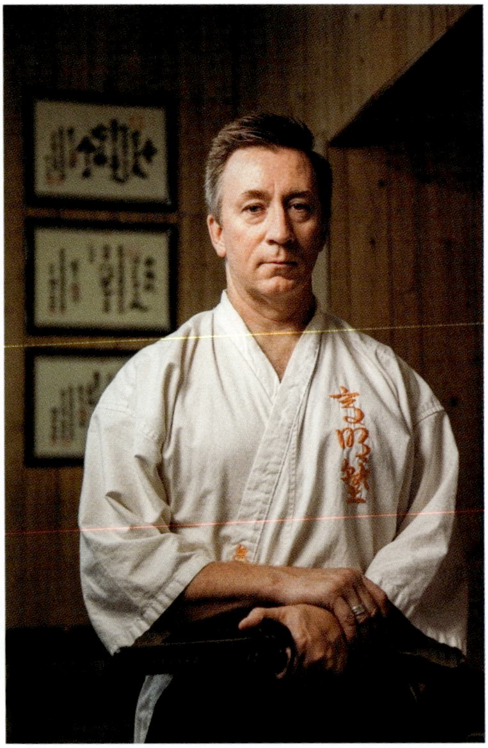

Figure 2.14 When I moved him forward 3 feet, the wall and certifications appeared more out of focus, with the shift of the focal plane—on the subject's eyes—closer to the lens and away from the wall.

ISO 400 • 1/50 sec. • f/4 • 67mm

Do Lenses Have Inherent Depth of Field?

It is common to hear photographers say that lenses have different inherent levels of depth of field based on their focal lengths. Visually, this makes sense when you start comparing images shot at different focal lengths with the same aperture value. Wider focal lengths produce images that seem to have more depth of field at the same aperture than do longer focal lengths. A shot made at f/5.6 at 17mm appears sharper all the way through than does a shot at f/5.6 and 200mm. From a practical perspective, this is great information and may well inform our own decisions on how to visually size up a shot. However, this information is technically flawed.

Wider-angle lenses seem to offer more depth of field than their longer relatives at the same aperture simply because of the size relationship between the lens and the subject, as well as the optical perspective different types of lenses exhibit (more on perspective later in the chapter). When you are shooting from the same distance to the subject (be it a single person or a complex landscape), using a wider focal length produces a frame in which the subject is significantly smaller—everything is smaller—than if you were shooting at longer focal lengths. As a result of the wider *perspective*, everything in an image shot at a wider focal length from the same distance as a longer lens looks more in focus. However, the depth of field will be the same relatively.

Hyperfocal Distance

At times, achieving maximum depth of field is appealing (**Figure 2.15** on the following page). Many of the world's famous landscape, architecture, and street photographs were made with all of their content in focus, from the closest foreground content to the farthest background subject matter. Achieving maximum depth of field like this is often referred to as *hyperfocal distance,* and it is another one of those "tricks of the trade" to add to your bag of techniques.

Hyperfocal distance actually refers to the distance at which you can place your focal plane and render everything in the frame sharply. Although there is a great deal of optical science defining hyperfocal distance, that distance is basically one-third of the distance *into* the scene in which you're shooting. For example, if you were shooting into a room that measured 100 feet long, you would focus at about 33 feet. Easy enough, right? Well, you're probably not photographing in 100-foot-long rooms very often. You are looking off into canyons, photographing people walking down a street that has no end, and shooting macro images of flowers in a field. All instances offer up varied distances in which to shoot, leaving you to take a visual stab at where a third of the distance into the scene may be (**Figure 2.16** on the following page).

Figure 2.15
Everything from the closest waterfall to the mountaintop in the background is in focus, illustrating maximum depth of field, or hyperfocal distance.

ISO 50 • 4 secs.
f/22 • 31mm

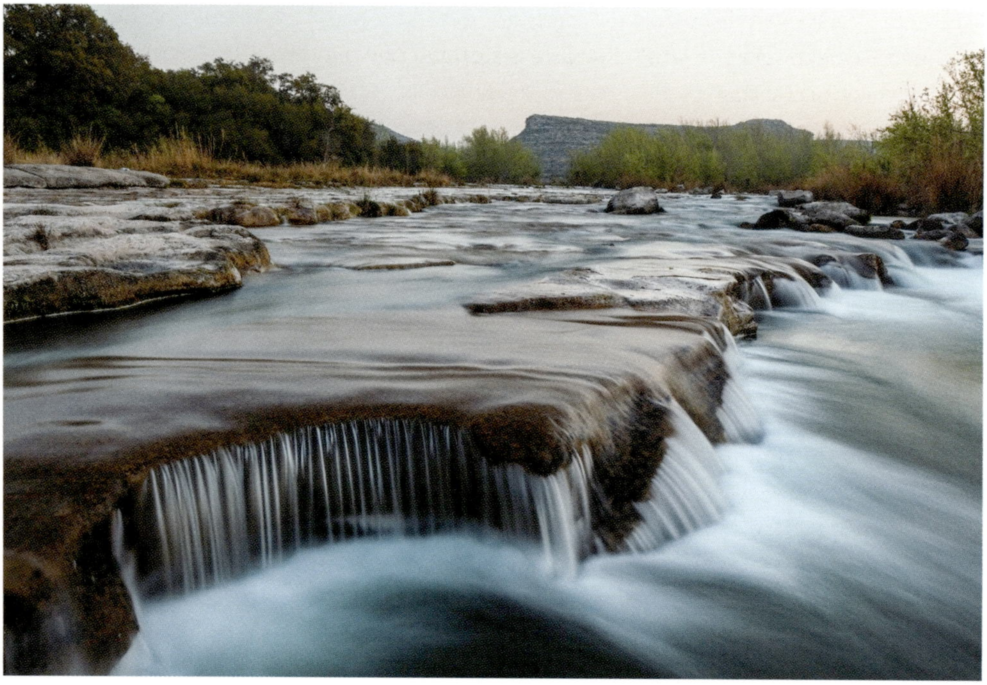

Figure 2.16
With the aperture stopped down all the way on a telephoto zoom lens, I tried to focus one-third of the distance into the entire scene (indicated by the red arrow) to ensure maximum depth of field.

ISO 100 • .6 sec. •
f/32 • 70mm

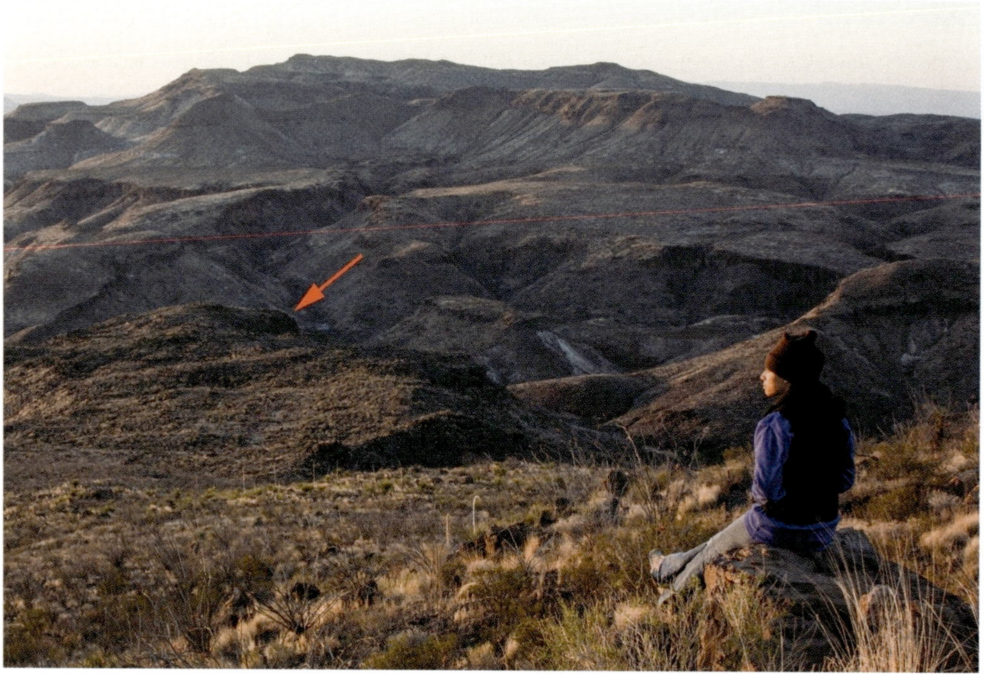

On top of focusing a third of the distance into a scene for maximum depth of field, you need to make sure the lens's aperture is stopped down all the way. For most wide and standard lenses, this means stopping down to f/22. For telephoto lenses and lenses capable of zooming to telephoto focal lengths, it might mean stopping down to f/32. Combining appropriate hyperfocal distance focusing and stopping the aperture down all the way will result in a sharp image throughout.

I've learned over the years that achieving hyperfocal distance is a bit easier (and more common) with wider focal lengths. They are less sensitive to minute adjustments of the focus ring—adjusting the ring on a telephoto lens may mean shifting focus dozens of feet, versus inches with a wide-angle lens. Wider focal lengths are often used in situations where maximum depth of field is desired, such as landscape photography.

Keep in mind that although you can use autofocus to focus one-third of the distance into a scene, it might be less frustrating to use manual focus. Additionally, shots like Figure 2.16 often require the use of a tripod, particularly when stopping the aperture down all the way means shooting with shutter speeds slower than the minimum sustaining shutter speed (see Chapter 1).

Depth of Field Preview Button

Wish there was a way for you to check out how much depth of field you will achieve before you push the shutter button? Sure, you can always snap a test shot and zoom in to the LCD display to check your focus throughout the image. However, it's nice to know that your Canon camera has a way to check the depth of field before you even put your finger on the shutter. It is called the Depth of Field (DOF) Preview button, a small button located below the lens on the camera body. Depending on the model of camera you are using, the placement and shape of the button may vary, but they all do the same thing.

When you press the DOF Preview button, the camera tells the lens to stop down to the selected aperture. At this point, you can look through the viewfinder (I usually hit the DOF Preview button while my eye is already at the viewfinder) and see how much of the image will be in focus. You'll notice as you press the button, the image in the viewfinder will dim. This is a result of the aperture closing down to the selected aperture, potentially restricting the amount of light passing through the lens into the camera. The dimming does not have anything to do with the shot exposure. However, in pressing the DOF Preview button, you are able to see what will appear sharp in an image and what will be soft due to the amount of depth of field.

I use the DOF Preview button frequently, especially with environmental portraits and landscape photography. I consider it one of the more valuable functions of the camera and lens combination. It is also particularly helpful for macro photography, where it seems the depth of field drops off drastically, no matter which aperture you use.

Perspective

In addition to considering the aperture—more specifically, depth of field—when I size up a shot, I envision its perspective before composing within the frame. Perspective refers to the size of and spatial relationships between objects in a two-dimensional image. Photographers use different perspectives to accomplish many things, one being to provide the viewer with a more three-dimensional perception of their work. When it comes down to it, photographs are dimensionally flat, but lenses, in conjunction with good composition, allow us to augment this feeling. Just as compositional technique emphasizes use of foreground, midground, and background to guide the eye through a shot, perspective deals with the size of the foreground to the midground and background, as well as the perceived distance between the three. Although it changes as focal lengths change, there are three categories we typically use to discuss perspective: expansive, compressed, and normal.

Expansive Perspective

The quintessential landscape shot is created with an ultra-wide-angle lens (think of the Canon 14mm f/2.8L or the EF-S 10–22mm f/3.5–4.5) pushed in close to a strong foreground subject, like an iconic plant or repetitious linear elements (**Figure 2.17**), with a sprawling mountain scene comprising the midground and background, topped off with an impressive sky that seems to stretch on forever. In this shot, the foreground looks to be miles away from the background structure, as well it might be, and it is so wide that you might as well be *in* the shot as opposed to looking at it. This feeling is closely associated with the type of perspective wider focal lengths offer: expansive.

Typically, focal lengths ranging from 8mm to 35mm provide an avenue to achieving expansive perspective. Several visual characteristics help highlight this common look. The first is that foreground subject matter—objects that are within several feet of the photographer—will appear much larger than subject matter of much larger size in the background (**Figure 2.18**).

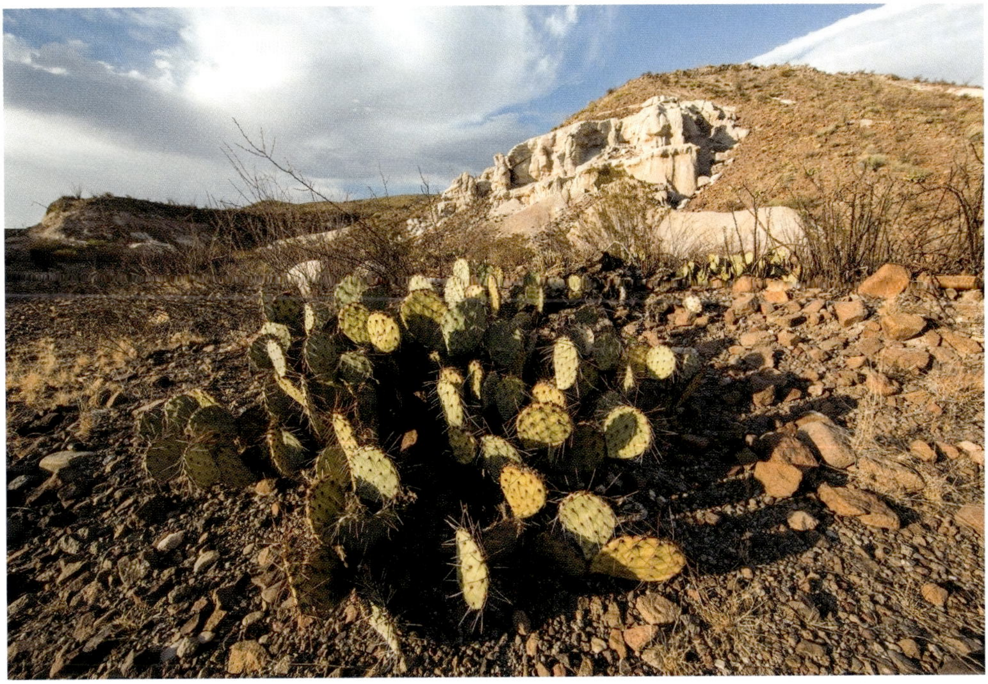

Figure 2.17
This extremely wide desert-landscape shot emphasizes and exaggerates the size of the foreground, expanding it toward the camera.

ISO 100 • 1/60 sec. • f/14 • 14mm

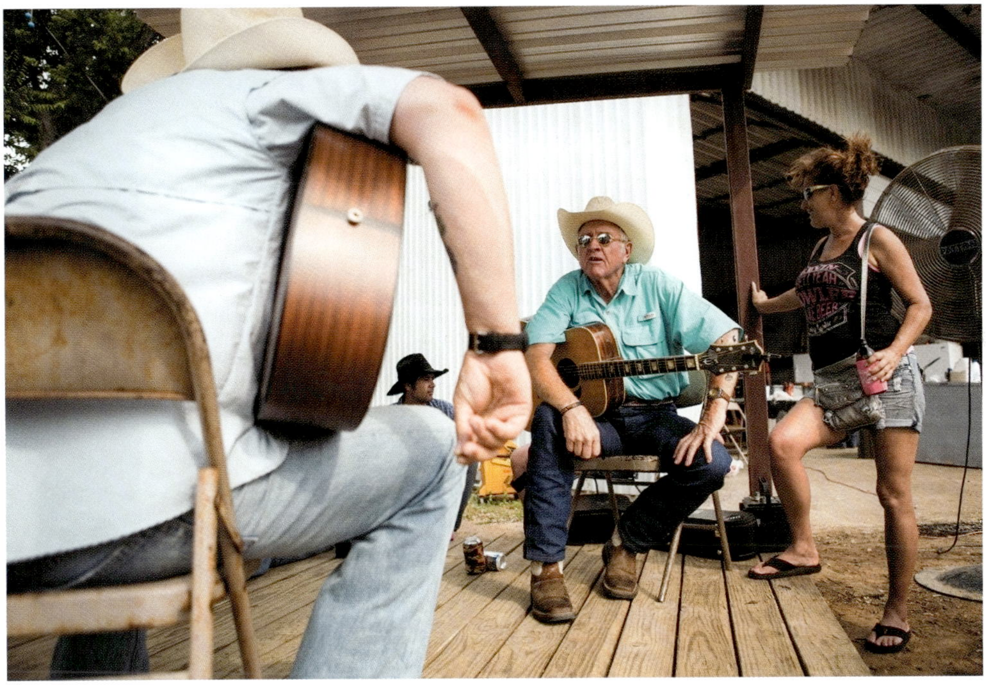

Figure 2.18
A wide-angle lens pushed in tight on the foreground makes it look like the man facing the camera is playing with a giant!

ISO 100 • 1/640 sec. • f/2.8 • 24mm

Want to drive visual significance toward a relatively small object while still showing off its environment? Throw on a wide-angle lens (**Figure 2.19**). The second image is an example of the signature expansive distance created between said foreground subject matter and midground and background material (**Figure 2.20**). The wider the lens, the larger the distance between points in the frame.

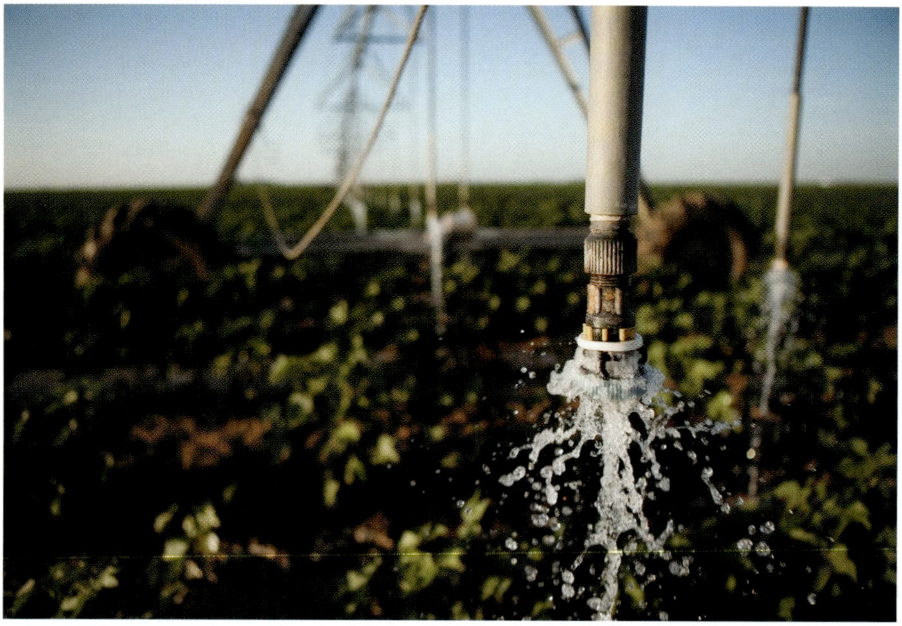

Figure 2.19
The value in a wide-angle, expansive perspective is its ability to showcase an important subject, like this irrigation head, and its relative environment.

ISO 100 • 1/640 sec. • f/2.8 • 24mm

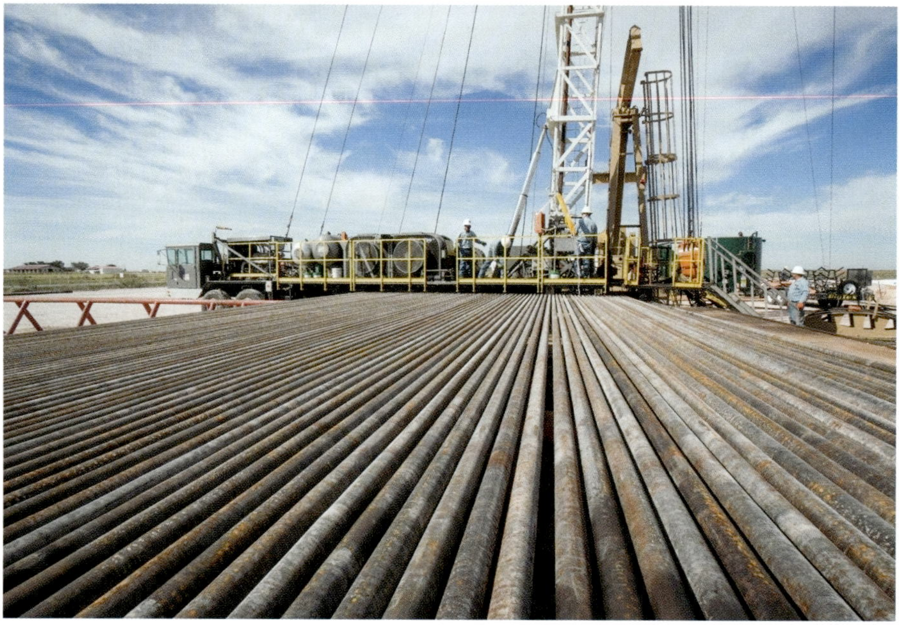

Figure 2.20
Expansive perspective exaggerates distance between foreground and background, making these oilfield pipes seem longer than the rig in the midground is tall. Truth be told, they are shorter than the vehicle.

ISO 200 • 1/60 sec. • f/22 • 17mm

I often use wider focal lengths, which result in expansive shots. I enjoy how you can drive so much attention to a particular part of the frame while also including the world around it for context and storytelling purposes (**Figure 2.21**). However, expansive perspective is not without its drawbacks.

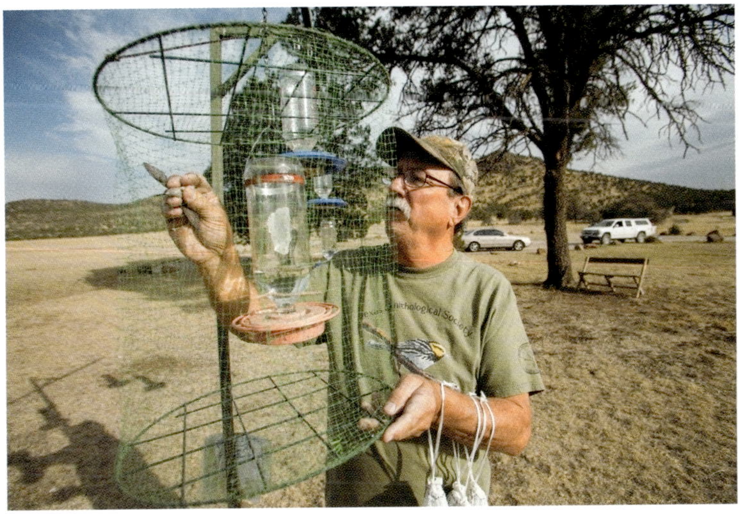

Figure 2.21
Pushing a wide-angle lens close to an active subject, such as this hummingbird researcher netting birds, engages viewers with the setting as if they were standing right there.

ISO 100 • 1/640 sec. • f/5 • 17mm

Distortion

All of the perspective goodness highlighted above can be considered serious optical distortion in some instances. In creating an expansive perspective, one is exaggerating the actual size and distances of subject matter in the frame. There are certain areas of photography where this is less acceptable or appropriate, such as in architectural and commercial photography (**Figure 2.22**), or even in areas of photojournalism.

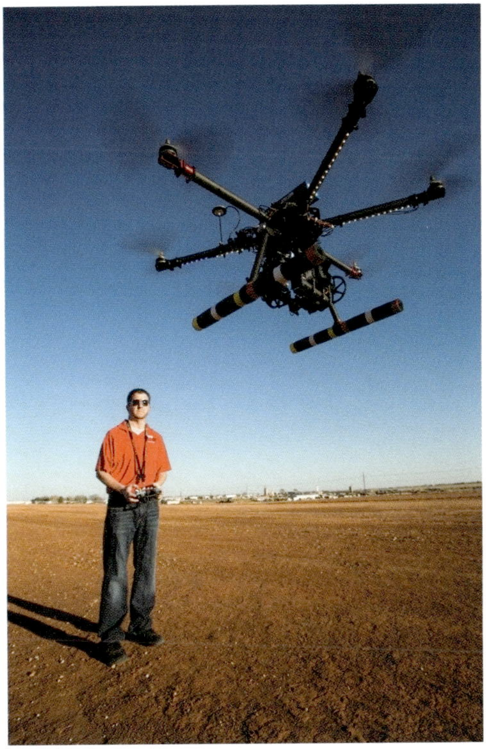

Figure 2.22
As interesting as the expansive exaggeration is, it distorts the length and, subsequently, the shape of the photography drone, as well as the length of photographer Kris Barton's legs.

ISO 100 • 1/250 sec. • f/7.1 • 18mm

Expansive perspective is also considered taboo in many portraiture circles. Consider for a moment the plight of a bride's nose if you pushed a 17mm lens close up on her face. The bride might not appreciate how her nose stretches and curves toward the outside of the frame as it follows the convex form of the lens elements, or perhaps the way her nose seems to bulge toward the viewer if she is facing into the frame. The distortion is caused by the actual curvature of the glass elements in the lens (**Figure 2.23**). They are responsible for this great perspective in many landscape shots—and some portraits if composed appropriately (**Figure 2.24**)—but they just might wreak havoc for a commercial portrait session.

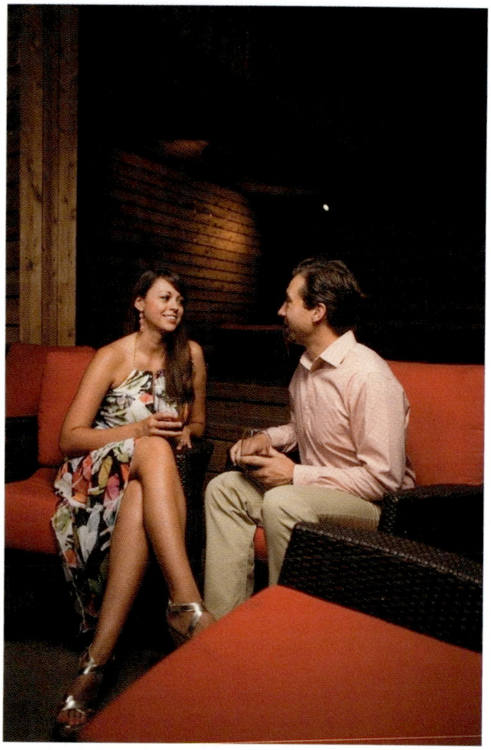

Figure 2.23 **Even at 32mm, wide-angle-lens distortion stretches the female model's legs since they exist near the left and bottom edges of the frame, areas where the curvature of the lens is extreme.**

ISO 100 • 1/30 sec. • f/2.8 • 32mm

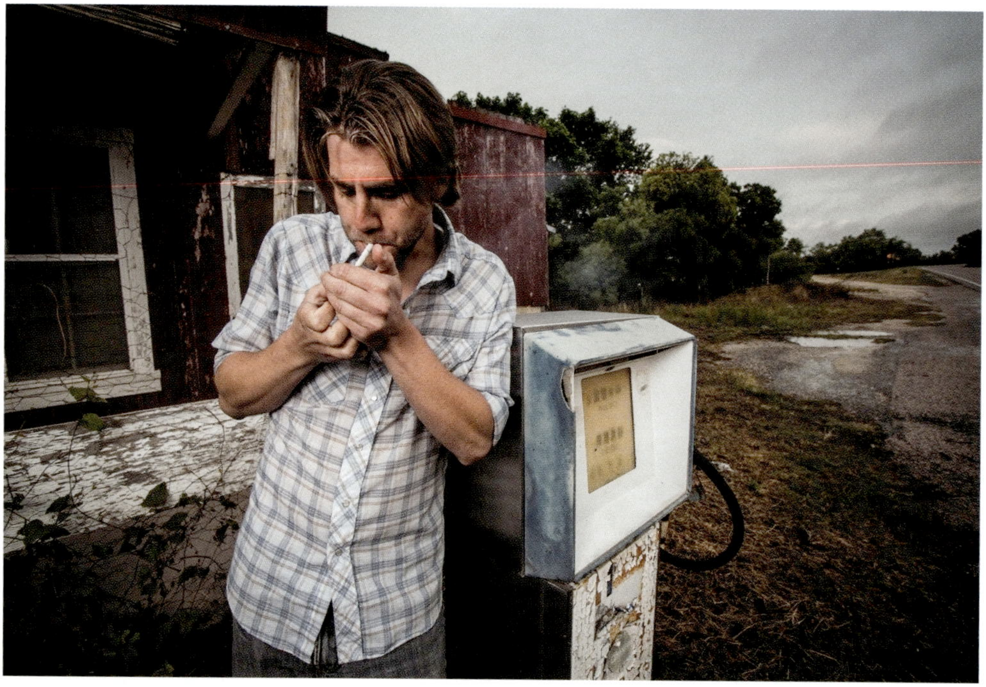

Figure 2.24 **Although this composition is stylistically appropriate, in my opinion, the model's head is not proportionately correct as a result of a wide-angle lens pushed in tightly for the portrait.**

ISO 200 • 1/60 sec. • f/8 • 17mm

Keystoning

Another issue wider focal lengths present is *keystoning*. Although technically not related to expansive perspective, it bears mentioning here since it is most evident when using lenses that achieve expansive perspective. Just as expansive perspective increases as you go wider with your focal length, so does this optical distortion. Keystoning refers to the convergence of vertical lines in a frame when a lens is pointed either up or down from being level with the horizon (**Figure 2.25**). A result of the shape of the lens elements, this converging of lines can express dominance or emphasize the importance of some subject matter in editorial contexts. However, it also severely distorts structures that we know to be level or square—not ideal for architects and others who value realistic depictions.

Tolerance of keystoning varies in different fields, and it is good to be aware of when keystoning happens. The nice thing about both keystoning and any other form of optical distortion or exaggeration is that you can see it through the viewfinder. If you are new to working with wider-angle lenses, test it out by zooming out to the widest focal length, focusing on a building, and moving your lens vertically up and down. Watch all of the lines in the frame that tend to be vertical start to lean in or out depending on the direction in which you are moving the camera. It is an interesting effect, but it bears repeating that keystoning doesn't go over well in some realms of image making. Note that keystoning occurs with all lenses; it is just more exaggerated with wider-angle lenses. Past 200mm, you might be hard-pressed to even notice it.

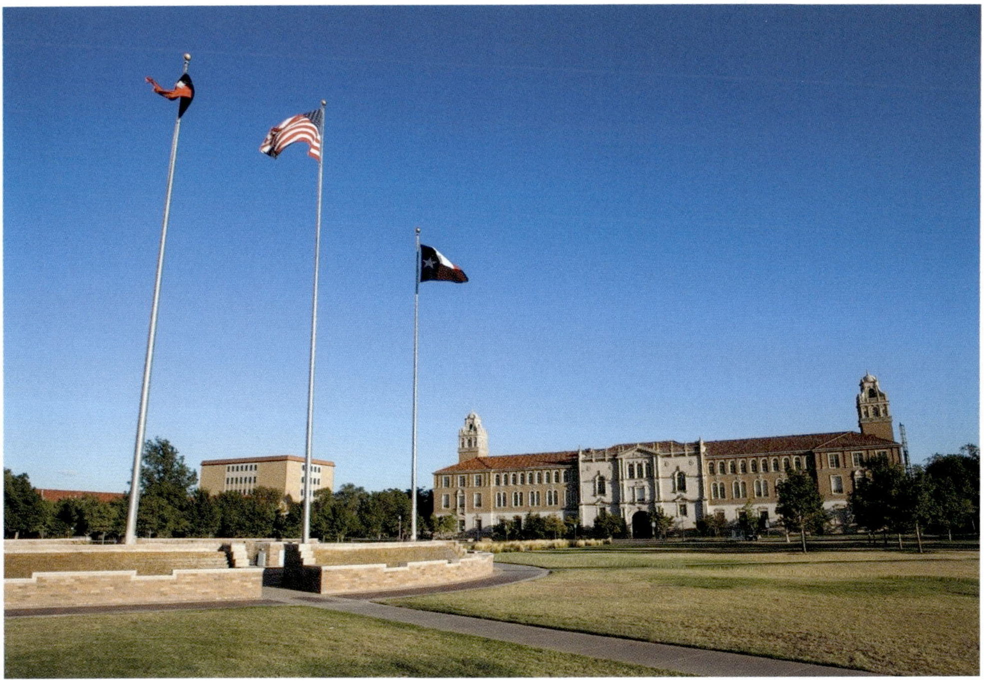

Figure 2.25
Normally, flag poles don't lean, and walls are usually built vertically straight. Keystoning forces vertical lines like these to lean in toward the middle of the frame when a wide-angle lens is pointed up (they lean the opposite way when the lens is pointed down).

ISO 100 • 1/250 sec. • f/8 • 24mm

Compressed Perspective

On the other end of the focal-length spectrum, a completely opposite look and feel emerges. Instead of expanding the distance between foreground and background, compressed perspective, wait for it, *compresses* that distance (**Figure 2.26**). Longer focal lengths—typically 105mm and beyond—smash foreground, midground, and background together, and the longer the lens, the more compression you get as a result (**Figure 2.27**). Portrait photographers like using a longer lens combined with a large aperture to place an out-of-focus, abstract background right behind the subject (**Figure 2.28**).

Landscape photographers use compressed perspective to draw out layers and patterns in vistas. Pulling backgrounds toward subject matter can be quite interpretive, and it is a great way to de-clutter an overly complex image. I enjoy using compressed perspective to create a sense of largeness in my landscape and outdoor work (**Figure 2.29**), and to highlight textural or pattern-like occurrences in environments that would otherwise go unnoticed without a longer lens's look (**Figure 2.30**).

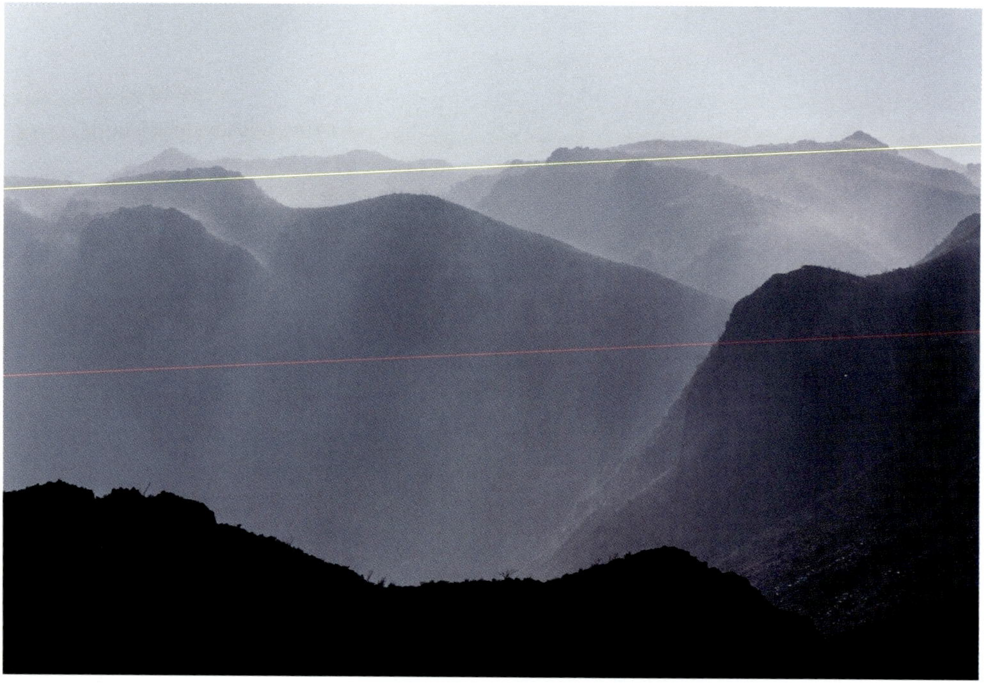

Figure 2.26 **In order to emphasize the amount of rain, I used a long 400mm focal length to compress all of the mountains together.**

ISO 200 • 1/1600 sec. • f/8 • 400mm

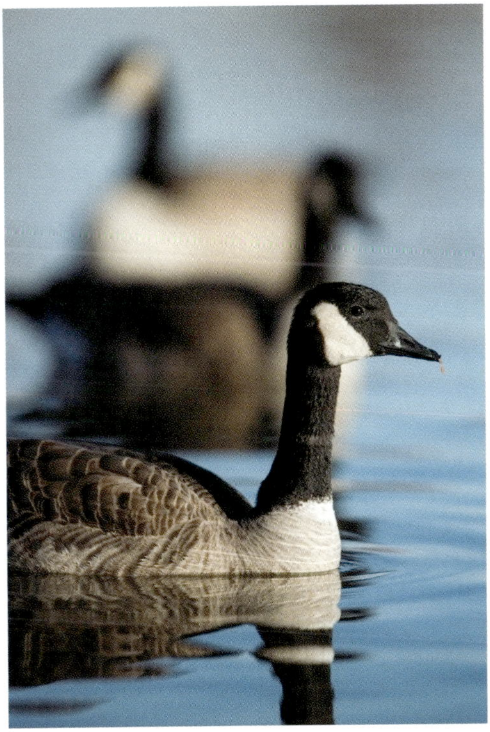

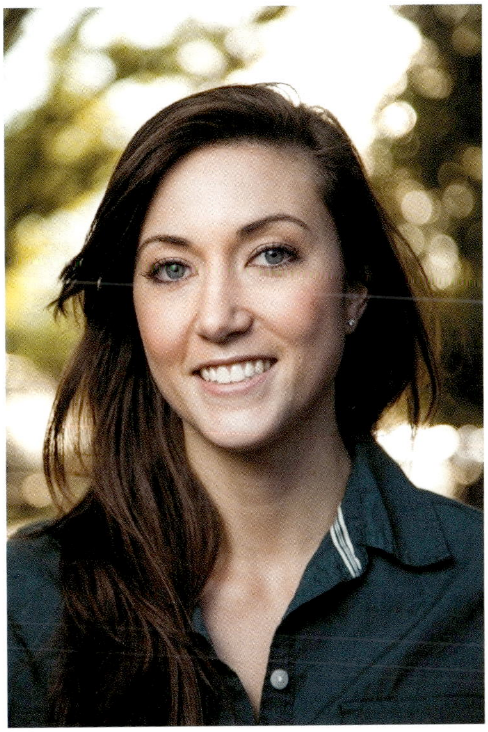

Figure 2.27 (left) Even though the other two geese are quite some distance behind the one in focus, a long lens will draw them together as a result of optical compression.

ISO 100 • 1/2000 sec. • f/2.8 • 400mm

Figure 2.28 (right) Compression perspective is useful for creating beautiful, abstract backgrounds for portraits.

ISO 100 • 1/100 sec. • f/4 • 105mm

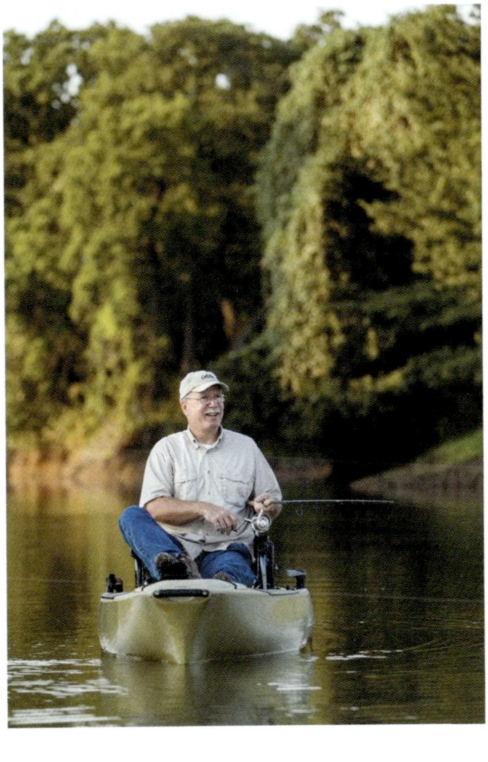

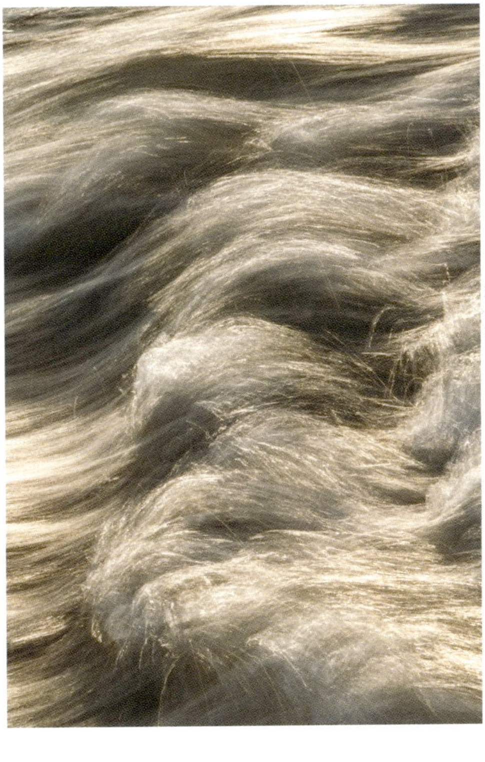

Figure 2.29 (left) With the wooded background pulled closer to the subject, the setting seems larger than the small creek on which the angler is paddling.

ISO 100 • 1/320 sec. • f/2.8 • 145mm

Figure 2.30 (right) Compression also allows for a nice way to isolate pattern and rhythm in small areas of a photo-worthy context, such as this one rapid in a larger set of them.

ISO 50 • 1/5 sec. • f/32 • 155mm

Compressed perspective is certainly another form of optical distortion, but it is treated less as such compared to expansive perspective. Although it does manipulate size—especially the relative size of the background compared to the foreground—it does not necessarily share the negative connotation. One thing to keep in mind is that compressed perspective threatens to make an already flat medium look even more flat. When working with longer lenses, pay close attention to photographic attributes such as color and light (and shadow) to increase or maintain the image's depth and dimension.

Normal Perspective

For a moment, lift your eyes from the book and look around you. Try to avoid using your peripheral vision and simply take in what is in front of you. Notice the size of the book compared to something of a similar size five feet away, then ten feet away. Gauge the distance from where you are sitting or standing to a wall or tree or another static object. In completing this simple visual exercise, you have experienced (as you have your entire life) normal perspective. This so-aptly named perspective highlights a lens's ability to replicate the way our eyes actually see everything in our environment.

So, what is the focal length that most closely matches the way our eyes take in relative size and spatial relationships? On a full-frame camera, the tried and true 50mm is considered a *normal* lens. On an APS-C crop-sensor camera, a 35mm (more like 31mm) lens would do the job. The normal perspective is extremely popular. Standard zoom lenses, such as the EF 24–70mm f/2.8L or EF-S 18–55mm f/3.5–5.6 are designed around the normal perspective. At the university, the only lens I require students in introductory courses to have is a zoom lens with a focal length that exhibits normal perspective.

Many photographers enjoy shooting with normal perspective because of their ability to capture what they actually see—or at least get pretty close (**Figure 2.31**). I know photographers who for extended periods of time would only shoot with a normal-perspective lens. It is the perspective in which many of the world's most famous, historical shots were recorded. Although a prime EF 50mm f/1.4 might not offer as much versatility as the Swiss Army knife of a lens, EF 28–135mm f/3.5–5.6 IS, it is still valued for its straight-ahead approach to making realistic images—not to mention its ultra-fast maximum aperture (**Figure 2.32**).

It is worth mentioning that in highlighting expansive, normal, and compressed perspective, I left out some ranges of focal lengths. As mentioned previously, perspective changes on a sliding scale from extremely expansive to extremely compressed as focal lengths change. The valuable thing to keep in mind is that as one moves to wider focal lengths, one will achieve more expansive perspective, and the longer the focal length, the more compressed. Going into a shoot knowing this helps you to both see and compose great shots and avoid being surprised later by unexpected perspective-influenced issues in your images. You will see in the following four chapters how perspective plays a large role in considering different types of lenses for making the most of different subject matter and their environment.

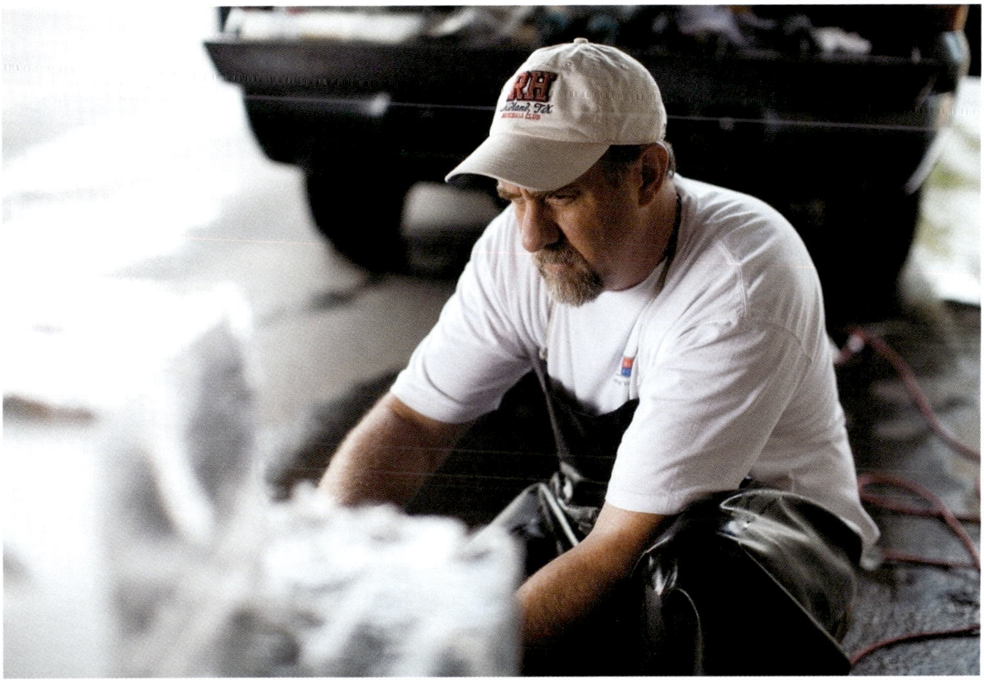

Figure 2.31
When on assignment photographing folks such as this ice sculptor, I like to make some images tight on the subject at 50mm to counter the expansive and sometimes distorted look of a wide-angle lens.

ISO 50 • 1/40 sec. • f/2 • 50mm

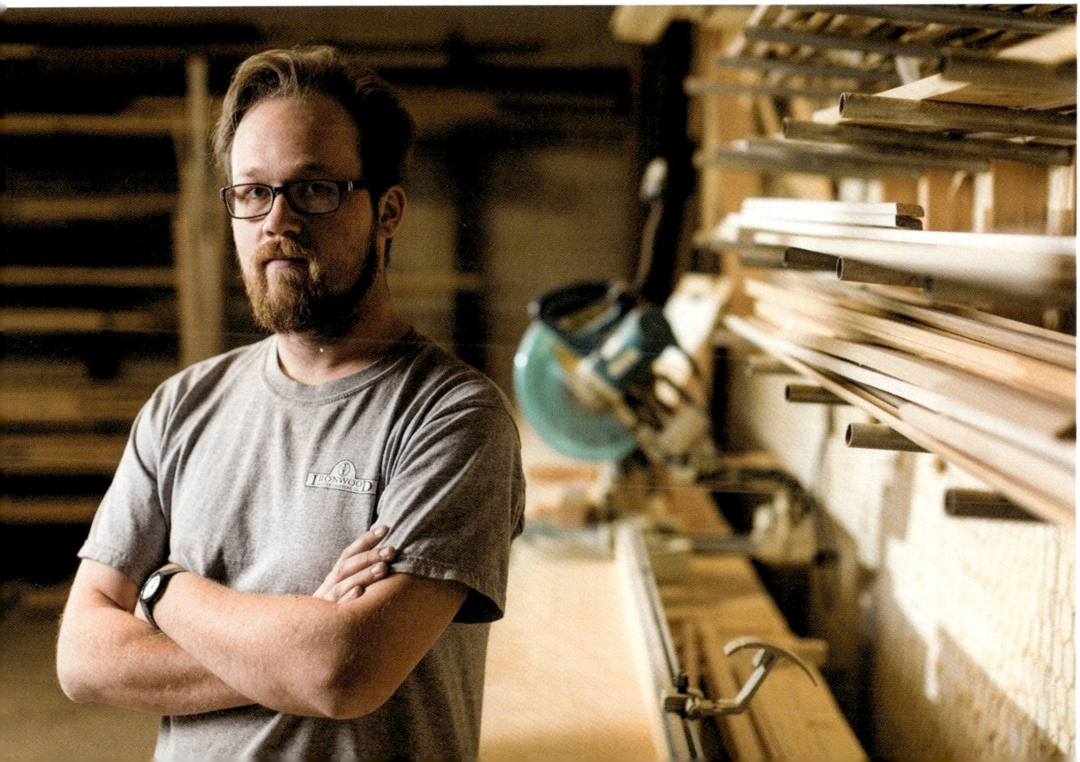

Figure 2.32
Because it captures subjects proportionately, a normal lens is great for environmental portraits.

ISO 200 • 1/200 sec. • f/2 • 50mm

Chapter 2 Assignments

Depth of field is so important to photographers! If there is one control that is a go-to technical and aesthetic consideration for folks new to photography, this is it. Below are a few assignments that will help you become more cognizant and confident in seeing and adjusting the depth of field your lens offers you.

It's all about the aperture

Thanks to relatively modern technology, there are multiple aperture values from which to choose, allowing you to make the finest adjustment to the amount of depth of field in the frame. Place your camera on a tripod and photograph a single subject (it could be a person or something inanimate, like a stuffed animal) positioned 5 feet from you. Start with your aperture wide open (the lowest value), and for each shot, stop your aperture down (up in value) by one stop until you cannot stop it down anymore. I recommend doing this in Aperture Priority (AV) mode, but if you are in Manual exposure mode, be sure to make equivalent adjustments to your shutter speed.

As you make these shots, check your LCD and notice how much depth of field you gain as you stop the aperture down each time. For more nuanced adjustments, stop your aperture down by a third of a stop each shot. Use this as a way to become more familiar with how the aperture's effect on depth of field will appear in your images. There are several variables that play into the appearance of depth of field, but this is the most fundamental of them all.

Move!

With the same subject, leave your lens at one focal length (50mm, for example) and the aperture at a fixed value (let's say f/5.6, but any will do). For this series of images, move closer by one foot every time you make an image, always maintaining focus on your subject. Move in closer until you pass your minimum focusing distance (the closest point you can focus on with that particular lens).

Now, start backing up a foot for each shot. Assess the level of perceived depth of field based on simply moving back and forth from your subject. You'll notice that the closer you move toward your subject, the shallower your depth of field becomes, and vice versa when you back out. This exercise will give you an idea of how to handle situations in which you've maxed out your aperture setting but may need more or less depth of field (especially handy when shooting portraits).

Go hyperfocal

Practice hyperfocal distance focusing by positioning yourself and your camera in front of a subject-heavy scene. It could be a landscape or cityscape with a strong foreground subject and a noticeable background subject. Place your camera on a tripod, compose your shot, and make your best guess at how far one-third of the distance between your background subject and the camera is. Focus on that point.

Stop your aperture down all the way, and make a few exposures. Check your focus. Is everything from the foreground subject to the background sharp? If it isn't, you might have to adjust where you placed the focal plane. If that doesn't work, you are more than likely too close to the foreground subject (remember minimal focusing distance). If it helps to do so before tackling a land or cityscape, set up four cones on a 100-foot stretch of pavement, two to indicate foreground and background, the other two to mark the points that split the distance into thirds. Focus on the second cone from the camera, and check your focus. Hyperfocal distance can be hard to judge when shooting in the field. Like anything, the more you work with it, the better you get at doing it.

Share your results with the book's Flickr group!
Join the group here: www.flickr.com/groups/canonlenses_fromsnapshotstogreatshots

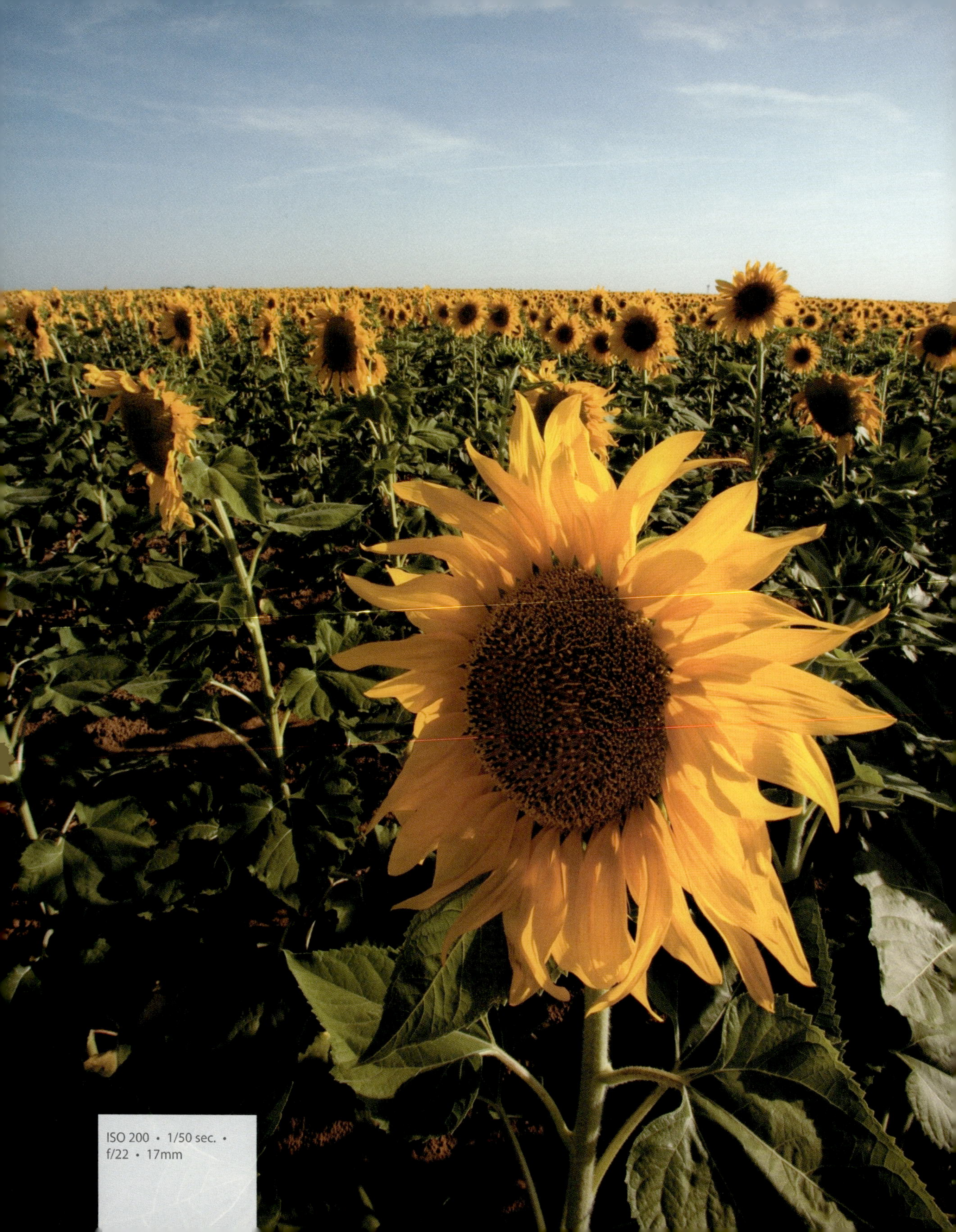

ISO 200 • 1/50 sec. • f/22 • 17mm

3
Ultra-Wides and Wides

Expansive opportunities

I have to be honest: I love wide-angle lenses. I love the extremely wide perspective, the bulbous glass at the end of the lenses, that they are not the size of telephotos, and that I can handhold wide-angle lenses using relatively slower shutter speeds. I am constantly drawn to images that showcase great use of wide-angle focal lengths, and I'm apt to *see* images in terms of wider focal lengths before considering longer lenses. Ultra-wide and wide-angle lenses have value in the photographer's camera bag, offering us really cool perspectives. I don't know anyone who has not had an "oh, wow!" moment after looking through a 14mm or 10mm focal length for the first time. Afterward, it's all about converting that moment to outstanding images!

Poring Over the Picture

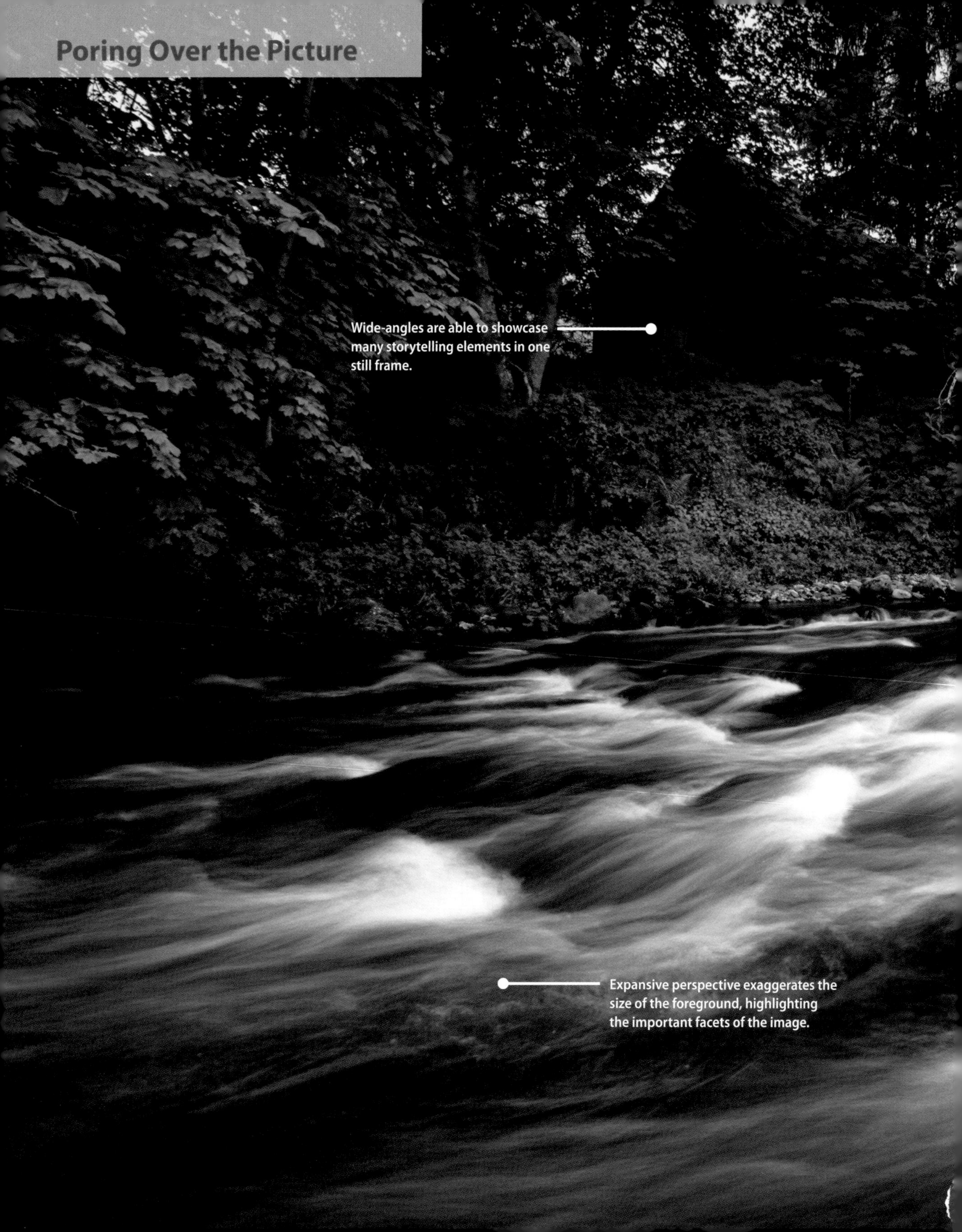

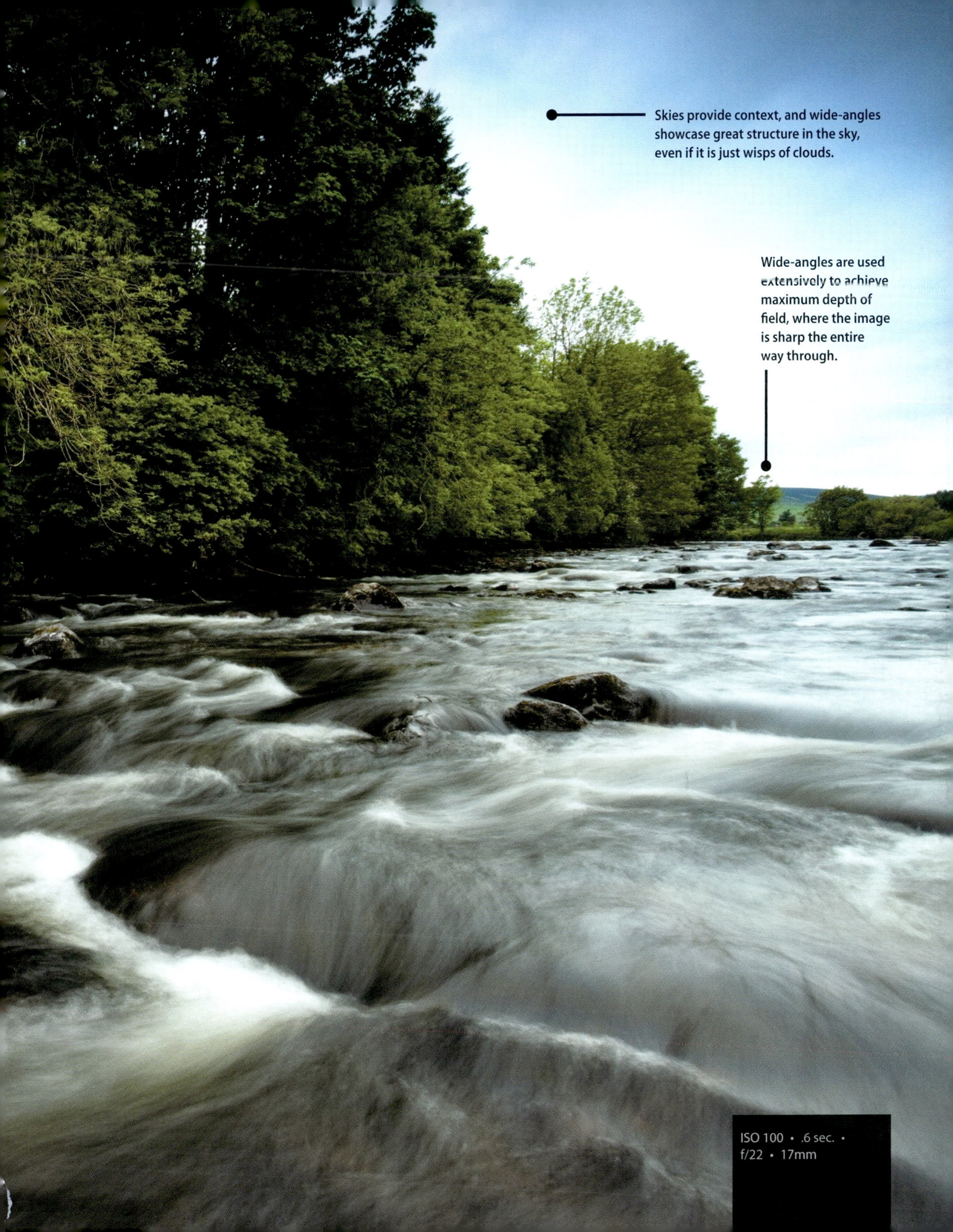
Skies provide context, and wide-angles showcase great structure in the sky, even if it is just wisps of clouds.
Wide-angles are used extensively to achieve maximum depth of field, where the image is sharp the entire way through.
ISO 100 • .6 sec. • f/22 • 17mm

How Wide Can You Go?

Really wide! As a matter of fact, 8mm is the widest focal length Canon lenses can reach. This is the widest end of the widest Canon zoom lens, the EF 8–15mm f/4L Fisheye (**Figure 3.1**). Wide-angle focal lengths typically comprise focal lengths of 24mm to around 35mm (these are full-frame focal lengths), and those wider are designated as "ultra-wide."

The EF 8–15mm f/4L Fisheye is ultra-wide, one of two fisheye lenses Canon manufactures at the time of writing, the other being the EF 15mm f/2.8 Fisheye. A *fisheye* lens exhibits the visual qualities of its moniker, offering a 180-degree angle of view. What does this mean? It means if you point the lens straight at the horizon, you'll more than likely capture your shoes in the shot, as well as the sky straight above you! As a result, everything within the frame of a fisheye lens is distorted, seemingly stretching outward toward the image's viewer. When you see a fisheye perspective, you immediately know it for the extreme distortion and curvature of straight lines, such as the horizon, building corners, and the like.

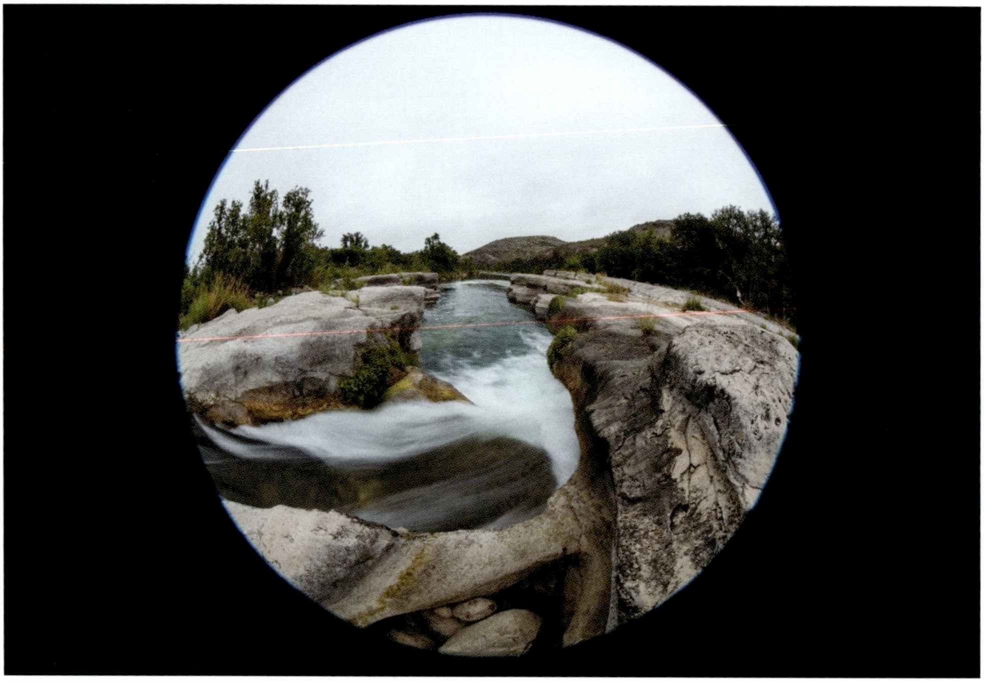

Figure 3.1
Canon's widest focal length is 8mm, as shown through this fisheye zoom (the EF 8–15mm f/4L).

ISO 100 • 1/4 sec. • f/22 • 8mm

Circular and Full-Frame Fisheyes

Although fisheye lenses have been around for more than a century, they gained wide appeal about 50 years ago and are still considered a popular niche lens. The EF 8–15mm f/4L Fisheye exhibits the two different types of fisheyes generally discussed: circular and full-frame (not to be confused with full-frame sensors).

Circular fisheyes produce a classic fisheye look in that the angle of view—all 180 degrees—is contained in a circular image in the middle of the frame (**Figures 3.2** and **3.3**). This is a result of the focal length being so wide that real estate on the camera's sensor (or film) has to be sacrificed. As you zoom out from 15mm to 8mm, you start to notice a circular visual manifest through the viewfinder. (Tip: make sure you take the lens hood off to ensure a circular image as opposed to another shape.)

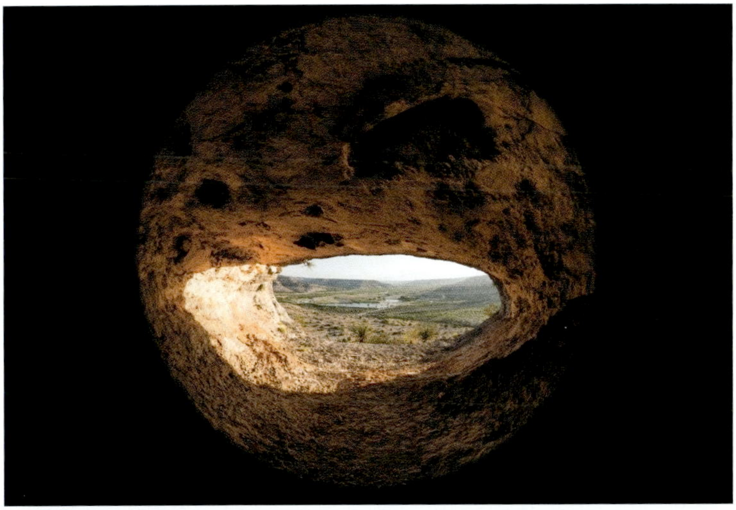

Figure 3.2
At 8mm, the EF 8–15mm f/4L is a circular fisheye, capturing a 180-degree angle of view, forcing one to be aware of where his or her feet rest.

ISO 100 • 1/40 sec. • f/11 • 8mm

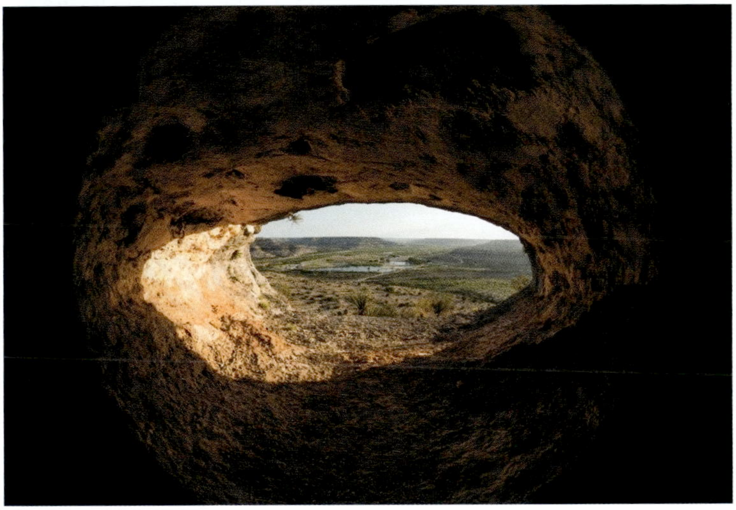

Figure 3.3
Zooming a bit tighter in the cave takes up more real estate on the camera's sensor without giving up too much detail in the shot.

ISO 100 • 1/40 sec. • f/11 • 10mm

Full-frame fisheyes, such as the EF 15mm f/2.8 and the longer end of the EF 8–15mm f/4L, project an image onto all of the camera's sensor, albeit still extremely distorted (**Figure 3.4**). Lest your hands move the zoom ring easily, the EF 8–15mm f/4L Fisheye includes a "Limit" switch, which locks the focal length at 15mm and avoids the circular vignetting that would occur at shorter focal lengths.

As I stated earlier, fisheye lenses fulfill a fairly niche function. The extreme curvilinear distortion and warping of the image is a unique visual, and although these lenses are downright fun to play with, they are not for everyone. I don't own one—they just don't fit my style. Others have a ball with them, seeing everything from landscapes to cityscapes in new, bulbous ways!

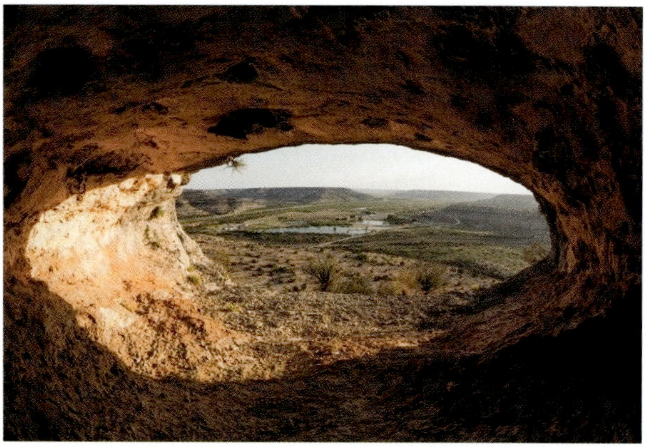

Figure 3.4 A full-frame fisheye perspective, where the bulbous aesthetic of the lens takes up the entire sensor and image area. Note the curved nature of the horizon in the far background.

ISO 100 • 1/40 sec. • f/11 • 15mm

Rectilinear Lenses

For those who want to avoid the fisheye look, Canon's EF 14mm f/2.8L offers an extremely wide perspective without the distortion that reveals the curvature of the lens elements (**Figure 3.5**).

The 14mm is a *rectilinear* lens, which means it maintains straight lines as visually straight, despite the accompanying wide-angle distortion that occurs when focal lengths get more and more expansive (**Figure 3.6**). This feature paired with this focal length makes for an incredible landscape lens (**Figure 3.7**), as well as one that can be used to really push up on high-action activities and show off the environment at the same time (**Figure 3.8**).

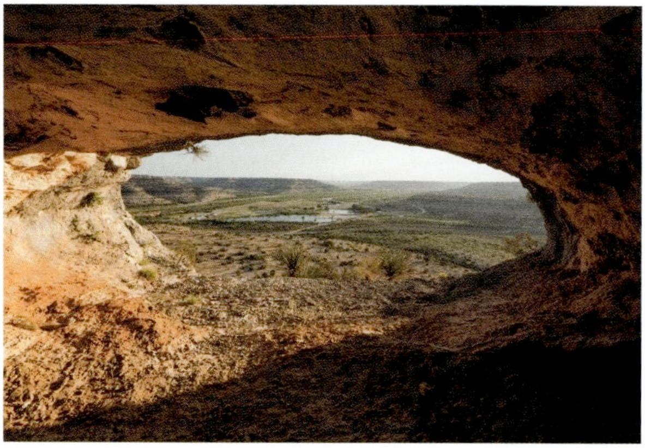

Figure 3.5 Fisheye lenses exhibit a curvilinear look, but the EF 14mm f/2.8L and all other wide-angle lenses showcase a rectilinear perspective, reducing the extreme bulge seen in previous images.

ISO 100 • 1/40 sec. • f/11 • 14mm

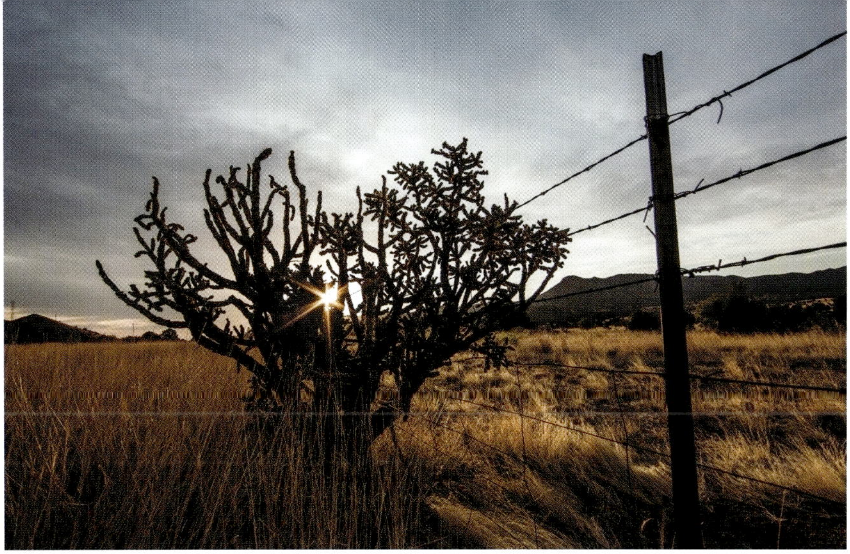

Figure 3.6 **Even though it is extremely wide, the rectilinear EF 14mm f/2.8 still keeps linear subject matter straight, such as the fence post and the barbed wire.**

ISO 200 • 1/200 sec. • f/11 • 14mm

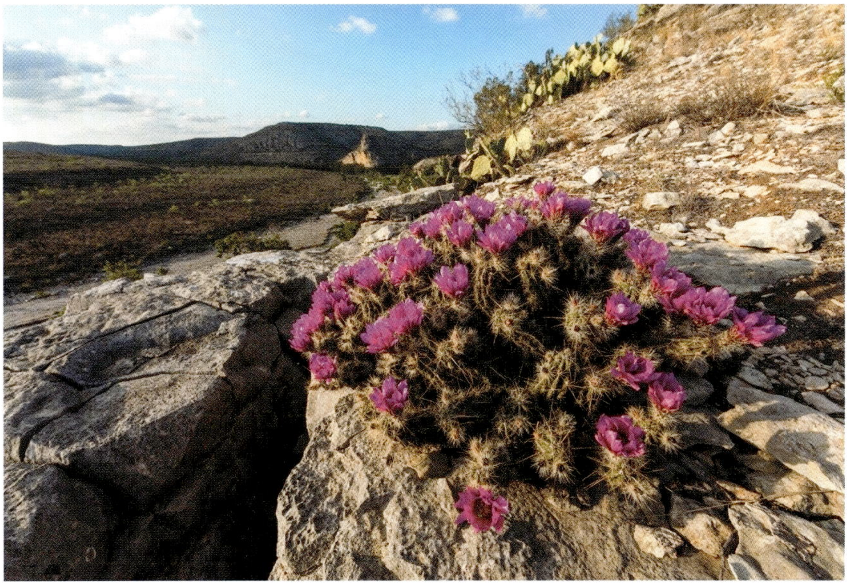

Figure 3.7 **Extremely wide-angle lenses typically have short minimal focusing distances, allowing the shooter to compose tightly on significant subject matter.**

ISO 100 • 1/40 sec. • f/16 • 14mm

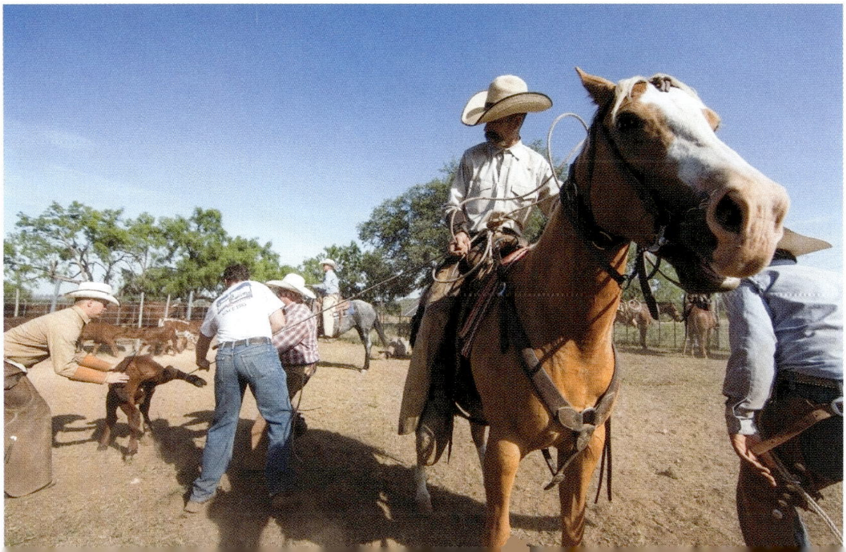

Figure 3.8 **Want to make your viewers feel like they are part of the action? Take a wide-angle like the EF 14mm f/2.8L into the thick of it.**

ISO 200 • 1/1000 sec. • f/5.6 • 14mm

Although it is difficult to use in all instances, given that subject matter diminishes in size greatly if just a few feet away, the EF 14mm f/2.8L is an extremely well made and highly functional lens for those wanting the widest rectilinear focal length possible. Unfortunately for some, this lens also comes with a premium price tag, so it might be worth renting before purchasing. If you're anything like me, though, you'll find an affinity for this chunk of glass.

Keep an Eye on the Glass

One thing to keep in mind with all lenses, but especially the widest of the wide, is the importance of taking care of the outer lens element. I'll touch on lens care in Chapter 8, but since we're on the subject of lenses that feature bulbous front elements, it is worth reiterating here: It is just too easy to put a greasy thumb- or fingerprint on that glass, or bump it into a hard corner. Consider always placing the lens cap on the lens when it is not in use, carry a lens cloth (always) with you, and, as my buddy Alan Hess taught me a few years ago, sling your camera over your shoulder with the lens pointing toward you instead of away from you. This way, the lens element is less likely to come into contact with grubby hands, brick walls, and the like.

Ultra-Wides for Every Day

Wide-angle lenses for Canon typically range in focal length from 8mm to 35mm. Technically, anything wider (or shorter) than 50mm can be considered wide-angle, but the closer the lens is to normal perspective, the more it loses that visual essence. For me and many others, the perfect wide-angle lens—which is part of the trinity written about earlier in the book—is a lens that covers the ultra-wide and wide alike. Wide-angle zoom lenses such as the EF 16–35mm f/2.8L, the EF 17–40mm f/4L, and the EF-S 10–22mm f/3.5–4.5 (for crop-sensor cameras) provide such an offering. They move from extremely wide-angle perspectives perfect for landscapes (**Figure 3.9**) to a longer focal length loved by many photojournalists and street photographers (**Figure 3.10**).

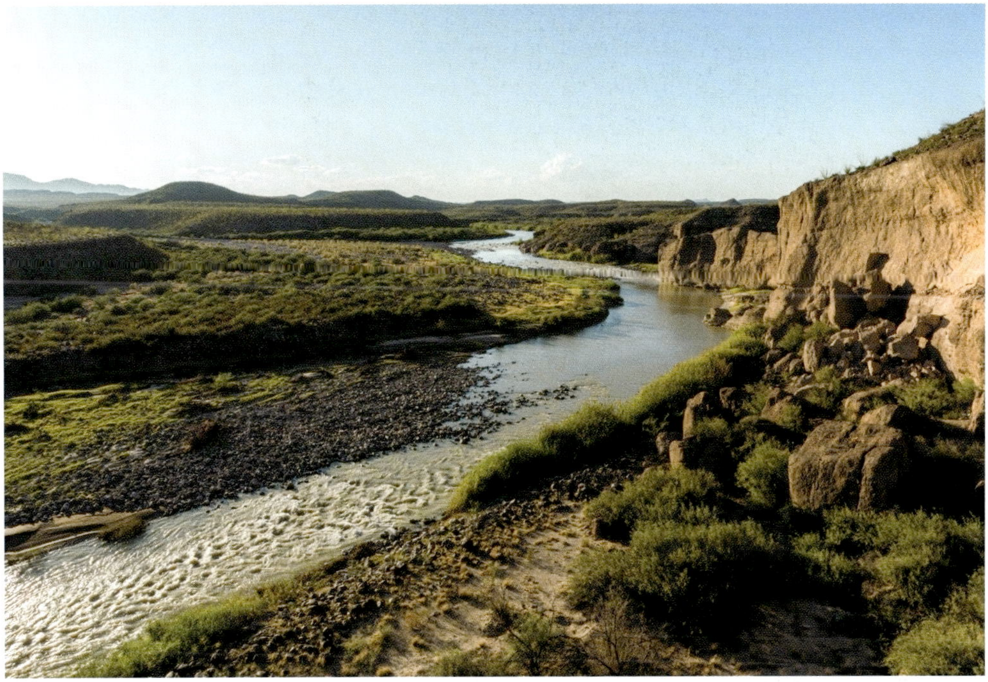

Figure 3.9

My first thought when I see a river like the Rio Grande in the Texas Big Bend is to go wide!

ISO 100 • 1/40 sec. • f/16 • 24mm

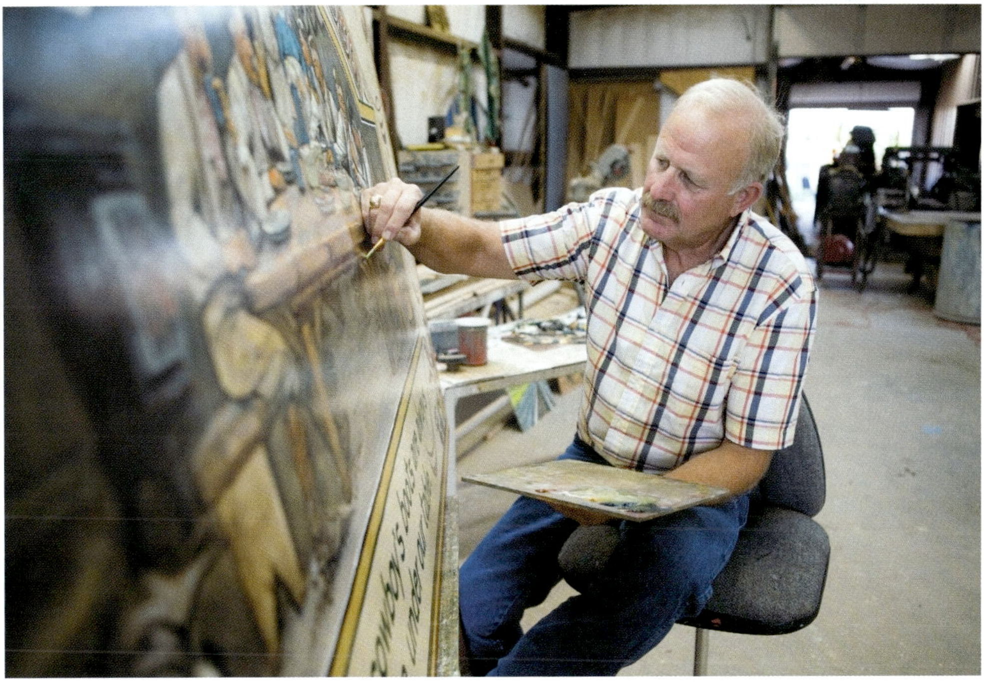

Figure 3.10

On the longer end of wide-angle focal lengths, 30mm was perfect for showcasing the artist, his work, and his studio without sacrificing the context to distortion.

ISO 400 • 1/100 sec. • f/2.8 • 30mm

A lens that covers landmark focal lengths, such as 16mm, 24mm, and 35mm, is ideal for an all-around wide-angle zoom. I prefer a wide-angle zoom that covers this range. Like many shooters, I tend to move from one extreme of the lens to the other and not hit much in between. I might use 17mm to tighten up on a feature-heavy portion of a desert landscape, and then move somewhere close to 35mm to make an environmental portrait. Somewhere near the middle is 24mm, a popular focal length for wide-angle prime lenses, as well as the starting point for the higher-end standard zoom lenses (**Figure 3.11**). It is also a very flexible focal length that doesn't quite distort like 16mm or 17mm but can still be used effectively to establish a visual context in the shot (**Figure 3.12**).

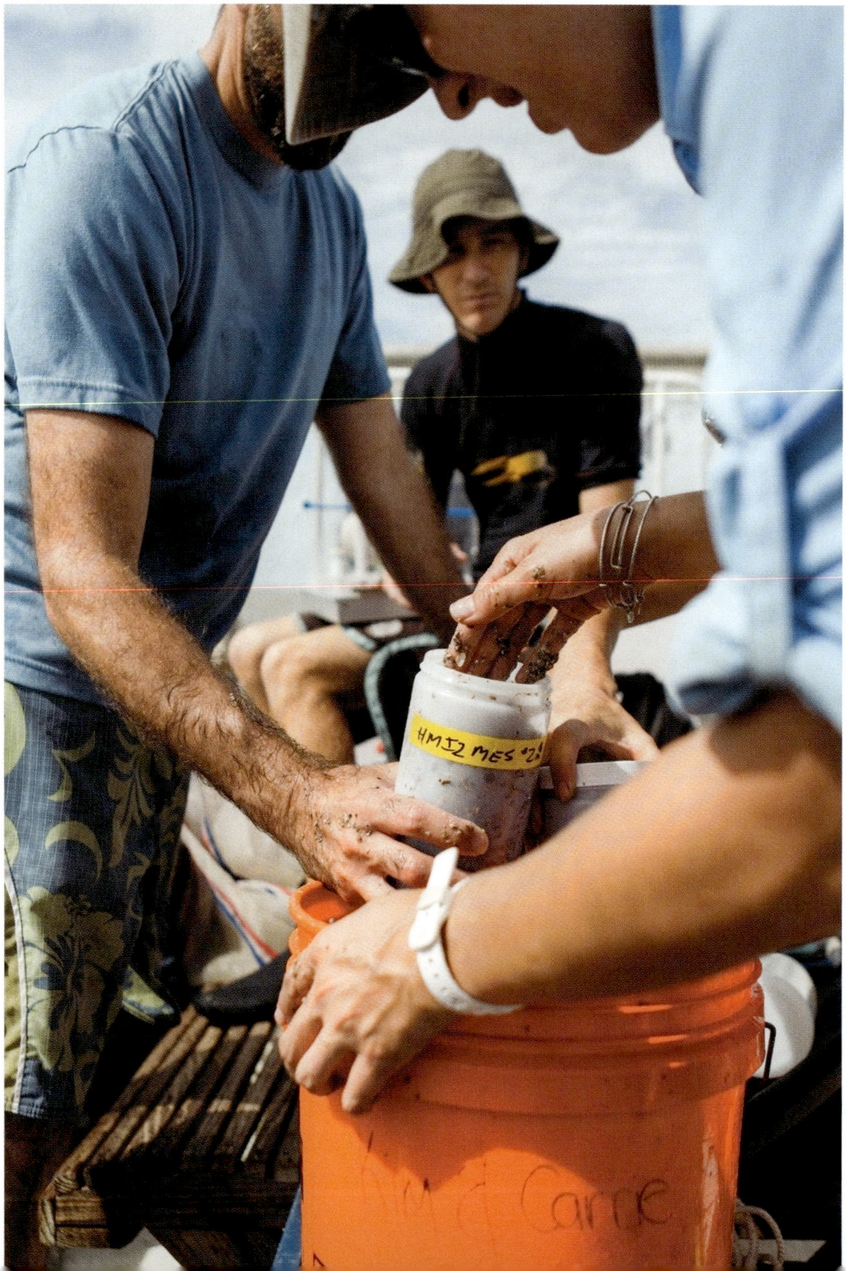

Figure 3.11
I used a 24mm focal length to move in tight on research activities of several marine biologists while also keeping the team's diver relevant to the story.

ISO 100 • 1/2000 sec. • f/2.8 • 24mm

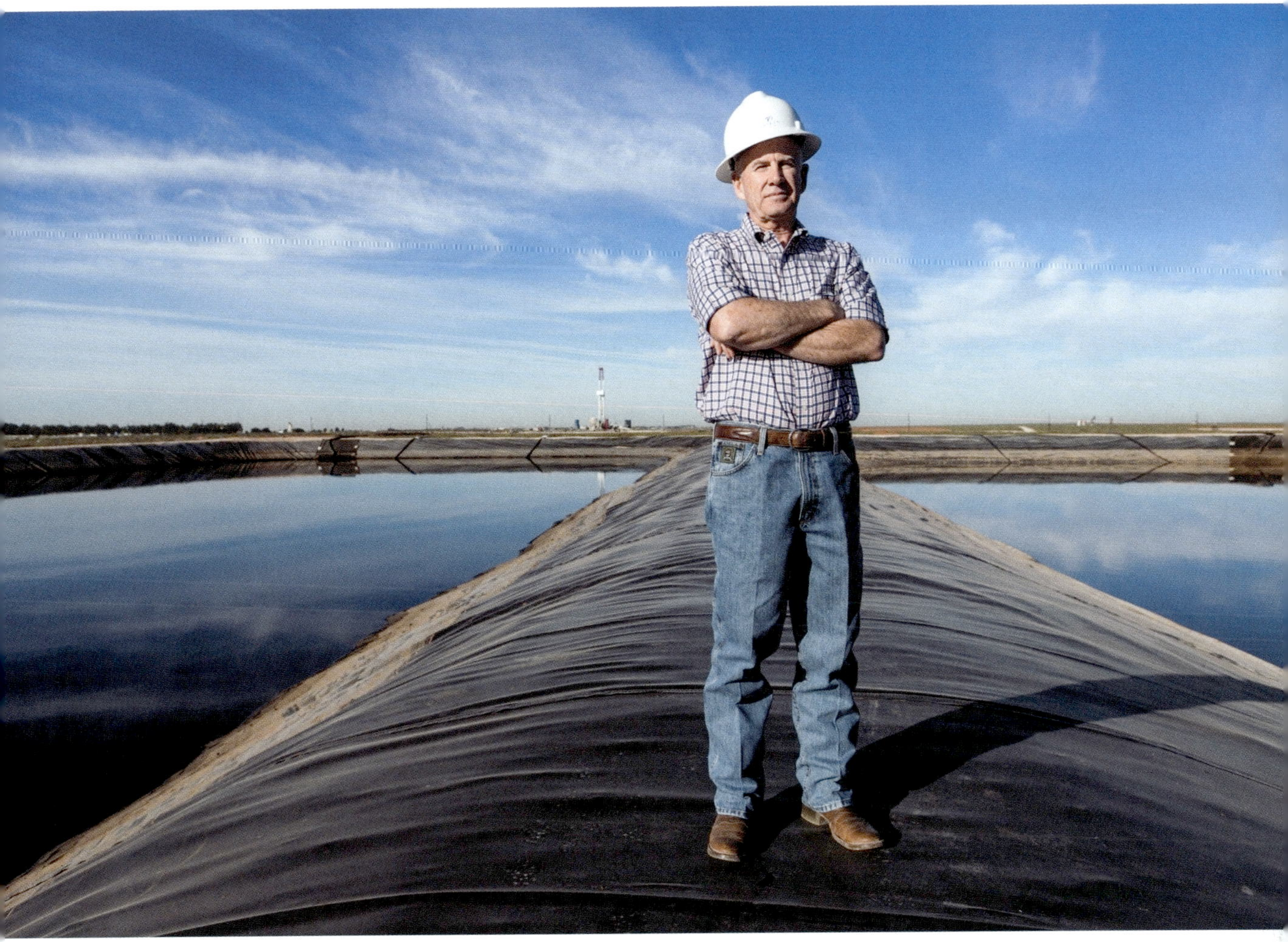

Figure 3.12 **Since 24mm does not distort as much as wider focal lengths, I tend to see environmental portraits at their widest starting at this focal length.**

ISO 100 • 1/1600 sec. • f/5.6 • 24mm

If I Had to Choose: My Favorite Wide-Angle

It is easy to fall in love with wide-angle lenses. I certainly did with my first one, and guess what? I still have it and use it on just about every shoot. Now discontinued, the EF 17–35mm f/2.8L holds a very special place in my camera bag. It is the first L-series lens I ever purchased, and it was the very first ultra-wide-angle lens I every owned. I bought it used from a colleague who recognized when I was starting out in photography that I had a hankering for wide-angle. He cut me a deal on a Canon EOS 1N (that's an older film camera body) and the lens. These were strong upgrades to what I was using previously, even if the camera and the lens were already at the time several years old and had been put through their paces. I kept that lens on my camera for six months straight, and during that time, I became comfortable shooting at extremely wide focal lengths—some might say too comfortable. Nevertheless, it was my first move into the professional gear arena, and the lens convinced me of the quality of Canon products.

Since then, the EF 17–35mm f/2.8 has been replaced twice with two versions of the EF 16–35mm f/2.8. Although the newer lenses are great pieces of glass, I have yet to see a real reason to upgrade. It's not that I have an emotional attachment to the lens (okay, just a bit), but rather it is this lens's flawless operation, sharp optics, and quick focus that keep it in my bag. Like I said earlier, I see in wide focal lengths (**Figure 3.13**), and I enjoy every time I put this lens on a camera. I'm certain it will remain a part of my kit for many more years to come!

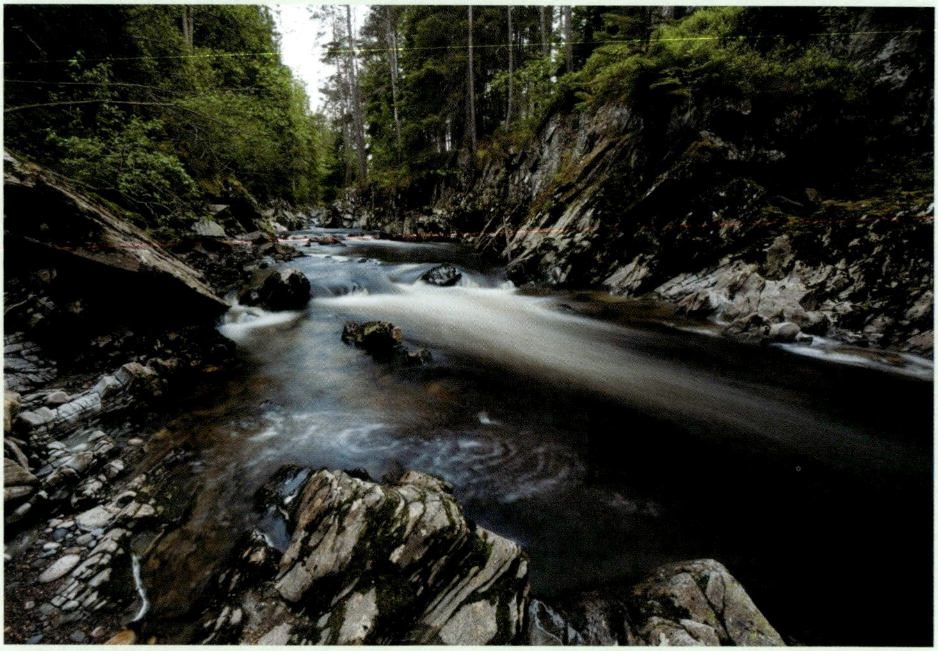

Figure 3.13 **I often shoot at the extremes of lenses, hence my tendency to shoot at 17mm on my favorite wide-angle, the EF 17–35mm f/2.8L. Rugged, structure-heavy Scottish streams invite this perspective.**

ISO 50 • 5 sec. • f/22 • 17mm

Composing With Wide-Angles

Most folks new to ultra-wide-angle photography point the camera up and watch the sky (or high rises, depending on where they live) stretch on forever. Wide-angle lenses can be extremely fun to play with, but taking that play to the next level means being attentive to composition and noticing how everything that is arranged in the shot is affected by the focal lengths used. This is where wide-angle images go from being neat pictures to being compelling and engaging photographs.

Work the Sky

Where I live in West Texas, the sky is one of our strongest visual assets. This region is extremely flat, and the sky is the biggest thing around. It is also a playground for photographers, offering up some of the best color, clouds, and storms to shoot in the world. As a result, local photographers are very conscientious and almost snobbish about the skies we use as both the main subject and background for our images. And it is all about the structure.

Simply put, skies with unique cloud structures are more interesting than if they were empty. The sky is not something we can control, and bald (cloudless) skies are simply a part of shooting outside. However, we can take advantage of the shapes and forms the sky presents some days (**Figure 3.14**).

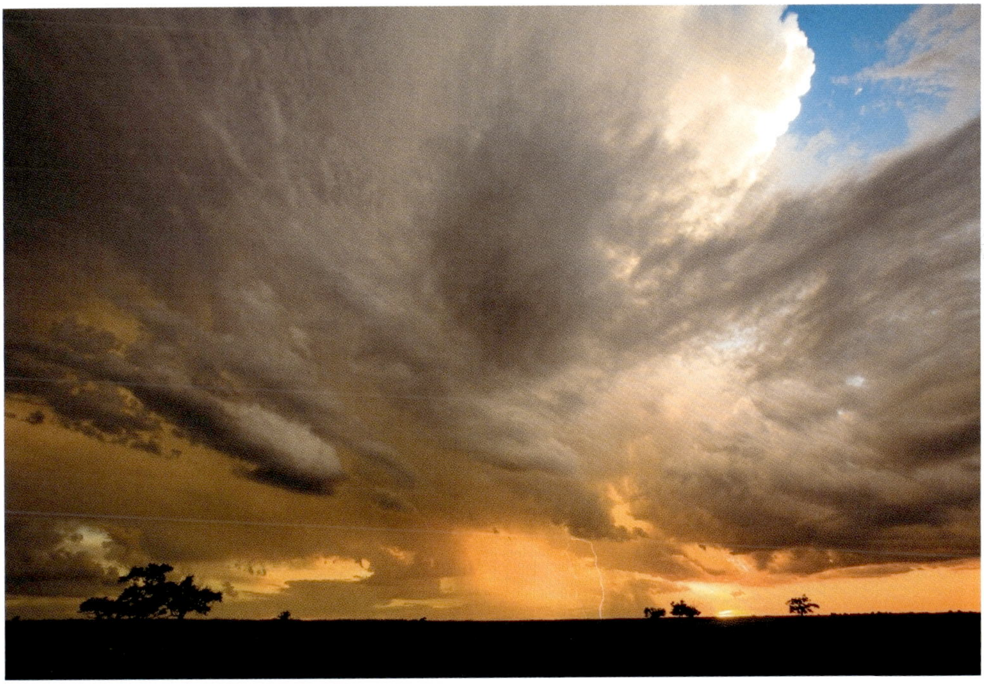

Figure 3.14

I'm a sucker for great thunderstorms, and I favor shooting them with extremely wide focal lengths for the expanse that often parallels a ferocious one.

ISO 50 • 1 sec. • f/22 • 17mm

Outstanding sunsets and layered color at sunrise or sunset, striated clouds cutting diagonally across the sky, and intense overhead thunderstorms are good reasons to compose a wide-angle shot with little more than the sky itself. When presented with these types of skies, move to a position so the structure fills the frame (**Figure 3.15**). Sometimes this means moving closer to the storm (while being safe) or farther under the clouds.

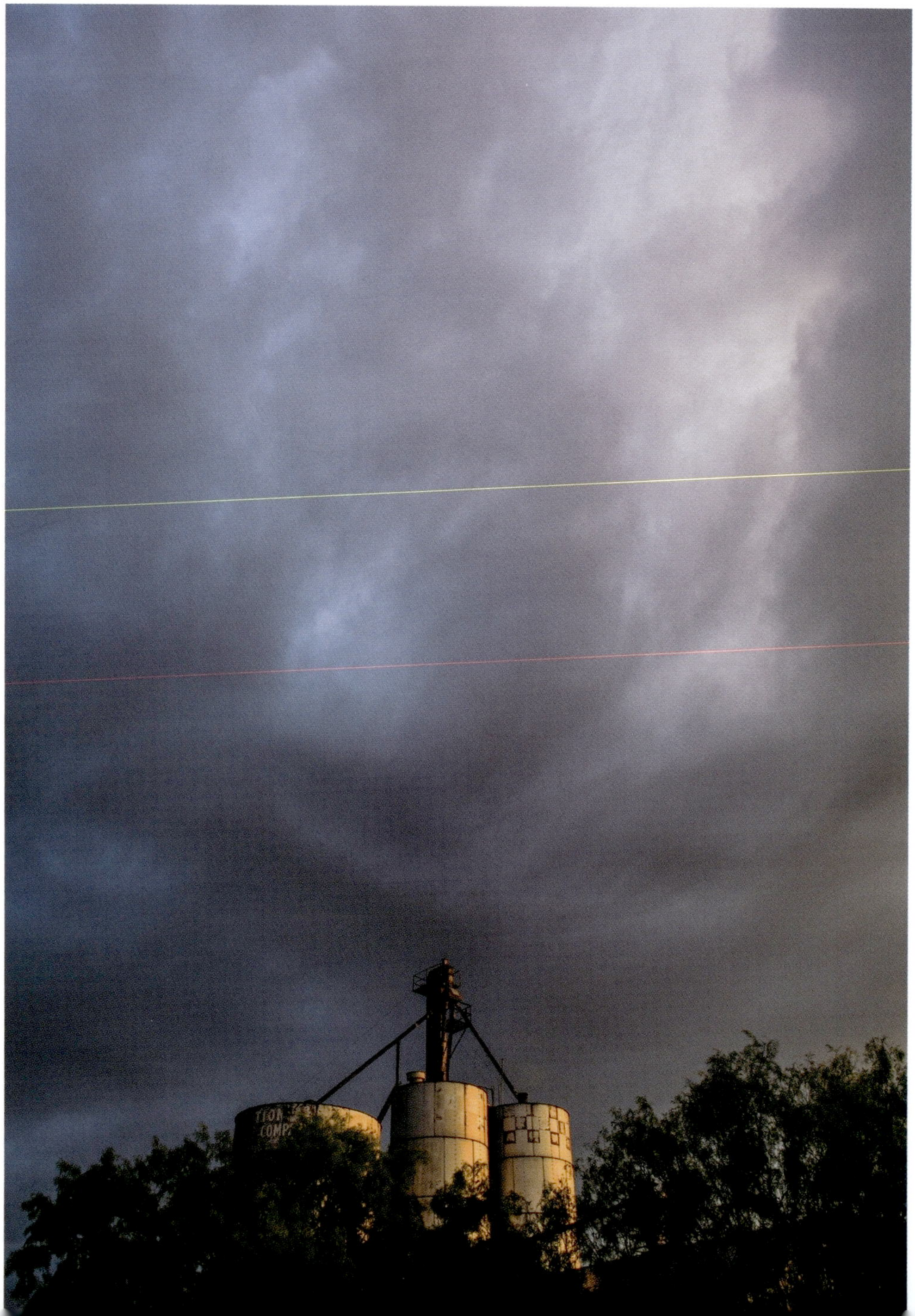

Figure 3.15
With a wide-angle, one can move into a unique and sometimes extreme cloud structure to produce the feeling of being under it.
ISO 100 • 1/6 sec. • f/5.6 • 24mm

Even though the sky is the champion in shots like this, remember to place at least a sliver of the earth's horizon in the shot (**Figure 3.16**). Showing a bit of land does two things: It provides both perspective and scale, and it showcases context and a sense of place. A very colorful sky full of performance can seem massive when tied to a minute structure on the ground, and that structure on the ground gives the viewer an idea of the environment in which it was shot (**Figure 3.17**). Power lines (which I desperately try to avoid at a small visual scale) and city buildings suggest an urban backdrop; mountaintops silhouetted against the sky indicate something more natural.

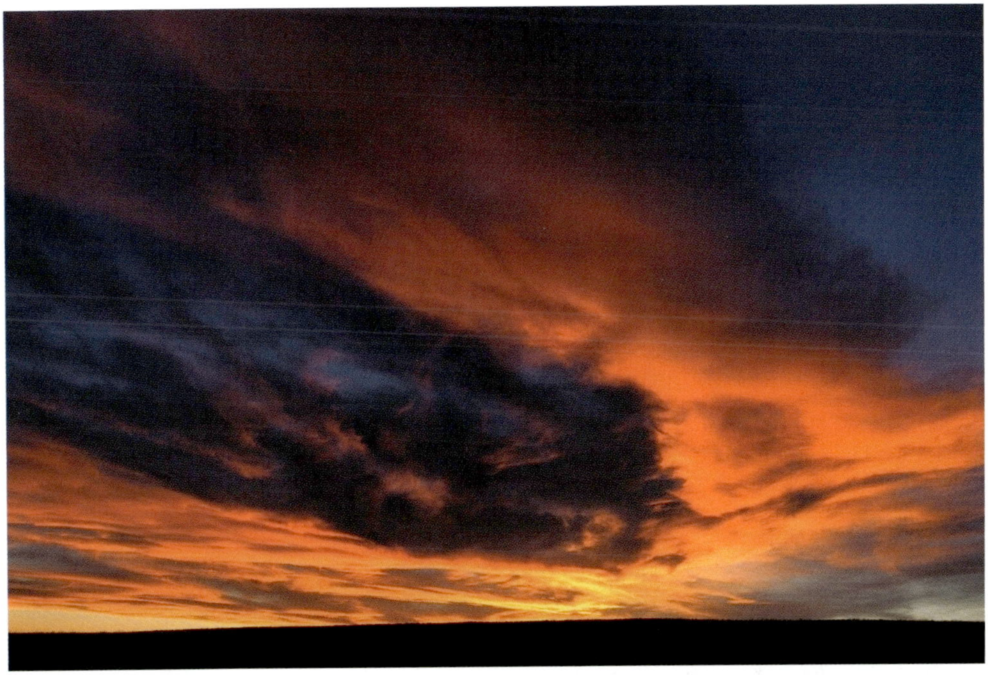

Figure 3.16
Placing a sliver of the flat West Texas horizon at the bottom of the frame gives a sense of scale to this impressive, colorful sky.

ISO 100 • 1/30 sec. • f/5.6 • 24mm

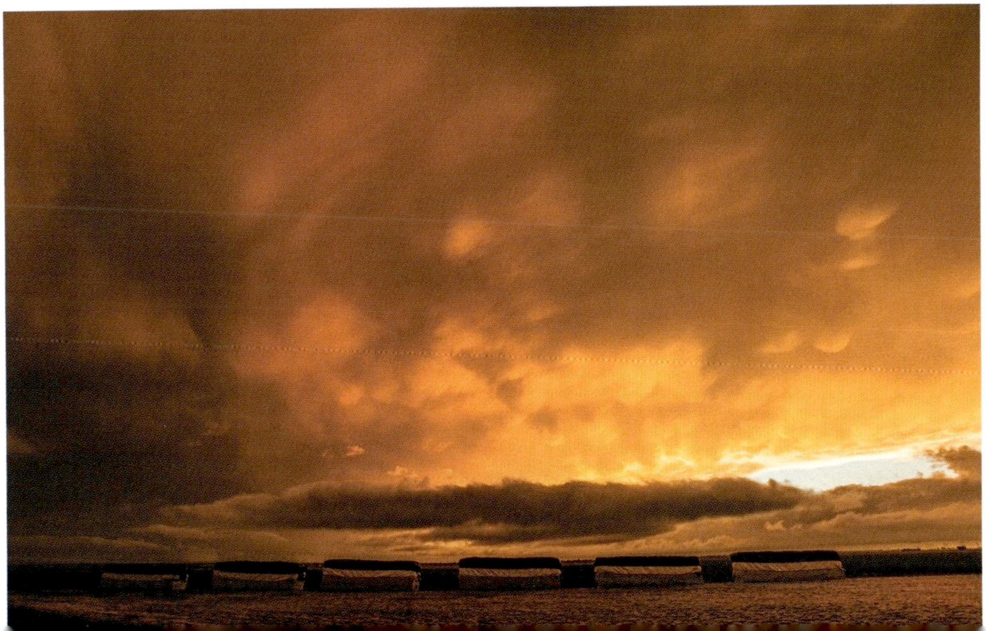

Figure 3.17
Just the tiniest bit of structure composed well in a shot can give storytelling clues, like these large cotton modules waiting out a massive thunderstorm.

ISO 200 • 1/100 sec. • f/5.6 • 17mm

Working the structure in a sky and filling a wide-angle frame up with great clouds and color help a shooter avoid capturing a lot of unwanted and unnecessary void space. For the most part, you want to avoid shooting an empty sky (**Figure 3.18**). Sometimes the void is what you want, perhaps for unique color or interpretive value (**Figure 3.19**). The void can be very powerful as a way to show emptiness and critical depth. When I am confronted with bald skies or clouds lacking character, I look for other natural or artificial structures, such as the overhanging branches of a large tree or a creative feature of a building downtown (**Figure 3.20**).

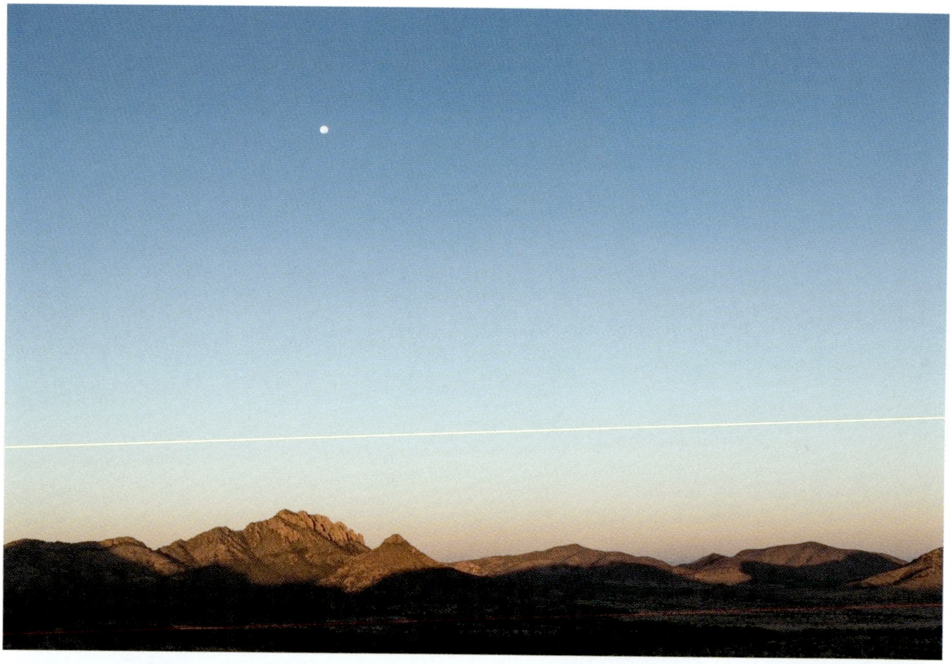

Figure 3.18
I wanted the full moon to work for this shot of Sawtooth Mountain, but it was simply too small and too far above the mountain, poised in an otherwise uninteresting, featureless sky.

ISO 100 • 1/125 sec. • f/5.6 • 34mm

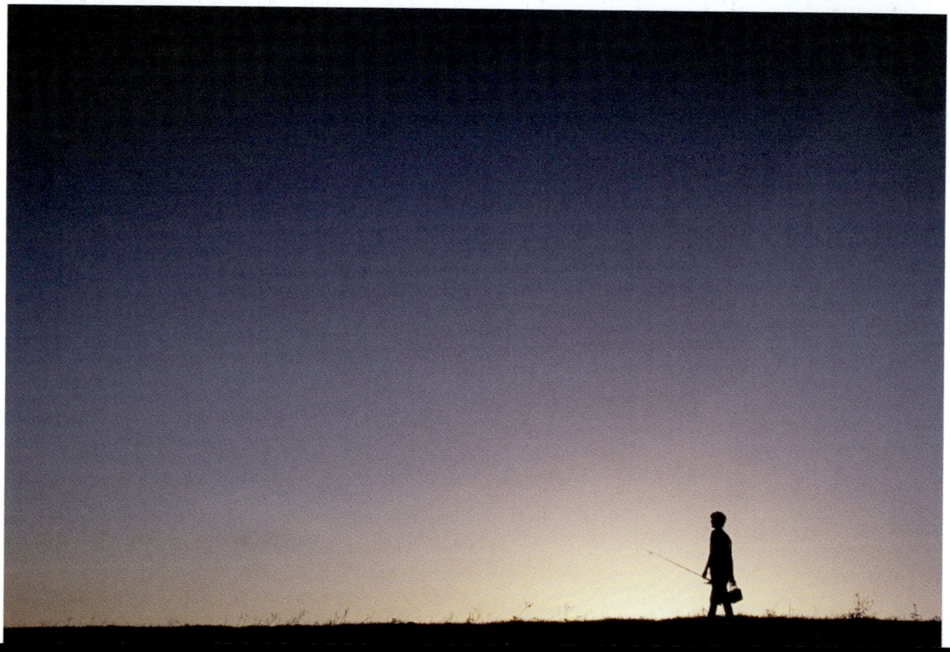

Figure 3.19
The large, open sky, combined with a unique color gradation and the silhouette of the primary subject, conveys feelings of nostalgia, youth, or just smallness.

ISO 100 • 1/250 sec. • f/5.6 • 17mm

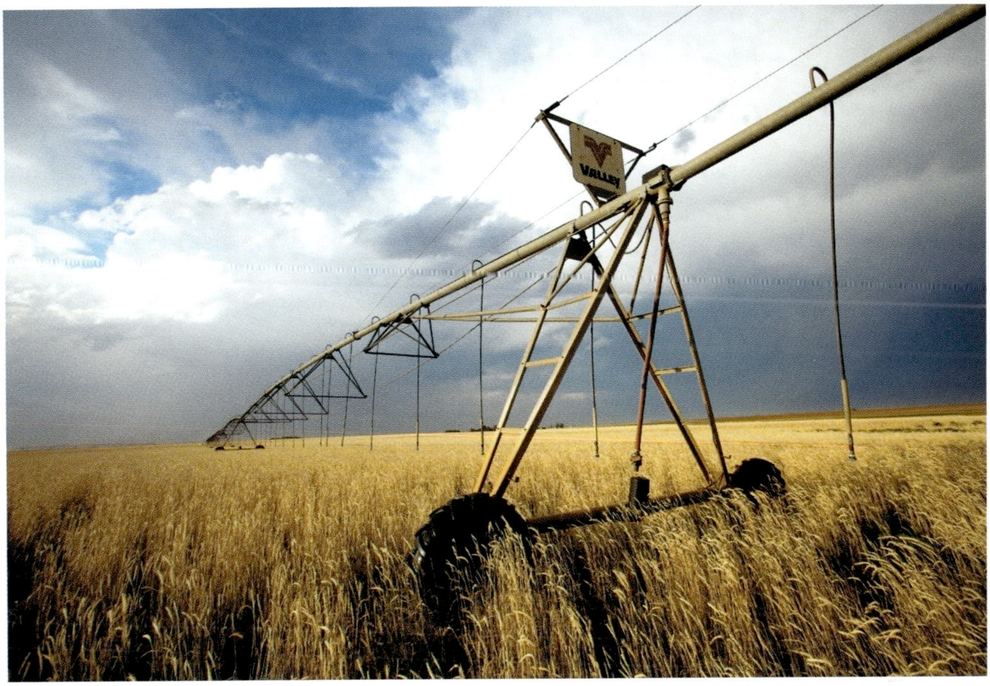

Figure 3.20
For skies lacking strong structure, lines or leading composition, I will add artificial components like this irrigation system to increase interest and a sense of place to the shot.

ISO 100 • 1/160 sec. • f/8 • 17mm

Push In on the Foreground

One of my favorite things to do with a wide-angle lens is find something of importance to the environment in which I'm shooting and make *it* the foreground (**Figure 3.21**). The nice thing about wide-angle lenses is that the minimum focusing distance is fairly short, allowing you to maintain focus on the subject while being just inches from it (**Figure 3.22**). Another asset of wide-angle lenses—their expansive perspective—keeps you from losing the environment. Concentrate the lens on a visually appealing part of a story but keep the story world as part of the picture (**Figure 3.23**).

The rule of thirds—one of the Holy Grail composition guides, suggesting placement of significant subject matter on invisible lines that trisect the frame into vertical and horizontal thirds—comes in especially handy while using strong foregrounds and wide focal lengths. Keeping the primary subject matter near the left or right vertical third and on or in the bottom third of the shot leaves plenty of real estate for the mid-ground expanse, as well as the horizon line on or in the upper third of the frame (**Figure 3.24**). Design-wise, this type of composition also leaves room for placement of text or other graphics that complement the editorial use of an image.

Figure 3.21 (left)
A large prickly pear serves as a strong foreground subject against an expansive river valley.

ISO 100 • 1/40 sec. • f/16 • 32mm

Figure 3.22 (right)
Being able to focus inches away from the small purple flowers at a wide focal length offered me a way to also expose the riparian habitat that gives life to the vegetation.

ISO 200 • 1/500 sec. • f/2.8 • 24mm

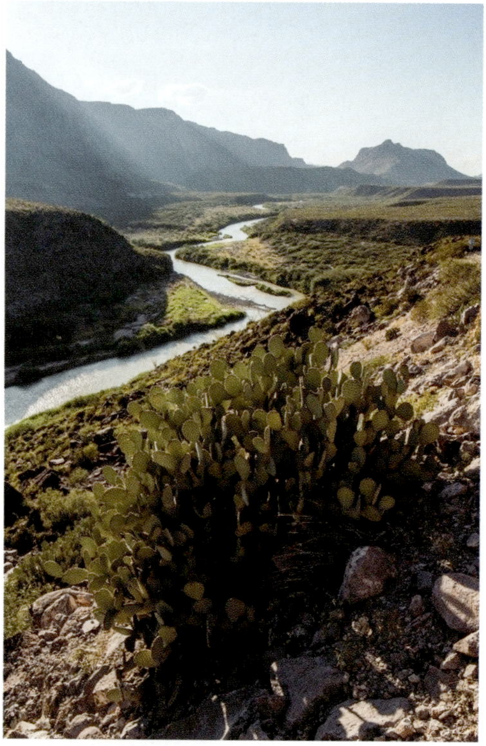

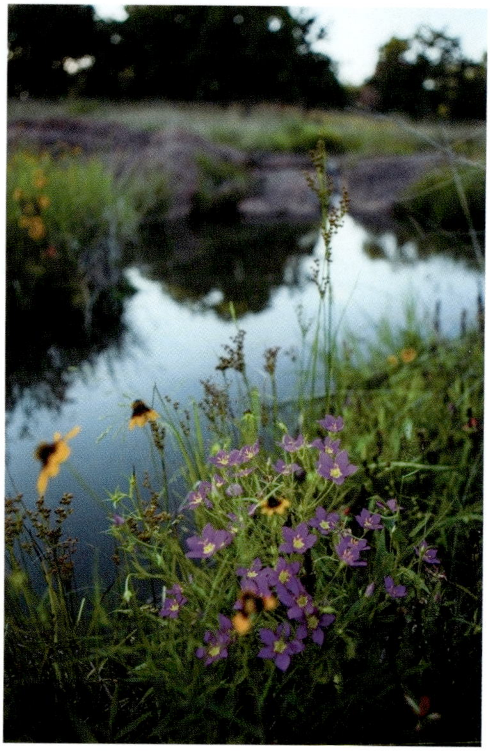

Figure 3.23
The curved feature of this small waterfall on a desert creek is an accent worth pushing in on it tightly.

ISO 50 • 1 sec. • f/22 • 14mm

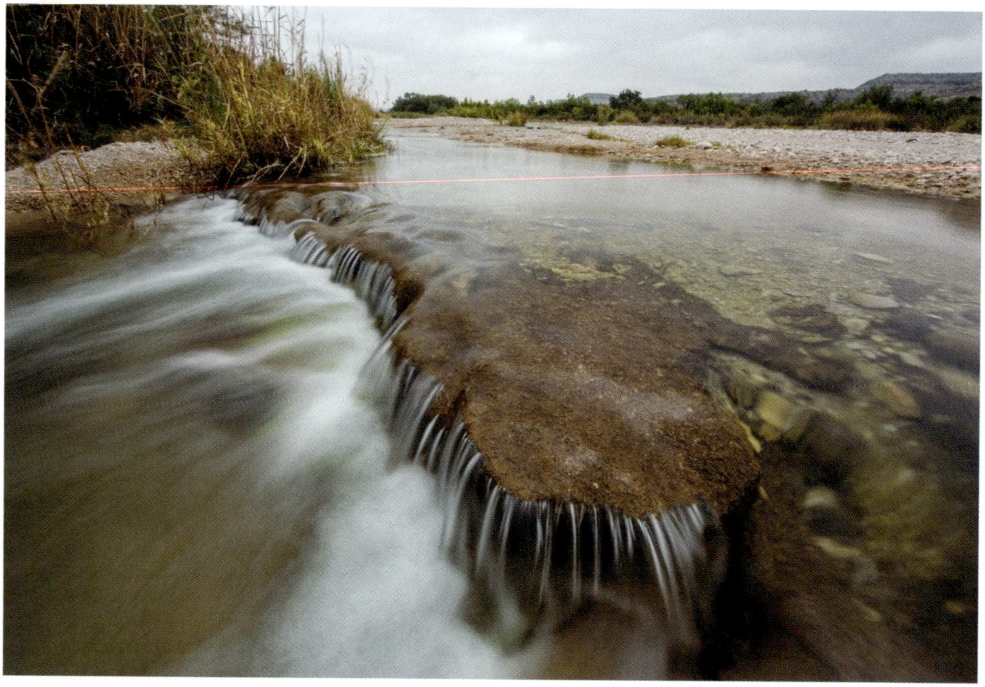

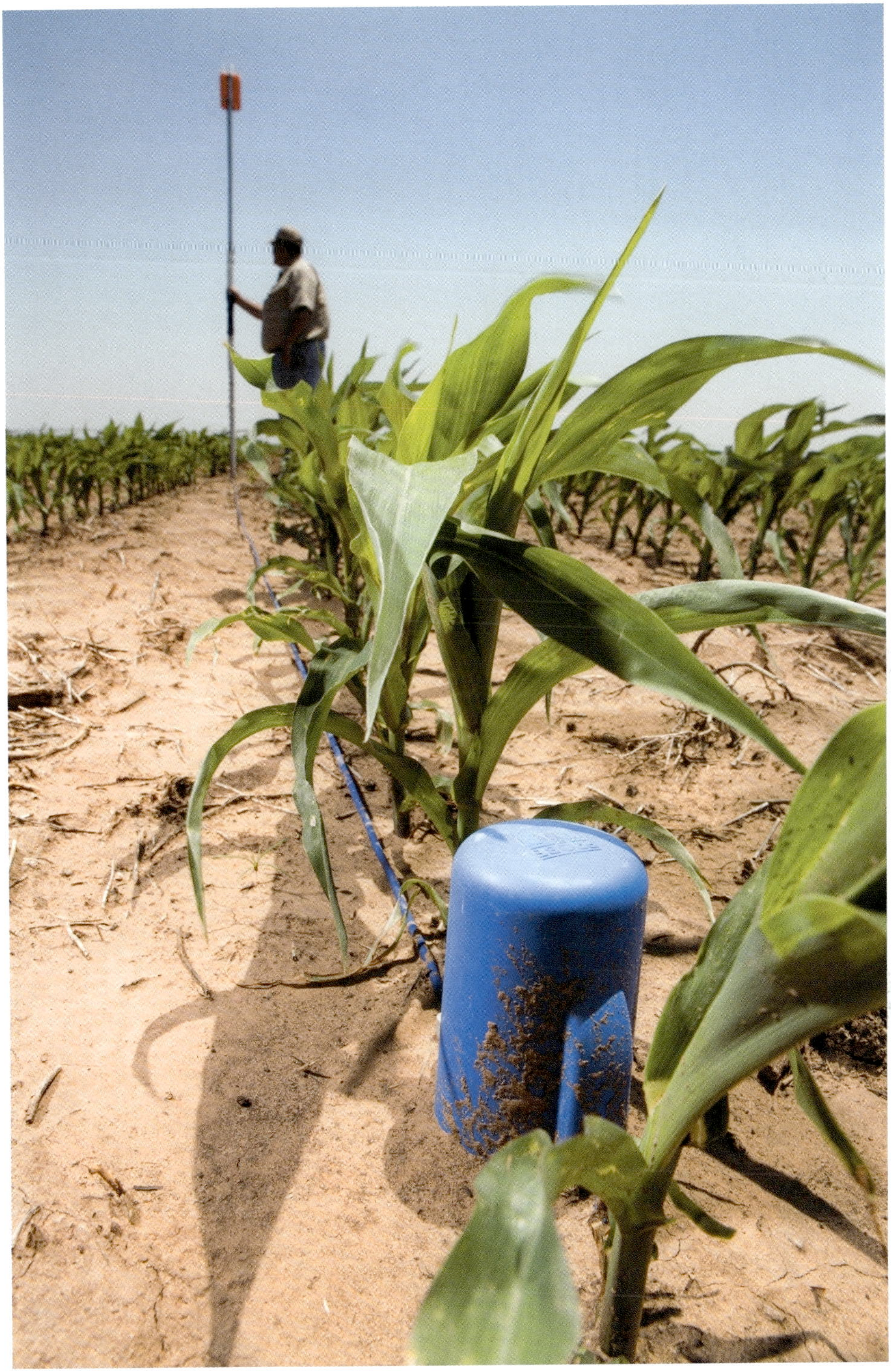

Figure 3.24

A wide-angle pushed close to the primary subject was essential in this shot covering new water conservation technologies that farmers are using.

ISO 100 • 1/125 sec. • f/14 • 24mm

Strong foreground subjects can also be used as guiding lines themselves. Explore the linear structure of subjects, considering it as a way to direct the eye through the frame. Wide-angle focal lengths allow us to exaggerate this direction, resulting in both aesthetic and strategic composition. One of my favorite places to discover new lines in unsuspecting subject matter is a large pink granite mountain in the Texas Hill Country (**Figure 3.25**). From high and low, I can find great wide-angle composition by simply pushing in tighter on nearby boulders and arranging myself so that other boulders fall in dynamic lines through much of the frame. I also use fragments of subject matter to help frame a shot (**Figure 3.26**).

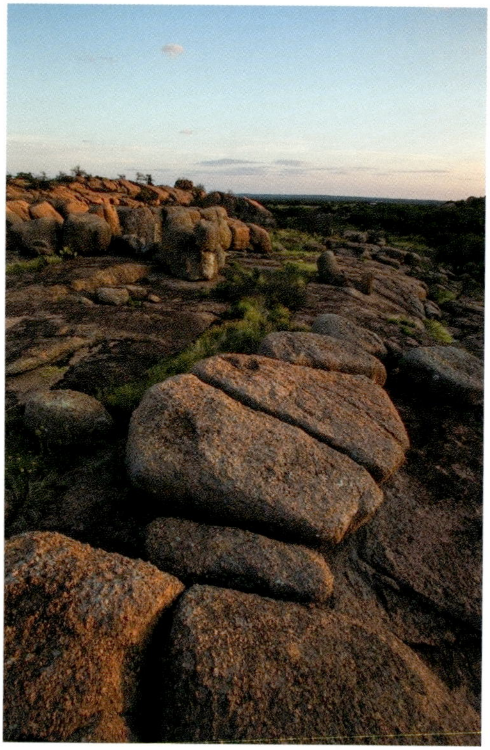

Figure 3.25 Looking through an extremely wide-angle lens and varying your position may uncover strong lines in subject matter you would normally not consider because of its form, such as these short granite boulders.

ISO 200 • 1/15 sec. • f/11 • 17mm

Figure 3.26
Wide-angle focal lengths such as 17mm make using a piece of an extremely close foreground subject (like the boulder at the right) useful for framing other subject matter while the foreground remains in focus.

ISO 200 • 1/25 sec. • f/11 • 17mm

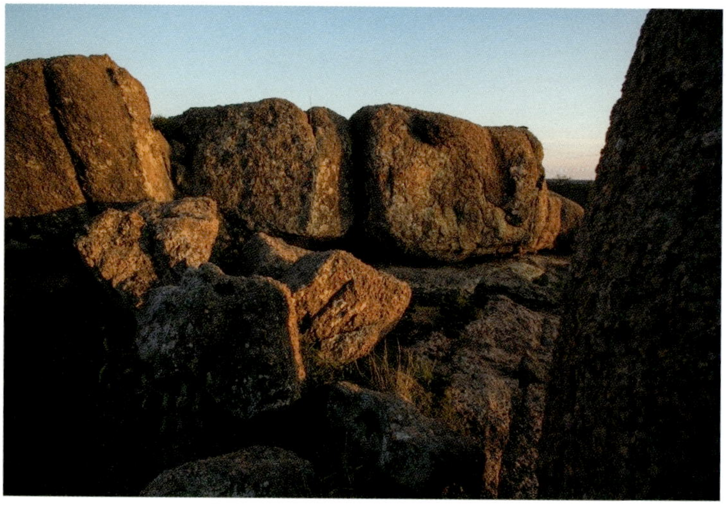

Break the Rules

Speaking of the rule of thirds, there are times when it should be ignored. This is the "rules are meant to be broken" part of the book.

Center the subject

When a subject is so valuable that you want to direct immediate attention to it, placing the subject in the middle of the frame will do it for you (**Figure 3.27**). Of course, haphazardly doing so might cause confusion, especially if the subject is very small compared to its surroundings. Instead, push in tight on the primary content. The curvature of wide-angle lenses—rectilinear or curvilinear—will force the subject to pop out toward the viewer (**Figure 3.28**). As the subject enlarges, you are being very deliberate about where your viewers' eyes go. Since wide-angles still let you keep the environment in the picture, consider using strong lines on either side of the subject to frame it and form an invisible vanishing point beyond it.

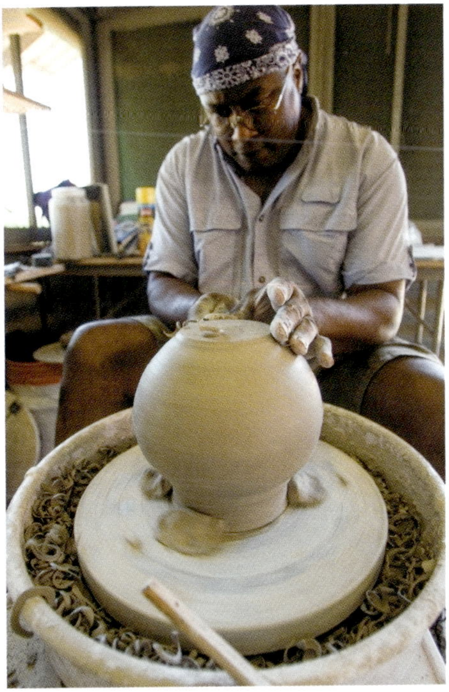

Figure 3.27 When centering subject matter in the shot, such as James Watkins's pot, consider filling the entire frame with the general form of the subject. The large circle of the potter's wheel is the foreground.

ISO 400 • 1/80 sec. • f/3.2 • 17mm

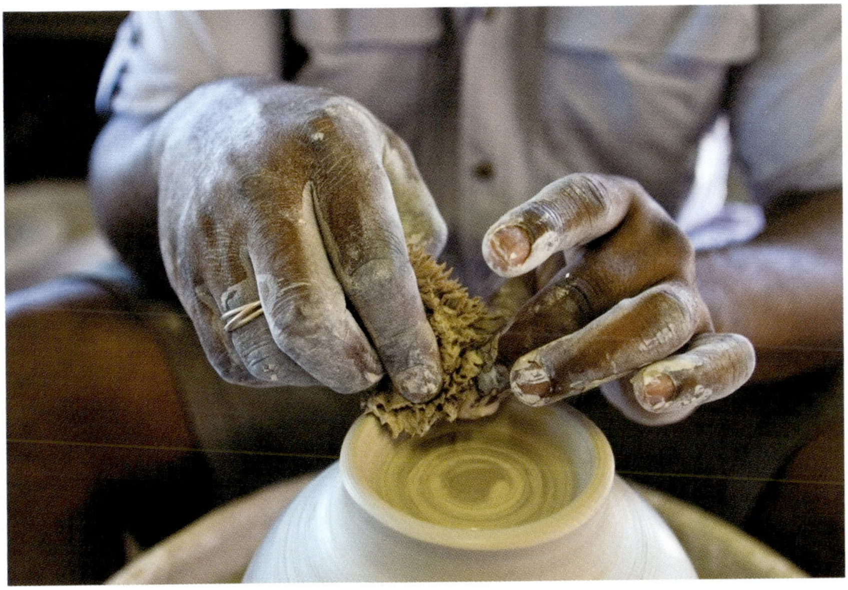

Figure 3.28 Placing Watkins's hands—a vital part of his artistic process—in the middle of the frame seems appropriate composition for this frame only because I shot tight on them and made them leap from the background with expansive perspective.

ISO 400 • 1/60 sec. • f/3.2 • 31mm

Warped perspective

Breaking compositional rules with a wide-angle lens, particularly the extremely wide ones, such as the fisheyes and the shorter extremes of the zoom lenses, is often kept in check by the focal lengths. While expansive perspective exaggerates the distance between foreground and background—something we are mostly in favor of when using these lenses—we also experience severe distortion (**Figure 3.29**).

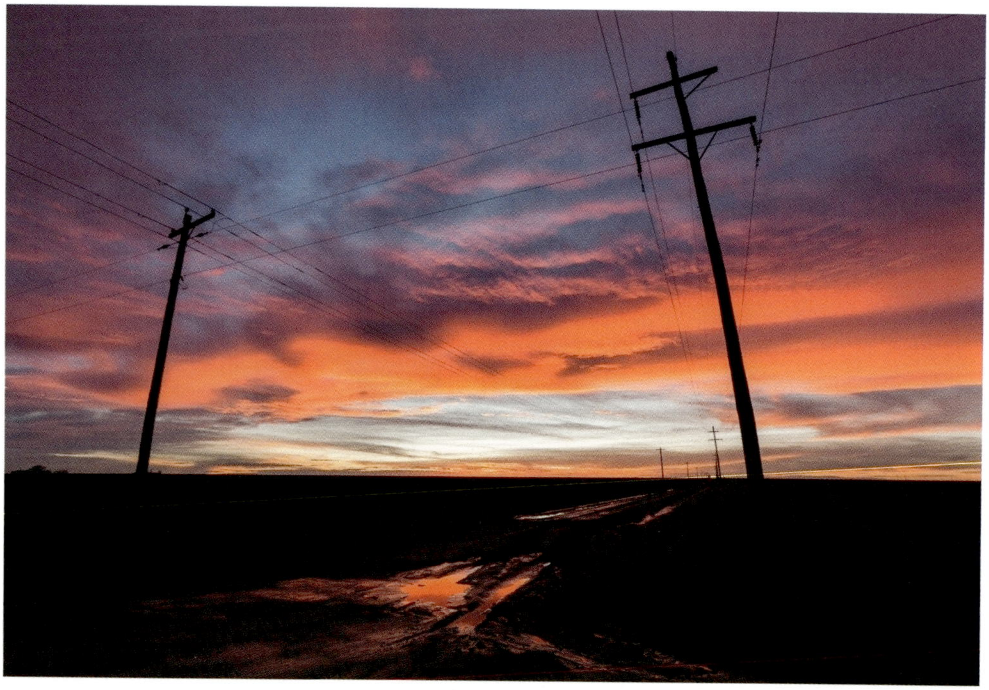

Figure 3.29
As windblown as West Texas is, the leaning of the electricity poles is a result of keystoning, a type of optical distortion common with wide-angle lenses.
ISO 250 • 1/30 sec. • f/5.6 • 17mm

Pointing a wide-angle lens up and down, and pushing it in on a subject and then backing it out all come with fairly drastic changes in perspective. It is the nature of the focal lengths to alter everything in the lens with the exception of the smallest part of the center of the frame (**Figures 3.30** and **3.31**). This area is like the eye of a hurricane, in which all is "normal." Outside this very small zone, lines are extended, subject matter grows or shrinks (depending on its distance from the lens), and contents near the edges of the frame begin to stretch so much it looks like they're trying to get out of the shot.

Distorting perspective is the nature of these lenses and wider focal lengths. It is handy, though, to know where this distortion can get us in trouble. I'm all for breaking the rules when it counts, but when something round (like the petals on flower plants) becomes extremely oblong, I re-adjust my composition, my physical position, or even the lens I'm using to negate this unwelcome warpage. I encourage shooting at wide focal lengths every chance you get just to see how subject matter reacts in the frame.

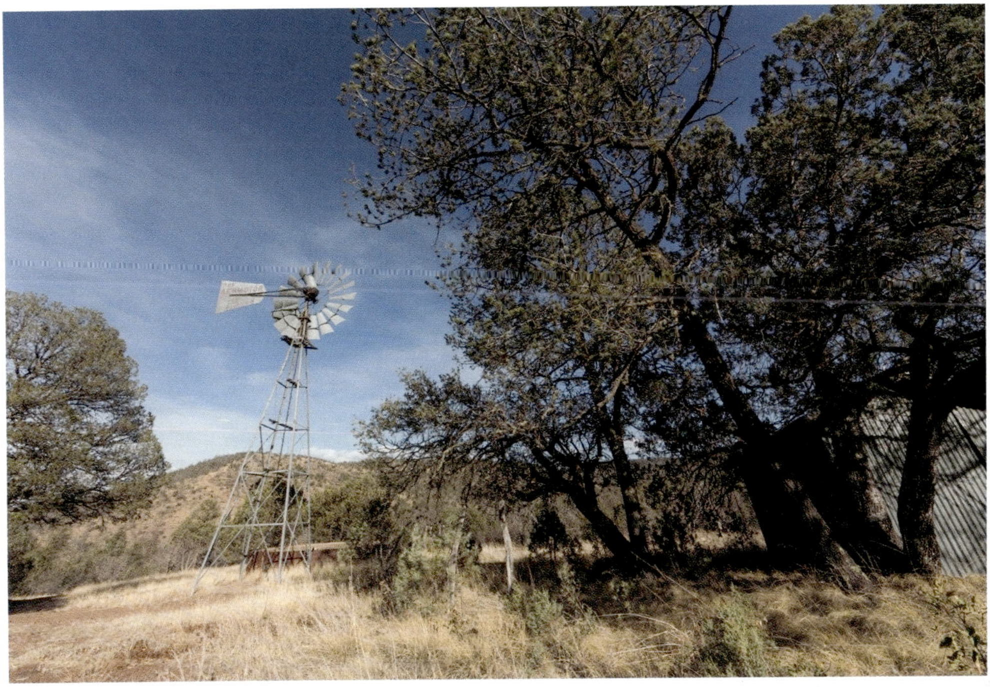

Figure 3.30
Keystoning is exaggerated when subject matter with vertical lines, like the windmill, are closer to the edges of the frame, where the curvature of the wide lens is most severe.

ISO 100 • 1/200 sec. • f/11 • 14mm

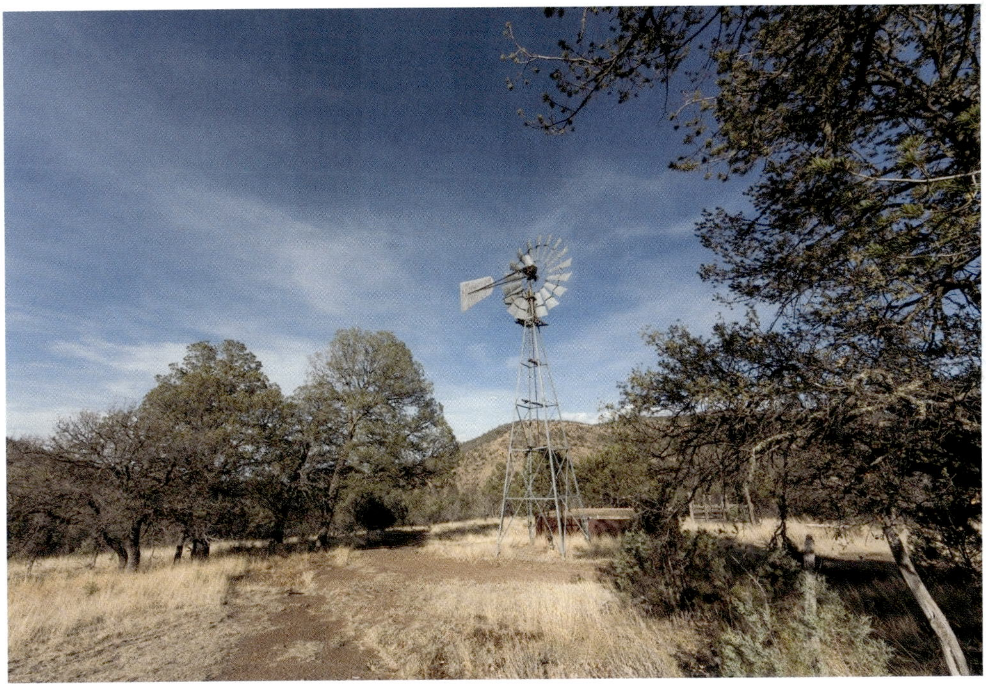

Figure 3.31
One way to mitigate distortion is by moving important subject matter closer to the center of the frame. The windmill is still keystoning but not as drastically.

ISO 100 • 1/200 sec. • f/11 • 14mm

The Wide-Angle Portrait

If you are new to photography, you may have heard that it is inappropriate to shoot portraits with wide-angle lenses. If you are not so new to photography, you may be telling this to newbies. There is validity in adhering to and offering up this piece of advice, but it is far from a rule to follow strictly. Some of my favorite portraits were made at 17mm, many others at 24mm. There are ways to make great portraits with wide-angles (**Figure 3.32**).

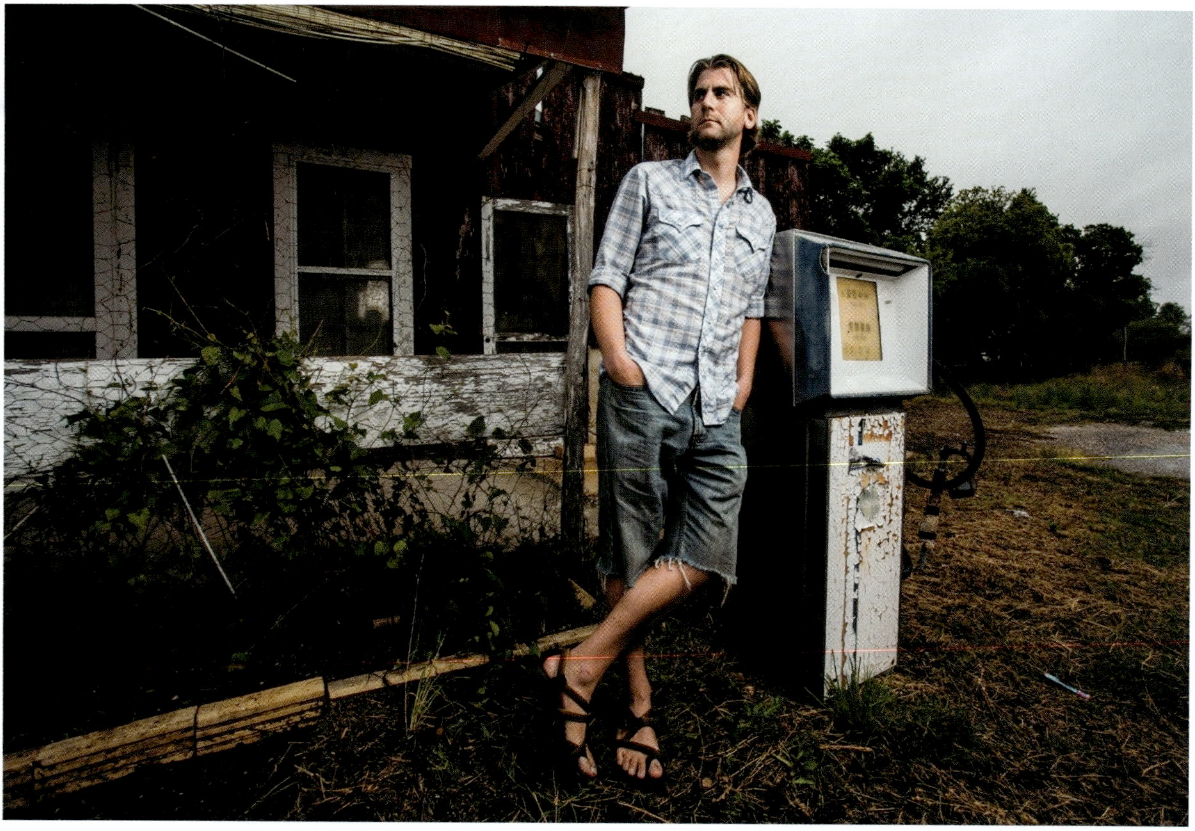

Figure 3.32 A wide perspective provides this portrait with context to go along with the character at the pump.

ISO 200 • 1/30 sec. • f/8 • 17mm

It all depends on the type of portrait you are wanting to make. More formal portraits may not benefit from the expansive perspective that wide-angles exhibit (**Figures 3.33**, **3.34** and **3.35**). For example, corporate headshots require the least amount of distortion possible to a face and body. Wide-angles don't surface much in bridal and traditional engagement and family portraits. Aesthetically, these types of portraits benefit more from longer focal lengths that compress distance between foreground and background, and more easily throw the background out of focus.

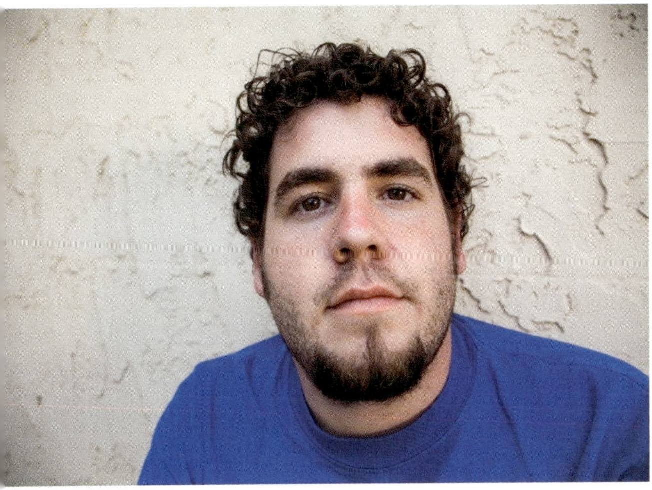

Figure 3.33 Push a wide-angle close to someone's face and features start to become more round and protruding.

ISO 100 • 1/100 sec. • f/5.6 • 24mm

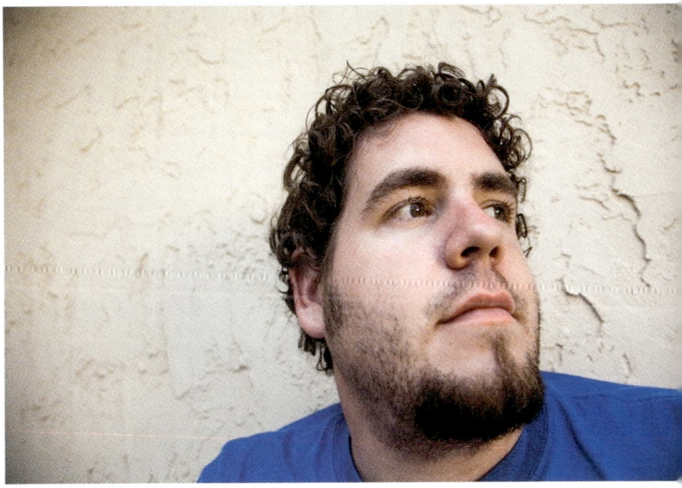

Figure 3.34 Photograph a face at the same distance from below and the chin starts to elongate, as does the nose.

ISO 100 • 1/100 sec. • f/5.6 • 24mm

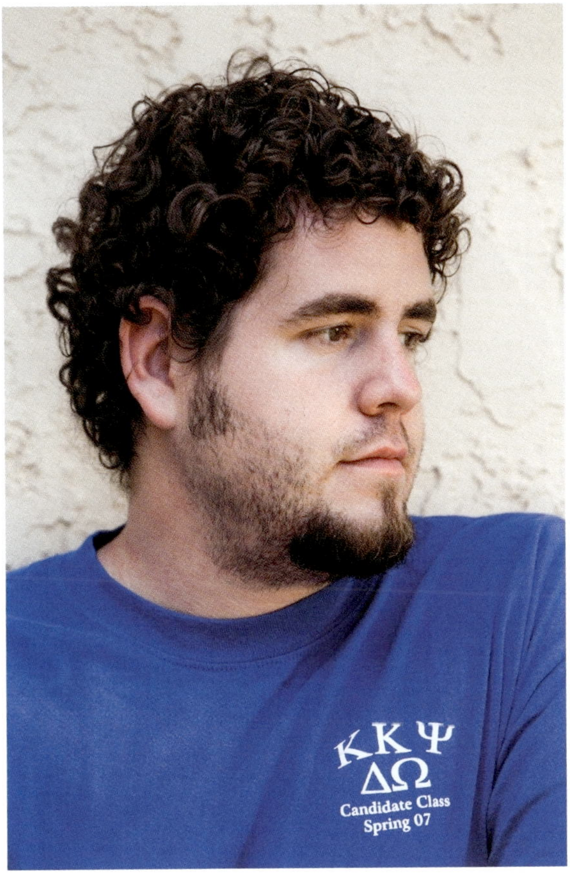

Figure 3.35 Headshots are best made at longer focal lengths that approach telephoto in order to keep facial and body features proportionate.

ISO 100 • 1/100 sec. • f/5.6 • 190mm

However, wider lenses are great for environmental portraiture and less traditional forms of portraits. As an editorial photographer, I'm constantly in environmental portrait mode, where showcasing the primary subject's context is important (**Figure 3.36**). Wider focal lengths allow the shooter to include a great deal of this environment while also powerfully composing the subject (**Figure 3.37**).

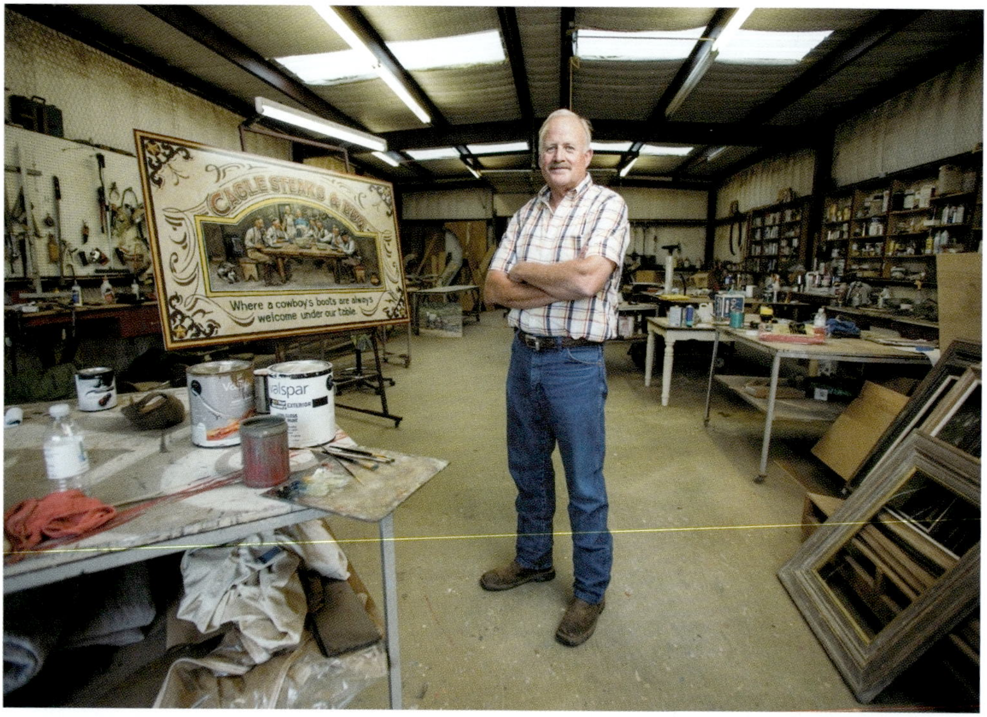

Figure 3.36
Wides are excellent lenses for environmental portraits, where showcasing the subject, like this western artist, in his space is important to telling a story.

ISO 200 • 1/60 sec. • f/2.8 • 17mm

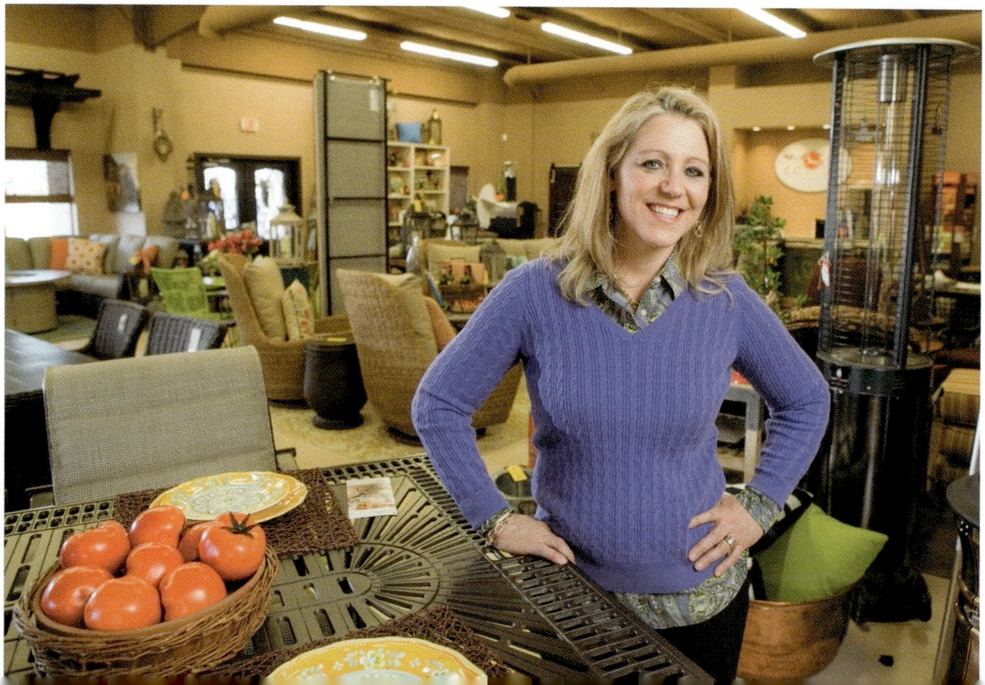

Figure 3.37
A boutique owner and her place of work. Wide-angle lenses are still good for pushing in to waist-high portraits, as long as the subject's body is not too close to the edge.

ISO 800 • 1/60 sec. • f/4 • 24mm

Full-body environmental portraits work well if the subject is kept from the edges of the frame, where her form may stretch too much because of the glass. Pushing in tight on a waist-up version of the same subject engages the viewer with the subject in a more stylized fashion. Family portraiture that resembles a photojournalistic look more than a traditional one can employ wide focal lengths to place the viewer in the "middle" of the action. Portraits that also exhibit interpretive drama and intensity are often wide-angle shots (**Figure 3.38**).

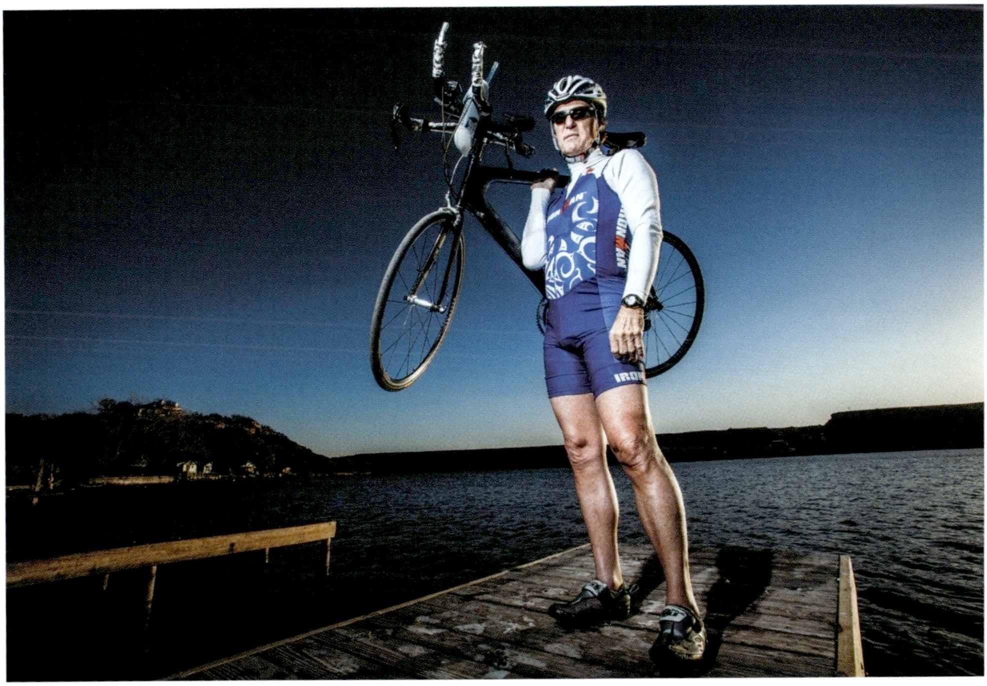

Figure 3.38
From below, wide-angles elongate the body, making the subject seem taller. For athletes, this perspective conveys power.

ISO 100 • 1/200 sec. • f/13 • 17mm

This look is not for everyone. Heavier people tend to gain more weight visually when wide-angles are pushed in on them, and while shooting subjects from below eye level may convey power for some, others may not like how it elongates their body. When shooting down on a subject with a wide-angle, you may turn the subject into a bobble-head doll (**Figure 3.39**) or make them top-heavy, seemingly leaning toward the outer edge of the frame along a slanted line (**Figure 3.40**).

Figure 3.39
Mike's no bobble-head doll, but shooting down on him at 17mm makes his head seem much larger than the rest of his body.

ISO 100 • 1/200 sec. • f/16 • 17mm

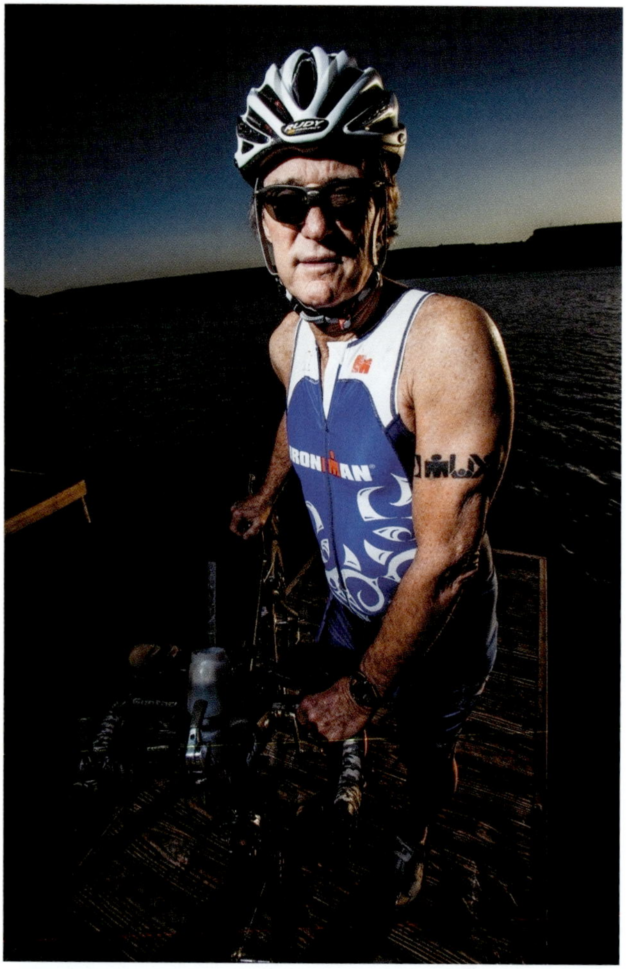

Figure 3.40
A farmer looks like he is leaning toward the edge of the frame due to the lens distortion, as it is pointed more downward than upward. Looking closely will also reveal that the lit side of his face stretches just a bit toward the edge as well.

ISO 100 • 1/200 sec. • f/11 • 17mm

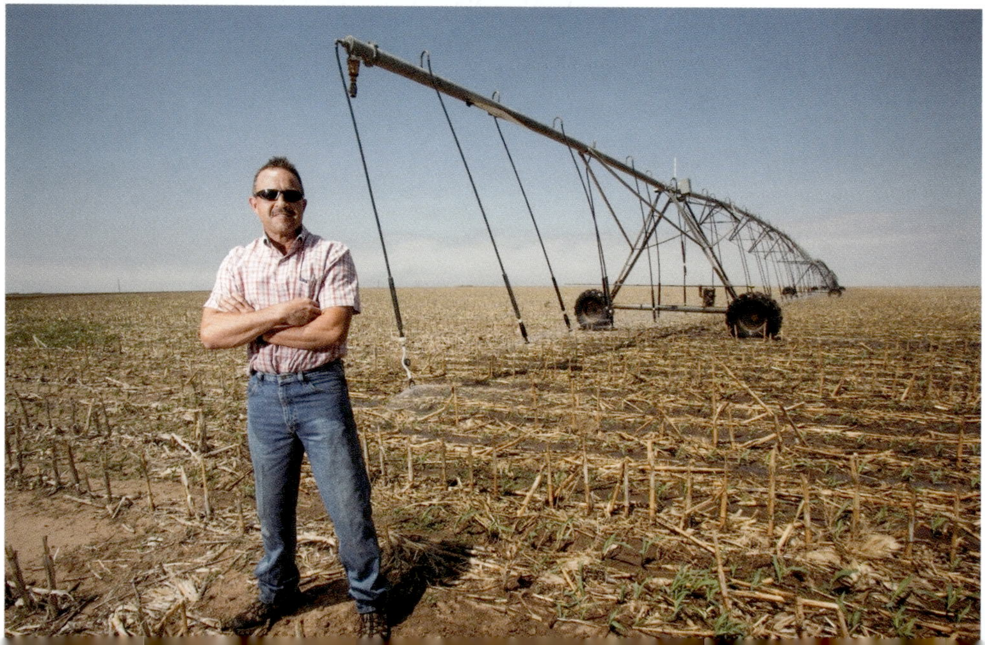

The wide-angle portrait is a balance act of context and perspective. Although lenses have no bias toward gender, people viewing portraits often do. Wide-angles are less prevalent in making portraits of women—especially in commercial settings—than of men, due to the level of distortion that comes with these lenses (**Figure 3.41**). Again, it all depends on the type of portraiture you are looking to create (**Figure 3.42**). Practice and knowledge of how the lens will affect the portrait's look are key to successfully using it (**Figure 3.43**).

All this being said, extremely wide focal lengths are generally not used for portraiture. The next chapter will cover a vast range of lenses and focal lengths that are more popular for this type of work, as well as a great many other forms of photography.

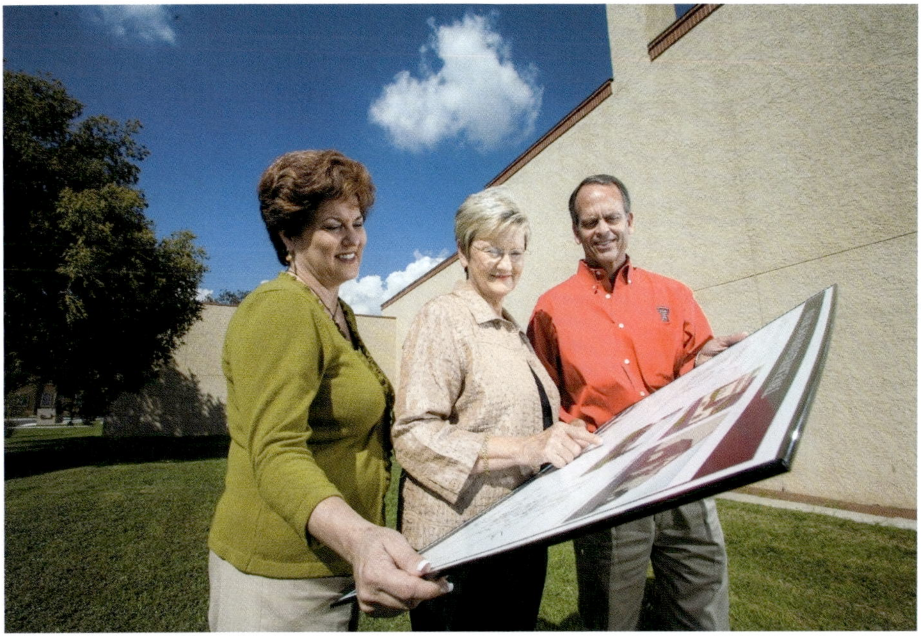

Figure 3.41
An interesting portrait of a building-planning committee, but I don't believe the woman in green appreciates the enlarged size of her hand. Since it is closer to the wide-angle lens, it falls victim to expansive perspective.

ISO 100 • 1/160 sec. • f/13 • 17mm

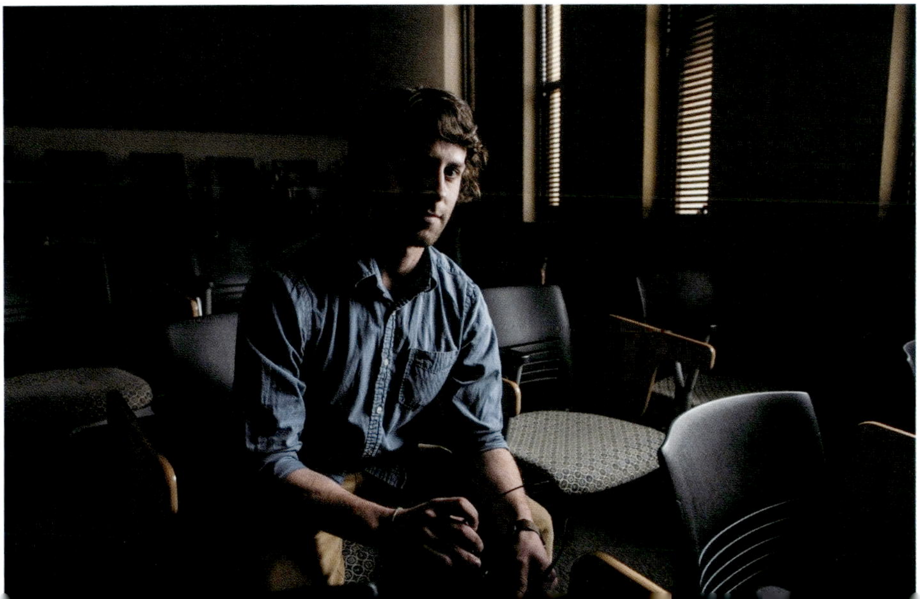

Figure 3.42
Wide-angle lenses are great for portraits that are highly stylized or dramatic, where the distortion that occurs is insignificant, such as in this short-lit portrait of a literature student.

ISO 500 • 1/125 sec. • f/4 • 24mm

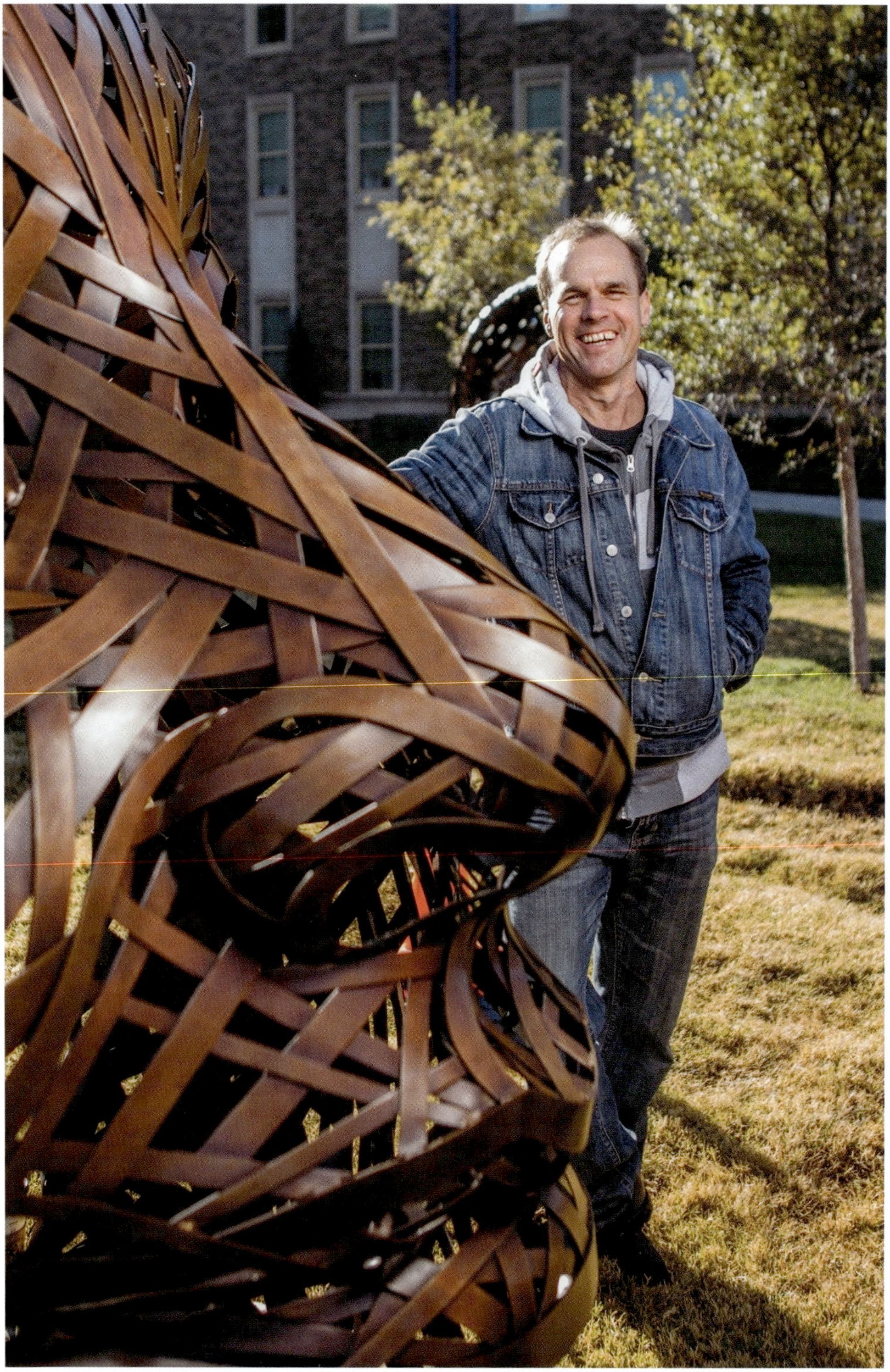

Figure 3.43
Knowing that a wide-angle lens would severely distort Michael Stutz's artwork, I decided to go with the longer end of the wide spectrum and use just a part of the art for this full-length portrait.

ISO 50 • 1/250 sec. • f/2.8 • 32mm

Chapter 3 Assignments

When I got my first wide-angle lens, it didn't come off my camera for six months. I worked with it tirelessly to get acquainted with it and learn how to compose different types of shots without getting too out of hand, perspectively speaking.

Lock it to the left

Walk outside with your wide-angle lens and zoom it out to the widest focal length (if you have a prime lens, just walk outside). Whether it is 24mm, 18mm, 10mm, or 8mm, stay at one focal length and work on composing with an extremely expansive perspective. Look around for strong subject matter to place in the foreground of some landscape shots, such as a knee-high plant or small rock formation. If you are downtown, look for street signs to compose with iconic buildings or roads to showcase strong lines. Working with the widest focal length you can will allow you to get comfortable with it, and as a result, develop some very interesting images.

Study the structure of the sky

Point your camera up to the sky and look for great composition up there. The next time a thunderstorm rolls your way, or the sky looks like it will offer up a nice sunrise or sunset, position yourself under it and look for structure. Strong lines created by striations or stretches of clouds, identifiable forms like circles and triangles, and layers of color make for not only interesting skies but often intriguing shots.

Portraits with a purpose

Choose a person—friend or family member—and photograph her in her environment. Create several portraits of your subject at varying wide-angle focal lengths and camera-to-subject distances. Seek out compositional elements and prime spots in which to place your subject. When moving in and away from your subject, recomposing the person in the frame, pay special attention to the distortion the focal length creates for the environment and your subject. Shoot full-length shots as well as waist-up portraits, and see what works best with the environment and the subject.

Share your results with the book's Flickr group!
Join the group here: www.flickr.com/groups/canonlenses_fromsnapshotstogreatshots

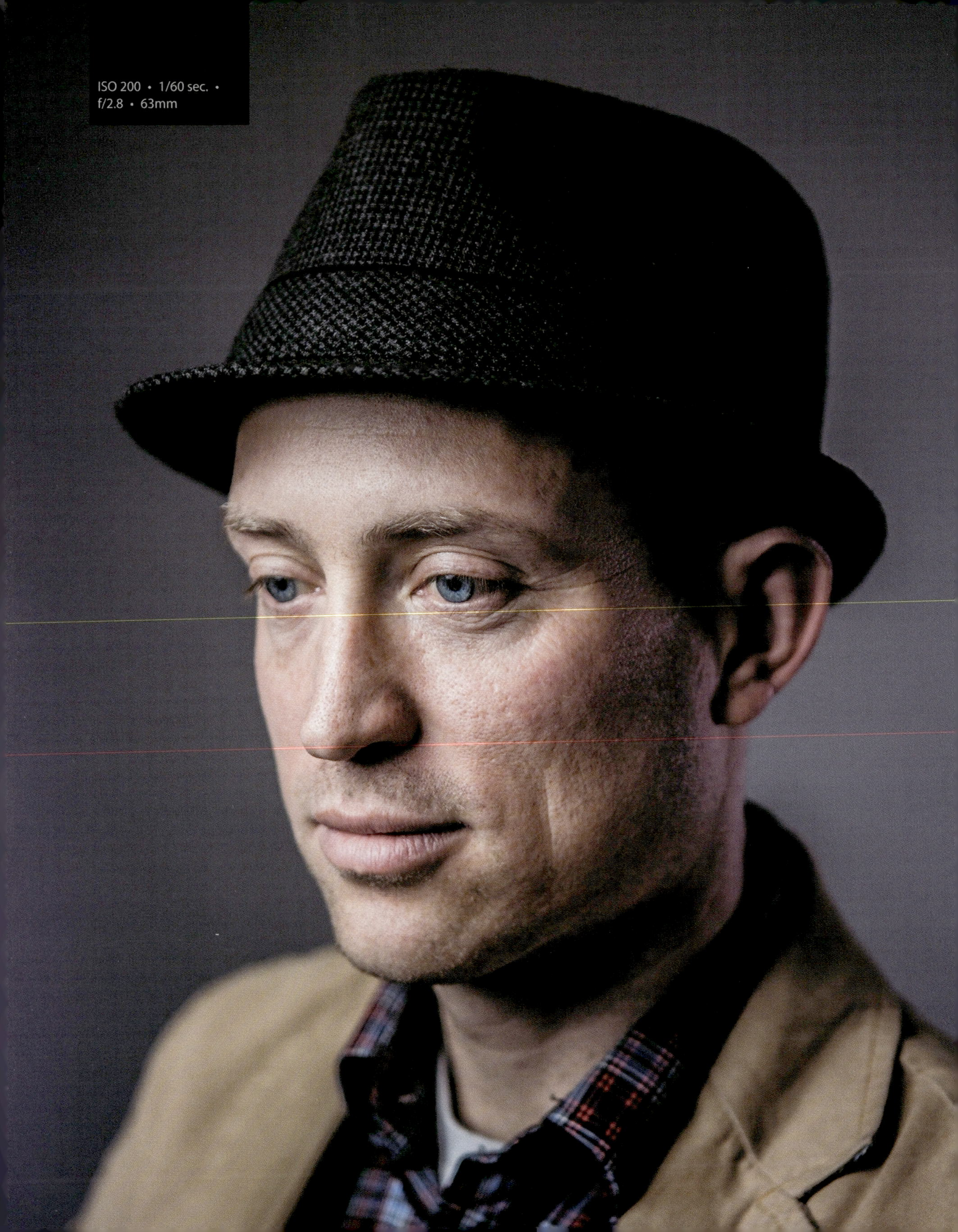

ISO 200 • 1/60 sec. • f/2.8 • 63mm

4

Standard Zooms and Primes

Image-making with the most popular lenses

Standard. That is a word that describes a necessity, the basis against which all else is judged, or around which everything is designed. It makes sense, then, that a large number of the lenses Canon makes belong to two groups dubbed standard primes and standard zooms.

Standard, in the case of lenses, refers to a range of focal lengths that photographers can maximize for the largest amount of image-making. All 19 lenses (as of this writing) in this category offer photographers the most options available in one lens for making great pictures—pictures that vary in focal length but do not deviate much from the familiar human perspective.

Poring Over the Picture

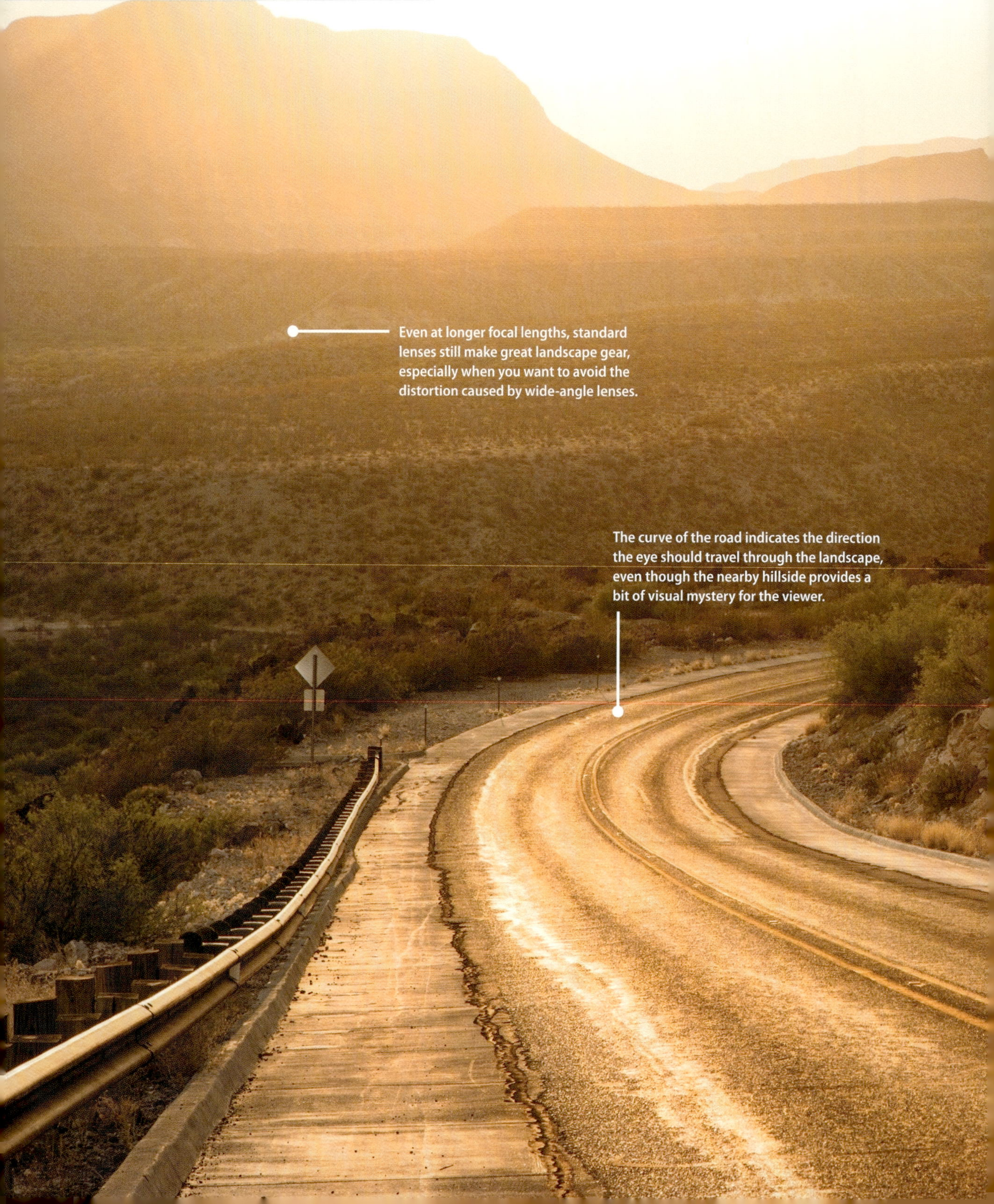

Even at longer focal lengths, standard lenses still make great landscape gear, especially when you want to avoid the distortion caused by wide-angle lenses.

The curve of the road indicates the direction the eye should travel through the landscape, even though the nearby hillside provides a bit of visual mystery for the viewer.

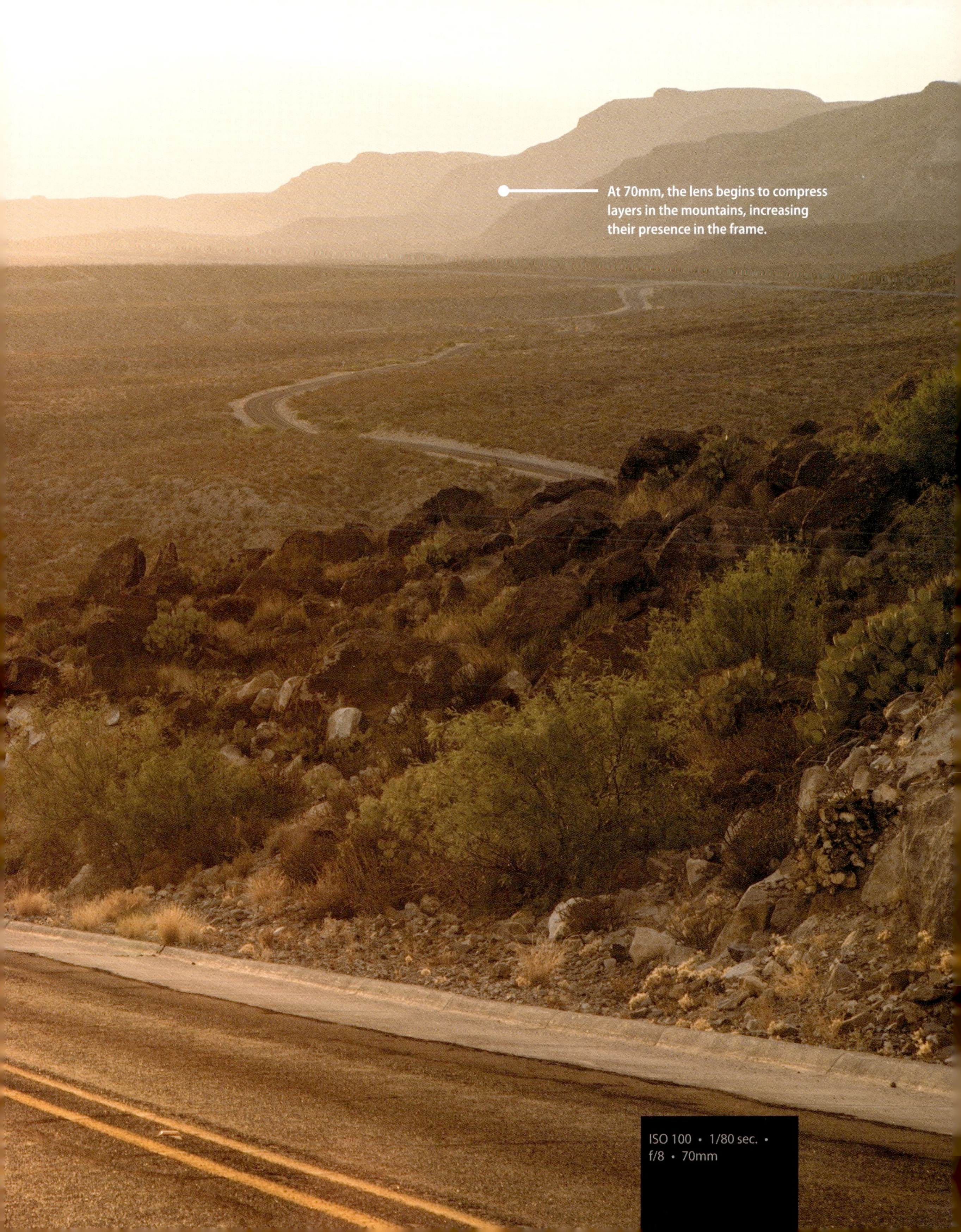
At 70mm, the lens begins to compress layers in the mountains, increasing their presence in the frame.
ISO 100 • 1/80 sec. • f/8 • 70mm

The Go-To Lenses

If you recently purchased an EOS Rebel-series camera, you more than likely purchased an entire kit that included an EF-S 18–55mm f/3.5–5.6 lens. If you purchased an EOS 5D Mk III or EOS 6D (full-frame sensor cameras), instead, you had the option of purchasing a kit version of the camera that included in the price an EF 24–105mm f/4L IS. Some retailers put together full-frame kits, including the EF 24–70mm f/2.8L in lieu of the EF 24–105mm f/4L IS. All lenses are excellent standard zooms and are intended to be photographers' go-to lenses for much of their work (**Figure 4.1**).

For the most part, any time you purchase a kit, the lens fits somewhere in this standard zoom range. Most folks consider standard focal lengths to be ranging from 24mm to 105mm on a full-frame sensor camera (dictated by design as opposed to a strict regulation), hence the popularity of the EF 24–105mm f/4L IS for the full-frame kit mentioned above. For the purposes of this chapter, we'll go with these focal lengths as well when discussing standard lenses.

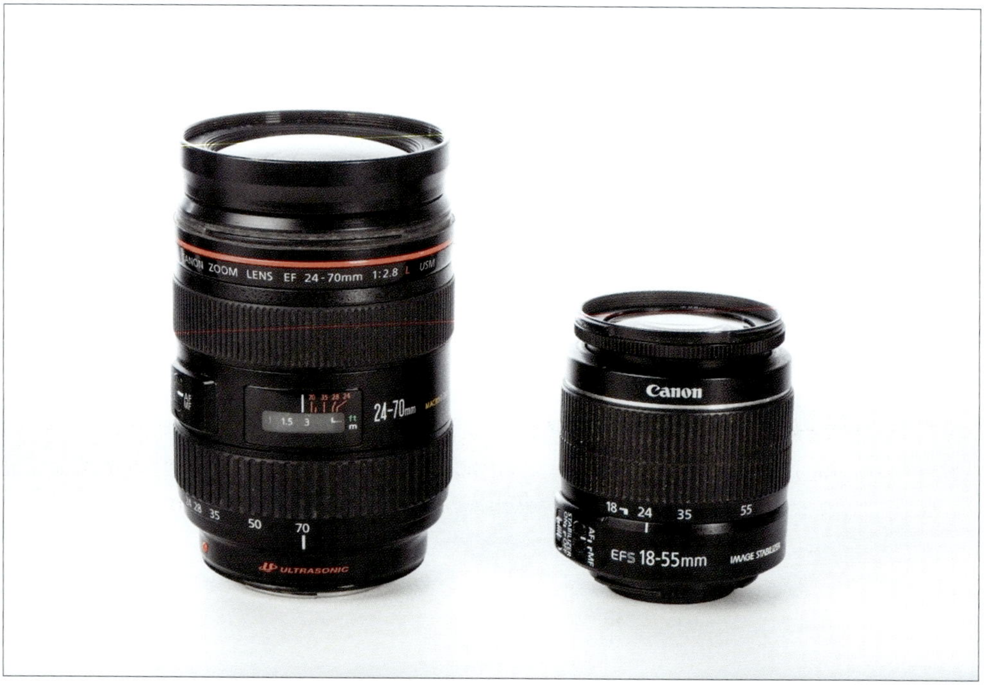

Figure 4.1
The EF 24–70mm f/2.8L (left) and the EF-S 18–55mm f/3.5–5.6 IS (right) are two popular Canon standard zoom lenses.

Range and Flexibility

The obvious advantage of a standard zoom—as well as a few standard primes if you choose to go that route—is its versatility. Rightly so, a standard zoom lens is built for the amount of flex a photographer demands of any one lens. I can't think of another lens that sees a variety of focal lengths actually used when shooting. As I mentioned in the previous chapter, wide-angle zooms are typically used at their widest focal length, and the opposite happens for many telephoto-zoom lenses. However, the 40-some-odd millimeters of focal length many standard zoom lenses offer (some more) tend to get used.

The standard zoom lens creeps into the wide world, especially if the lens reaches as wide as 24mm or its EF-S equivalent (18mm on an EF-S lens is comparable to a 29mm full-frame perspective). At the same time, many reach 70mm or more, which is medium-telephoto territory. Not too shabby for one lens. For photographers on a budget or wanting to carry a minimum amount of gear, the standard zoom lens is ideal. It is the foundation for the lens trinity highlighted in Chapter 1, and it is the one I recommend that all novice photographers obtain first. Standard zooms run the gamut in terms of build quality and lens speed and features.

An additional advantage of the standard zoom lens is its coverage of landmark focal lengths, including 35mm and 50mm. Both focal lengths are valuable to many photographers, particularly those interested in photojournalism. We'll spend more time discussing the 50mm lenses later in this chapter. However, it is important to mention—especially for those new to selecting gear for rental or purchase—that a standard zoom lens also allows the photographer to learn if she leans toward these two focal lengths and whether or not it is advantageous for her to purchase dedicated 35mm and/or 50mm prime lenses.

Real-Life Applications

Aside from the mechanical flexibility of standard lenses, especially standard zooms, they are also useful for a diverse range of photographic subject matter. More than anything else, this is the reason to own either a standard zoom or a couple of standard prime lenses, like a 35mm and a 50mm.

Landscape photography

Consider the flexibility of focal lengths the standard category includes, and then consider what you can adequately shoot with this range. I used to think that all of my landscape shots had to be made with an ultra-wide lens. Nowadays, I probably use 24mm as the widest focal length more than I do 17mm or wider (**Figure 4.2**). Why? It doesn't distort as much as 17mm, it's wide enough to showcase a lot of environment but tight enough to mitigate large void spaces in the sky or foreground, and probably most convenient, it is the widest extreme on a zoom lens that lets me quickly move from fairly wide to long with the twist of my wrist. This is useful for shooting in a river environment (**Figure 4.3**), where a wide perspective will provide one shot, and a tighter perspective will offer another in literally seconds (**Figure 4.4**).

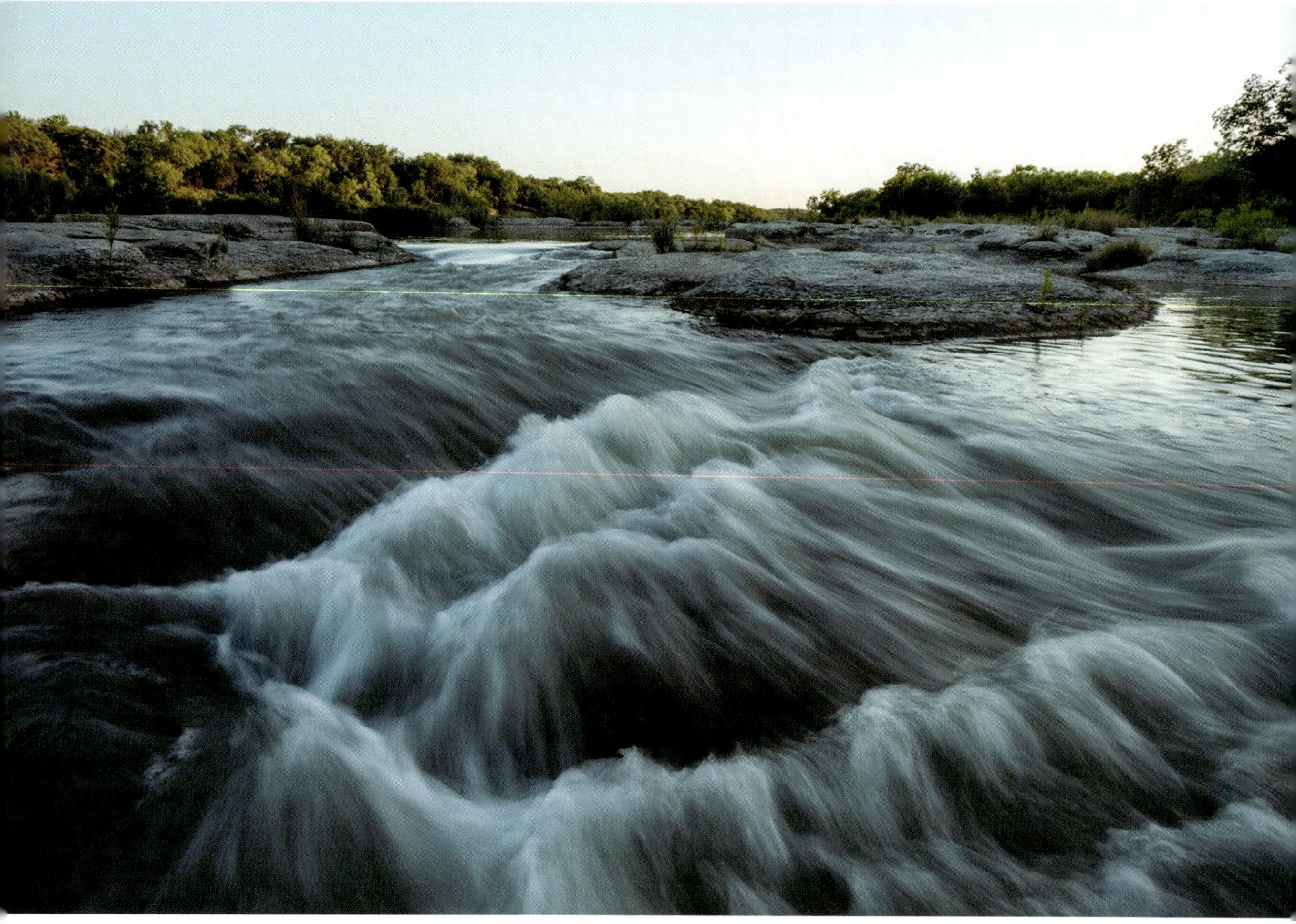

Figure 4.2 At 24mm, a standard zoom lens is very capable of helping to create expansive landscape shots.

ISO 100 • 1/6 sec. • f/22 • 24mm

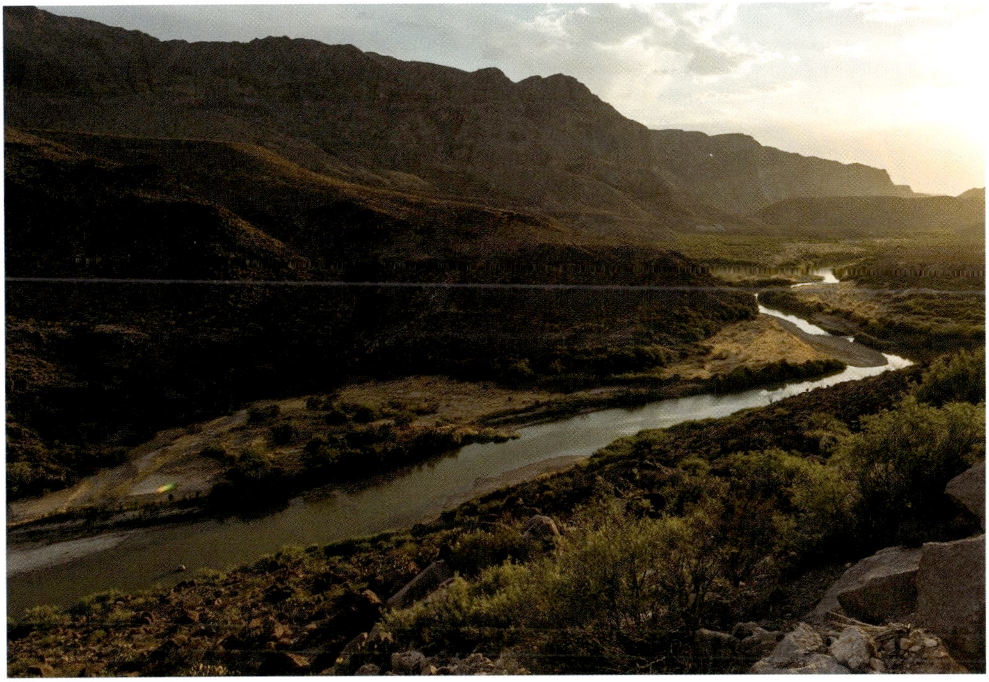

Figure 4.3
A standard zoom lens like the EF 24–105mm f/4L IS offers up great wide views of desert riparian landscapes.

ISO 100 • 1/125 sec. • f/8 • 24mm

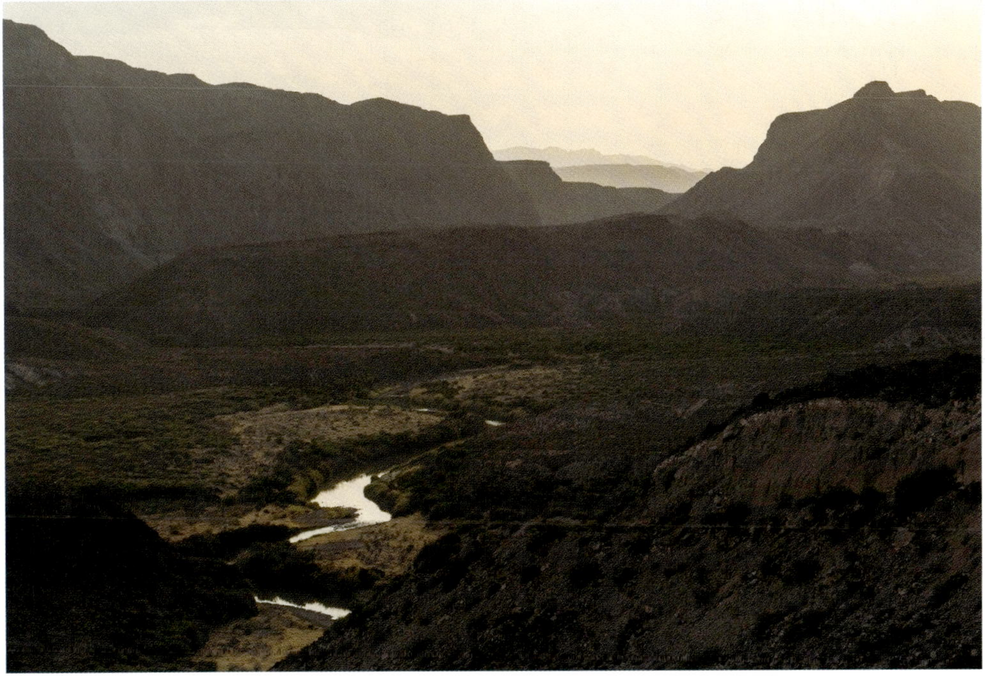

Figure 4.4
At the same time, the long end of an EF 24–105mm f/4L IS helps compress the layers of the same landscape, making for a rather different image.

ISO 100 • 1/125 sec. • f/11 • 105mm

Photojournalism

The standard lens range is also very popular in the photojournalism and documentary fields of photography (**Figure 4.5**). It not only allows the photographer to work closely with his subject matter, but it also forces him to produce more intimate images based on physical proximity of the camera to the subject(s) (**Figure 4.6**). Some of the most compelling images ever made were created with a 35mm or 50mm lens. Technological limitations and availability prevented photographers in the 1930s, '40s, and '50s from obtaining longer lenses, which would have provided a different perspective. Yet the 35mm and 50mm lenses offered these photographers a great way to tell stories from a close yet observable distance. Because of this, the standard focal length range has remained popular for photography since photo essays were first popularized.

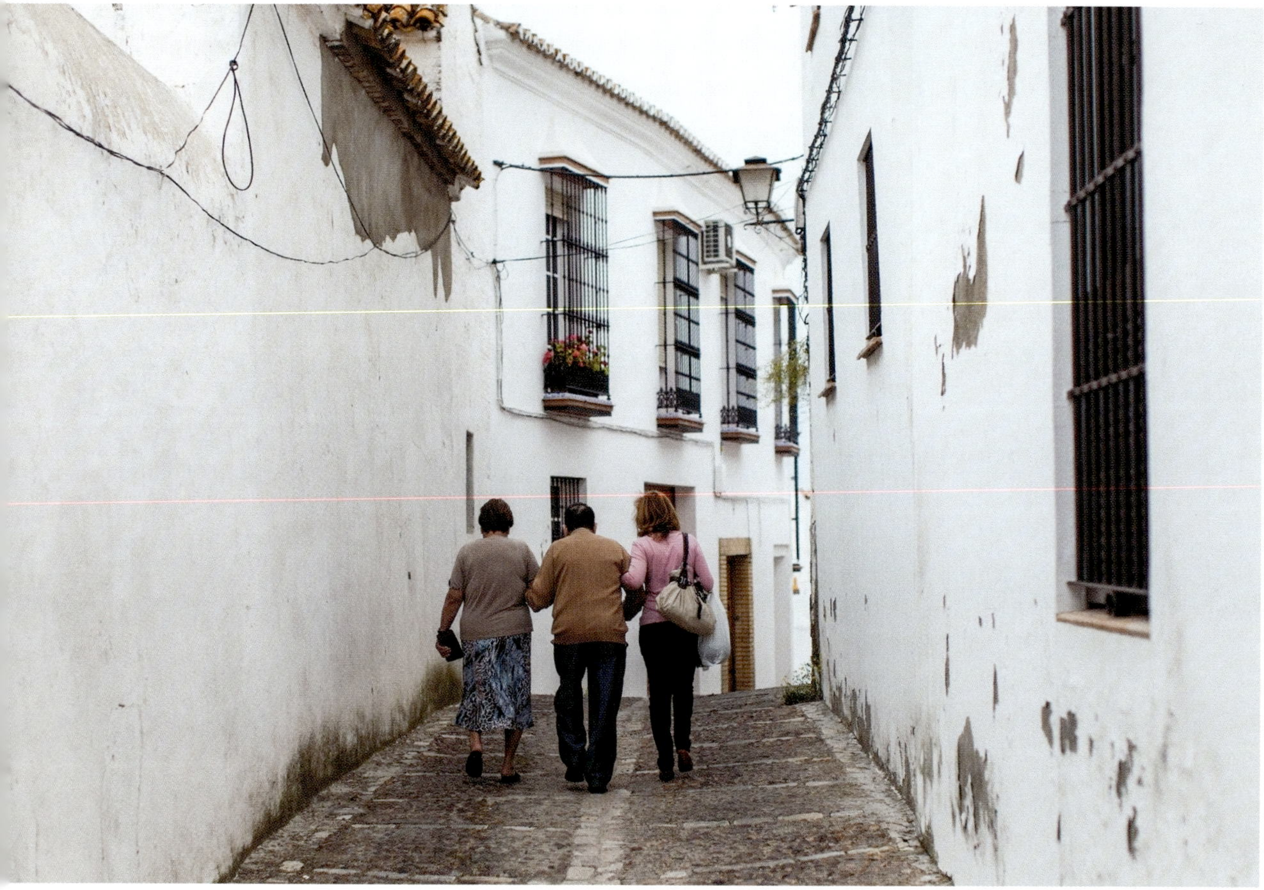

Figure 4.5 A 50mm lens is nice to take on a photo walk, perfect for finding candid moments, like this family walking home in Carmona, Spain.

ISO 200 • 1/4000 sec. • f/2.2 • 50mm

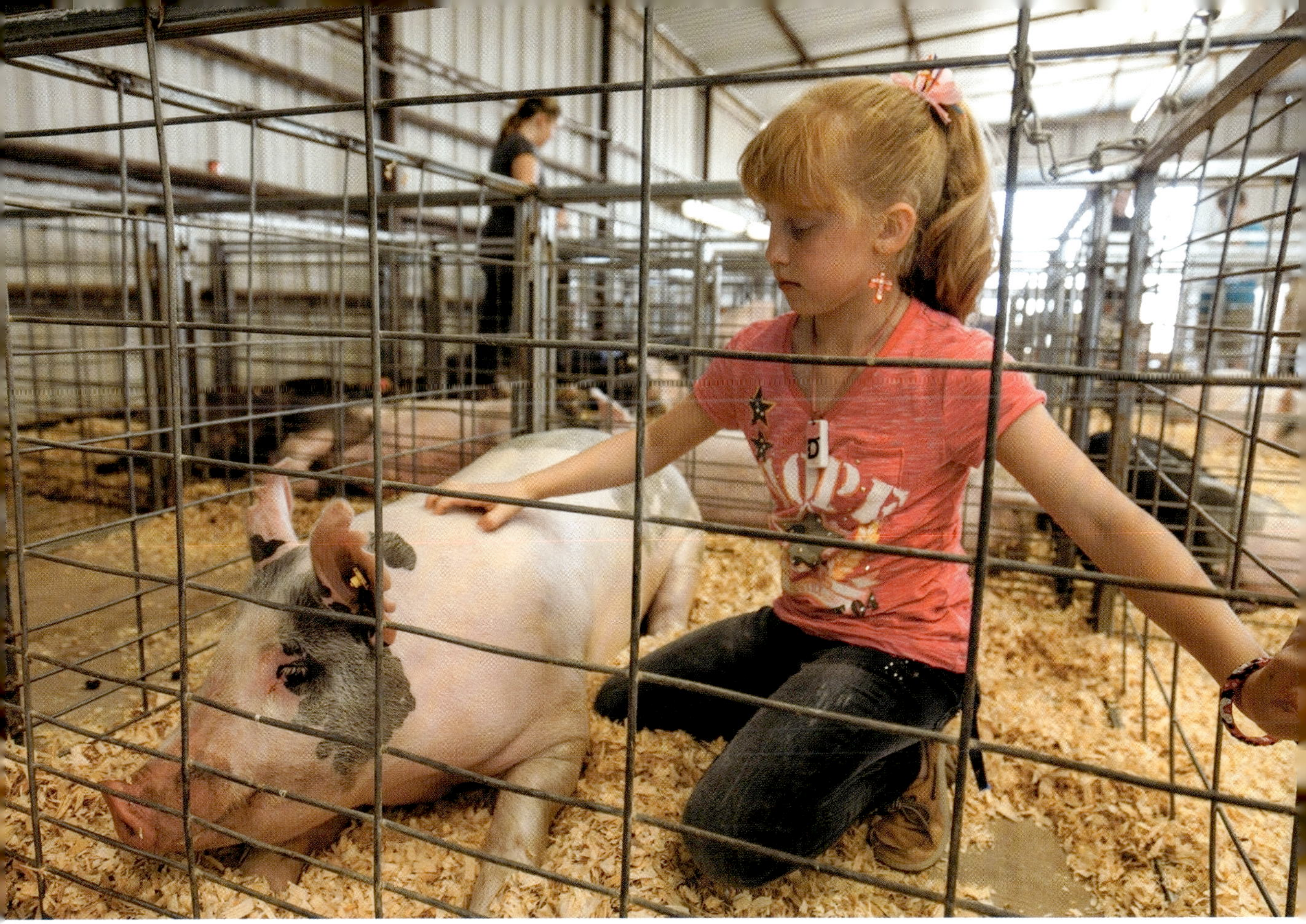

Figure 4.6 **Standard lenses keep the distance between the subject and the photographer close and engaging, helping to create a feeling of actually being there for the viewer.**

ISO 400 • 1/60 sec. • f/4 • 24mm

Portraiture

Standard focal lengths are also valuable for portraits. I know many environmental portrait photographers who consider their standard zooms the most important lenses in their bags. Whether you are shooting full-length portraits with the wider side of the lens (**Figure 4.7**) or head shots with the longer end (**Figure 4.8**), the standard zoom is as flexible for portraits as it is for landscapes. Keep in mind that the wider focal lengths exhibit higher levels of distortion and keystoning, which might prove disadvantageous for fashion work. Subsequently, many waist-up, or medium, portraits are made at the longer focal lengths in the standard range (**Figure 4.9**), including perhaps the most popular portrait focal length Canon makes, the 85mm (which we will touch on shortly).

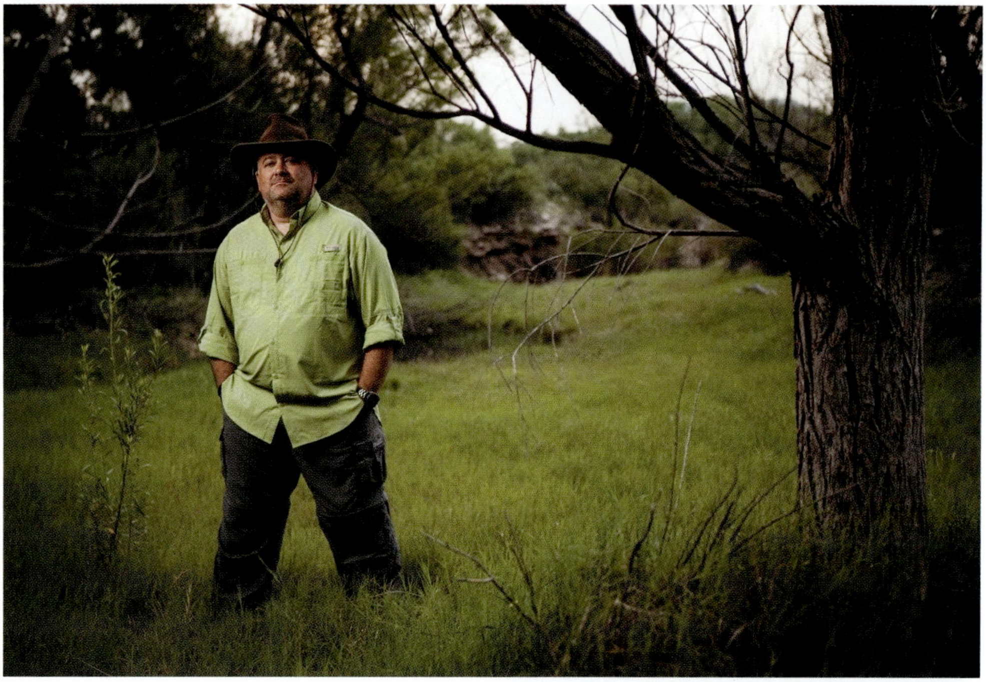

Figure 4.7
A standard lens is my favorite lens for making full-length portraits.

ISO 100 • 1/125 sec. • f/2.8 • 50mm

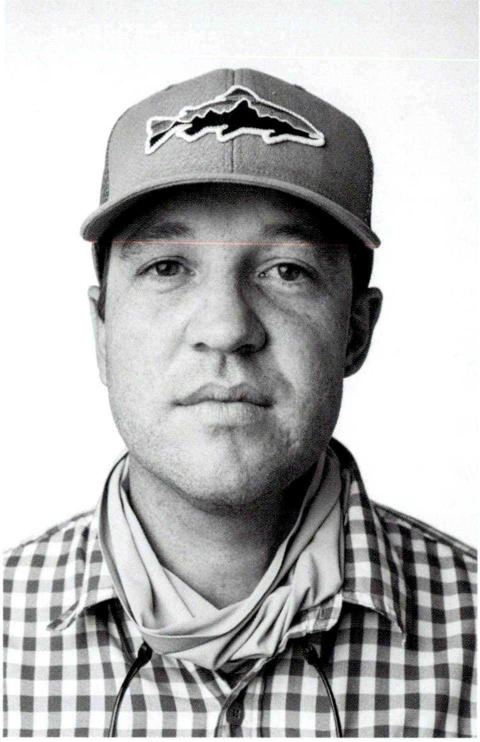

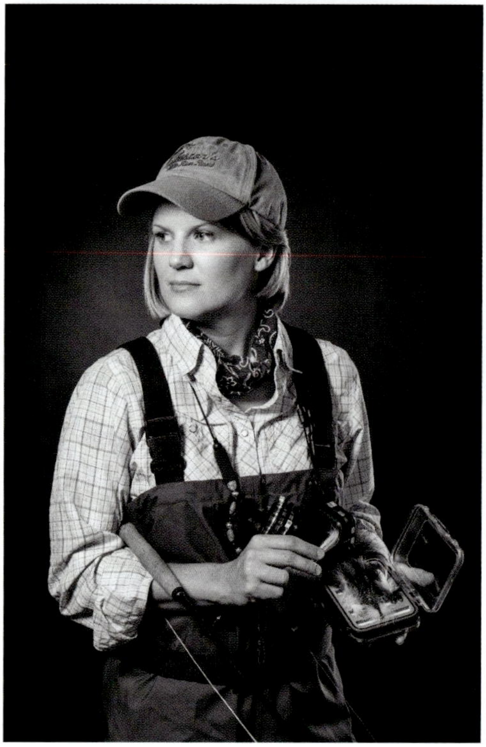

Figure 4.8 (left)
The long end of a standard zoom lens is the preferred focal length I use for studio work, as illustrated in this portrait of angler Byron Kennedy.

ISO 200 • 1/160 sec. • f/8 • 70mm

Figure 4.9 (right)
Angler Lindsay West Kennedy poses for an in-studio shot made at 70mm, a great focal length for a variety of portrait work.

ISO 200 • 1/160 sec. • f/8 • 70mm

Sports and wildlife photography

We can't leave out the sports and wildlife folks here. Although the majority of sports and wildlife work is achieved using telephotos and super-telephoto lenses, I don't know a single photographer interested in these areas who does not own a standard zoom lens or at least one lens that fits within the standard focal length range. Take American football photography, for example. When the action on the field gets closer and closer to the end zone, there is only so much a 400mm lens will offer you. A standard zoom, like the EF 24–70mm f/2.8 L, keeps the photographer prepared for a play that moves closer to her side of the field, but it is even more useful for those milder activities like halftime (**Figure 4.10**).

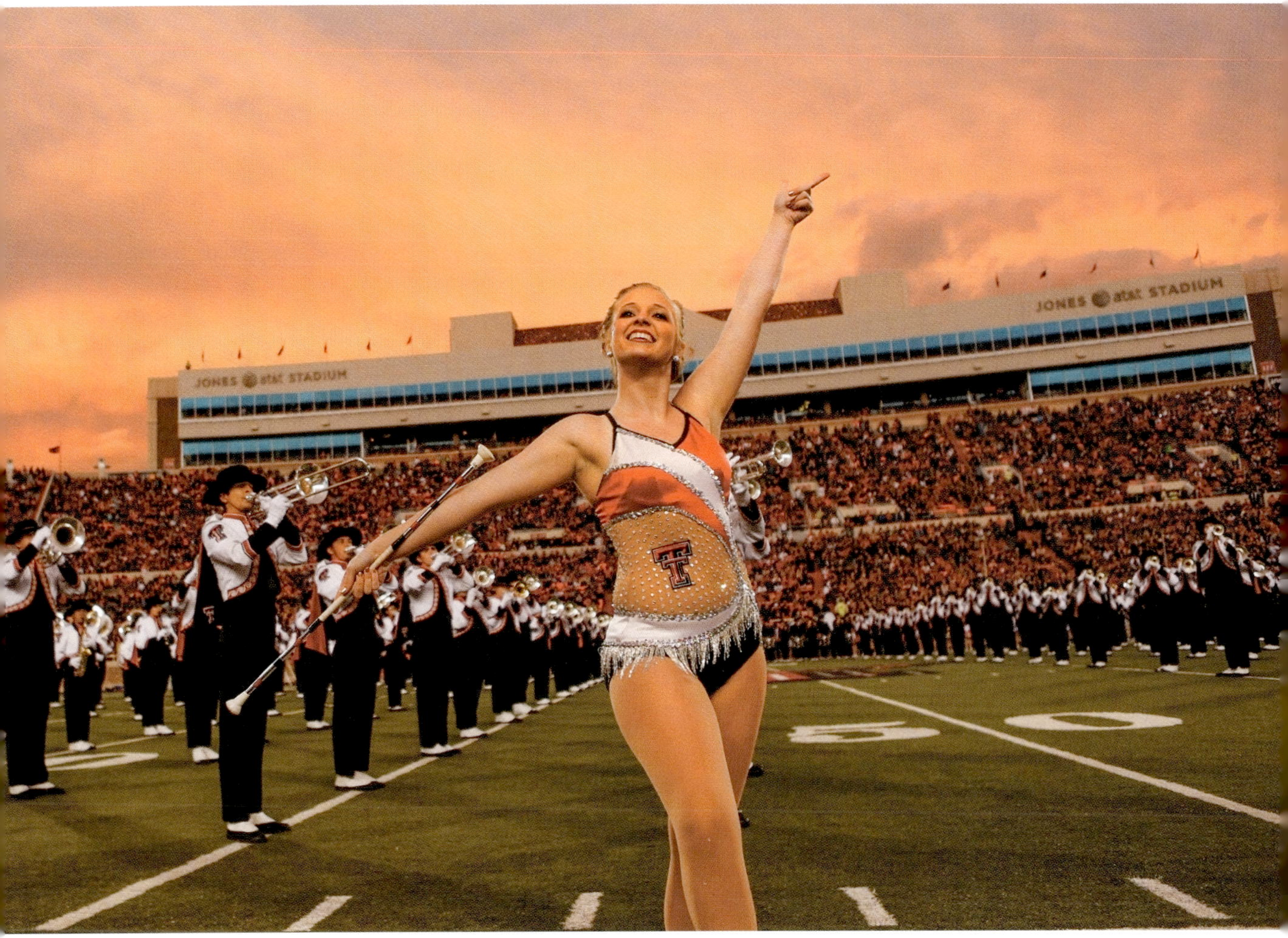

Figure 4.10 **A standard zoom lens is nice to have on the football field, especially for capturing the halftime show, where being close to the action doesn't mean getting knocked down.**

ISO 800 • 1/1250 sec. • f/2.8 • 24mm

Other sports that allow spectators a close look at the action, such as cycling, are great activities to shoot with both wide-angle and medium-telephoto perspectives (**Figure 4.11**). As so many photographers have stated over the years, being closer to the action makes for more interesting images, and a standard zoom lens or a few prime equivalents allow you to do just that.

Wildlife photography may offer a few more challenges than sports do, even at the longer end of the standard range of focal lengths, but certain subjects allow the shooter to use shorter lenses (**Figure 4.12**). Shorter focal lengths are also easier to use in conjunction with remote cameras set up to shoot wildlife from hidden areas.

And, although I have never had the pleasure of testing this myself, I hear a standard zoom is ideal for underwater photography.

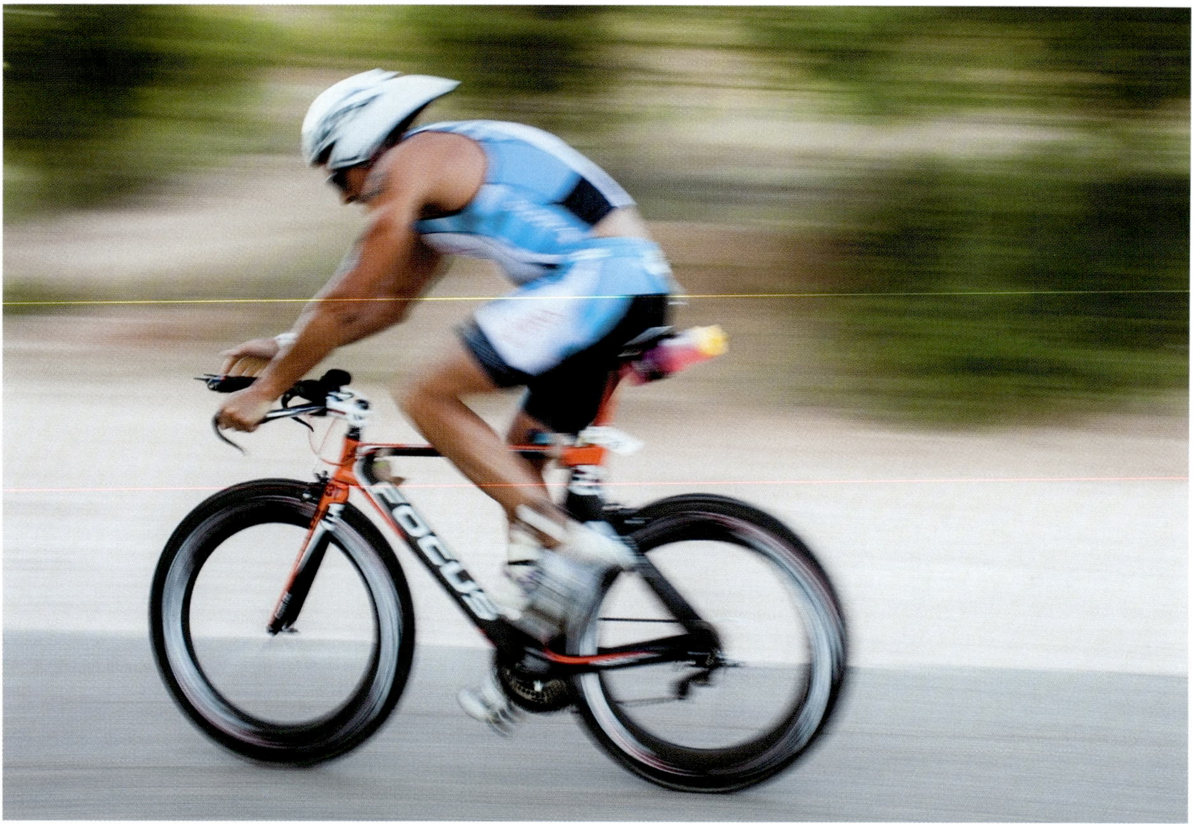

Figure 4.11 **You can make a pan of a cyclist easily with a standard lens from the side of the road.**

ISO 100 • 1/20 sec. • f/5 • 50mm

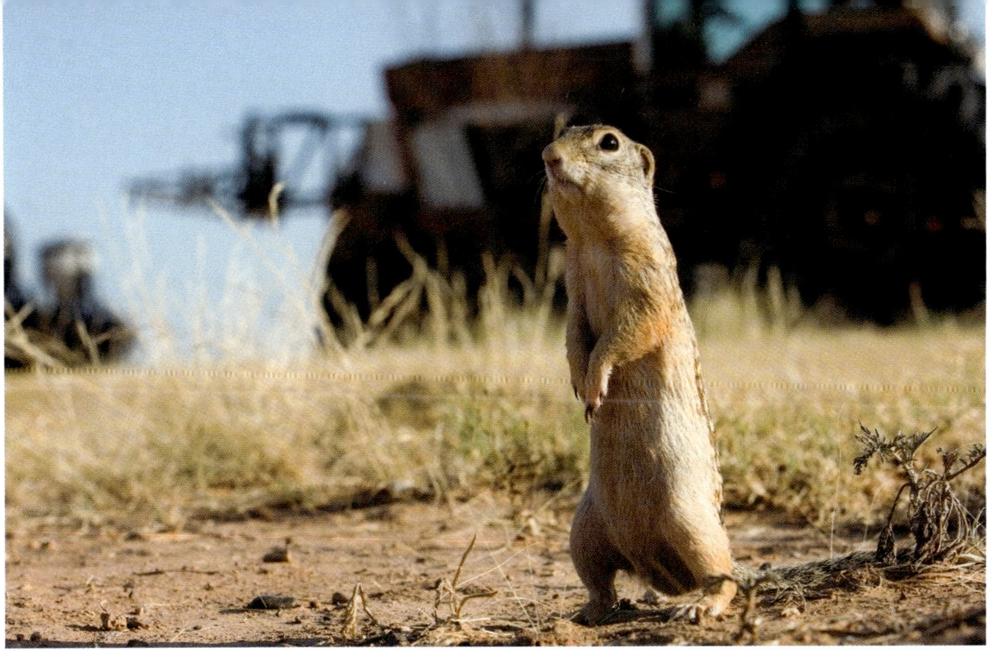

Figure 4.12
Wildlife can be tough with a standard zoom lens, but with enough patience, you can make a comical shot of the smallest animals.

ISO 100 • 1/200 sec. • f/9 • 73mm

If I Had to Choose: EF 24–70mm f/2.8L

I am very pragmatic about my lens choices. I want a lens to be sharp, tough, and simple. I want it to function for me in any environment—especially if it is the lens I will use the most. This is what I love about the EF 24–70mm f/2.8L. Long considered the core of a professional's Canon lens trinity, it has only recently (within the past three years) made its way into my bag. Like many, while I was shooting film I started out with an older Canon EF 28–90mm f/4–5.6, a standard kit lens for folks with film versions of the Rebel series (no longer in production).

When I started shooting digital, I upgraded to an EF 24–105mm f/4L IS. This is still one of the sharpest lenses I have ever used, as well as one of the most versatile given the range to 105mm. For a landscape shooter, I can't see a better standard zoom lens. However, my work started to move toward the more editorial, where shoots were in a variety of environments. The f/4 of the 24–105mm was a bit hindering on some locations where the light was dim. Hence my move to the EF 24–70mm f/2.8L. Although it lacks Image Stabilization, and it weighs a ton (I have the previous version—Canon shaved off some ounces with the current iteration), it is on my camera the most, and it is everything I described above—high quality and extremely reliable. Like with the EF 24–105mm f/4, the build quality is outstanding. Believe me, it can take a hit, and it feels good in the hand. It is sharp at f/2.8, a major concern for lenses that open up extremely wide, and I feel confident handholding it at relatively slow shutter speeds.

Although it is a zoom lens, the EF 24–70mm f/2.8 is the one I use the most for my environmental and studio portraiture work. I find myself moving in and out of active situations, shooting portraits and other subject matter at a variety of focal lengths to test out different shots and achieve interesting angles and perspectives. They say that gear shouldn't matter that much when it comes to vision, but I feel visually nimble with this lens.

Composing With Standard Zooms and Primes

Composing with the standard range of focal lengths isn't necessarily different from composing with any lens. Finding and using strong lines, following the rule of thirds, and the like, are standard compositional techniques. However, trying to envision those things coming together with so many useful focal lengths can be daunting, especially while on location, when everything is coming at you at once, or when you want to maximize the most from your photography in a short amount of time.

Points of Interest

Envisioning shots with wide-angle lenses is relatively easy. I'm not saying wide-angles are easy to use successfully, but the wide-angle look is very familiar. Therefore, seeing in a wide perspective, where compositional interests such as lines are strongly emphasized, isn't as intimidating as *seeing* with other perspectives. It's more work envisioning images with the standard range of lenses. I am a fan of simplifying, though, and that's what I want to encourage in your own use of standard focal lengths.

Primary, secondary, and tertiary

Using all (or some) of those components of great composition covered in the previous chapter, focus on finding and providing a way for viewers to notice significant points of interest in your shots. You can use these points to guide the eye through the shot, from one direction to the other (**Figure 4.13**), or use them to isolate strong subjects over minor ones or a complementary background (**Figure 4.14**). Also consider being able to showcase multiple points of interest as if there were a visual hierarchy to how they should be physically viewed. A primary interest point—one that is the most important to the shot—may be placed in the foreground, a secondary interest point behind it (staggered

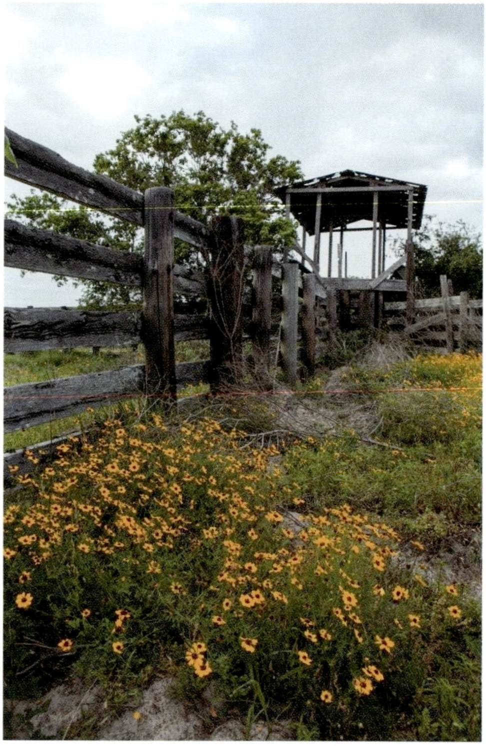

Figure 4.13 **The flowers in the foreground serve as a primary point of interest, which lead the eye to a secondary point—the lines of the fence—and on to the abandoned cattle station, the tertiary interest point.**

ISO 400 • 1/40 sec. • f/8 • 24mm

to an opposite side perhaps), and a tertiary point placed as the least significant of the three (**Figure 4.15**). You may choose to have only one real point of interest in the frame, or as many as you can keep organized for the human eye.

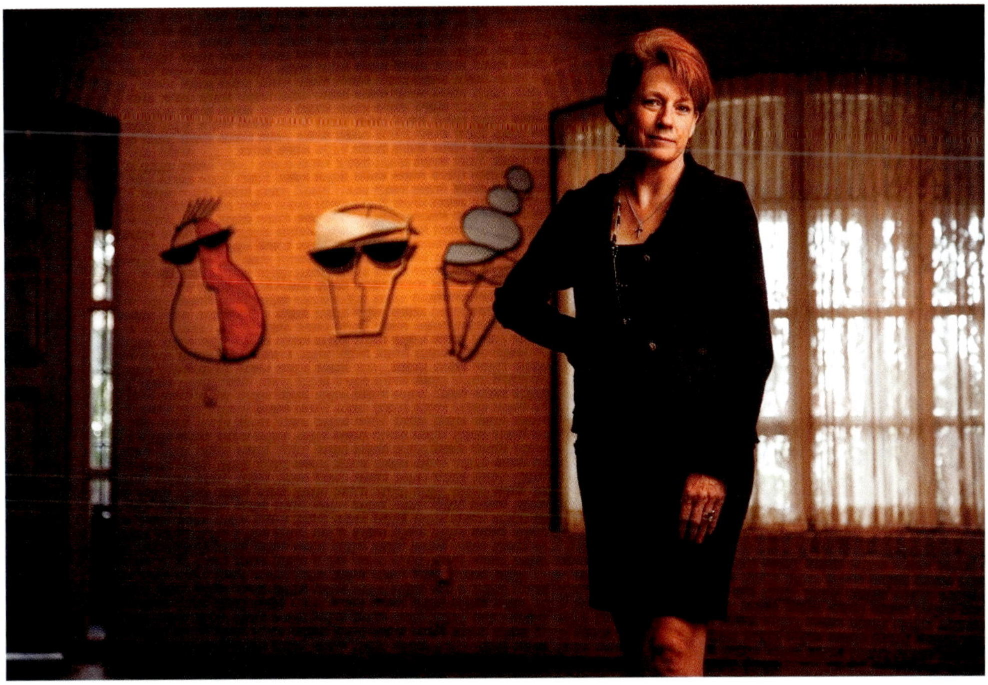

Figure 4.14
Artist Charice Adams in front of some of her work in a local gallery. Using points of interest for composition can be as simple as one subject placed in front of the other.

ISO 320 • 1/30 sec. • f/4 • 82mm

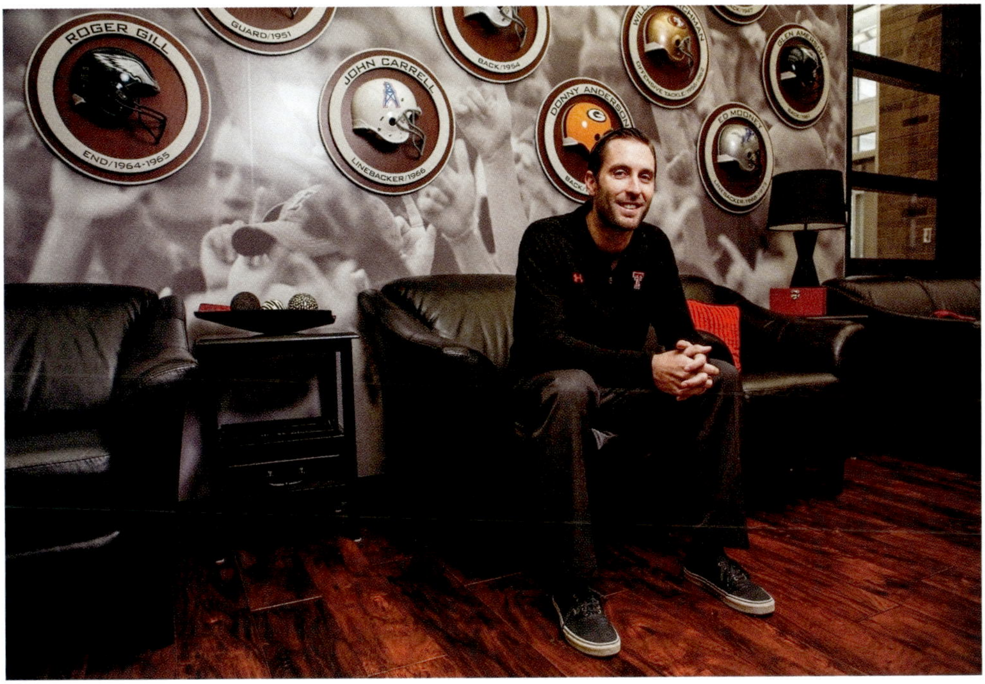

Figure 4.15
With football coach Kliff Kingsbury serving as the primary point of interest, a wide-angle portrait includes the helmets as secondary interest points, and the image of the fans on the wall as a tertiary point.

ISO 400 • 1/60 sec. • f/3.5 • 24mm

Using this points-of-interest technique is by no means relegated to standard focal lengths only. I encourage everyone to use it at any focal length. However, it is a great way to simplify working with lenses and a range of focal lengths that cross the wide-to-telephoto divide. Although this divide is not over 100mm, it is incredible the visual difference one extreme has to the other (**Figures 4.16** and **4.17**).

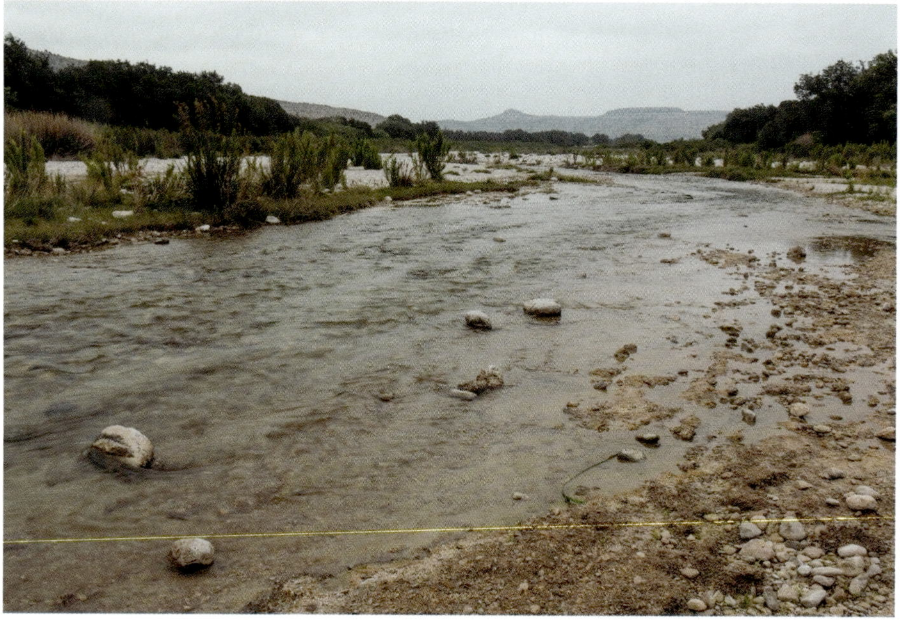

Figure 4.16
At 35mm, you can see a line among diminished points of interest.

ISO 200 • 1/8 sec. • f/22 • 35mm

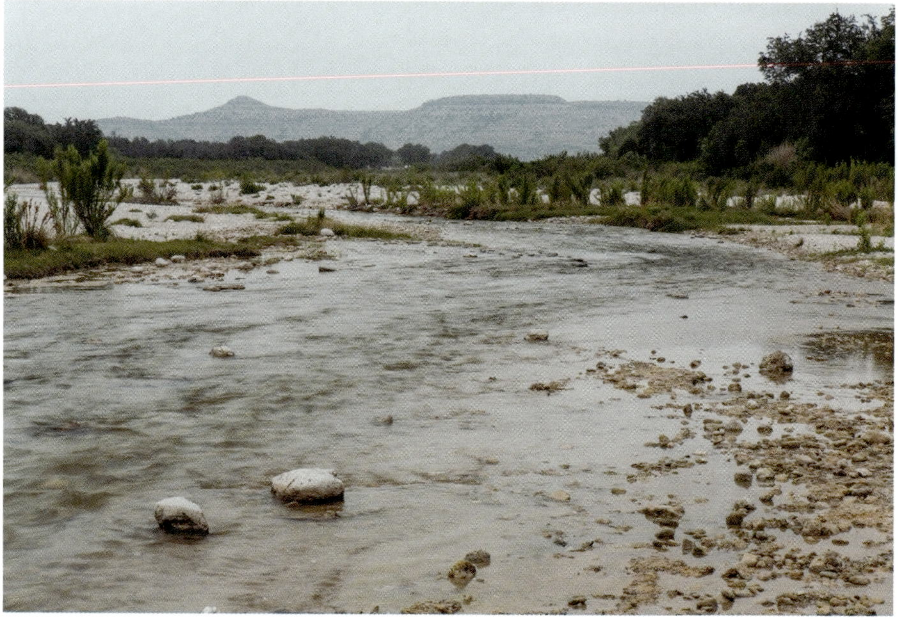

Figure 4.17
Yet, at 70mm, the hills in the background compress more with the foreground elements, new lines are formed, and interest points are more strongly exhibited.

ISO 200 • 1/4 sec. • f/22 • 70mm

No matter how much you zoom in (or out) on your subject matter, create a visual roadmap the viewer can follow from one strong point of interest to the other. Sometimes this requires looking through the lens at various focal lengths before snapping the shot.

Storytelling with lenses

An added benefit of shooting points of visual interest is the storytelling that results. In any given environment, a point of interest serves as a component of the visual story that exists in an image (or multiple images). When these points of interest are tied together, a visual narrative is created based on our own ability to comprehend their connection (**Figure 4.18**).

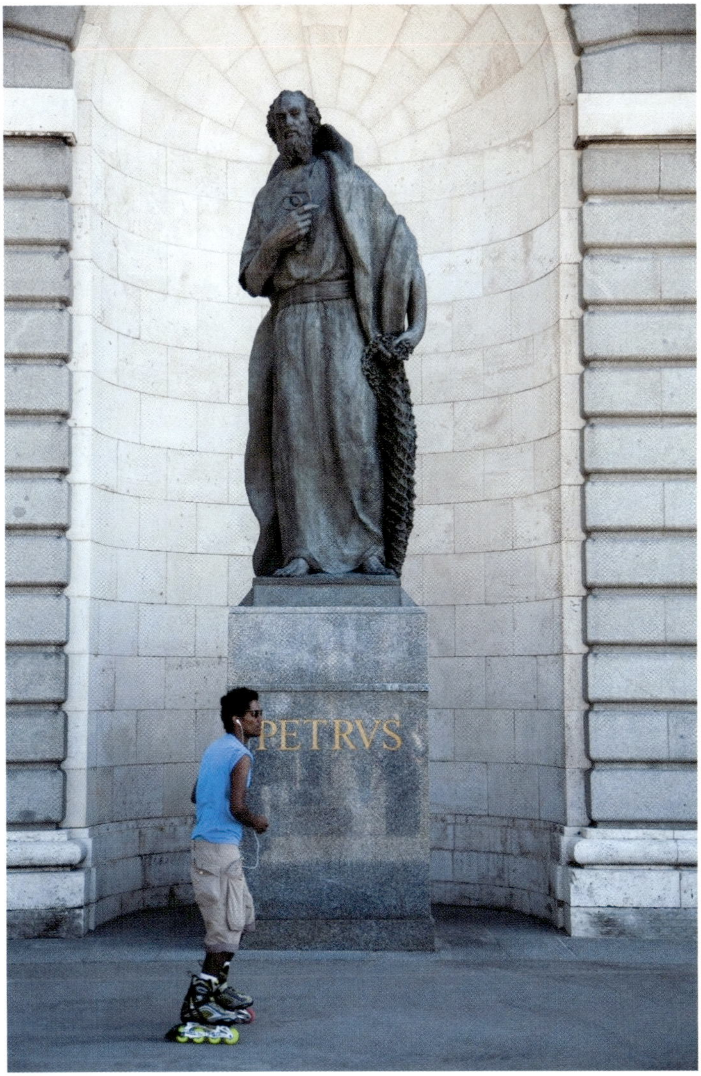

Figure 4.18
A skater riding past a statue of Saint Peter in Madrid conveys a modern society set against the backdrop of tradition.

ISO 200 • 1/500 sec. • f/4 • 55mm

Photography can be rather interpretive, and there's a sliding scale as to how much interpretation is required when creating *and* viewing an image (**Figure 4.19**). As image makers, though, we are at the visual helm of creating meaning with our images.

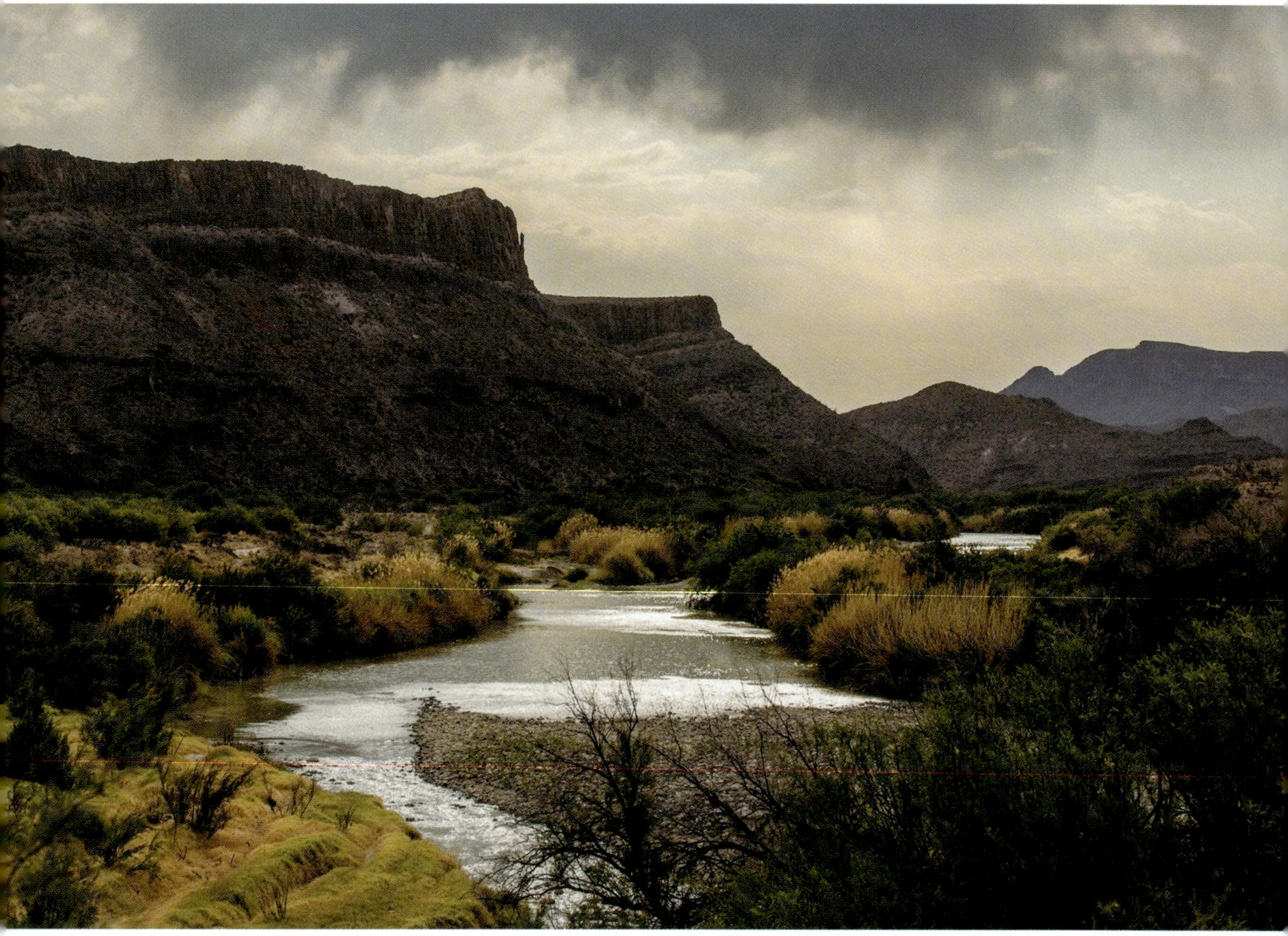

Figure 4.19 **The gloomy look of the Rio Grande and the U.S./Mexican border in far West Texas sets up an image for quite a bit of interpretive value.**

ISO 200 • 1/500 sec. • f/11 • 90mm

Fortunately, standard focal lengths have always been right alongside this storytelling process. Since the look of these types of lenses isn't as visually defined as, say, a 14mm or a 500mm, a photographer's attention to composition is even more key to an image's success. Combine that with points of interest that increase a viewer's understanding of a context or engage a viewer in a more active way (**Figure 4.20**), and the lens helps the photographer do what he set out to do.

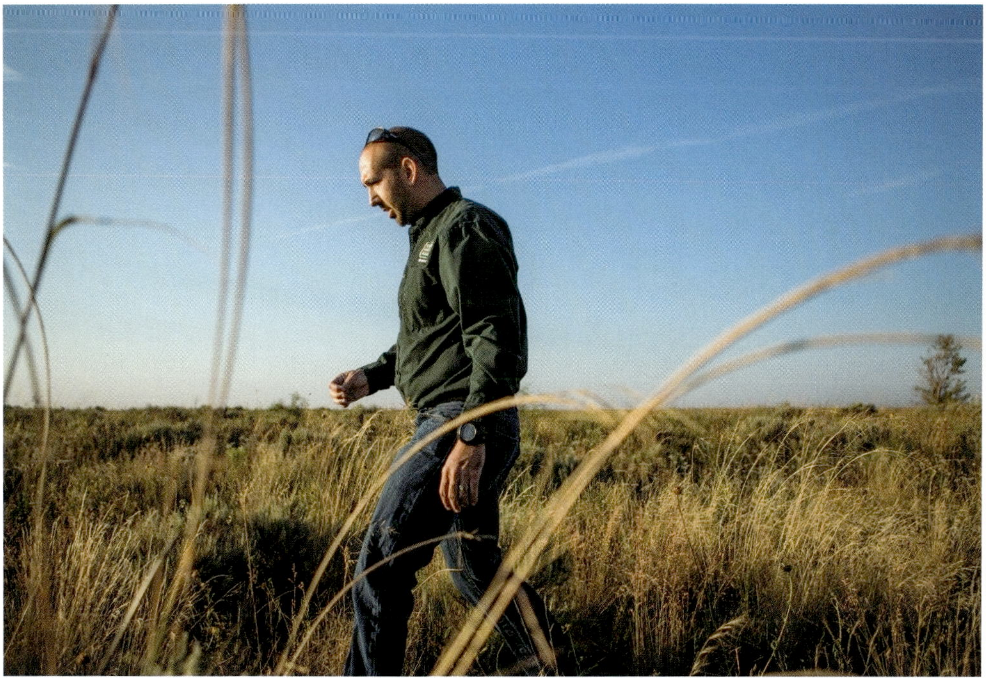

Figure 4.20
Pushing in tight on the secondary interest point—the West Texas grassland—helps highlight the primary subject of interest, a staff member of the Texas Parks and Wildlife department.

ISO 100 • 1/1600 sec. • f/2.8 • 24mm

Framing

Although not unique to the standard range of focal lengths, one key compositional technique I find myself using quite a bit when I have a standard zoom lens in hand is *framing.* Framing, the use of content within an image to drive attention toward the subject, is a great technique to employ when you cannot rely largely on a perspective effect of a lens (**Figure 4.21**). An overhanging tree or the architecture of a building can visually frame up the subject of a portrait (**Figure 4.22**) or activity of interest.

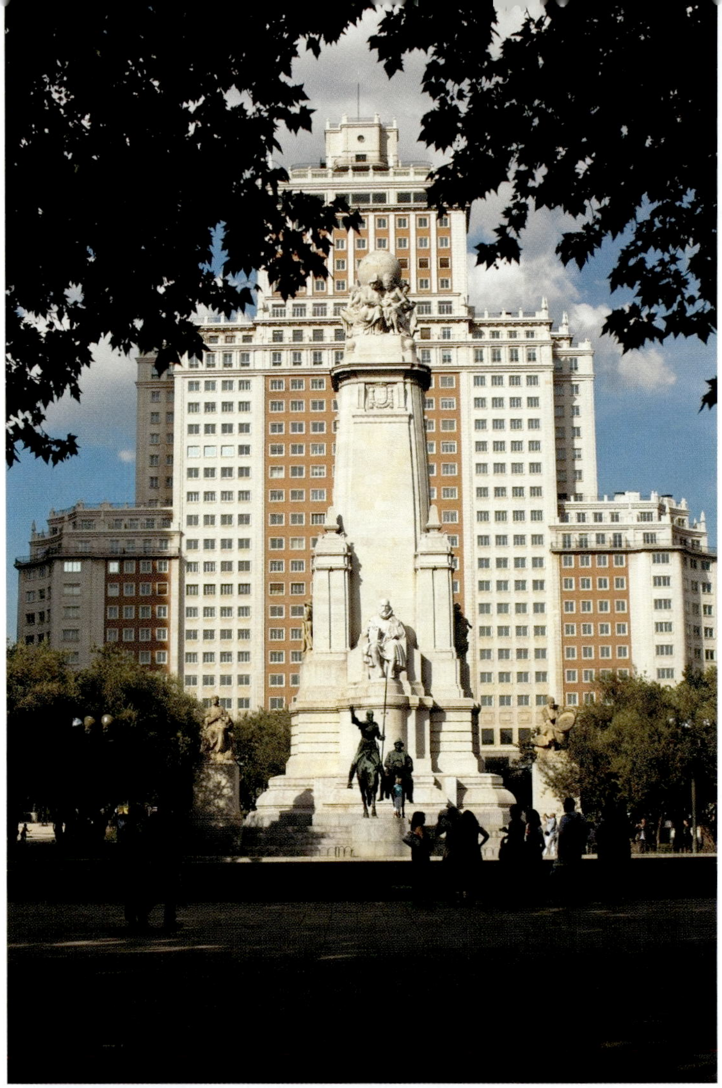

Figure 4.21
The shadowed trees and foreground frame the Cervantes Monument in Madrid, Spain.

ISO 50 • 1/1000 sec. • f/4 • 50mm

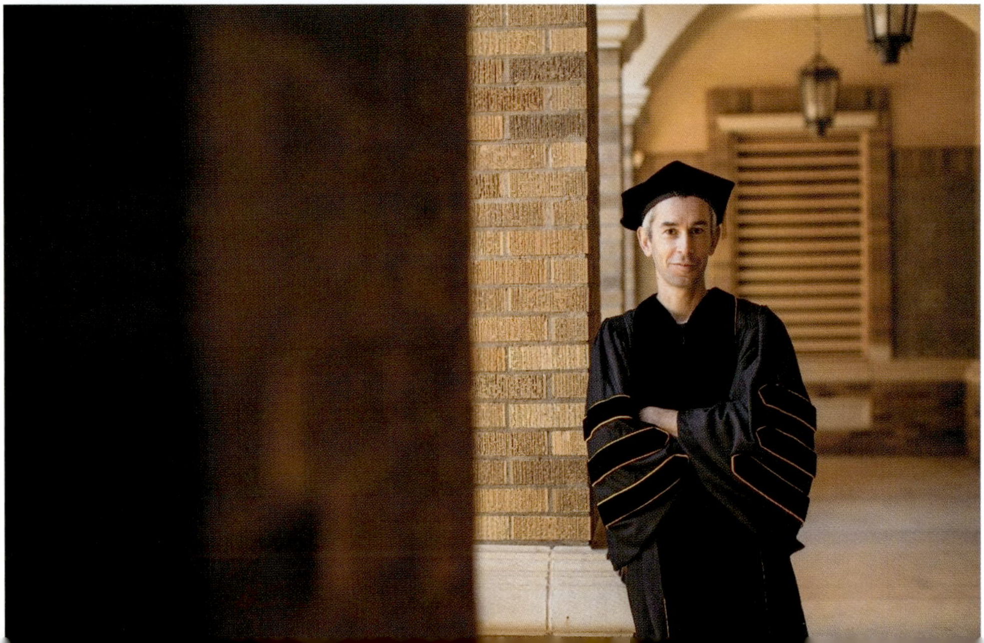

Figure 4.22
I used an out-of-focus square column on the left to force the eye to the right and toward doctoral graduate Patrick Merle.

ISO 100 • 1/320 sec. • f/2 • 50mm

I often find myself using arches and walls as framing devices, where shooting at 35mm or longer allows me to keep most of the straight lines of an environment in perspective. Just about anything can serve as a frame, and sometimes all it takes to find frames is putting your eye to the viewfinder. Again, when you are not using a lens effect—e.g., wide-angle lens—to draw the eye to what is important in the frame, you'll want to take advantage of framing devices while also employing other compositional techniques with a standard lens (**Figure 4.23**).

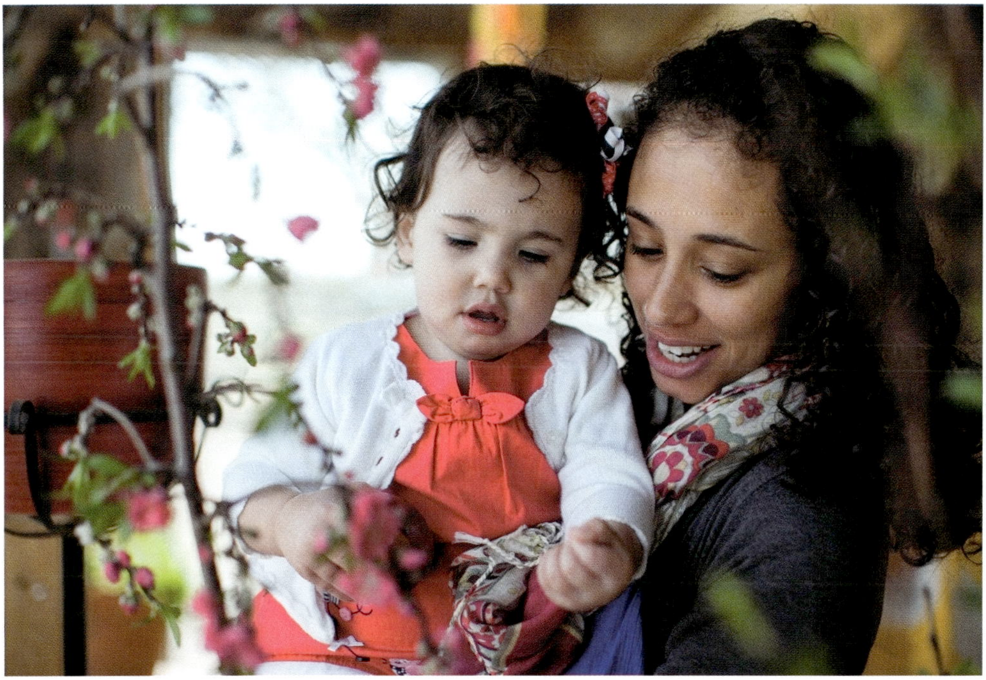

Figure 4.23
Using foreground material to frame up a shot of mother and daughter—who are placed along the right-third line of the frame—creates an appealing way to direct the viewer to the right side of the frame.

ISO 100 • 1/800 sec. • f/2 • 50mm

Over the Shoulder

Speaking of framing, one technique that's useful with the longer extremes of standard focal lengths is what we'll call the over-the-shoulder shot. These are popular shots of people using out-of-focus foreground material—many times they are the shoulders of other people talking to the subject—to push attention toward the person being photographed. Think corporate public-relations shots of employees enjoying their jobs (**Figure 4.24**). As cheesy as that example sounds, this technique forces the eye to look directly at the most important part of the frame without sacrificing environmental details, such as the person connected to the shoulder being used to frame the primary subject (**Figure 4.25**).

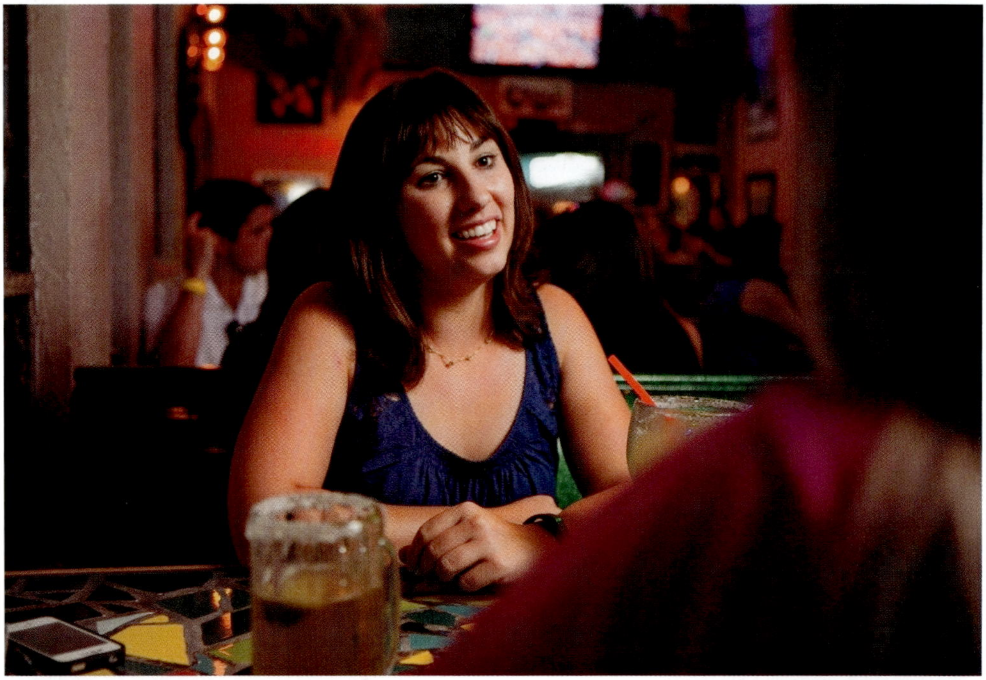

Figure 4.24
Over-the-shoulder shots made at longer standard focal lengths are a great way to make viewers feel as if they are with the primary subject of interest.

ISO 1600 • 1/60 sec. • f/2.8 • 40mm

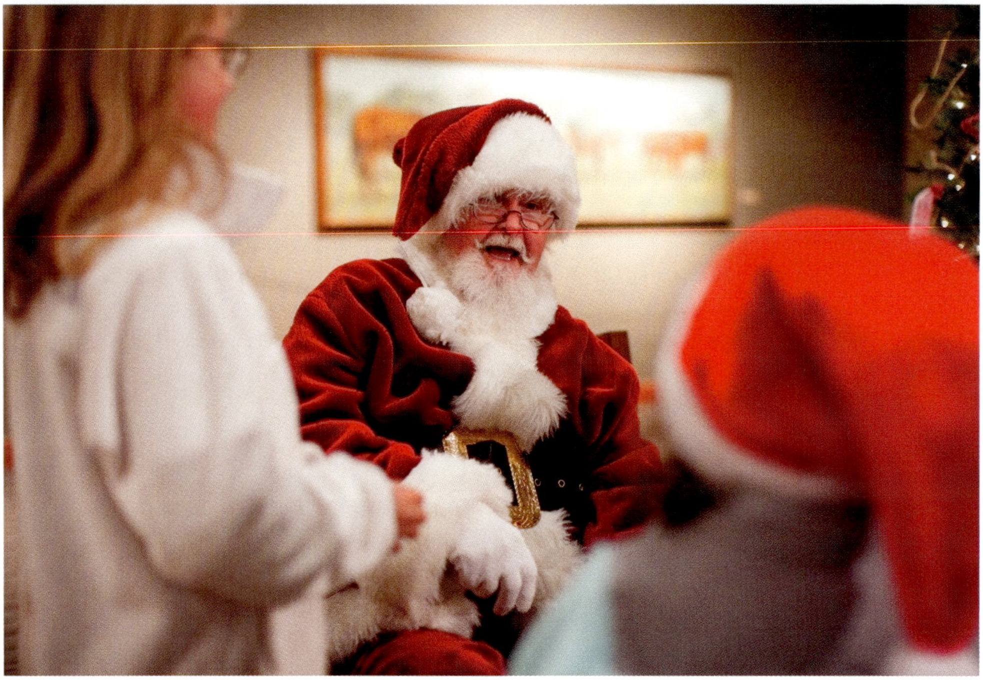

Figure 4.25
Getting the camera low and behind the children gives the viewer a childlike perspective while encountering Santa Claus.

ISO 800 • 1/200 sec. • f/2 • 50mm

Of course, this type of composition is not limited to human subject matter. Nor does it have to involve a shoulder. The idea here is to draw attention to important subject matter by reducing the focus of the foreground and background (open up those apertures), de-cluttering the shot by moving in tight, and isolating the subject through simplifying the composition (**Figure 4.26**). I recommend using longer focal lengths, such as 70mm to 105mm, for these types of shots because of the increased compression. Using wider focal lengths may enlarge the size of the foreground—the lesser important subject—and create an expansive distance between it and the primary subject.

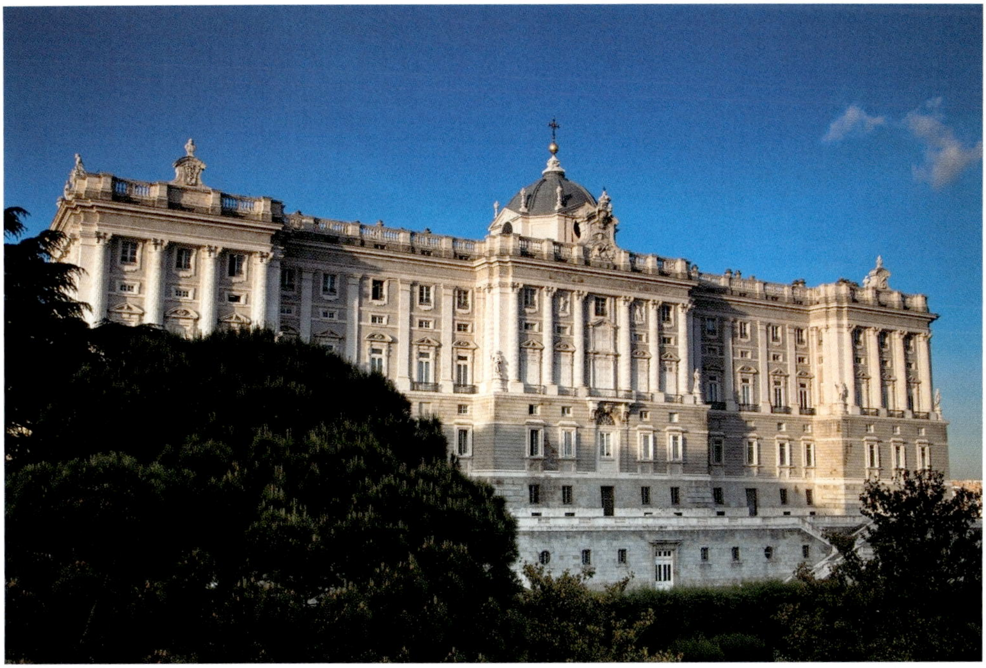

Figure 4.26 **Trees surrounding the royal palace in Madrid serve as a great "shoulder," or framing device, for the magnificent building.**

ISO 200 • 1/80 sec. • f/5.6 • 32mm

50mm: Normal Perspective

If you were going to get only one prime lens in the standard category, I would have a hard time recommending any lens other than the 50mm. After all, it is the standard around which the standard range of focal lengths is based (**Figure 4.27**). The 50mm is widely known as the focal length that provides a perspective most similar to human perspective. It lacks the peripheral vision we have, but in terms of the relationship between all of the content we see—their sizes and distances from each other—50mm gets pretty close (**Figure 4.28**). Hence the moniker *normal perspective*.

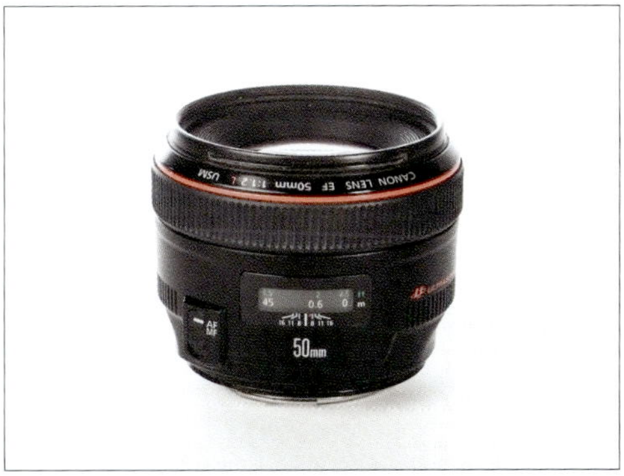

Figure 4.27 **The EF 50mm f/1.2L, Canon's flagship normal or prime lens.**

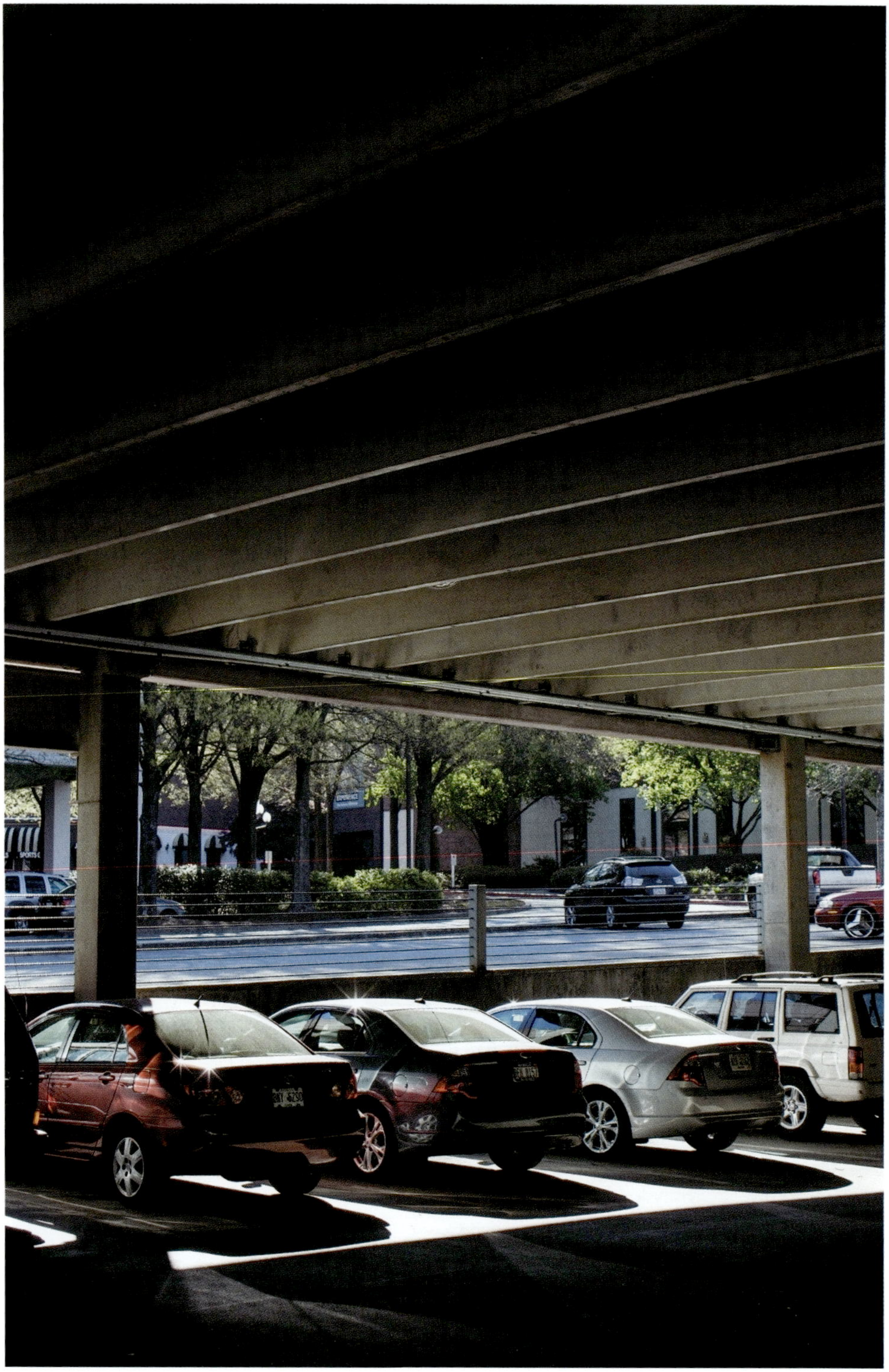

Figure 4.28
On a full-frame camera, 50mm maintains our own eyes' perspective of our surroundings, minus our peripheral vision. You get the same perspective with a 31mm lens on an APS-C crop sensor.

ISO 200 • 1/125 sec. • f/8 • 50mm

Also known as normal lenses, 50mm lenses have been around a while, and they're not going anywhere. I would dare say they are some of the most popular lenses available to photographers. They were the kit lenses of choice decades ago. Since they relate so well to our own eyes, 50mm lenses are extremely popular with photojournalists and documentary photographers because of their straightforward, non-manipulative perspective, their relatively small size, and their simplicity (**Figure 4.29**).

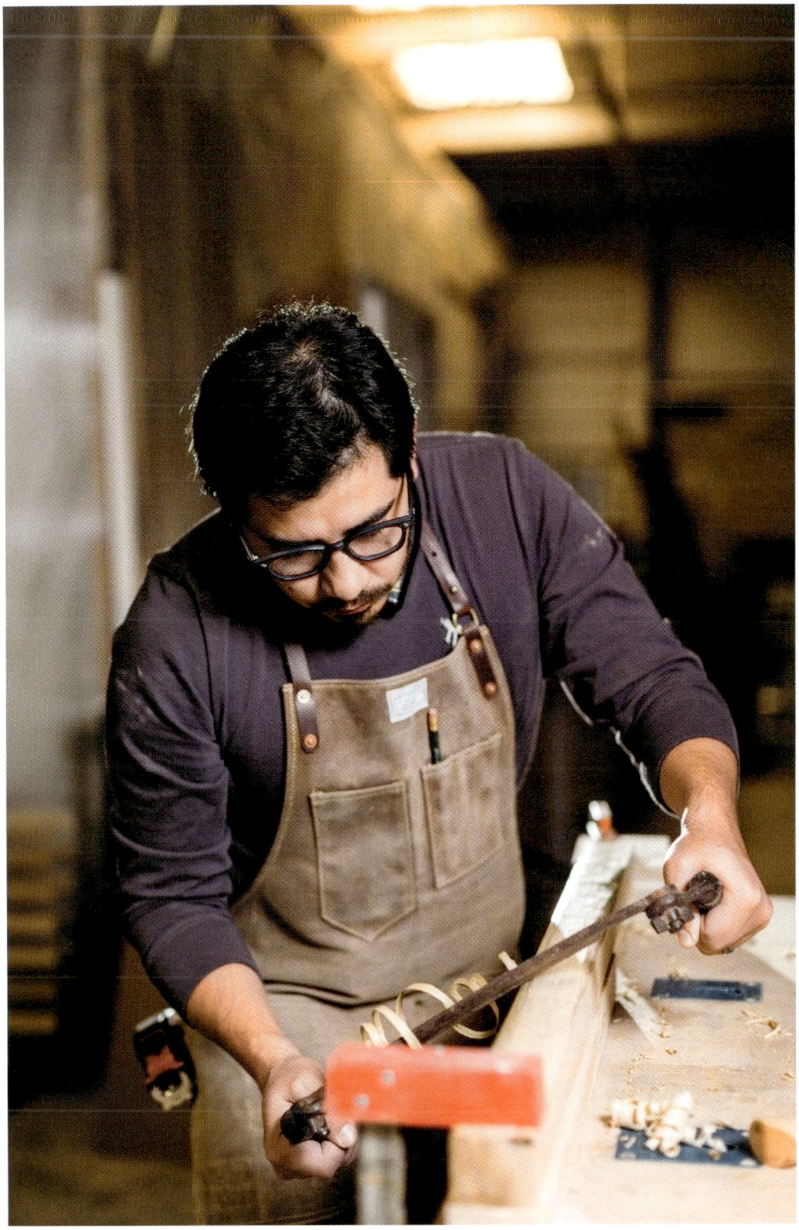

Figure 4.29
At 50mm, the shot can be pushed in fairly tight on carpenter Sly Luna without distorting his form or the form of other structures around him.

ISO 200 • 1/200 sec. • f/2 • 50mm

Like most prime lenses, 50mm lenses are also popular in part due to their extremely fast apertures. Canon offers three 50mm lenses (EF 50mm f/1.8, EF 50mm f/1.4, and EF 50mm f/1.2L) that differ on, among other features, maximum aperture openings. All other features aside, each of Canon's 50mm lenses has an extremely fast aperture (**Figure 4.30**). Achieving fast shutter speeds in dimly lit environments is possible when you're using apertures that open this wide (**Figure 4.31**).

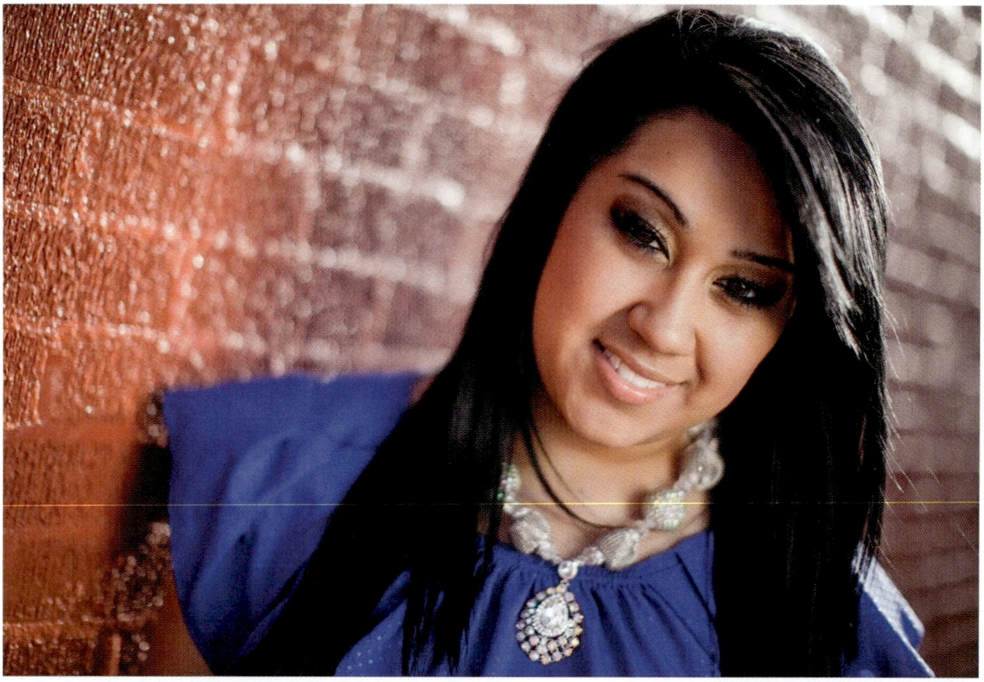

Figure 4.30
Achieve extremely low depth of field easily with any of Canon's three 50mm lenses.

ISO 100 • 1/3200 sec. • f/1.2 • 50mm

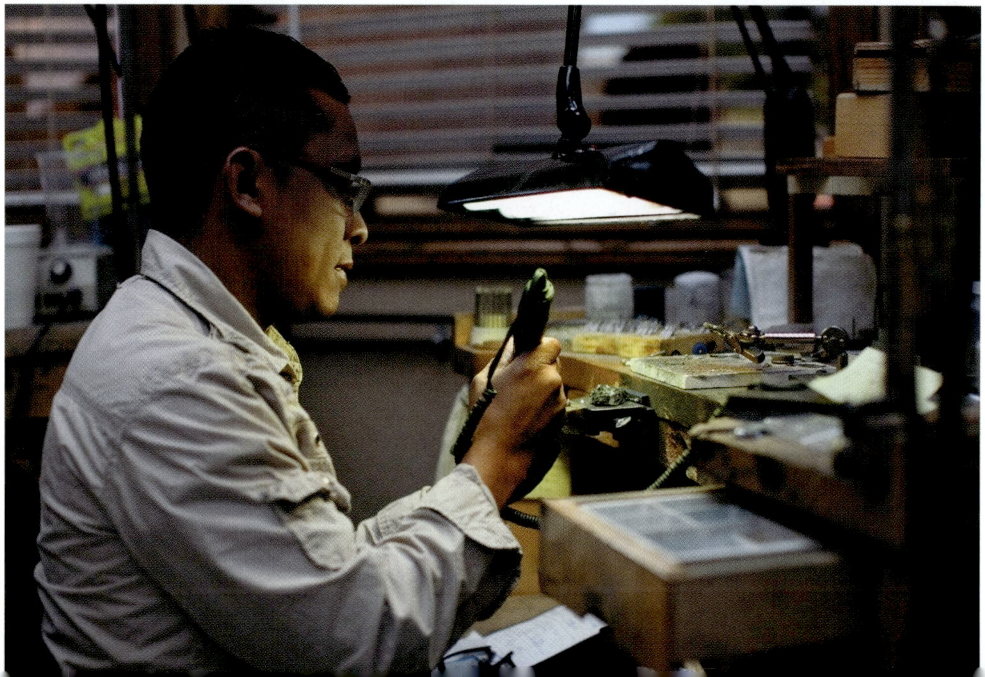

Figure 4.31
The fast apertures of most prime glass, especially Canon's 50mm lenses, help in creating images in dimly lit environments, such as this jeweler's desk.

ISO 400 • 1/640 sec. • f/2 • 50mm

These large apertures also provide extremely shallow depth of field. Soft, creamy, out-of-focus areas are unique to apertures larger than f/2.8, and given the right distance from the subject, the 50mm lens has a look all its own (**Figure 4.32**). When zoomed in to capture medium waist-up shots of people in action and street photography, a 50mm lens offers superior isolation value. The depth of field is so shallow that the primary subject in focus sometimes looks as though it was digitally composited into the frame later.

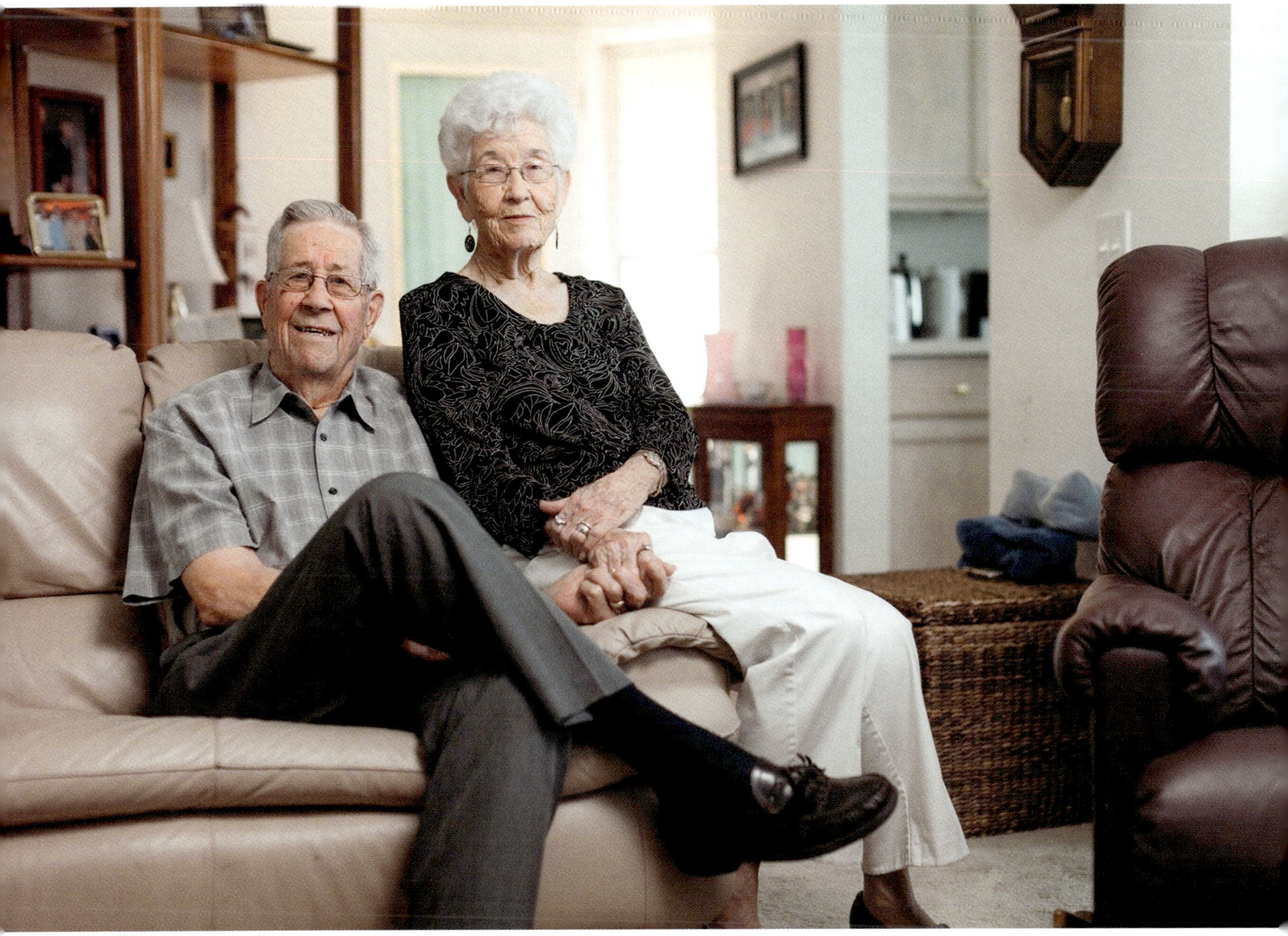

Figure 4.32 A soft bokeh keeps the visual attention on the couple while providing a signature 50mm lens look to the entire frame.

ISO 100 • 1/200 sec. • f/2 • 50mm

Which 50mm Lens?

Fortunately, Canon gives the photographer interested in purchasing a 50mm lens a few choices. Three, to be exact: the 50mm f/1.8 (the cheapest of the three), the 50mm f/1.4, and the 50mm f/1.2L (the only premium-series lens of the three). For the conscientious shopper out there, here are a few issues to consider and features to compare among the three lenses before you make a purchase.

Although salespeople won't agree with me, the first thing to consider is cost. At just over US$100, the 50mm f/1.8 is less than a tenth of the pro-line 50mm f/1.2L cost. Even the 50mm f/1.4 is only a quarter of the price of the L-series iteration.

The second issue to consider is build quality. There's a reason the f/1.8 version is the least expensive of the three (actually the cheapest Canon lens currently manufactured). The glass is contained in an all-plastic barrel, and the lens mount is also plastic. The focus ring is very small, and I've known a number of them to structurally fail under ordinary but often semi-rough treatment by the photographer. The f/1.8 is also the slowest to autofocus since it does not contain the ultrasonic motor technology most other Canon lenses feature. It is incredibly lightweight, though. The f/1.4 version also has an all-plastic barrel, but the lens mount is metal, and the focus ring is constructed of a large, rubber belt found on many other higher-quality lenses—all without adding too much weight. The f/1.2L, though, is heavy. It contains the most glass, and like the majority of other L-series lenses, it features an all-metal barrel. Simply put, it is a tough lens. Some folks care nothing about the extra weight, but it does tug a bit on the camera strap during a long photo walk. Both the f/1.4 and f/1.2L lenses focus quickly and well.

The third issue to consider is the quality of the lenses' glass. Although the f/1.2L version is the only premium lens in the lineup, it takes a bit of pixel peeping to discern much of a difference between it and the f/1.4 lens. It certainly contains the highest-quality glass of the three, and it will only continue to get better in future iterations. The f/1.4 is extremely sharp, especially for a non-L lens, but the least-expensive f/1.8 isn't as sharp as the other two 50mm lenses.

The last issue to consider is the size of the maximum aperture for all three lenses. This seems like a crucial issue, but when you are comparing aperture values that are the widest for all Canon lenses—varying only one stop from f/1.8 to f/1.2—it becomes the least of all the issues. Certainly, f/1.2 offers incredibly shallow depth of field when the aperture is wide open, but so does f/1.4 and f/1.8. The bokeh is a bit smoother for the f/1.4 and f/1.2 lenses.

So, which one do you buy? Find the feature or combination of features (including price) most important to you and go with the lens that offers them. I own the 50mm f/1.2L, and here's why: It is one of the strongest lenses I have ever used, and I use it quite a bit. If you see yourself using the lens a lot, meaning you will put it in a variety of scenarios, and glass quality matters to you, go with the more expensive L-series lens. That said, I believe the best bang for your buck is the 50mm f/1.4. If you don't anticipate using this focal length a lot, or you don't have the budget for the L- series price tag, there is absolutely nothing wrong with the f/1.4 version. It focuses quickly, it handles nicely, and it's sharp.

To be brutally honest, the 50mm f/1.8 is just not that great of a lens. Some people call it the "nifty fifty." Others call it a throwaway lens because they believe it's not *if*, but *when* it fails, and it doesn't cost that much to replace. If you want to avoid a US$1,000+ price point, save up enough to get the 50mm f/1.4. If you want a lens that will last you for 100 years, the f/1.2 version might be the one.

85mm: Standard Portrait Lens

Want to cause lens envy? Roll into a photography party (do they have those?) with an EF 85mm f/1.2L on your camera. Heck, even the lesser expensive—but sharp as a tack—EF 85mm f/1.8 will have people looking (**Figure 4.33**). The first thing people will think: portrait shooter (regardless of whether or not that's how you would describe your work).

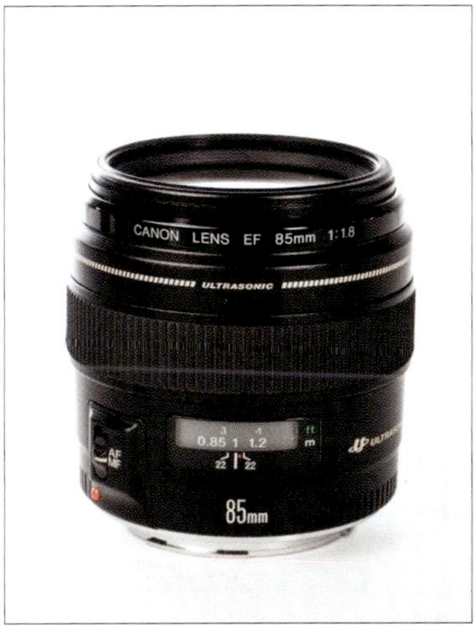

Figure 4.33
The EF 85mm f/1.8, one of two Canon 85mm lenses, is my favorite based on focusing speed, sharpness, and price.

Why It's Great

In terms of it being the perfect portrait lens, the 85mm focal length has several things going for it. First, in any iteration, it is an extremely fast lens. Like the 50mm trio from Canon, both 85mm lenses sport wide opening apertures and an incredibly shallow depth of field. Popular among environmental portrait photographers, wedding shooters, children photographers, and folks producing great Hollywood head shots, both 85mm lenses offer superb bokeh (**Figure 4.34**). When pushed in tight to the subject and left wide open, the lens makes just about everything out of focus except for the focal point on a subject's face (**Figure 4.35**). Distracting backgrounds are manipulated into abstract blobs of color and light with these lenses, perfect for cleanly isolating your subject in the frame.

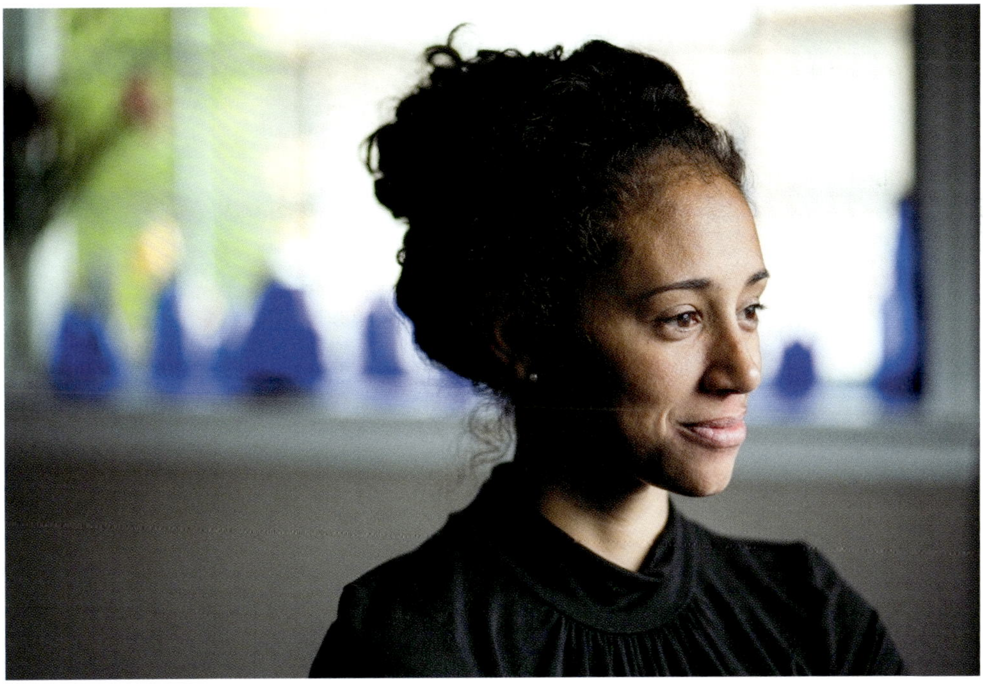

Figure 4.34
Great for tight portraits, the Canon 85mm lenses are made for taking advantage of light as well as interesting backgrounds.

ISO 200 • 1/160 sec. • f/1.8 • 85mm

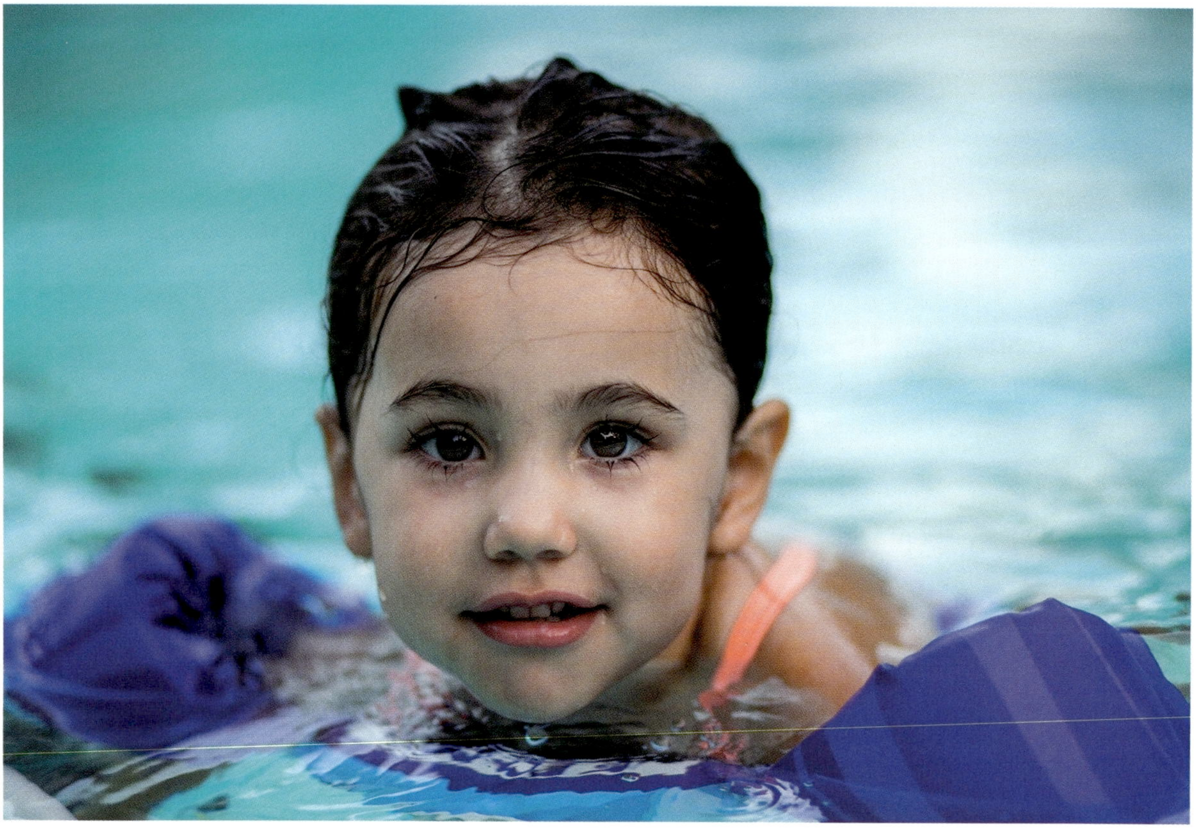

Figure 4.35 **Backgrounds fade easily into beautiful, blurred color and light when either of the Canon 85mm lenses is pushed close to its minimum focusing distance from the subject.**

ISO 200 • 1/500 sec. • f/1.8 • 85mm

The second feature of this great-for-portraiture focal length is that it is long enough to create a bit of foreground-to-background compression, but it is still short enough that the photographer can stay relatively close to her subject. The compression caused by the lens is nice because it helps simplify shots, particularly when combined with very shallow depth of field (**Figure 4.36**). Keep an eye out for sharp, clean backgrounds. The proximity of the shooter to the subject is nice because it enables a tight relationship between the two. They can have conversations easily. The photographer can give instructions without yelling and can simply make the experience comfortable for the subject, who may feel removed from the action if the shooter is farther away than an 85mm focal length will allow for a head shot or other tighter portraits.

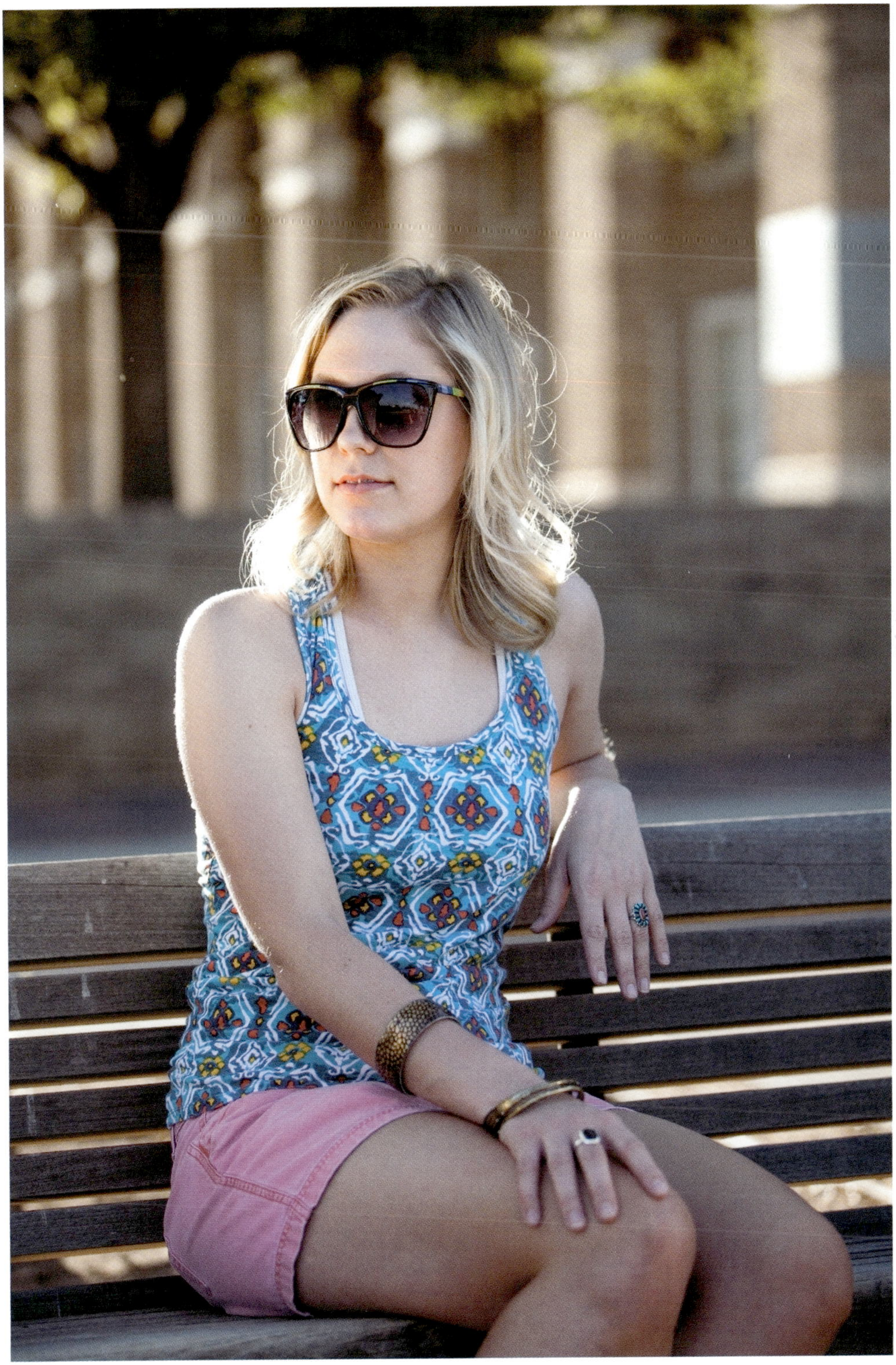

Figure 4.36
There is just enough compression at 85mm to keep the background close to the subject, but not so much that it becomes decontextualizing should you choose not to use a wide-open aperture.

ISO 100 • 1/400 sec. • f/2.8 • 85mm

The Cost of Owning an 85mm

Like the Canon lineup of 50mm lenses, the two 85mm lenses differ on a few features and price points. The EF 85mm f/1.8 is a more affordable iteration of the lens, featuring an all-plastic lens barrel (although it comes with a metal mount), and of course, a smaller maximum aperture. Many believe—including yours truly—that the f/1.8 version of the lens focuses faster than the f/1.2L. (The L-series version features an electronic focus requiring electricity from the camera to operate as opposed to a mechanical focus like most EF and EF-S lenses—ultimately, it makes it a slower-focusing lens.) In my opinion, this is a big issue, especially when the f/1.8 version is tack sharp. However, for those shooting mostly posed portraits, the slower focusing speed of the more-expensive f/1.2L may not be such a downside. The difference in price? There is a difference in price between the lenses of over US$1,500. But, with that price comes a very stout and heavy metal barrel, excellent glass, and the admiration of all of your photo buddies (well, maybe...).

Although I was willing to splurge on the L-series 50mm, my own style of shooting doesn't justify the expense of the EF 85mm f/1.2L. Instead, I opted to purchase the more affordable EF 85mm f/1.8. Both are excellent pieces of glass, and a choice between the two—like with all lenses—is based on personal preference.

Nail the Focus With Wide Apertures

With the extremely wide maximum apertures of Canon's standard prime lenses, like the EF 50mm f/1.8 and f/1.4, the EF 85mm f/1.8, and especially the EF 50mm f/1.2L and EF 85mm f/1.2L, it is worth pointing out that they are sometimes difficult to focus. You may think a particular area of your image is in focus while the aperture is wide open, but then realize you are off when you see the images on the computer later.

Lenses that open up extremely wide—especially the f/1.2 variety—create planes of critical focus with depths of field that in some cases are less than a couple inches deep. The closer you move the lens to your subject, the seemingly shallower that depth of field becomes. So, it makes sense that when you first focus on someone's eyes and then shift the camera (on axis, no less) to compose your shot, the plane of critical focus may move off of the original point of focus. At this point, the focus may be more on the subject's nose, and with such shallow depth of field, you miss the shot because the eyes are slightly out of focus. This is not as much of a problem with lenses that open only as wide as f/2.8 or less because the shallowest depth of field created with these lenses is much deeper than at f/1.2.

continues on next page

Nail the Focus With Wide Apertures *continued*

So, what do you do about it? Old-school shooters would recommend just dealing with it. Shoot at a more stopped-down aperture, which is what I usually end up doing (**Figure 4.37**), work harder at seeing and nailing focus, and possibly go to manual focus (a great recommendation—just don't take deep breaths while focusing). Others recommend re-calibrating your camera's autofocus to focus in front of or behind the plane of critical focus in order to compensate for this type of shifting. Many Canon cameras allow users to fine tune focusing marks like this, and all it takes is knowing whether or not you are focusing in front of or behind where you think you are (and checking the operator's manual). Simply put, there is no go-to fix for this issue; it's just good to know that it is an issue that you will more than likely encounter.

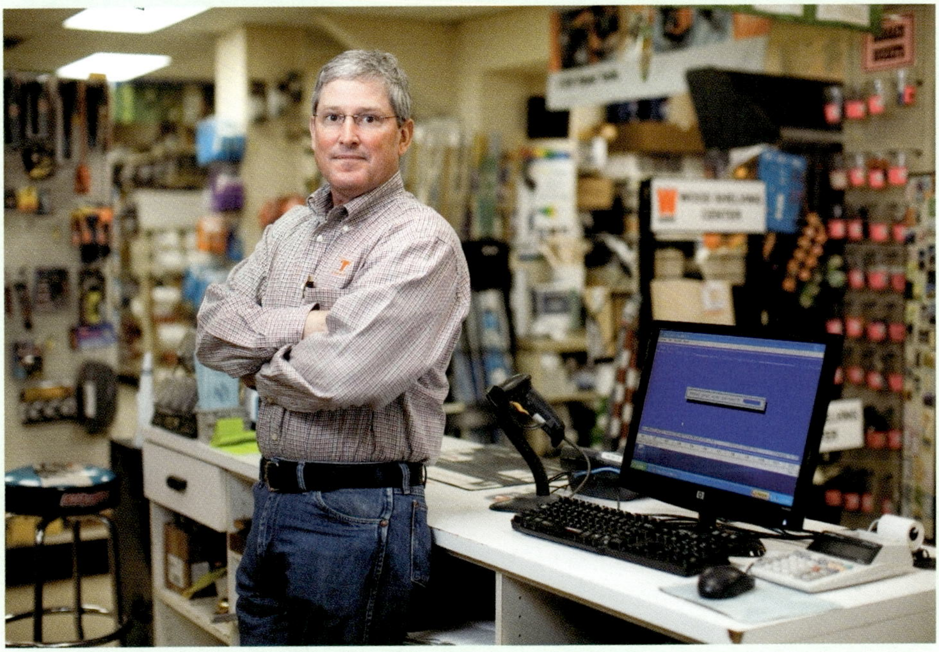

Figure 4.37 I often shoot at f/2 when I'm using the EF 50mm f/1.2L and want to mitigate a distracting background.

ISO 100 • 1/80 sec. • f/2 • 50mm

The All-Around Lens

Every year I teach a 15-day editorial field course to 14 students at the university. At least one student will ask me if I can recommend one lens that will work for the large majority of photography we produce in the class (but won't break the bank). Having had a few meals on the cheap while I was in college, I sympathize with their wanting to save money. Luckily, I'm quick to recommend the EF-S 18–200mm f/3.5–5.6 IS (**Figure 4.38**).

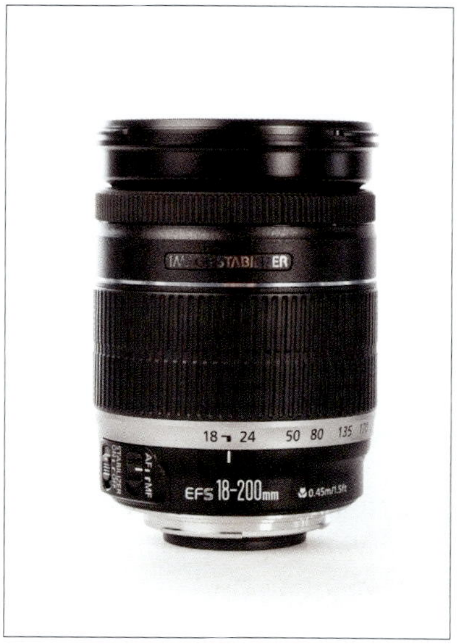

Figure 4.38 For Canon APS-C crop-sensor-camera users, the EF-S 18–200mm f/3.5–5.6 IS is the perfect lens—focal length flexibility at a great value.

The 18–200mm focal length range is, for one thing, incredibly long. Not only is it long, though, it offers the photographer some of the most useful focal lengths he will need and use, all in one lens. A fairly wide perspective all the way to reaching telephoto perspective lets the photographer make the most of many different environments and types of photography. It truly is an all-around lens. To be honest, I have always been skeptical of lenses that try to cover this much ground in a zoomable package. For example, I've always been wary of the EF 100–400mm f/4.5–5.6L IS because lens sharpness tends to suffer when extremely long ranges are incorporated into zoom lenses like this. However, the EF-S 18–200mm f/3.5–5.6 IS has not given me cause to shudder, especially at a price point well below US$1,000.

Another nice thing about a lens like the EF-S 18–200mm f/3.5–5.6 IS is that it doesn't have to be removed from the camera body much, if at all. This comes in handy when you might need to change lenses in poor weather (think rain or a dust storm) that may pose great risk to your camera body.

There is one catch. The lens highlighted here is an EF-S lens, only available for photographers using crop-sensor cameras, like any in the Rebel series. For those using full-frame cameras that only accept EF mount lenses, such a long range of coverage does not exist in a zoom lens—at least one that covers much of the standard focal range discussed in this chapter. However, there are several lenses that do include a great range, such as the EF 24–105mm f/4L IS and the EF 28–135mm f/3.5–5.6 IS. Of course, there is also the EF 28–300mm f/3.5–5.6L IS, but at more than US$1,000 more than the EF 24–105mm f/4L IS, it is cost prohibitive for a lot of folks. All, however, are nice EF alternatives to the popular EF-S 18–200mm f/3.5–5.6 IS.

Chapter 4 Assignments

Here are a few aesthetic and technical workouts that will help you improve your vision with, and operation of, the many lenses in the standard 24mm to 105mm range.

Working up interest

Let's flex some serious composition muscles. Find a location that is important to the surrounding area. It could be something cultural like a fountain statue or museum, or something playful like a piece of playground equipment or outdoor basketball court. When you are on location, search for different ways to compose shots of it. Start dissecting the different kinds of subject matter that make up the location. Determine what is the most important. Consider that a primary interest point to which you want to direct the eye or use as an initial leading device to other areas of the location. After identifying the primary subject, find secondary and even tertiary points of interest to build into your composition. Again, use them to either lead the eye to the primary interest point, or use them to compositionally complement a dominating foreground interest point. Make several shots using different points along different lines, and think about foreground, midground, and background. To make it even more interesting, add a person (or people) to the mix.

Just be normal

On your next photo outing, shoot only at 50mm. That's it. For those of you using an APS-C crop-sensor camera like a Rebel, 60D, or 7D, you'll need to shoot at 31mm (or close). Get a feel for only shooting at this focal length and from this perspective. We often go really wide or really long, and we need practice seeing and shooting at normal perspective. Assess the size and distance between all of the components of the subject matter, gauge the distances you need to be from subjects for certain types of shots, and as always, work the frame's composition!

Shoot shallow

While you are out on that photo walk, spend some time shooting with the aperture wide open. This works best if you have a 35mm, 50mm, or 85mm prime lens. Set the lens to its maximum aperture, and work at varying distances on one subject to nail focus. If possible, use a human subject and focus on her eyes. Once you do so, re-compose for the shot, and see how far your focus drifted (if at all) away from the eye. Did the focal plane move forward or backward? Determine how you might best be able to overcome this disadvantage of the extremely wide aperture settings inherent in many primes. Move to manual focus to see if you can eyeball it any better. Work on this technique continually to ensure you do not come away with out-of-focus shots.

Share your results with the book's Flickr group!
Join the group here: www.flickr.com/groups/canonlenses_fromsnapshotstogreatshots

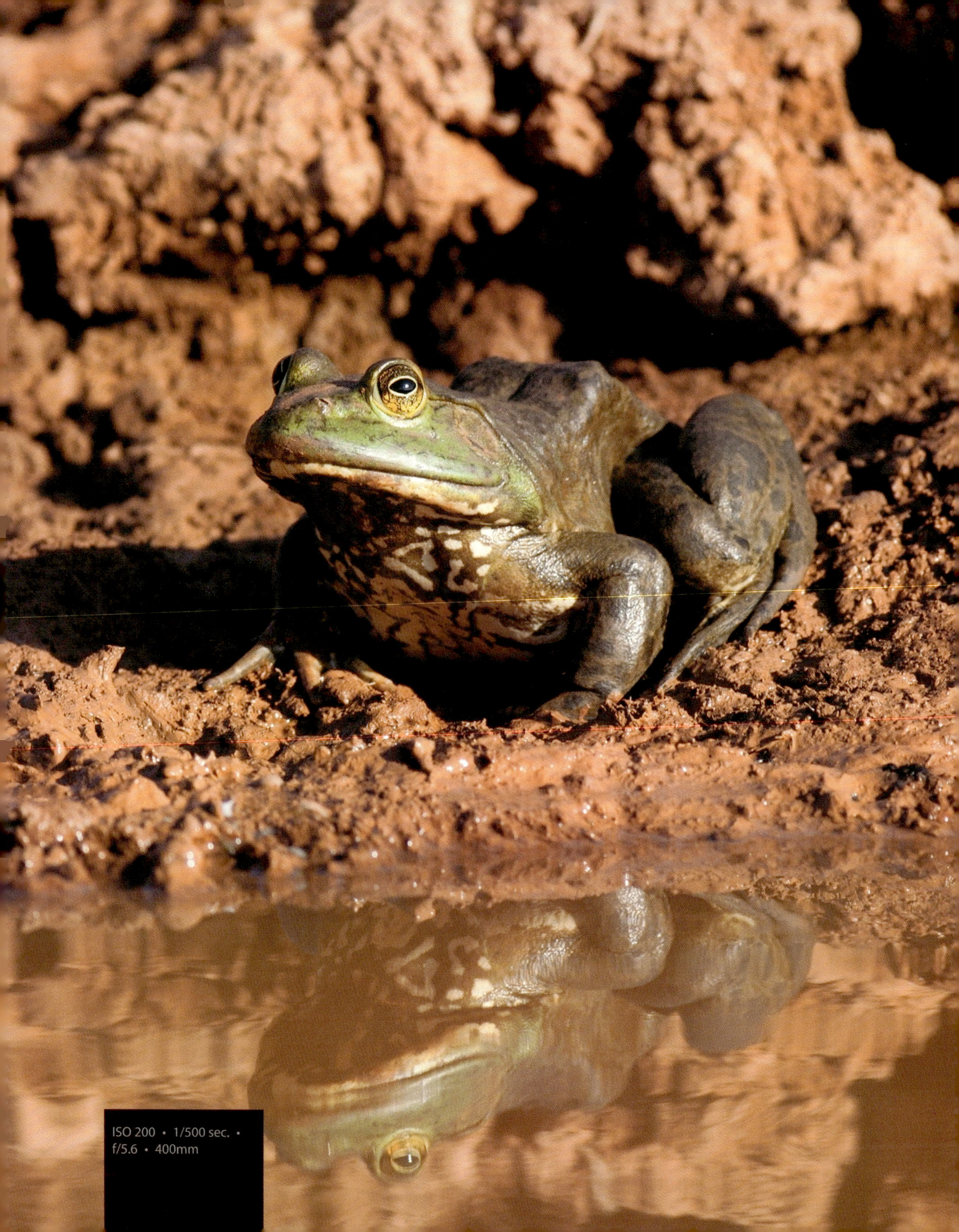

ISO 200 • 1/500 sec. • f/5.6 • 400mm

5 Telephotos

The big glass

"Whoa!" That's usually the response I get from folks when I show up to photograph a local sporting event with a large, white-barreled telephoto lens in tow. It doesn't matter which telephoto lens it is—they all draw attention. But that's not what the longer lenses in the Canon lineup are for. Sure, they may attract a few more eyes than the average standard lens, but they also fulfill a useful purpose in the photographer's camera bag: Literally, they are for reaching out.

Poring Over the Picture

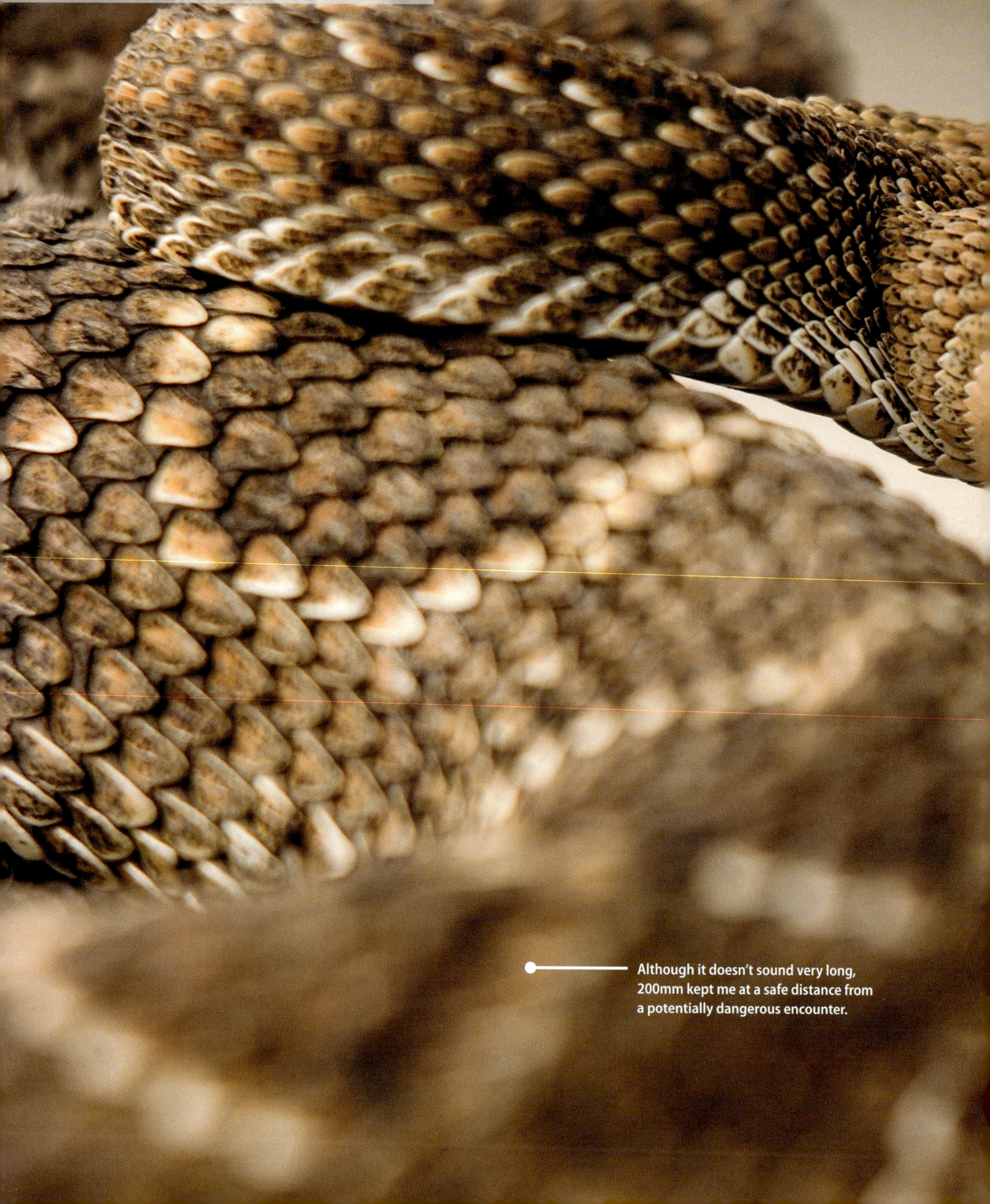

Although it doesn't sound very long, 200mm kept me at a safe distance from a potentially dangerous encounter.

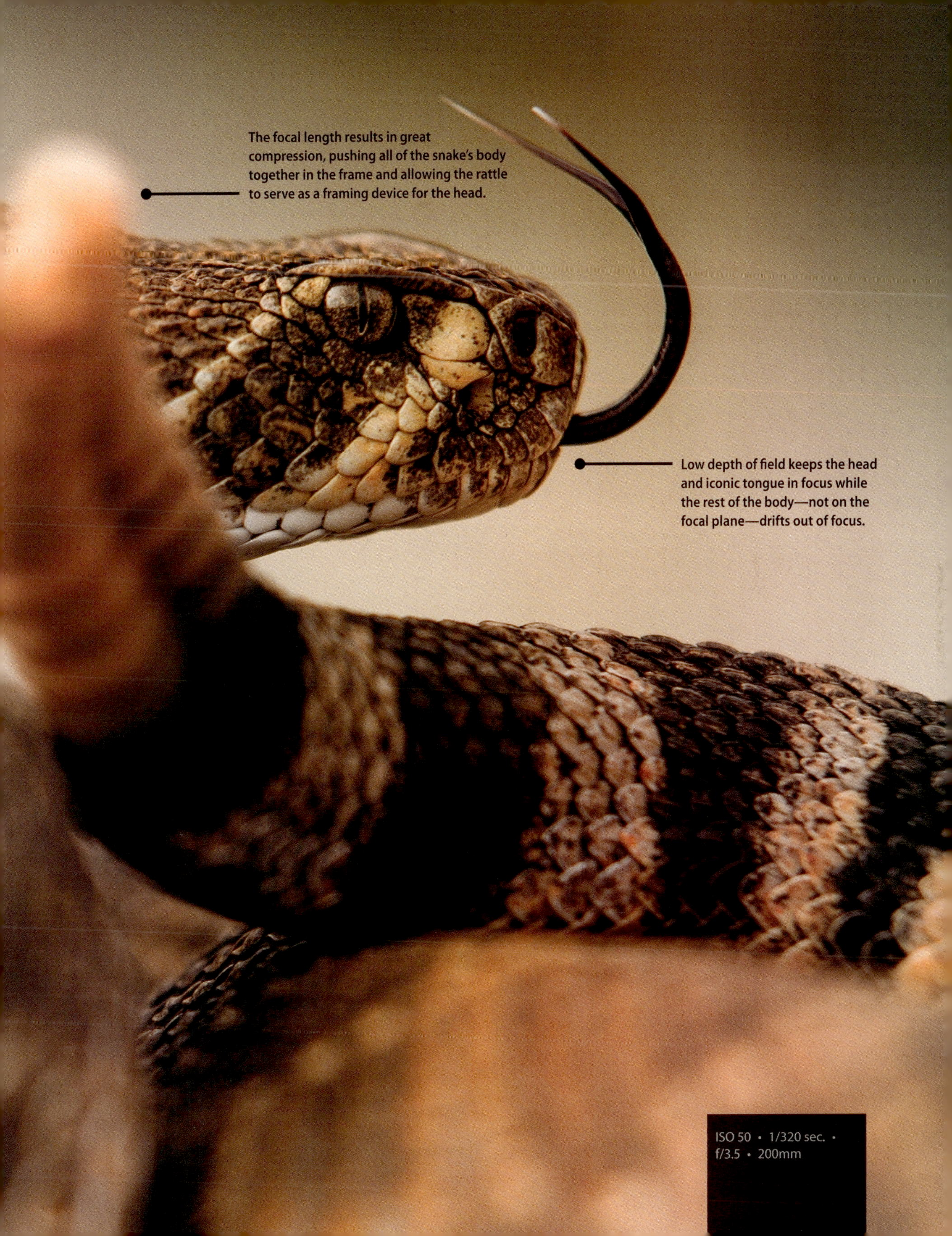
The focal length results in great compression, pushing all of the snake's body together in the frame and allowing the rattle to serve as a framing device for the head.
Low depth of field keeps the head and iconic tongue in focus while the rest of the body—not on the focal plane—drifts out of focus.
ISO 50 • 1/320 sec. • f/3.5 • 200mm

Go Big or Go Home

Telephoto focal lengths generally start at 105mm and, for Canon, reach 800mm (although there are a few discontinued and very elusive EF 1200mm f/5.6L lenses out there). Generally speaking, telephotos are heavier and larger than other Canon lenses, although some non-L-series telephotos are similarly sized as L-series standard lenses. Telephotos are bulky, but with that size comes a world of focal lengths perfect for a variety of special purposes (**Figure 5.1**). The longer the focal length, the more specialized a lens becomes, and while not any one lens is completely relegated to a particular type of photography, we can look at popular uses for some lenses and focal lengths.

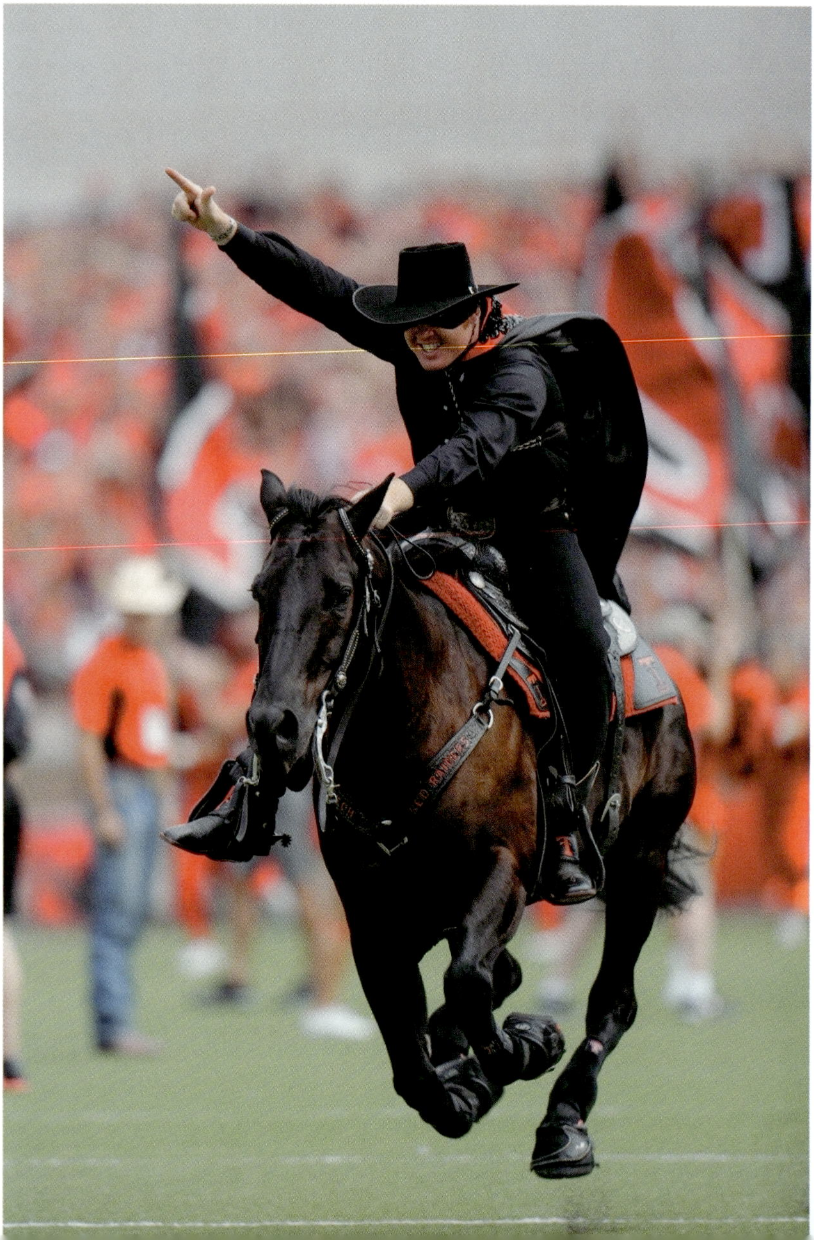

Figure 5.1
The sports-photography world wouldn't be the same without the 400mm focal length.
ISO 200 • 1/800 sec. • f/2.8 • 400mm

Medium Telephoto Zooms and Primes

As part of many photographers' trinity of lenses, a medium telephoto holds a special place in the camera bag. A medium telephoto zoom makes for a nice lens purchase after the initial camera and standard zoom lens, when a photographer wants to reach out a little farther than his standard zoom allows. Probably the most popular segment of the telephoto lenses and focal lengths Canon offers, medium telephotos typically range from 70mm to 200mm. Canon makes several variations on this range. Some of the more popular lenses include the EF-S 55–250mm f/4–5.6 IS for crop-sensor camera bodies and the EF 70–300mm f/4–5.6 IS and EF 70–200mm f/2.8L IS. These lenses are so popular that Canon makes several versions that differ on aperture size, glass quality, and Image Stabilization capability.

Why are these lenses in such demand? Medium telephotos (zoom or prime) are extremely useful lenses for just about any genre of photography. A 70–200mm or 70–300mm lens can be used creatively and effectively for everything from landscape (**Figure 5.2**) to portrait photography (**Figure 5.3**), from photojournalism (**Figure 5.4**) to sports and wildlife (**Figure 5.5**). Throw on an extension tube or two and you have a great macro lens (**Figure 5.6**). (We'll talk more about macro lenses in Chapter 6.)

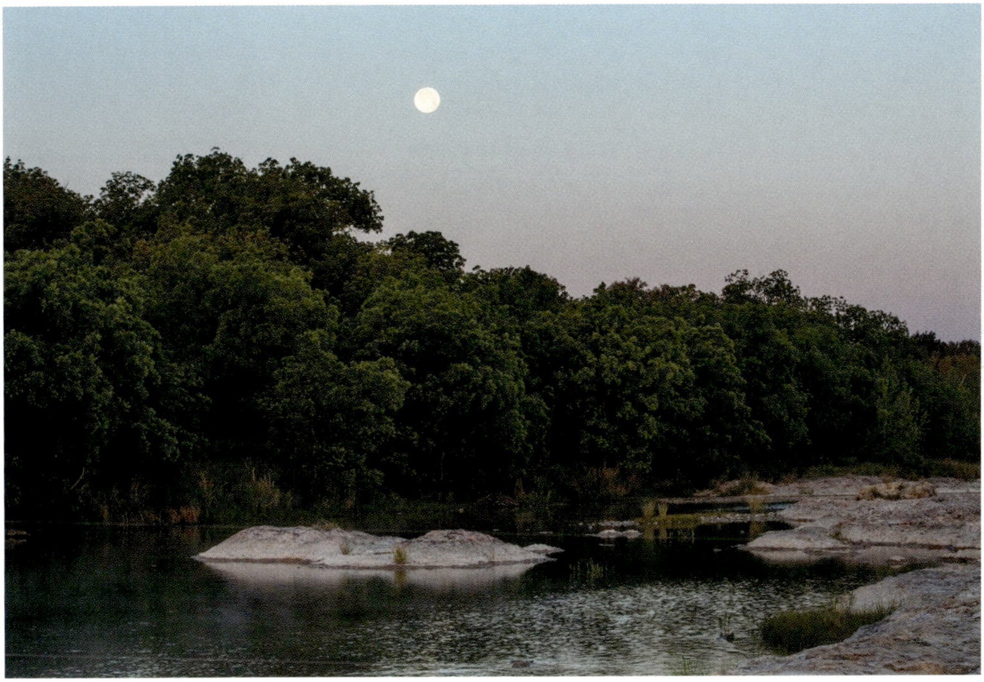

Figure 5.2
Longer focal lengths allow you to concentrate on composition that is not necessarily right in front of you.

ISO 100 • 1/5 sec. • f/22 • 98mm

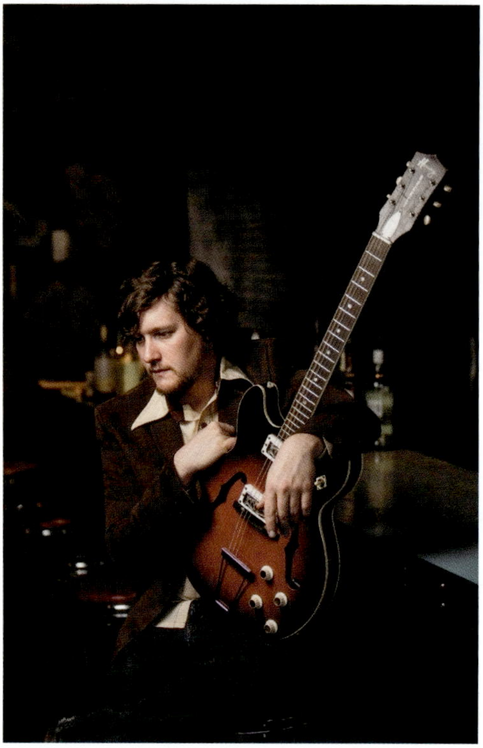

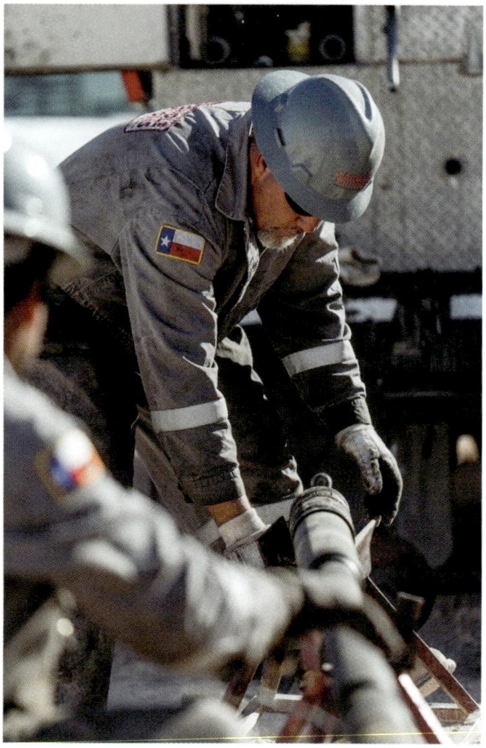

Figure 5.3 (left)
The compression at long focal lengths helps bring many elements together in an environmental portrait.

ISO 100 • 1/80 sec. • f/2.8 • 100mm

Figure 5.4 (right)
Telephotos often keep the photographer from intruding on the authentic unfolding of events (and they keep her safer from potential danger).

ISO 100 • 1/1000 sec. • f/2.8 • 135mm

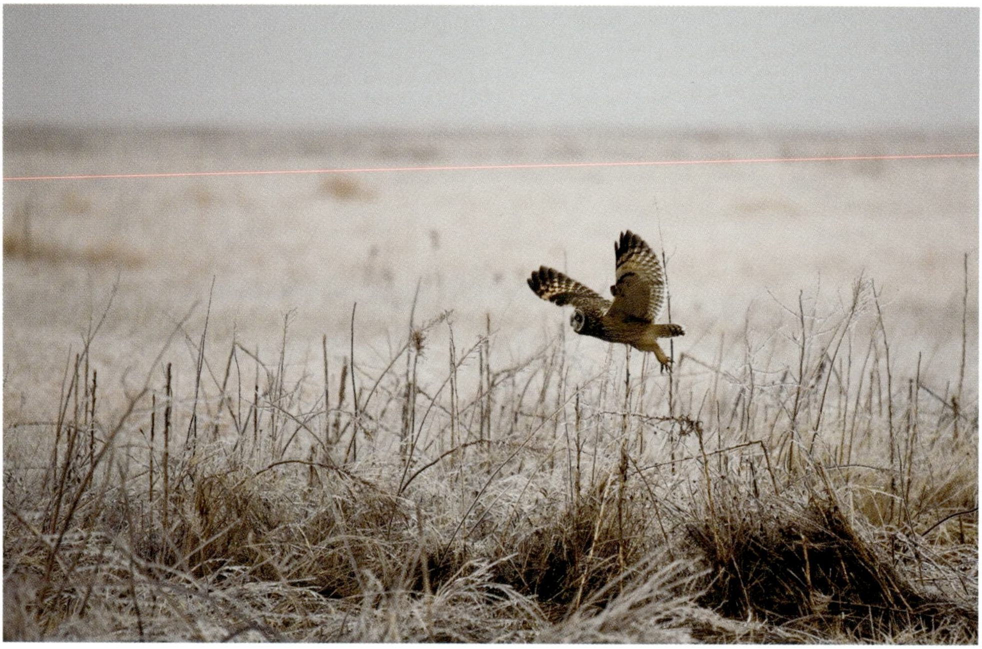

Figure 5.5
Telephoto lenses work well for wildlife and sports photography.

ISO 100 • 1/1600 sec. • f/2.8 • 200mm

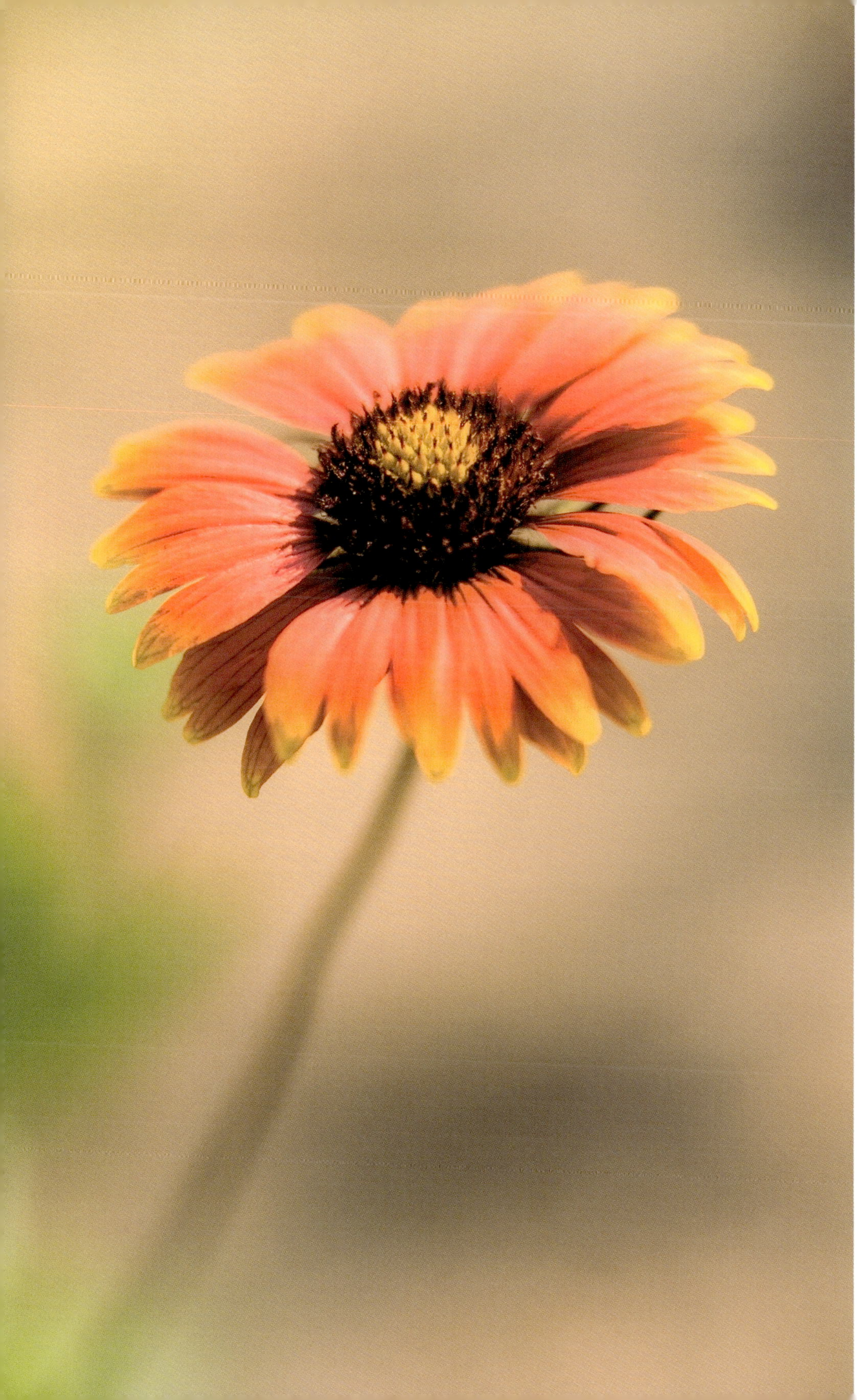

Figure 5.6
An affordable extension tube can turn a telephoto lens into a very effective macro lens.

ISO 200 • 1/400 sec. • f/2.8 • 180mm

For Portraits: 85mm, 135mm, or 200mm?

From medium telephoto to full-on telephoto, Canon makes several lenses that are great for portraiture. In the previous chapter, I highlighted the two 85mm primes as the iconic portrait lenses for wedding, family, and cultural photographers. The 85mm is not exclusive for portraits, though. Many folks decide—based on price, flexibility, and other factors—that other lenses may suit their needs better.

The 135mm (for which Canon makes two versions) is a great focal length for portraiture (**Figure 5.7**). The EF 135mm f/2L is extremely sharp, and it comes at less than half the cost of the EF 85mm f/1.2L. At 135mm, the photographer does not have quite the intimacy with the subject as she would have with an 85mm, but she's not as removed as she would be using a 300mm.

Another great focal length for portraits is 200mm. More compression and longer reach, the 200mm is the bread-and-butter portrait length for some (**Figure 5.8**). Sometimes the distance between subject and shooter is appealing, allowing subjects to be themselves by themselves, particularly for full-length portraits. At the same time, 200mm makes for a great head-shot focal length, easily throwing the background into an abstract blur of light and color (**Figure 5.9**).

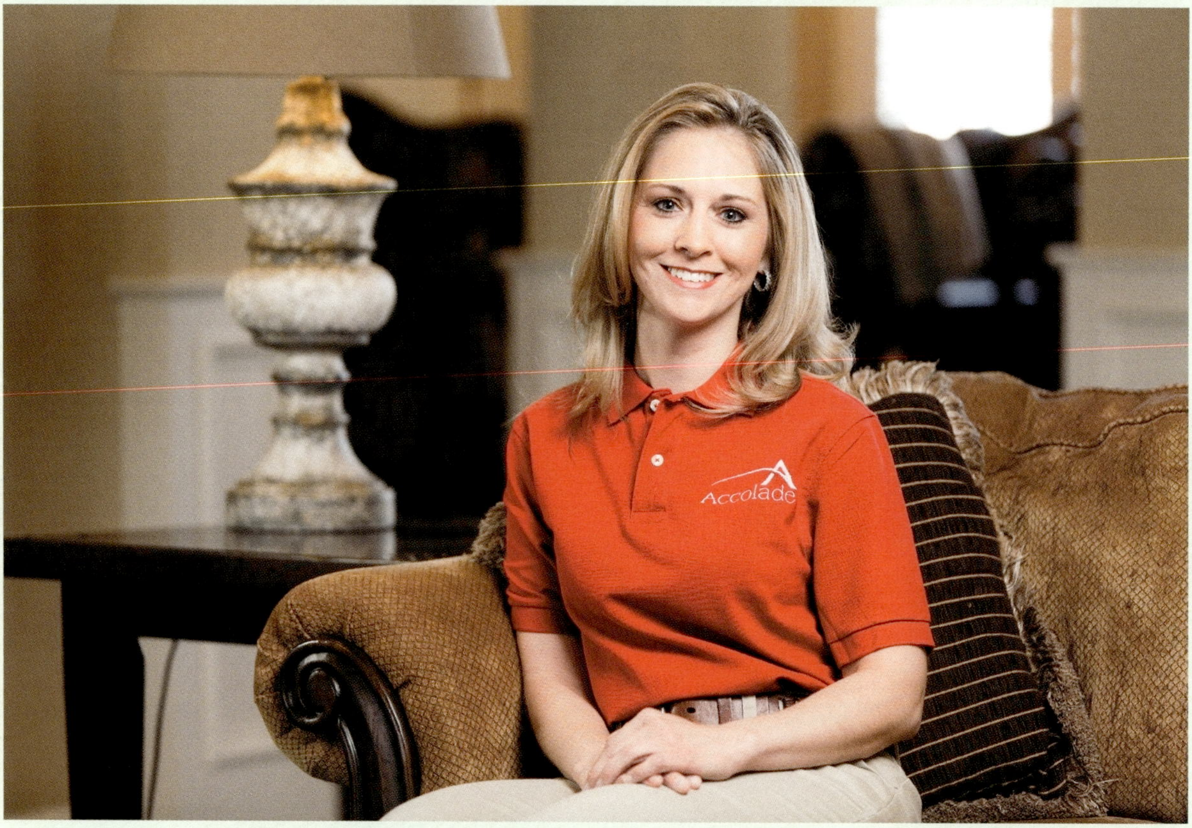

Figure 5.7 The 135mm is a nice alternative to the 85mm or 70–200mm lens for many portrait shooters. Although longer than 85mm, 135mm still keeps you at a nice talking distance from the subject.

ISO 400 • 1/100 sec. • f/2.8 • 135mm

Canon offers several ways to get into the 200mm focal length. The most affordable options are the EF-S 55–250mm f/3.5–5.6 IS, the two versions of the EF 75–300mm f/4–5.6, and the popular EF 70–300mm f/4–5.6 IS. There is also a DO and an L-series version of the last lens, but they come at a premium. For the money, the EF 75–300mm f/4–5.6 IS may be the best of the group. More expensive than the non-IS versions of the group, it is still half the cost of an L-series or f/2.8 lens. Canon makes 16 lenses that reach or include 200mm in their focal range, including several versions of the famed 70–200mm lens. And for those seeking prime versions, the EF 200mm f/2.8L and the EF 200mm f/2L IS offer two great but pricier (especially in the case of the latter) alternatives to many of the zooms.

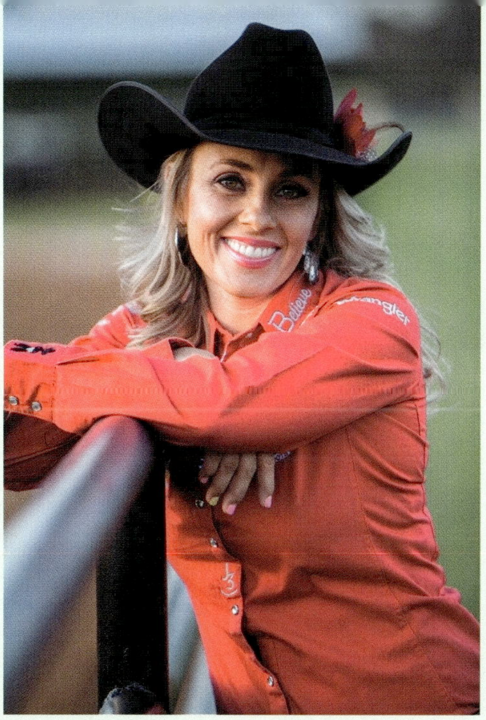

Figure 5.8
I favor 200mm for many portraits due to its ability to bring an abstract background seemingly close to the subject.

ISO 100 • 1/500 sec. • f/2.8 • 200mm

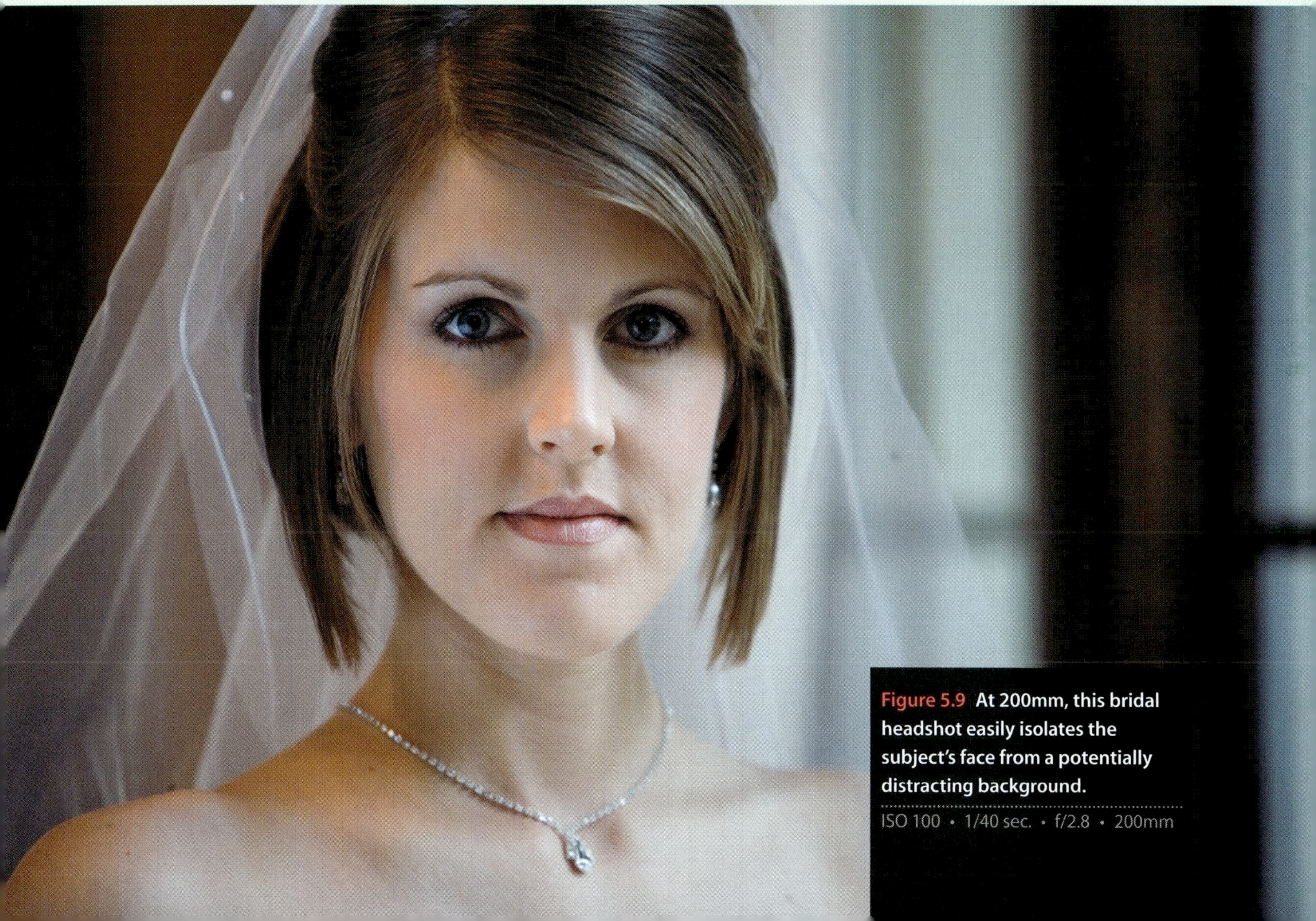

Figure 5.9 At 200mm, this bridal headshot easily isolates the subject's face from a potentially distracting background.

ISO 100 • 1/40 sec. • f/2.8 • 200mm

Folks buying an EF-S 55–250mm f/4–5.6 IS or an EF 70–300mm f/4–5.6 IS to photograph their children playing sports are happily surprised when they see how functional the lens is for portraits. Landscape photographers employ these focal lengths for a number of reasons, including quasi-*macro work* (zooming in from a long distance on something small, such as a flower) and creating patterns and textures in long shots with compression (see later in the chapter).

Sports photographers use these lenses to concentrate on action that gets within a range too tight for their super-telephoto lenses. And just about every photographer enjoys being able to throw a background out of focus easily when zoomed into a subject and using a wide-open aperture (**Figure 5.10**). Medium telephotos are extremely versatile lenses, just as long as the shooter accommodates for the extra focal length, which is greater than on most standard zooms.

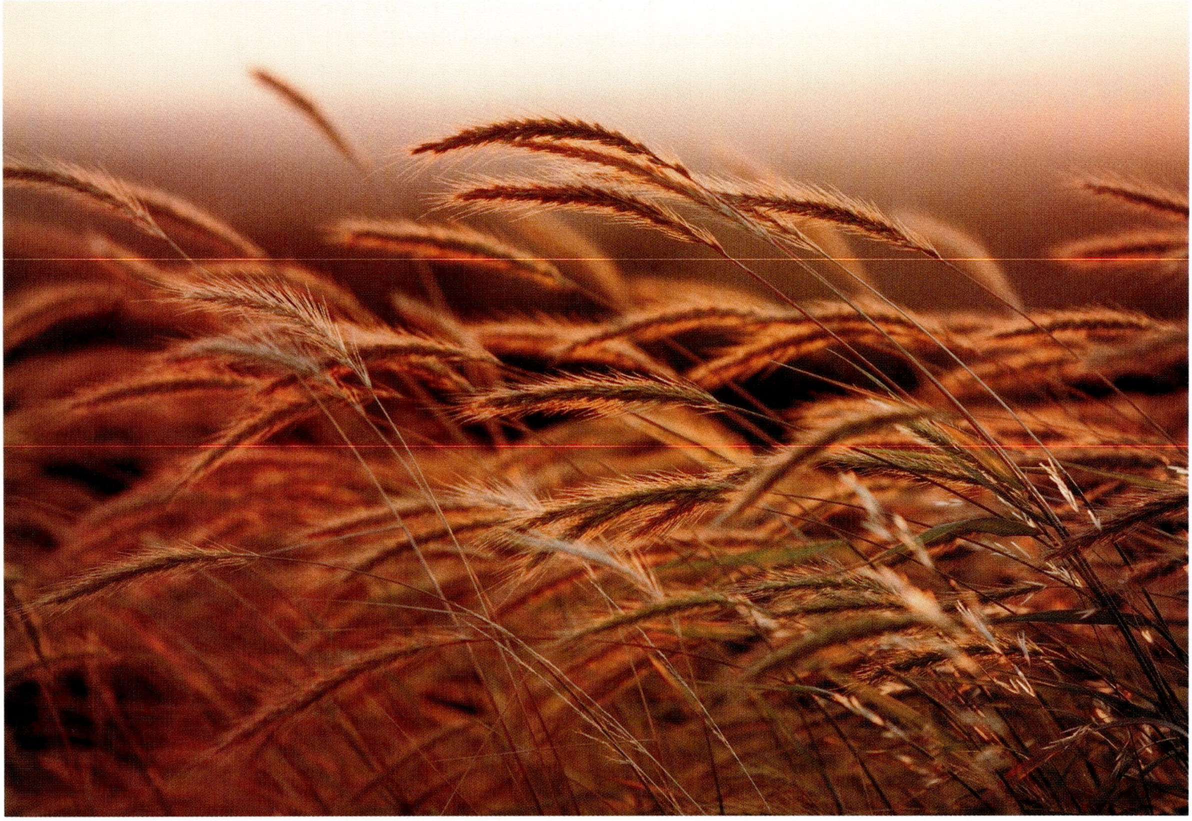

Figure 5.10 The shallow depth of field, resulting from a long focal length and wide maximum aperture, highlights the subject and combines it with a colorful, aesthetically pleasing background.

ISO 400 • 1/500 sec. • f/2.8 • 165mm

300mm: A Bit More Reach

There was a point in my career when I honestly didn't know what to do with 300mm. I knew it was the long end of the popular EF 70–300mm lenses, but I didn't have much use for it in my landscape work, and it was a tad bit too long for my portraiture work (the lens put me too far from subjects). At 200mm, I could be productive, but not at 300mm. As it turns out, my problem had to do with how I was seeing my images before making them, and to some degree, the content I was shooting.

In the grand scheme of telephoto focal lengths, 300mm is just a bit more reach than 200mm. But in that distance, the lens goes from being an all-around image maker to somewhat of a specialty lens. It's not so specialized that it can only be used for one thing, like wildlife, but this long focal length moves into super-telephoto range. When I started photographing animals (**Figure 5.11**) and sports (**Figure 5.12**) and started concentrating on landscape composition that took full advantage of the long focal length's great compression (**Figure 5.13**) and ability to isolate individual subjects (**Figure 5.14**), I entered into another world of photography.

Figure 5.11 (below left) **With more compression than 200mm, a 300mm lens readily pulls the background and foreground together, adding the brown calf as another point of interest in the frame.**

ISO 100 • 1/500 sec. • f/4 • 300mm

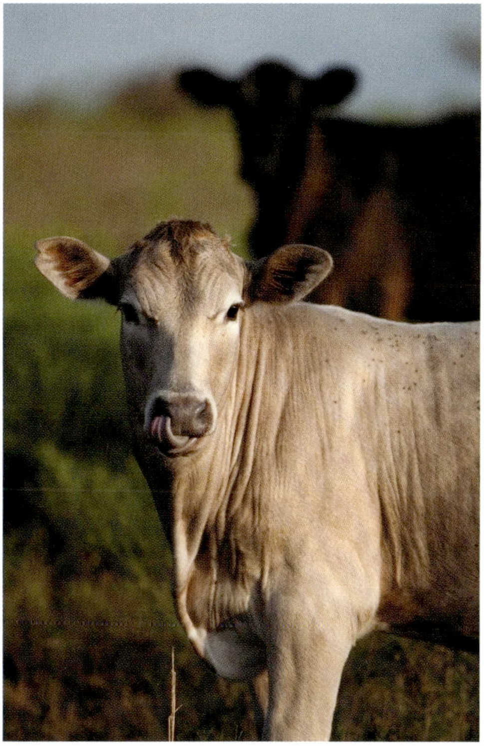

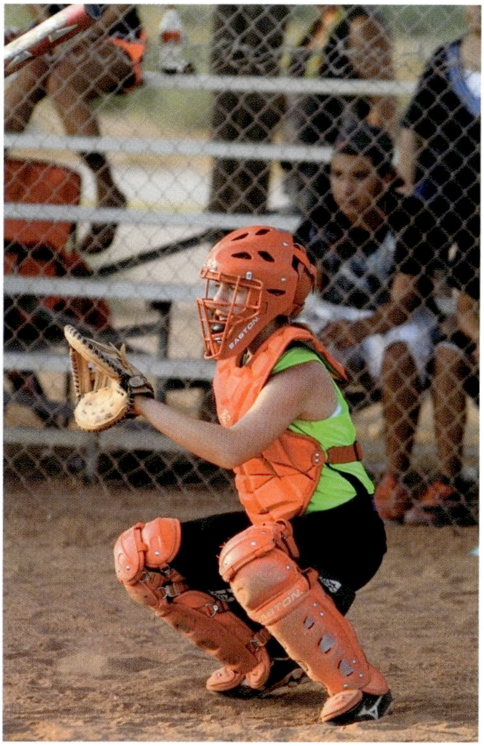

Figure 5.12 (right) **Little League baseball is a great environment for the 300mm focal length. The photographer can get closer to the action than he can at college or professional sports events, which generally require at least 400mm.**

ISO 320 • 1/400 sec. • f/4 • 300mm

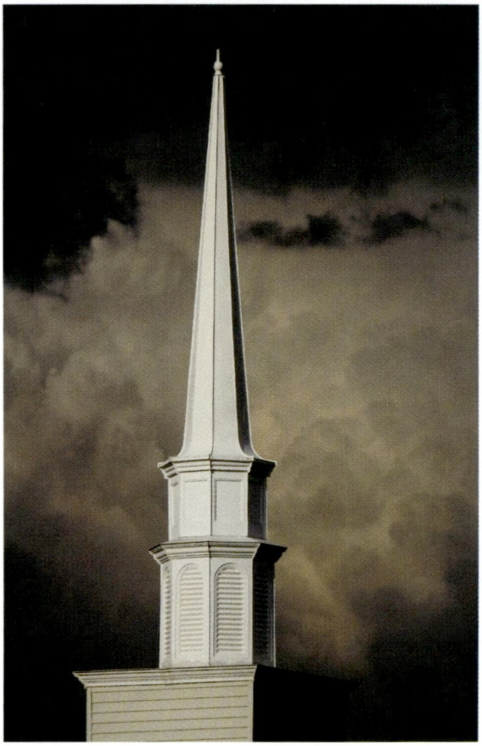

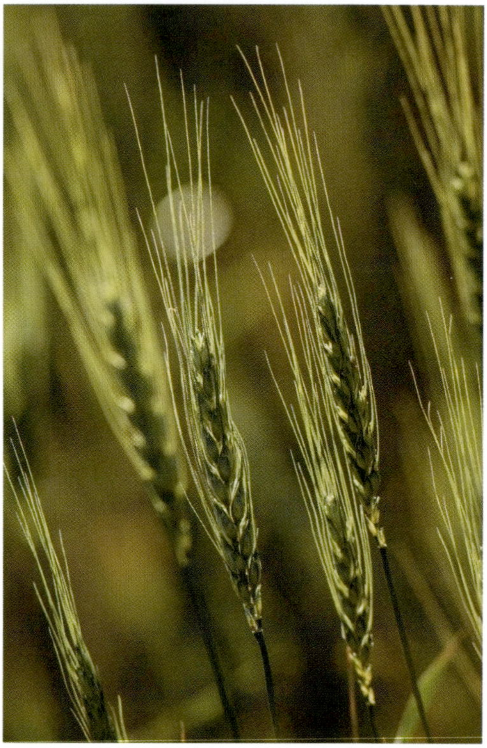

Figure 5.13
A large thunderstorm brewing miles away from the church creates an ominous background for the steeple.

ISO 200 • 1/8000 sec. • f/4 • 300mm

Figure 5.14
Pushed in tight, 300mm is a great focal length for isolating subject matter against a soft background.

ISO 100 • 1/500 sec. • f/4 • 300mm

Many popular starter telephoto lenses include 300mm, such as the EF 70–300mm assortment mentioned in the previous section, as well as the more expensive EF 28–300mm f/3.5–5.6L IS, the EF 100–400mm f/4.5–5.6L IS, and the new (and very pricey) EF 200–400mm f/4L IS. I personally like the EF 300mm f/4L IS. Although pricier than the zoom lenses, it is tough as nails, extremely sharp, and very light, especially compared to its heavyweight cousin, the EF 300mm f/2.8L IS. I primarily use it for sports and some wildlife, and occasionally landscapes.

400mm: The Ultimate Telephoto?

Designated as the little guy in the super-telephoto range, the 400mm is often considered the ultimate telephoto lens. I would not call it an all-around lens, but it is one of the most useful lenses for wildlife and sports (especially sports).

The EF 400mm f/2.8L IS

Every other Saturday in the fall, I pack up my camera bags and head up to Texas Tech's football stadium. As 60,000 fans fill the seats, roughly 40 photographers start preparing for the game on the field. All of a sudden, you see numerous large, white lenses placed on monopods. Possibly the most iconic lens in sports, the EF 400mm f/2.8L IS is noticeable by fans and shooters alike (**Figure 5.15**). And it is a performer. Fast to autofocus, it is the optimum chunk of glass for sports when paired with a camera that has a great autofocus system (**Figure 5.16**). For the focal length, the EF 400mm f/2.8L IS also has an outrageously fast aperture (**Figure 5.17**) for extremely low depth of field. This comes in handy when shooting sports in dimly lit environments, such as most high school football and soccer fields. The shallow depth of field is nice, but the wide aperture opening is more about getting the fastest shutter speed possible with all of the light hitting the sensor (**Figure 5.18**).

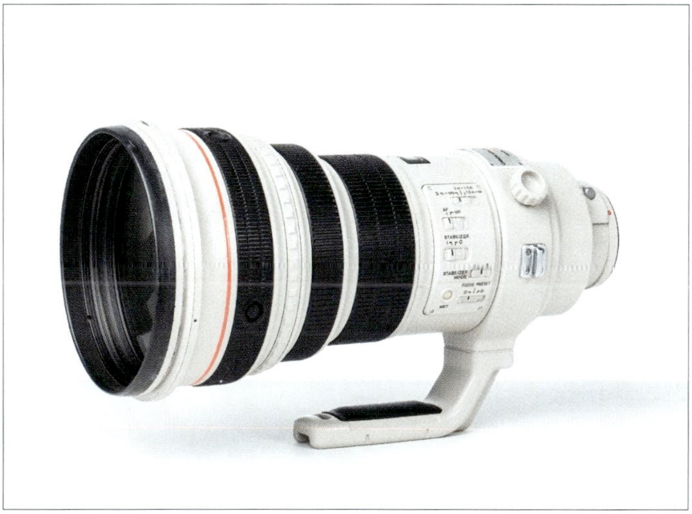

Figure 5.15 The EF 400mm f/2.8L IS is a treasured lens for many sports and wildlife photographers.

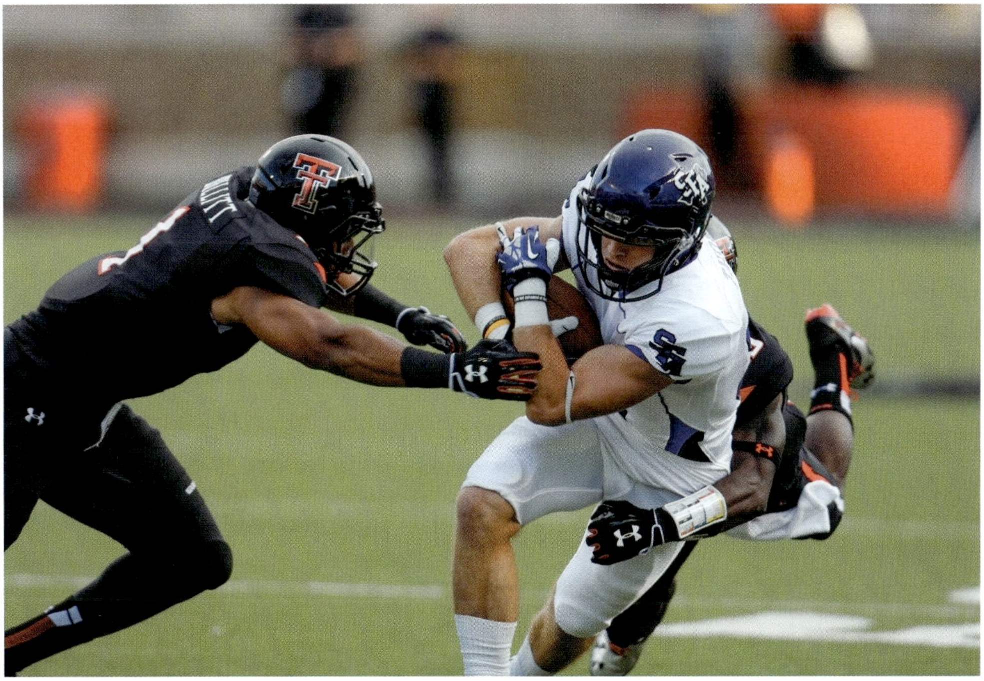

Figure 5.16 The 400mm f/2.8's quick ultrasonic motors ensure snappy autofocus when engaged on quick subject matter.

ISO 400 • 1/1600 sec. • f/2.8 • 400mm

Figure 5.17

At f/2.8, the background fades into an abstract indication of the environment in which the rider is competing.

ISO 100 • 1/2500 sec. • f/2.8 • 400mm

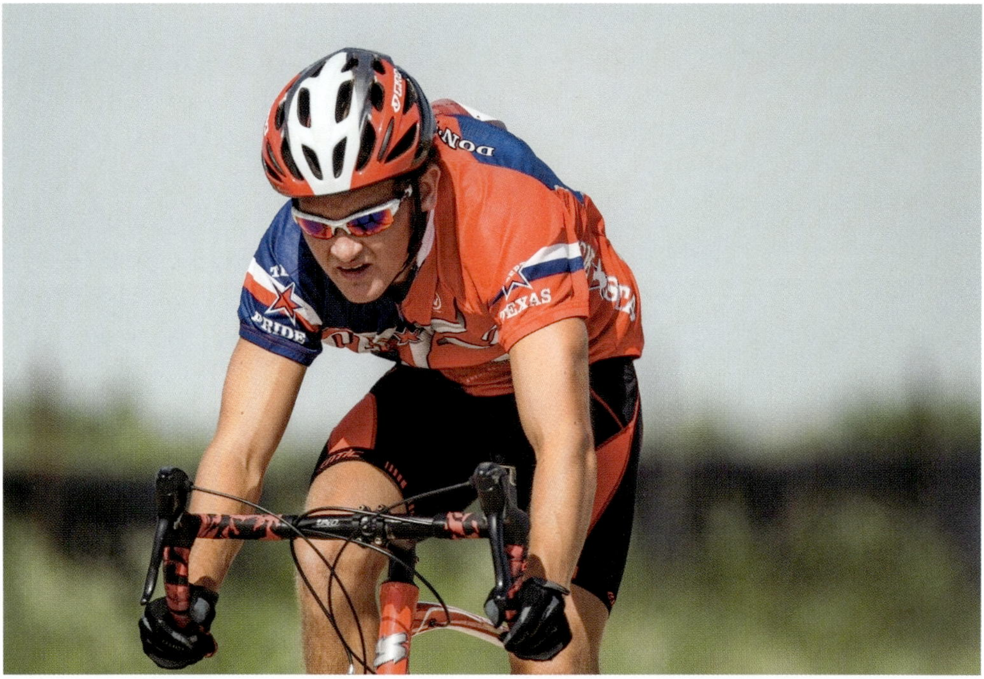

Figure 5.18

Under dim stadium lighting, f/2.8 apertures are almost necessary given the low amount of light for fast shutter speeds on high action.

ISO 3200 • 1/1250 sec. • f/2.8 • 400mm

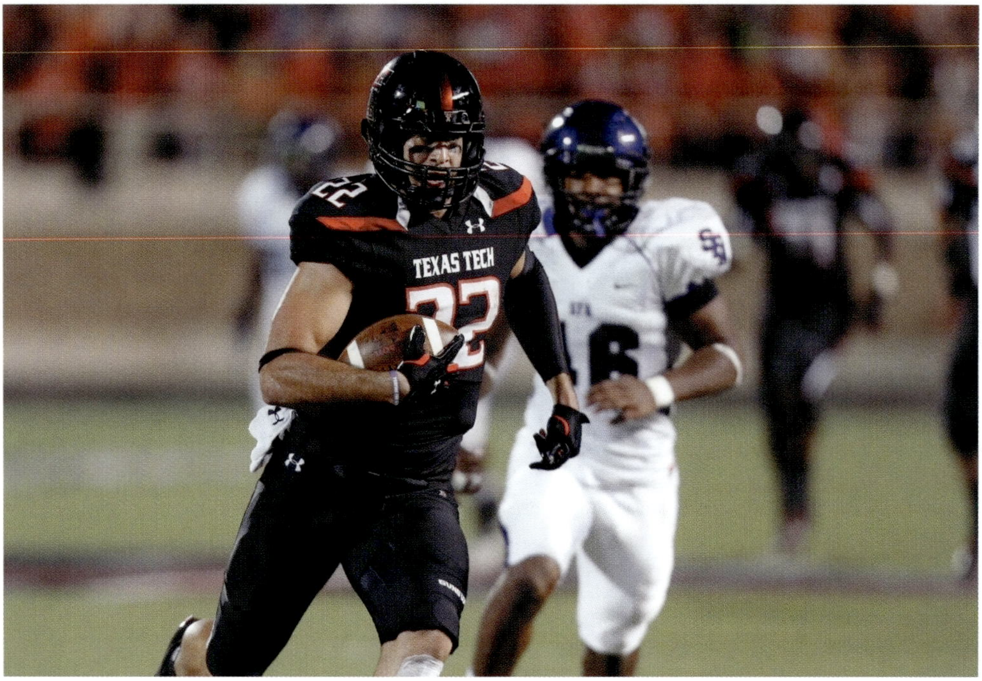

Shop around

There's only one big disadvantage of the EF 400mm f/2.8L IS: It is super expensive! As of this writing, a new EF 400mm f/2.8L IS will set you back US$11,500. The other disadvantage is its weight—something Canon is tackling in its latest version of the lens.

A 400mm f/2.8L really is for those committed to professional photography (or for those with deep pockets who appreciate high-quality gear). I know I couldn't do without one when shooting sports. Fortunately, Canon makes a few more lenses reaching 400mm that are less expensive without sacrificing build quality or the premium L glass. Two zoom lenses offer great focal length flexibility, the EF 200–400 f/4L IS and the EF 100–400 f/4–5.6L IS. A recent Canon addition, the 200–400mm is a powerhouse for wildlife and sports photographers; however, its price point is not far below that of the EF 400mm f/2.8L IS. Even though some folks do not like the push-pull zoom feature of the 100–400mm, it does offer the most flexibility of the lenses that reach 400mm.

Two other 400mm prime lenses are also worth considering: the EF 400mm f/4 DO IS and the EF 400mm f/5.6L. The DO in the former stands for Diffractive Optics, which means it is a much smaller and lighter lens than most 400mm packages, and the optics in it reduce the occurrence of chromatic aberration (color fringing). The EF 400mm f/5.6L is the least heavy of the 400mm lenses and also the most affordable (priced around US$1,500). As much as I like shooting the EF 400mm f/2.8L IS, it's just not feasible to carry it around except for sporting events and some wildlife photography. This is when I turn to the EF 400mm f/5.6. Sure, it is two stops slower and does not have Image Stabilization, but it is sharp as a razor and doesn't take up near as much room. In fact, I bought both the EF 300mm f/4L IS and the EF 400mm f/5.6L at the same time years ago to have great hiking telephotos (**Figure 5.19**), and I did it for a fraction of what it costs to buy the 400mm f/2.8L.

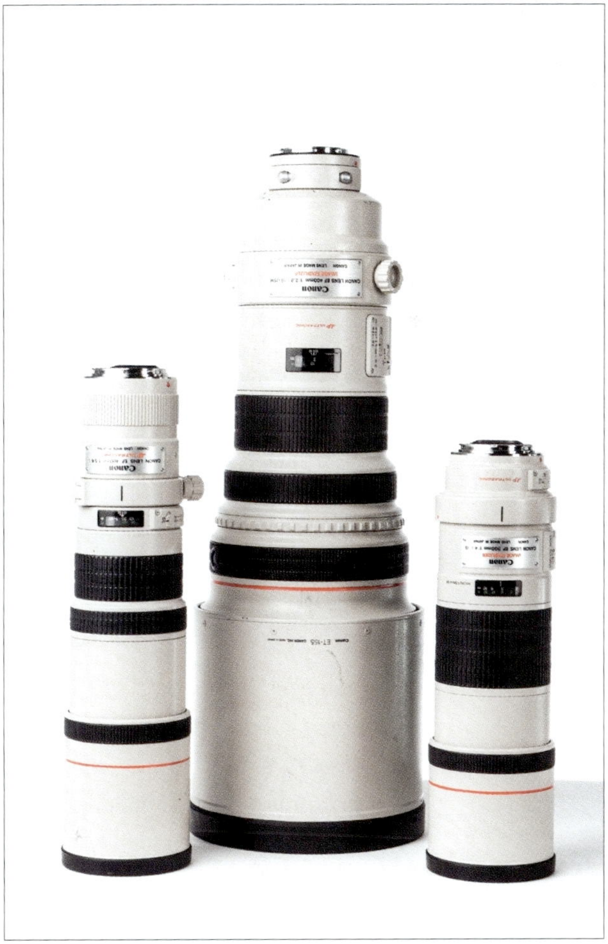

Figure 5.19 The EF 400 f/5.6L (left), the EF 400mm f/2.8L (middle), and the EF 300mm f/4L IS (right)

500mm, 600mm, and 800mm: Extremely Long Glass

In my short, three-season tenure of photographing NCAA football, I've seen a lot of 400mm f/2.8 lenses. However, I've only seen two photographers—two *Sports Illustrated* shooters—come on the field with anything longer. They both carried not only 400mm f/2.8s but a 500mm and a 600mm. You can also assume they each had an assistant to carry the load. With 400mm lenses, the nice images start at about the 50-yard line if you are standing in the end zone, but these guys could shoot clear down the field without a problem. Shooting with lenses over 400mm allows you to get close to the action without getting trampled or run over (**Figure 5.20**).

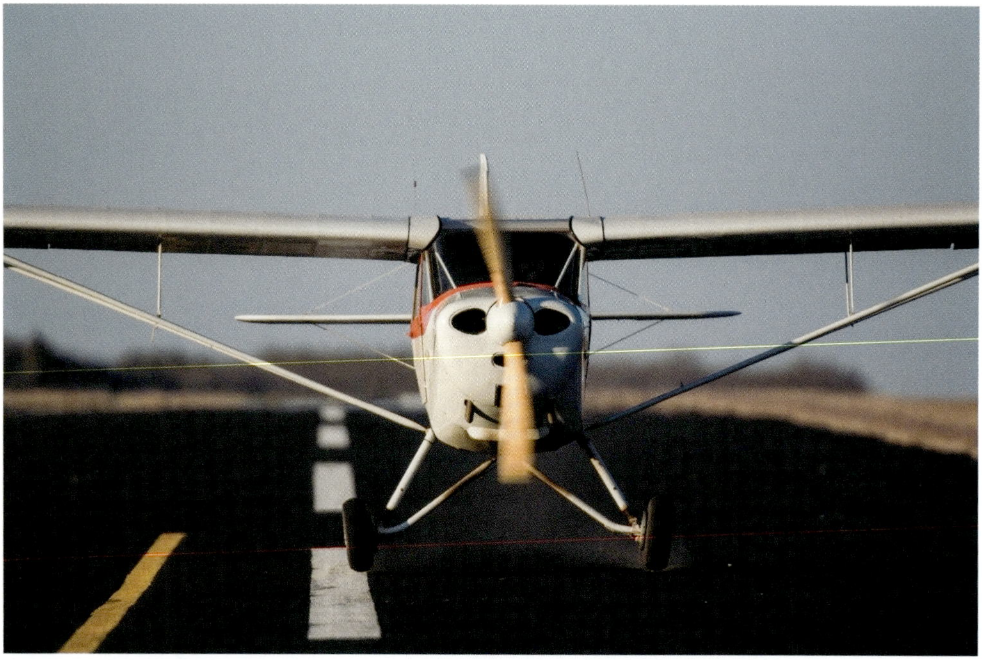

Figure 5.20
Shooting with extremely long glass often means being able to position yourself where you could not with shorter focal lengths.

ISO 400 • 1/1000 sec. • f/5.6 • 500mm

I'm bunching Canon's EF 500mm f/4L IS, EF 600mm f/4L IS, and EF 800mm f/5.6L IS together in a section because of their increasingly specialized use. They are heavy, a bit unwieldy for most folks, and like the EF 400mm f/2.8L IS, very expensive. The question to ask yourself is, "Can I use a 500mm, 600mm, or 800mm lens enough in my work to justify its US$10,000+ price tag?" Although many of us would like to answer, "YES!," I imagine it might be difficult to do so.

All that said, these lenses are highly functional for the right shooters, such as wildlife photographers. I know wildlife photographers who swear by their EF 500mm f/4L IS lenses for capturing everything from rabbits to deer to bears (**Figure 5.21**). Wildlife photography is hard work outside the zoo, and the incredible reach each of these lenses offers is suitable for animals that can be a bit unpredictable or skittish.

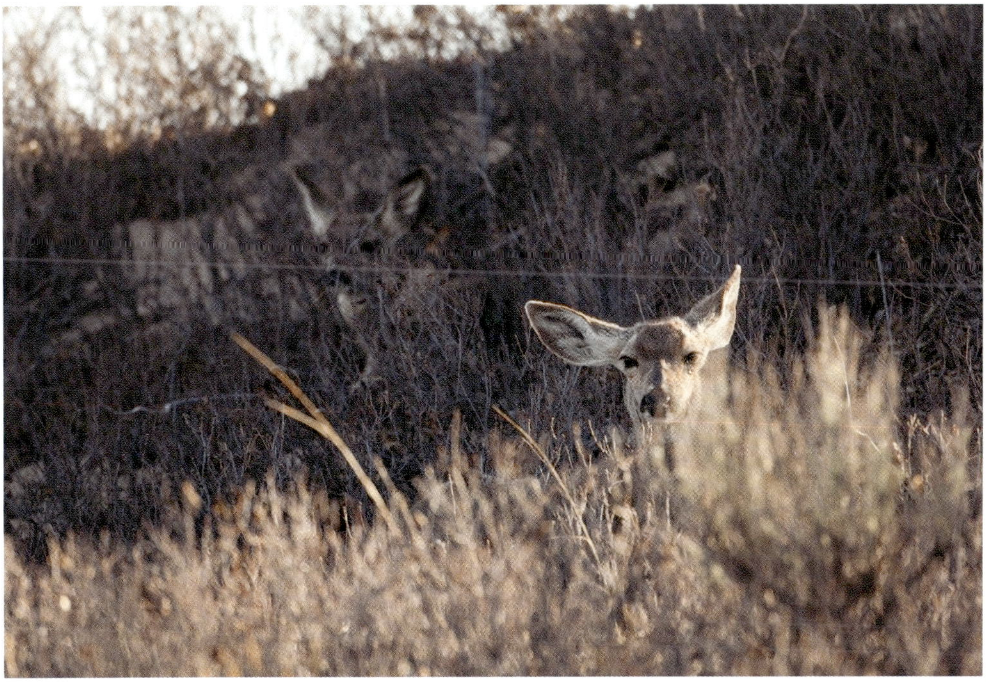

Figure 5.21
Many large-mammal wildlife photographers list the 500mm focal length as their favorite due to the wariness of their subject matter.

ISO 200 • 1/500 sec. • f/4 • 500mm

Bird photographers are especially drawn to these longer focal lengths due to the size of—and distance from—their subject matter (**Figure 5.22**). A super-telephoto lens lets a photographer shoot in tighter on wildlife from a distance, making for more authentic images of the animals. It also makes it easier to photograph potentially dangerous animals, such as bears or lions, safely.

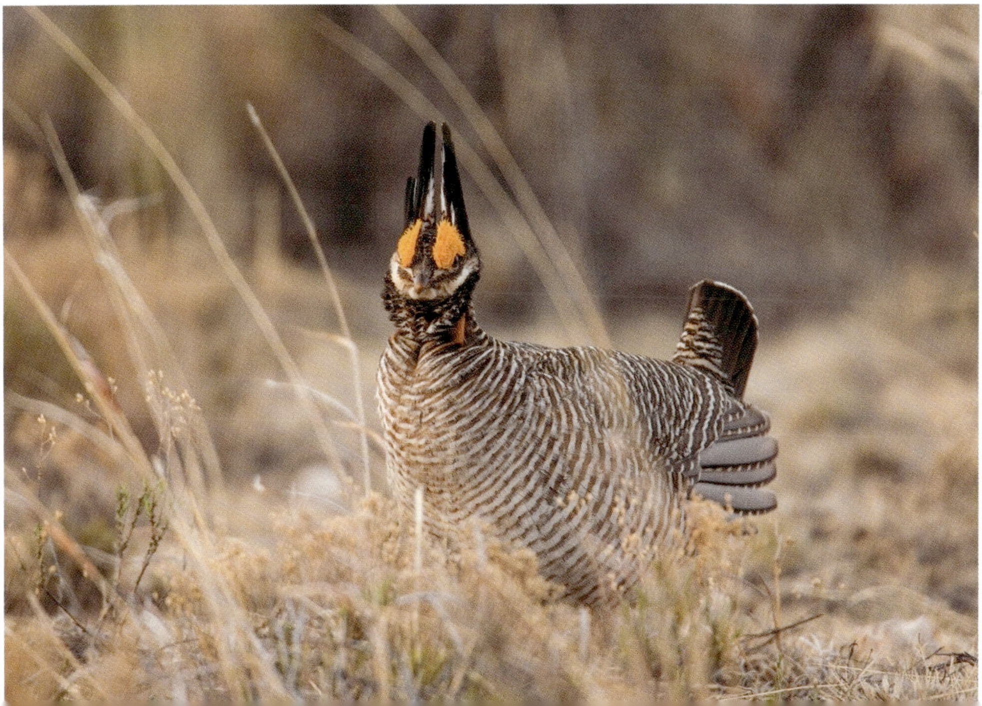

Figure 5.22
Photographing animals like the small and skittish lesser prairie chicken is all but impossible without focal lengths longer than 400mm.

ISO 800 • 1/500 sec. • f/4 • 500mm

If I Had to Choose: EF 70–200mm f/2.8L

To be honest, I'm not sure I have a favorite lens. However, if there was only one lens, it would hands down be the EF 70–200mm f/2.8L (**Figure 5.23**). I like to think that every lens in my bag is a workhorse, but this one is the Clydesdale. I've used this lens for every assignment I've had over the years. Landscapes, portraits, touchdown catches, western diamondback rattlesnakes—I find a way to use this lens for just about everything I shoot. You will find this lens or one of its iterations in most professional Canon users' bags.

Canon makes four 70–200mm lenses: an EF 70–200mm f/4L, an EF 70–200mm f/4L IS, an EF 70–200 f/2.8L, and an EF 70–200 f/2.8L IS (listed from least to most expensive). For predominantly landscape shooters, the f/4 versions of the lens are a bit smaller and lighter for those long hikes (not to mention the non-IS version is well under US$1000). That being said, the majority of shooters I know—landscape or otherwise—opt for one of the two f/2.8 versions. For many, that one stop of light gained and one stop of depth of field lost are worth the extra expense. The f/2.8s are built like tanks, and they weigh as much, especially those equipped with Image Stabilization. I use a non-IS f/2.8 version. I have had it for years, and not having IS only means that I keep a vigilant eye on my shutter speed and physical stability. But if I were shopping today for a new version, I would probably get the IS-equipped f/2.8.

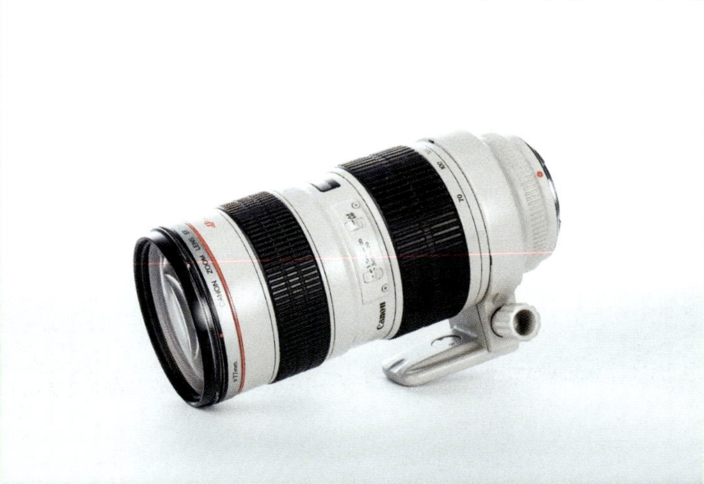

Figure 5.23
The EF 70–200mm f/2.8L is sharp and versatile.

Composing With Telephotos

I often find it difficult to compose well when using telephoto and super-telephoto lenses—it's simply hard to see composition at longer distances. The following are a few compositional tips to keep in mind when sizing up a long-lens frame.

Think Simplicity

Telephotos force you to think more simply about the images being made (**Figure 5.24**). Take a look at some of your favorite images made at long focal lengths like 200mm, 300mm, or longer. Chances are, they are not overly complex with many different definable subjects, and they might even contain a bit of mystery as to the context in which they were shot. In fact, telephoto lenses force us to heavily consider what must be left out of the frame in order to bring attention to what should be in it. Simplification is a good thing to consider at all focal lengths.

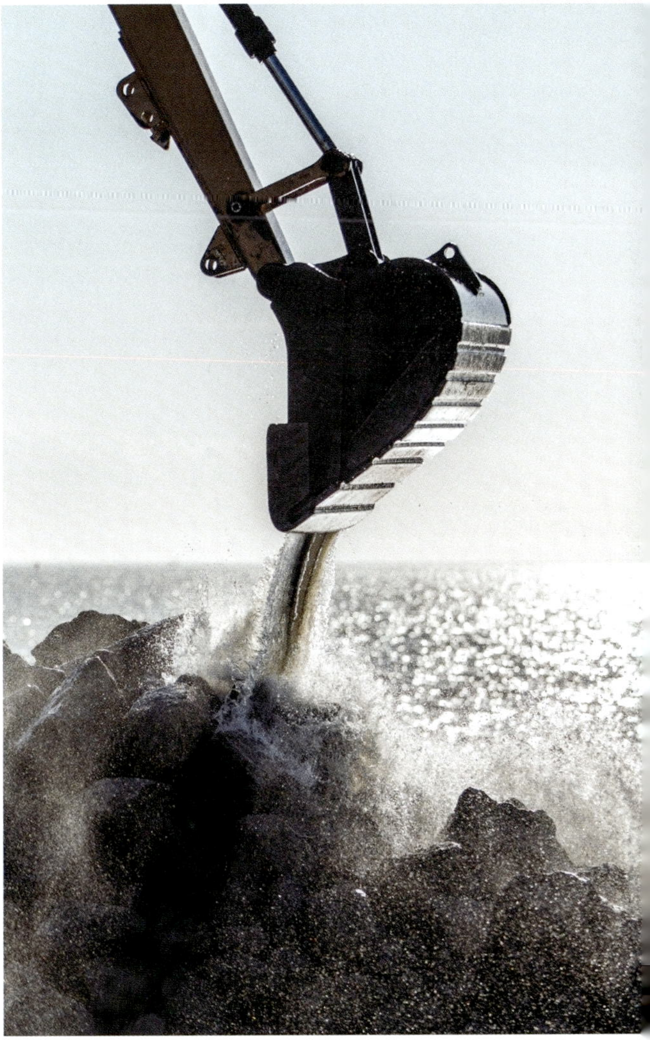

Figure 5.24 **Instead of trying to capture the entire machine, isolating and focusing only on the bucket makes for a much simpler but more dramatic shot of this reef rebuilding machine.**

ISO 200 • 1/1250 sec. • f/8 • 200mm

Learn to isolate

Telephoto lenses are good for mitigating distraction simply because they're too long to include everything. Decide what needs to go and what needs to stay. This is about making certain subject matter shine. Take sports photography, for example. Agencies often send photographers lists of players on which to concentrate, particularly if they are being considered for professional play. These agencies not only want action shots (**Figure 5.25**), but they also want what they call portraits (**Figure 5.26**), which are shots of the players standing or walking on the field. A long lens, such as an EF 400mm f/2.8L IS, is perfect for excluding anyone else close to the subject of interest from the frame. Telephotos are great at blurring the background in wildlife shots as well, no matter how fast the maximum aperture may be (**Figure 5.27**).

Figure 5.25
An isolated action shot of a football player draws attention to only the subject of interest, emphasizing his athleticism.

ISO 100 • 1/1000 sec. • f/2.8 • 400mm

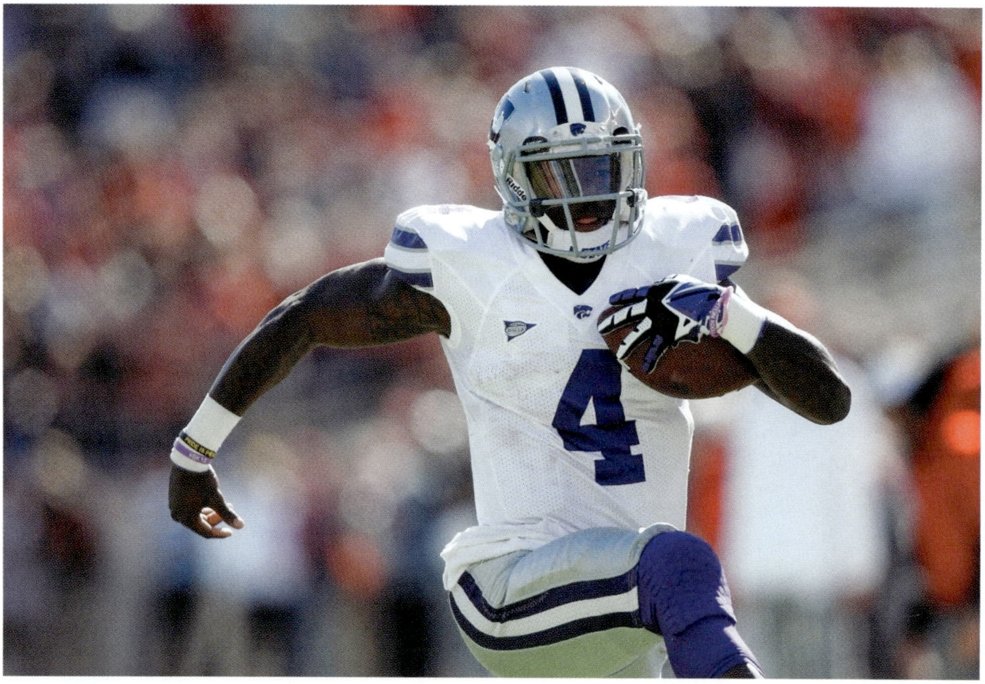

Figure 5.26 (left)
A fairly standard sports portrait of a player on the field

ISO 100 • 1/1250 sec. • f/2.8 • 400mm

Figure 5.27 (right)
De-cluttering an image is as simple as opening the aperture all the way. Even so, the background still contributes to the story of the image.

ISO 100 • 1/250 sec. • f/5.6 • 400mm

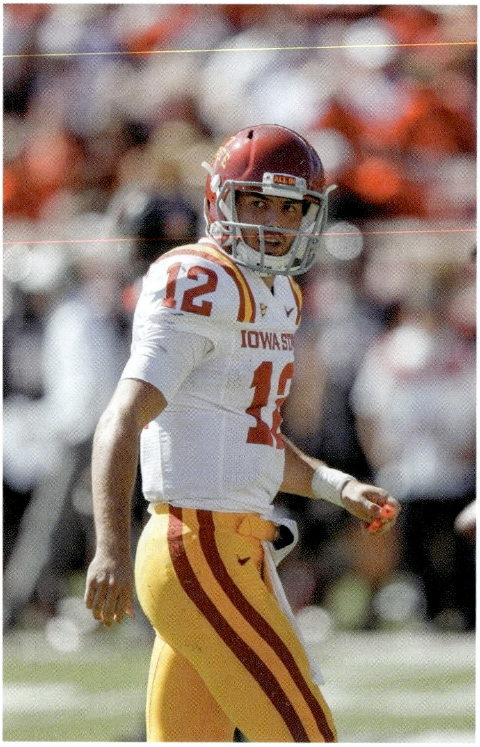

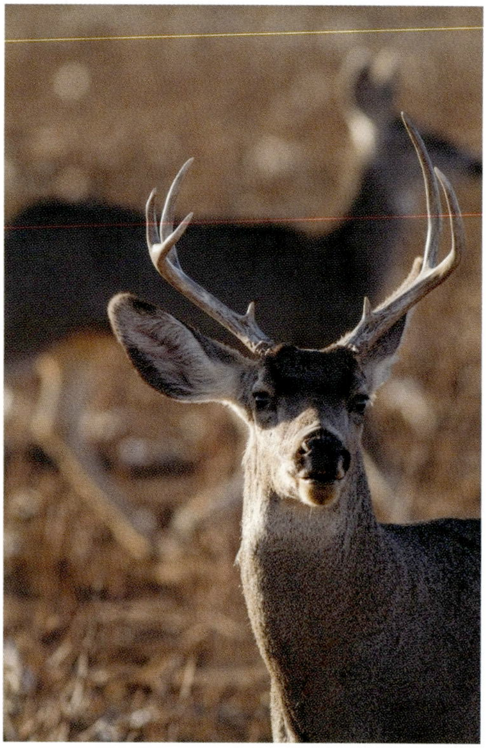

Because the focal plane is farther away when the subject is far away from the camera, the background remains more in focus (**Figure 5.28**). The closer the subject, the more isolating you can make the shot (**Figure 5.29**). In this case, the lens is saying, "Look at *this*!" Shots like these are fun to make, and they are extremely useful for portraiture and editorial purposes.

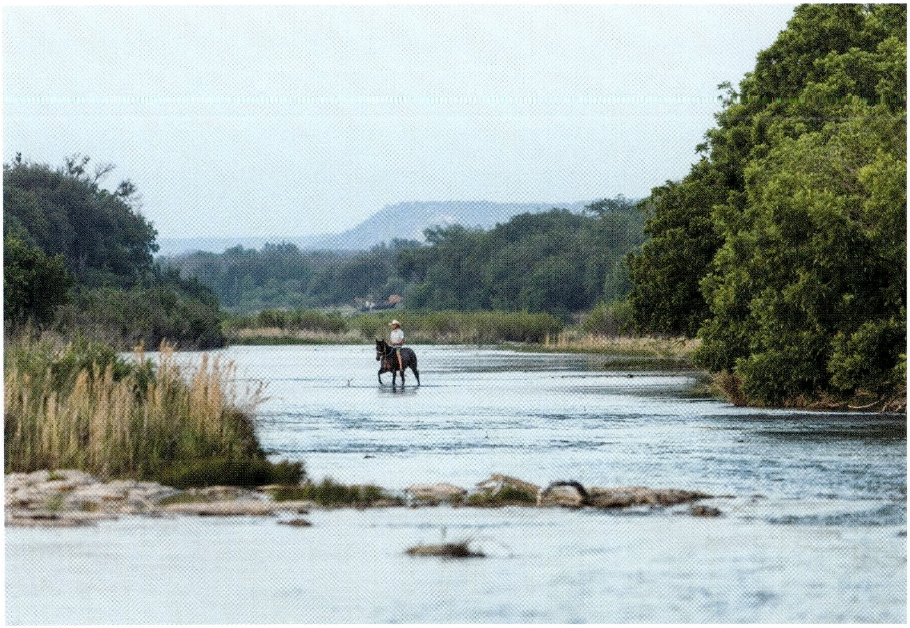

Figure 5.28
A cowboy walks his mount across the river a fair distance from the camera, and much of the background is in focus.

ISO 400 • 1/160 sec. • f/5.6 • 200mm

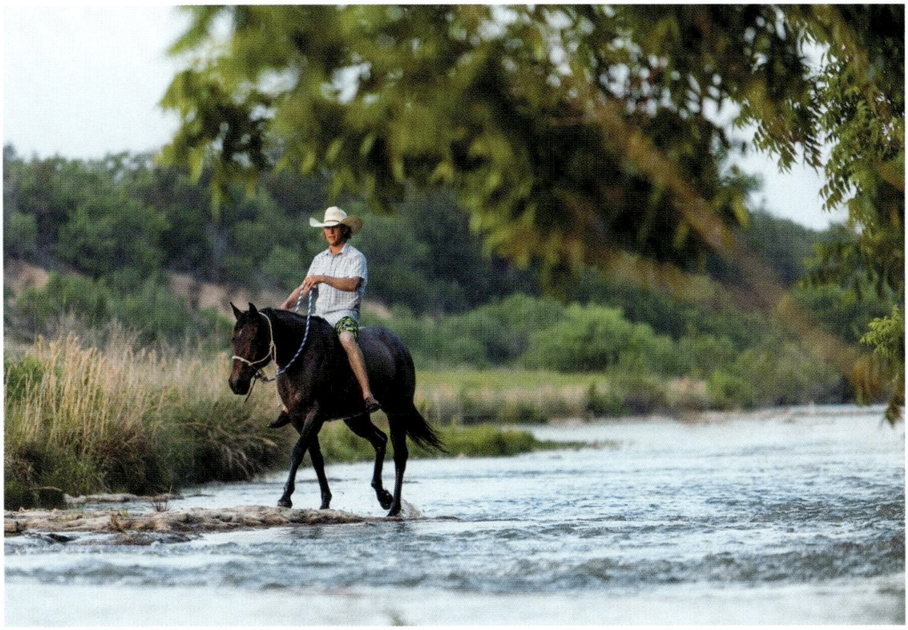

Figure 5.29
When you zoom closer, the background moves more into a visual abstraction of the environment. Yet, it is still a major part of the image's overall readability.

ISO 400 • 1/640 sec. • f/2.8 • 200mm

Pay attention to the background

Throwing a background out of focus is one of the surest ways to make a subject pop in an image, but too bright of a background can distract from a dimly lit subject (**Figure 5.30**), and that same subject can fade into a very dark background (**Figure 5.31**). A blurred background is nothing more than light values. Either moving your own position or moving the subject against a new, nondistracting background can overcome light values that are bothersome in your shot. It's always a good idea to consider the tonal values of what is behind the subject (**Figure 5.32**).

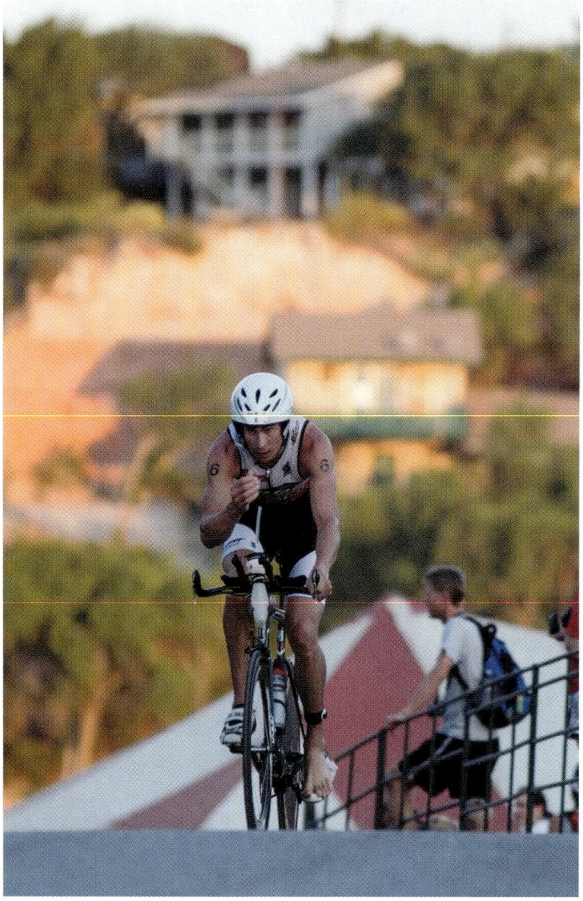

Figure 5.30 The bright canyon wall behind the cyclist overrides the eye's ability to maintain constant focus on the shadowed rider.

ISO 200 • 1/200 sec. • f/4 • 300mm

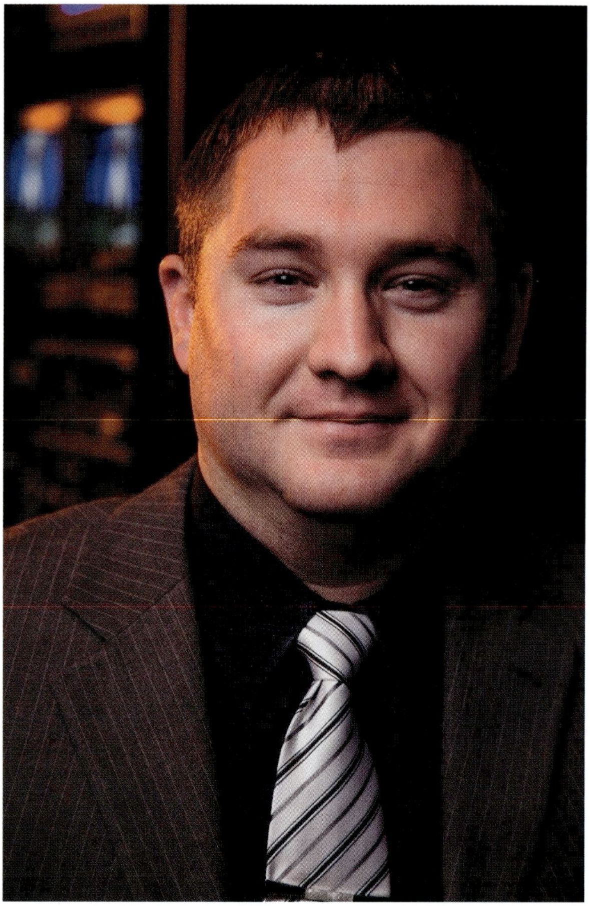

Figure 5.31 The subject's dark hair makes the outline of his head disappear into the black background.

ISO 200 • 1/25 sec. • f/4 • 105mm

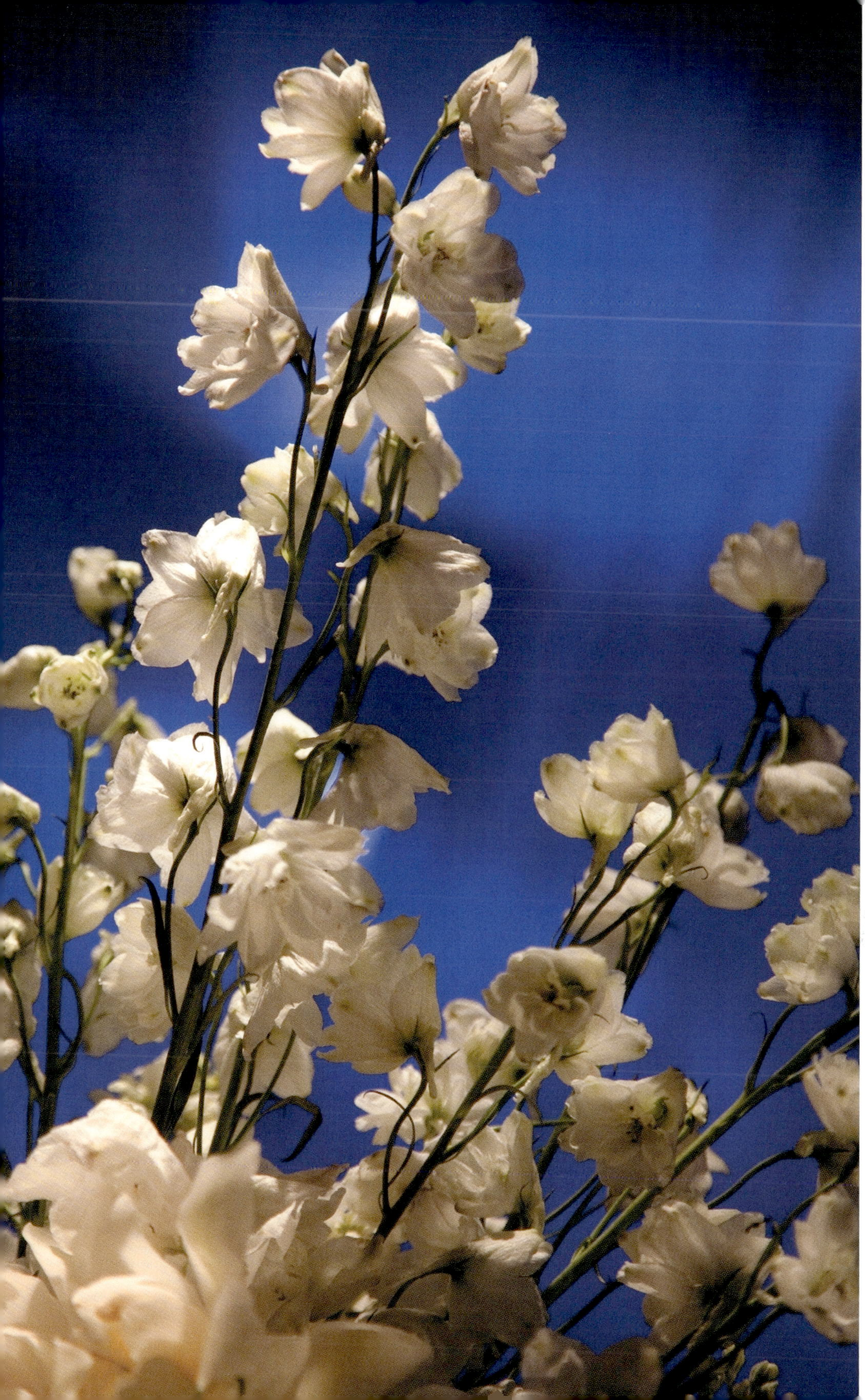

Figure 5.32

The flowers in this wedding reception balanced well against a blue-lit wall thrown out of focus in the background.

ISO 1600 • 1/160 sec. • f/4 • 105mm

Context vs. decontextualization

Consider how the strength of the bokeh (the degree to which a background is out of focus) has an effect on an image's meaning. With long lenses and wide-open apertures, it's fairly easy to isolate the subject by using extremely shallow depth of field. However, it is just as easy to delete any kind of meaningful, storytelling context the background may provide for the shot. In some cases, this is the photographer's intention. Head shots, for example, are supposed to focus on the person in them, not the background (**Figure 5.33**). These images demand the background just fade to a complementary shade of blurred color and light.

Other shots may call for the background to play a bigger storytelling role. Tight portraits or close-ups of static subject matter may need the background to say something more than just blurred color and shapes (**Figure 5.34**). Photographers have a tendency to use the shallowest depth of field for shots like this.

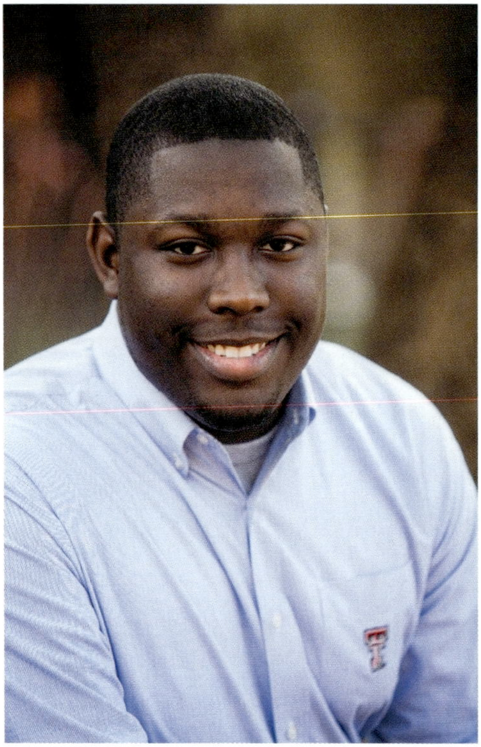

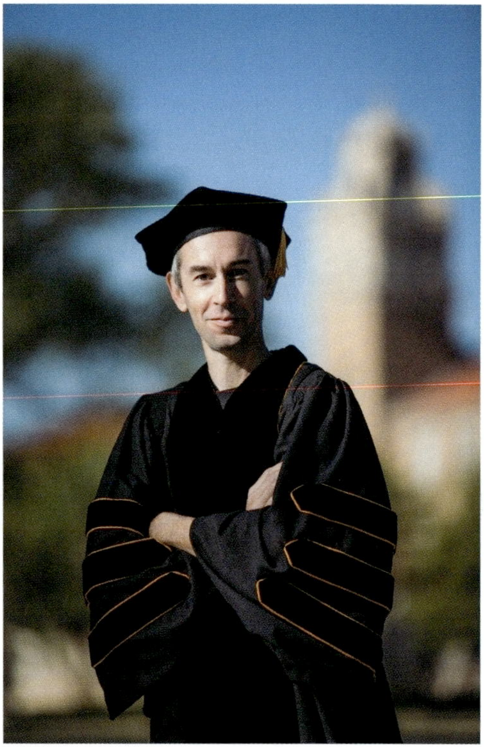

Figure 5.33 (left)
A headshot is all about the person in the frame, justifying a complete blurring of visual matter in the background.
ISO 200 • 1/250 sec. • f/2.8 • 200mm

Figure 5.34 (right)
Even at f/2.8, the distance of the primary subject and secondary subject (the tower) from the camera kept the background in focus enough to tie the graduate to an iconic feature of the university.
ISO 100 • 1/2000 sec. • f/2.8 • 190mm

It may be to your advantage to increase the depth of field sometimes, to draw a stronger connection between subject and the environment serving as a background. Instead of shooting at f/2.8 (**Figure 5.35**), perhaps use f/5.6 or f/8 (**Figure 5.36**). You can produce an image that is aesthetically pleasing yet not decontextualizing. You may also choose to move the subject closer to the background instead of stopping the aperture down.

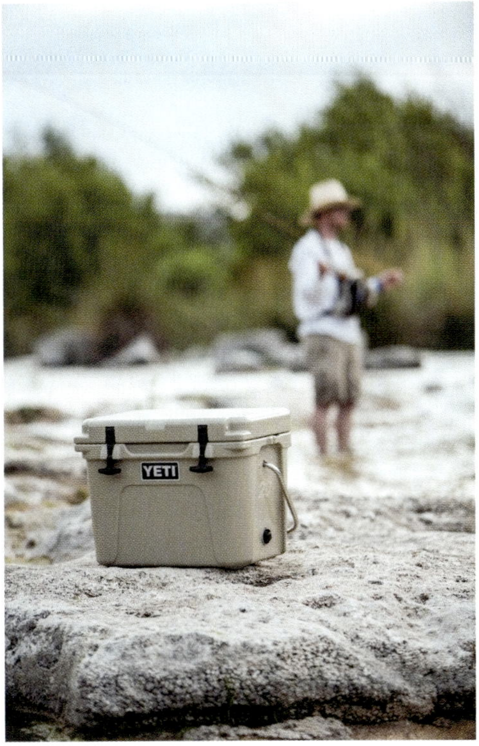

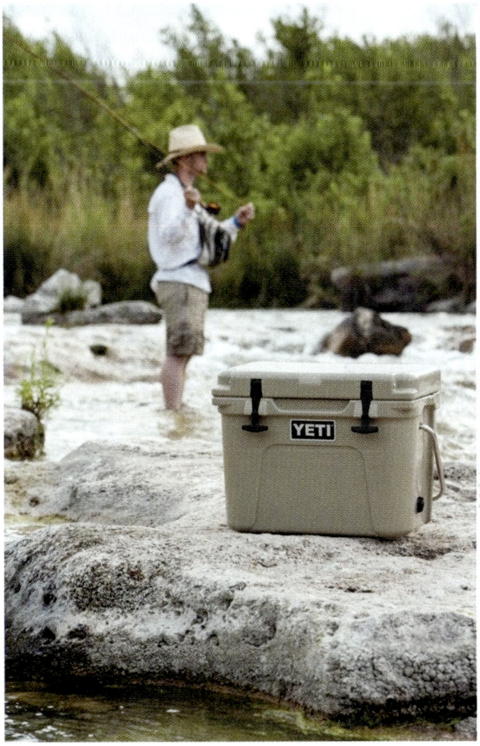

Figure 5.35 (left) At f/2.8, the cooler stands out well, but parts of the subject—like the fly rod he is holding—get lost in the light values of the background.

ISO 100 • 1/500 sec. • f/2.8 • 150mm

Figure 5.36 (right) Stopping down to f/8 brings the background more into focus, and the human subject immediately stands out against the vegetation farther back.

ISO 100 • 1/60 sec. • f/8 • 160mm

Compress

I described optical compression in Chapter 2, but it bears repeating that this is a visual element photographers should take advantage of when using longer focal lengths. Many of the interesting facets of the images in this chapter are a direct result of foreground and background being slammed together in varying degrees of compression (**Figure 5.37**). Learn to see how compression affects the images you want to make, helping you produce different looks for a subject. It will even help you make the most of unique atmospheric conditions, such as haze, fog, and water (**Figure 5.38**).

Figure 5.37
The mountains of Texas and Mexico along the Rio Grande seem dramatically close with a long focal length's compression.

ISO 100 • 1/250 sec. • f/9 • 200mm

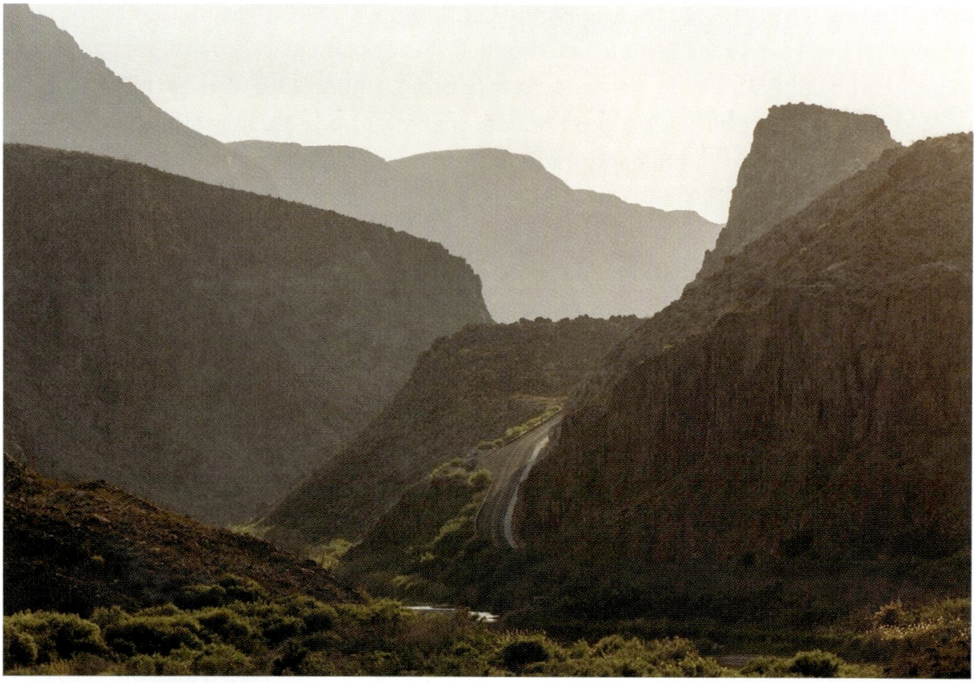

Figure 5.38
Certain subject matter can be made to look even more interesting with the right light and perspective, such as this tight shot of backlit irrigation water.

ISO 100 • 1/800 sec. • f/6.3 • 200mm

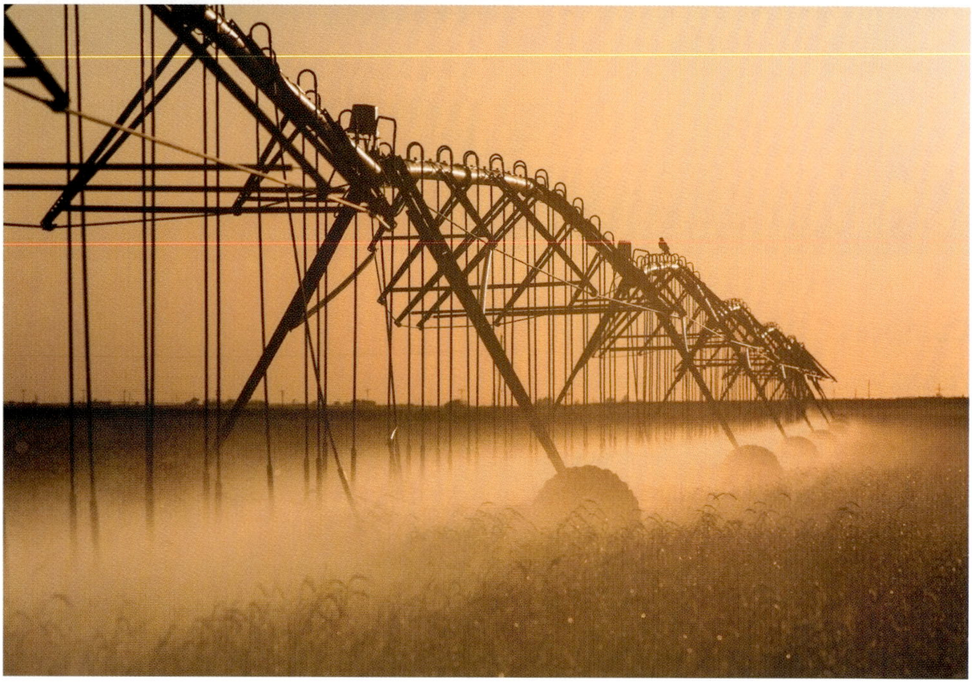

Look for Layers, Rows, and Patterns

One of my absolute favorite things to do with telephoto lenses is shoot repetition (**Figure 5.39**). I always have my eyes peeled for shapes and forms that occur in some sort of systematic fashion. I'm primarily drawn to three different visual elements that exhibit this repetition: layers, rows, and patterns.

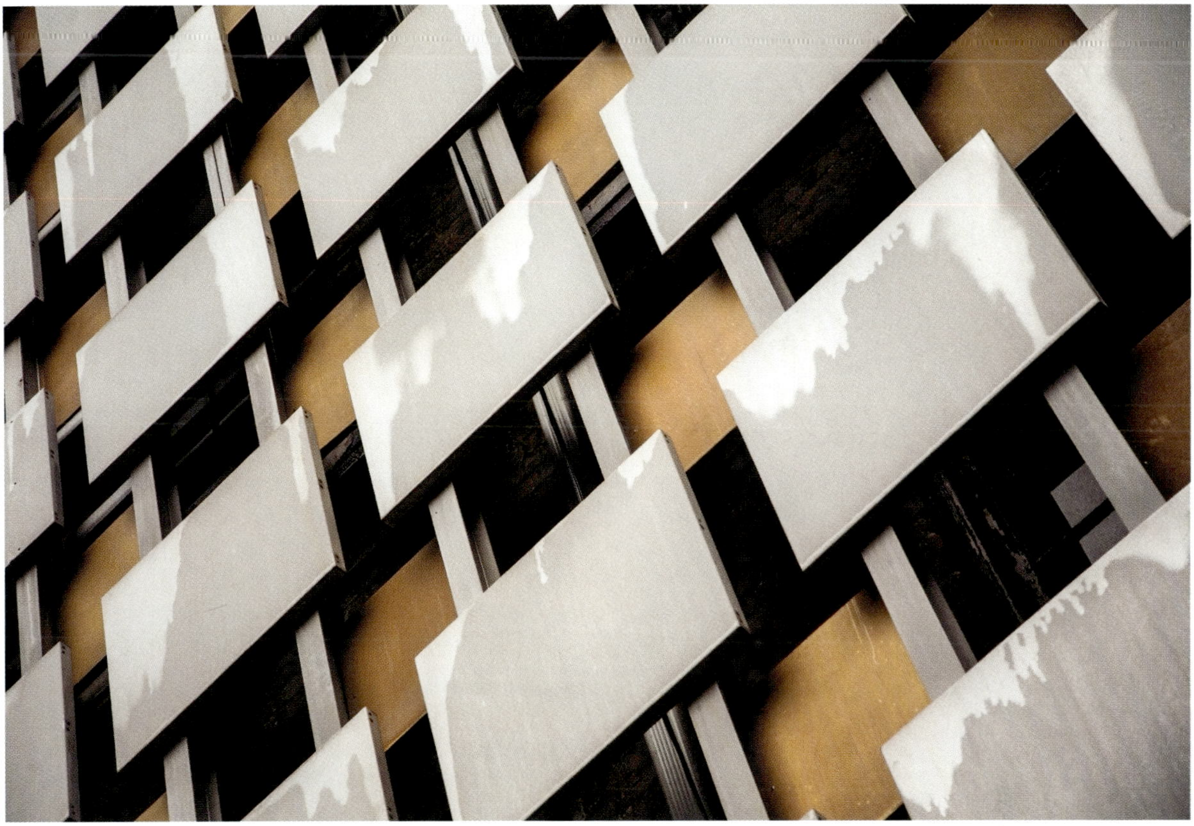

Figure 5.39 **Train your eye to look for repetitious subject matter, like this side of a building in New Orleans.**

ISO 200 • 1/400 sec. • f/4 • 82mm

These elements can be found just about anywhere, such as a hayfield or the clouds in the sky (**Figure 5.40**), windows on a building (**Figure 5.41**), or a small plant outside your apartment door (**Figure 5.42**). Of course, you can make great shots of these elements at any focal length, but longer lenses let you see them in a variety of ways, and certainly in ways that can be more abstract. They allow you to compress layers and other repetitious elements, forcing the eye to immediately notice something it would not otherwise in passing (**Figure 5.43**).

Figure 5.40
The layered structure and colors of the sky are made even more interesting with a compressing focal length.

ISO 200 • 1/125 sec. • f/9 • 200mm

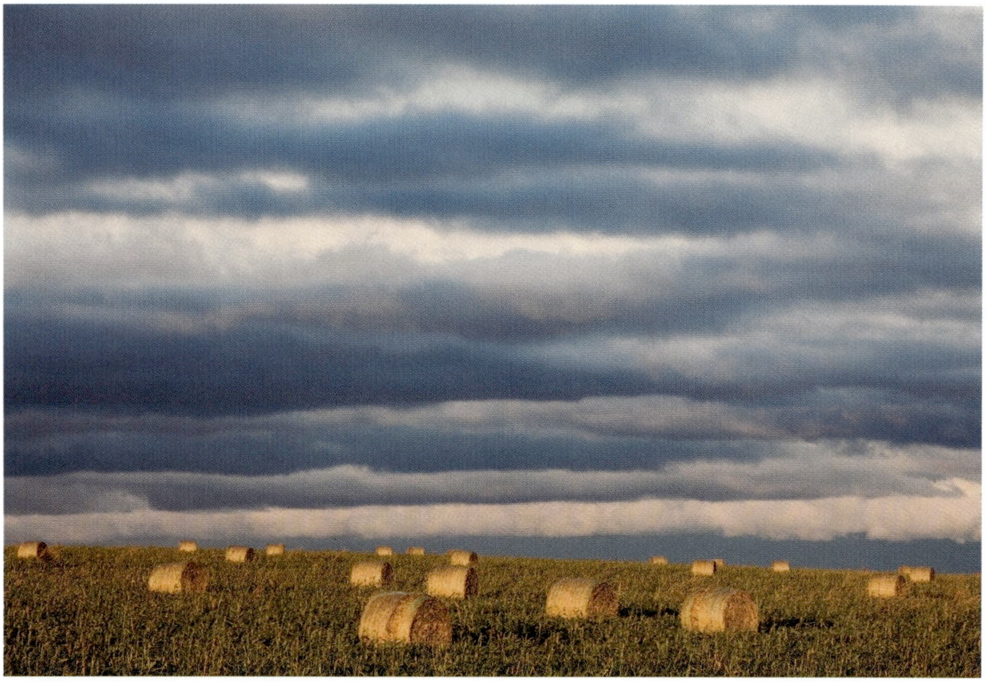

Figure 5.41
The human eye is attracted to patterns, like this wall of windows in Madrid's Plaza Mayor.

ISO 100 • 1/200 sec. • f/4 • 80mm

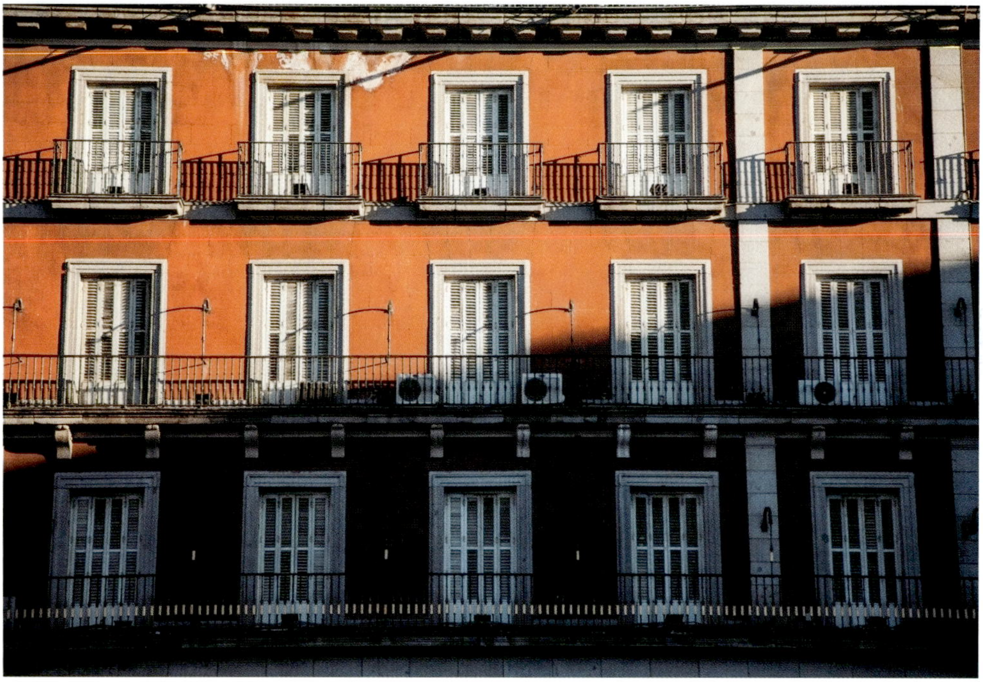

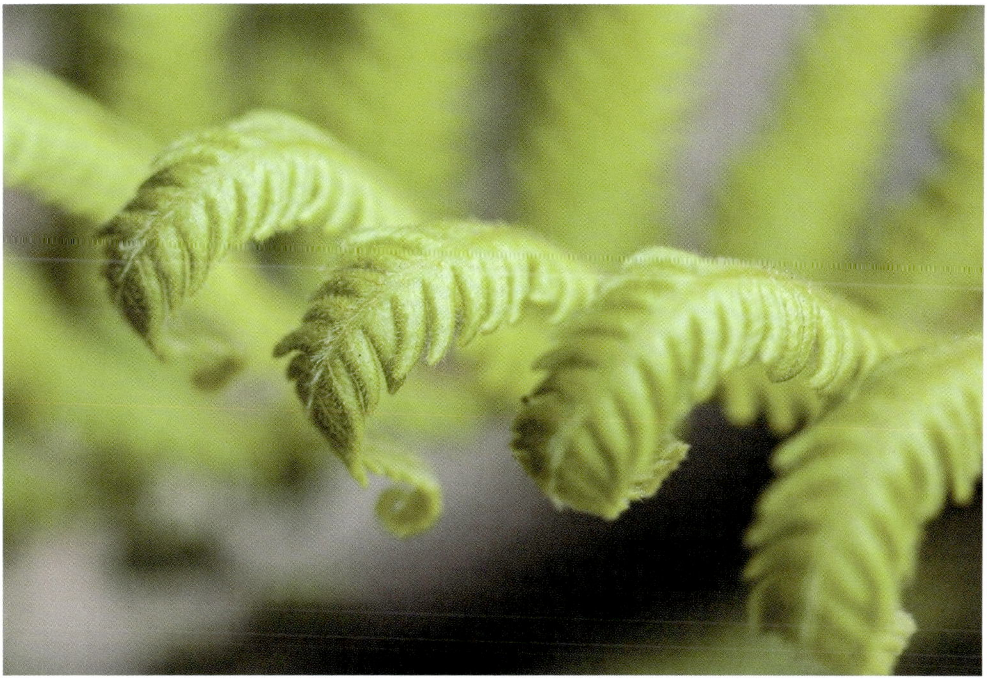

Figure 5.42
A macro shot of a fern reveals the patterned look of the plant.

ISO 100 • 1/10 sec. • f/8 • 90mm

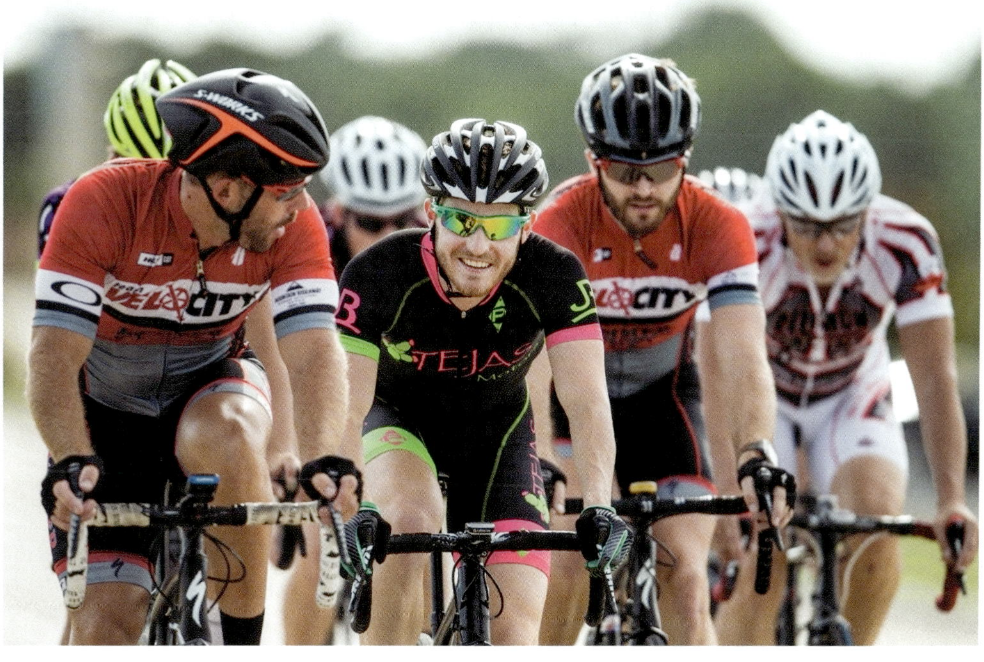

Figure 5.43
Wide-angle lenses would not capture patterns like this small peloton, even if it were closer to the camera. The longer focal length's compression helps the eye discern this layering of people and form.

ISO 100 • 1/800 sec. • f/2.8 • 400mm

Repetitious shots like this can often be a mystery, and aside from the playfulness of these images, they allow the photographer to produce a sensory connection with the viewer. I often describe close-ups as those shots that make someone use their sense of touch imaginatively. Although we cannot replicate this sense with the camera, a tight shot of the patterned texture of a rocky ledge or a small succulent plant (**Figure 5.44**) can help someone imagine how that subject feels.

Longer lenses let the photographer draw the viewer's eye to a pattern as if it were more important than the content itself (**Figure 5.45**). It is another interesting way of presenting subject matter, as well as a great way to create interest in other shots of the same subject or in the same story.

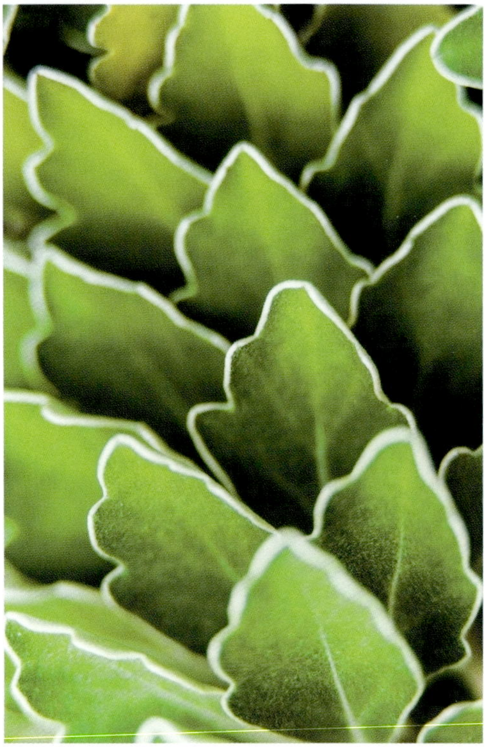

Figure 5.44 **Green-and-white repetition, with just enough evidence of what the subject is, makes for a great close-up.**

ISO 200 • 1/30 sec. • f/2.8 • 135mm

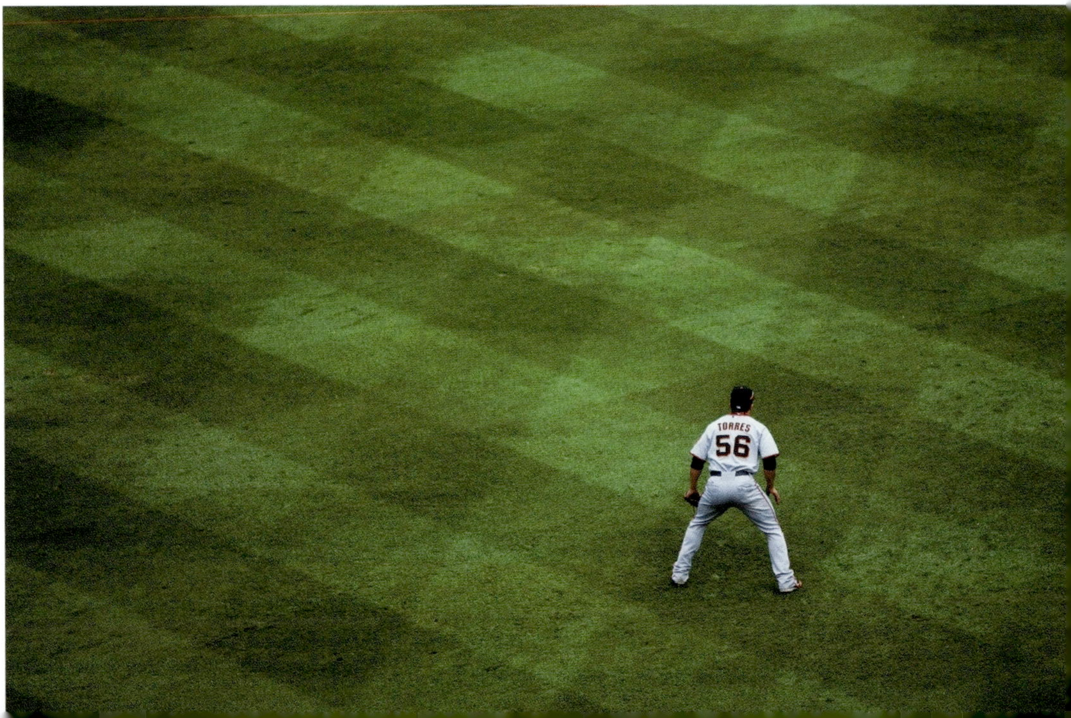

Figure 5.45 **Even though the outfielder is the primary subject of the shot, the patterned outfield makes the shot even more interesting.**

ISO 200 • 1/1250 sec. • f/2.8 • 200mm

Choosing Telephoto Lenses Wisely

Telephoto lenses are expensive, more so than most other lenses, and especially so when you get to the real big fellas: the 400mm, 500mm, 600mm, and 800mm. Even the non-L- designated lenses can be pricey, with the exception of the EF 75–300mm f/4–5.6 (between US$200 and US$300). As with all lenses, spend some time comparing features before purchasing, and remember, the longer the lens, the more specialized it becomes.

First, consider what it is you want to shoot with the telephoto, and more important, how frequently will you be shooting similar subject matter? If you are shooting mostly portraits, 200mm might be the longest lens you consider. There are several great lenses that include 200mm in their zoom range as well as prime lenses leading up to 200mm (like the EF 100mm f/2.8, the EF 135mm f/2L, and the EF 200mm f/2.8L). If you are shooting sports, consider your 300mm and 400mm options. I can't speak highly enough of the 400mm platform for football, baseball, and any sport that doesn't happen mere feet in front of you. For basketball, however, you can get away with a 70–200mm lens.

The second consideration is how much weight you are willing to lug around. Some telephotos can be fairly lightweight, such as the non-L-series zooms and several of the shorter L-series primes, like the EF 135mm f/2L and the EF 200mm f/2.8L. Beyond those, weight goes up dramatically, caused by the quality of the construction materials, the size of the maximum aperture (the amount of glass in each lens), Image Stabilization, and appendages like tripod mount collars. For most folks, the weight of the lens does not matter until the 300mm focal length, but even carrying around an EF 70–200mm f/2.8L IS might cause some backache. I favor carrying either the EF 300mm f/4L IS or the EF 400mm f/5.6L (or both) over the f/2.8 versions when I am out hiking strenuous landscapes—they are several pounds lighter and easier to pack in one bag.

The last thing to consider is the lenses' price points. Canon's long lenses range in price from US$200 (for the EF 75–300mm f/4–5.6) to US$14,000 (for the EF 800mm f/5.6L IS). Going into debt over a lens that you may pull out of the bag a couple times a year—or will never use to make money—would not be wise. If you're not a bird photographer, don't even look at the 600mm or 800mm lenses. When I need to photograph birds, I determine whether or not I can use my 400mm. And, if I can't, I rent. However, I do use my 70-200mm lens every time I go on a shoot. With that, I can justify investing in the higher-priced, higher-quality version. Ultimately, the decision to purchase a lens is up to you.

Practice, Practice, Practice

To get acquainted with any of your lenses, practice is key. The longer and heavier the lens, the more time you need with it. This might mean taking regular walks or excursions with your camera. Here are a few things to work on and consider when mastering the long lens.

Minimum Sustaining Shutter Speed

In the first chapter, I covered minimum sustaining shutter speed—the slowest shutter speed you can use while handholding a camera and lens to achieve a sharp shot. Any slower shutter speed will result in a body-caused motion blur. Knowing your personal minimum sustaining shutter speed with every lens, especially telephotos, comes in handy (**Figures 5.46** and **5.47**).

The surest way to find this out is to simply put a camera to your eye with your long lens on and make exposures with slower shutter speeds each time you snap a shot. Look at the shutter speed on the last shot in focus, and you'll know your minimum sustaining shutter speed for that lens. If you are new to photography, this shutter speed will more than likely have a denominator that is close in numerical value to the focal length you used.

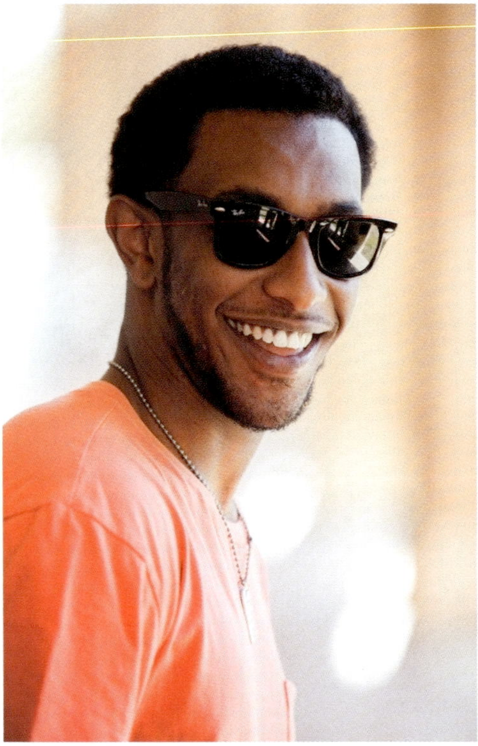

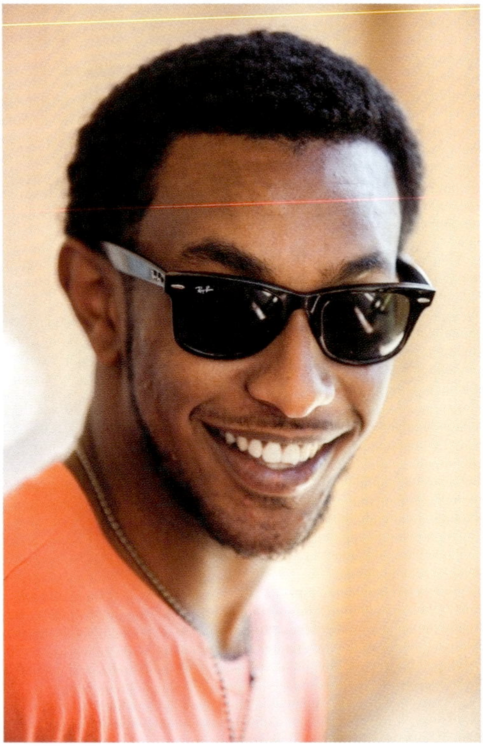

Figure 5.46 (left) This portrait is slightly out of focus, a result of shooting such a long focal length at a relatively slow shutter speed.

ISO 100 • 1/50 sec. • f/2.8 • 165mm

Figure 5.47 (right) Using a bit shorter focal length and moving in close, I was able to sustain the focus of the portrait at just a notch faster shutter speed.

ISO 100 • 1/80 sec. • f/2.8 • 150mm

For example, if you are shooting with a 200mm lens, the theoretical minimum sustaining shutter speed would be 1/200 of a second. The idea is to shoot at that shutter speed, or faster, to avoid your body movement forcing a shot out of focus. The longer the lens, the faster the minimum sustaining shutter speed becomes.

Of course, with practice, any photographer can reduce the minimum sustaining shutter speed for any lens. Using the lens enough to be familiar with how it handles is one way. The other way is through increased stability.

Finding Stability

Reducing your minimum sustaining shutter speed is all about finding and increasing your stability. The sturdier you make your camera and lens, the more able you are to handhold them while still retaining focus.

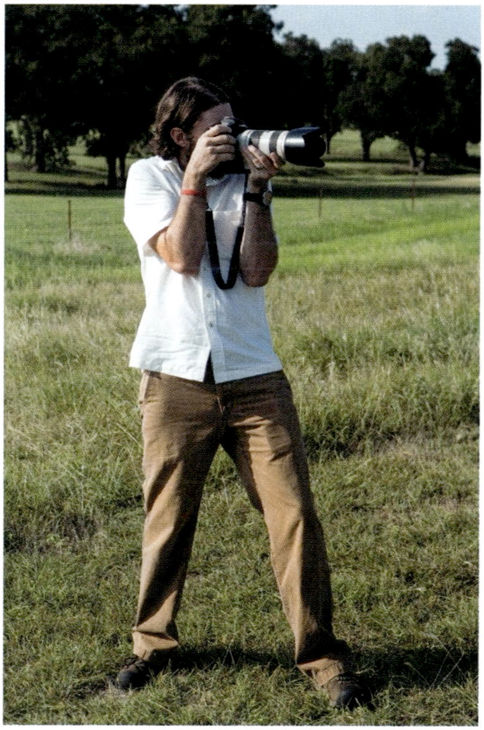

Figure 5.48
A stable stance: Place the lens on top of your left hand, lock both elbows into your body, and widen the position of your feet, one in front of the other.

The stance

Here's a sure-fire way to immediately add stability to your shooting: Put your left hand *under* the lens, and lock your elbows onto the side of your body (possibly on the top of your hips) to provide support (**Figure 5.48**). Widen your feet, placing one in front of the other, and you've just made yourself a much more stable human platform. Let your own weight settle before shooting, and press the shutter button when you exhale (you may not be able to do this when shooting things in flight or extreme motion). All of this is about tuning your body to reduce the minimum sustaining shutter speed and ensure sharp images. Again, this technique is not exclusive to telephoto lenses, but it really starts to make a mark here.

Adding weight

Heavier lenses are often more stable to handhold than the featherweight alternatives, especially if your stance is set well. Many folks would say that the EF 300mm f/4L IS is more stable than a more-flexible EF 70–300mm f/4–5.6 IS. Why? The prime lens has a bit more heft to keep it from bobbing around with the movement of the supporting arm and hand. It makes sense that adding weight (to a point) makes a platform more stable.

So, what if you own a non-L-series telephoto lens that seems to jump around with the slightest movement of your hand or body? I have seen photographers tape small weights to their longer lenses. I even know one wildlife photographer who wraps one-pound ankle weights around the circumference of his EF 400mm f/5.6L with camouflage tape. You probably can't put ankle weights around non-L-series telephoto zooms, and some lenses do not have enough room on the barrel for large weights, but there's always a creative way to add more weight. There are no rules about how much weight to add. It is simply worth experimenting if you experience more than normal movement of the lens when you are shooting.

Tripods

There are times when the human platform is just not stable enough. Once you pass under the minimum sustaining shutter speed, it is time to put the camera and lens on a tripod. Here are a few tips to make the most out of stabilizing your tripod.

If you have a lens that has a tripod mount collar, use it (**Figure 5.49**). Lenses that have these, such as the EF 70–200mm f/2.8L, the EF 300mm f/4L IS, and the EF 400mm f/2.8L IS, are simply too heavy for the tripod to be connected to the camera. If the lens doesn't break off the camera, the weight of the lens may tip the tripod over, or more likely, the instability of this kind of setup will rock the camera and lens up and down while you are trying to make a steady shot. If your lens did not come with a tripod mount collar or have room for one, it probably doesn't weigh enough to cause this issue. Set the tripod legs apart as far as they will go at the height you have the tripod. The closer the legs are together for any height, the more likely the rig will tip over. Add the weight of any telephoto lens on top, and it will tip more quickly.

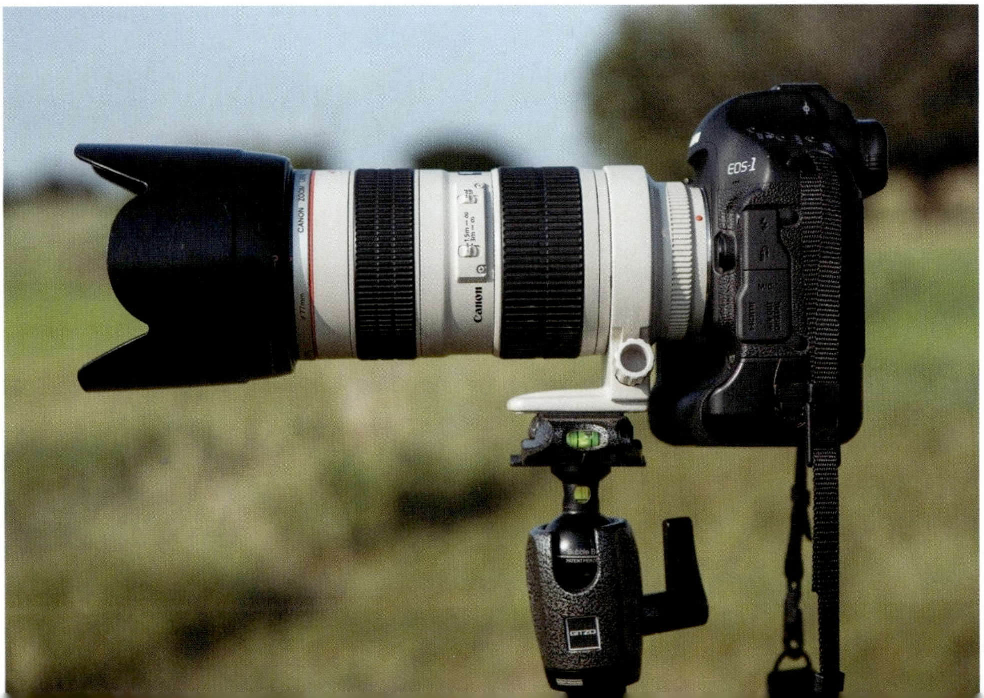

Figure 5.49
Using a tripod mount collar helps better balance the weight distribution of the camera and lens, resulting in less wobble and cleaner images.

Add weight to the tripod. Many tripods have hooks at the bottom of the center column. Hang your camera bag from this to further stabilize the platform (**Figure 5.50**). If you don't have a bag or anything that can hang from this hook, use your body to add weight. Make sure your tripod legs are secure and will not slip, and while you are shooting, hold onto one of the legs, adding a bit of your own weight for stability. This works for fairly quick shutter speeds, but I wouldn't trust your body for stability if your exposure is longer than, say, a second or two.

Also consider carbon. Carbon tripods are not heavy (quite the opposite), but they have one thing going for them in terms of stability that aluminum tripods don't: Carbon legs translate less vibration than aluminum legs. There have been times when I became frustrated with my aluminum tripod in a river because I could feel the water moving by the tripod legs. The vibrations were stronger the closer I got to rapids. Carbon legs are helpful in these situations, and you can always add more weight. Carbon sticks are more expensive than aluminum sticks, but there are some great companies making affordable carbon gear. I use both aluminum and carbon tripods, with Manfrotto being my go-to for aluminum sticks. They also have relatively affordable carbon alternatives to some of their most popular aluminum tripods.

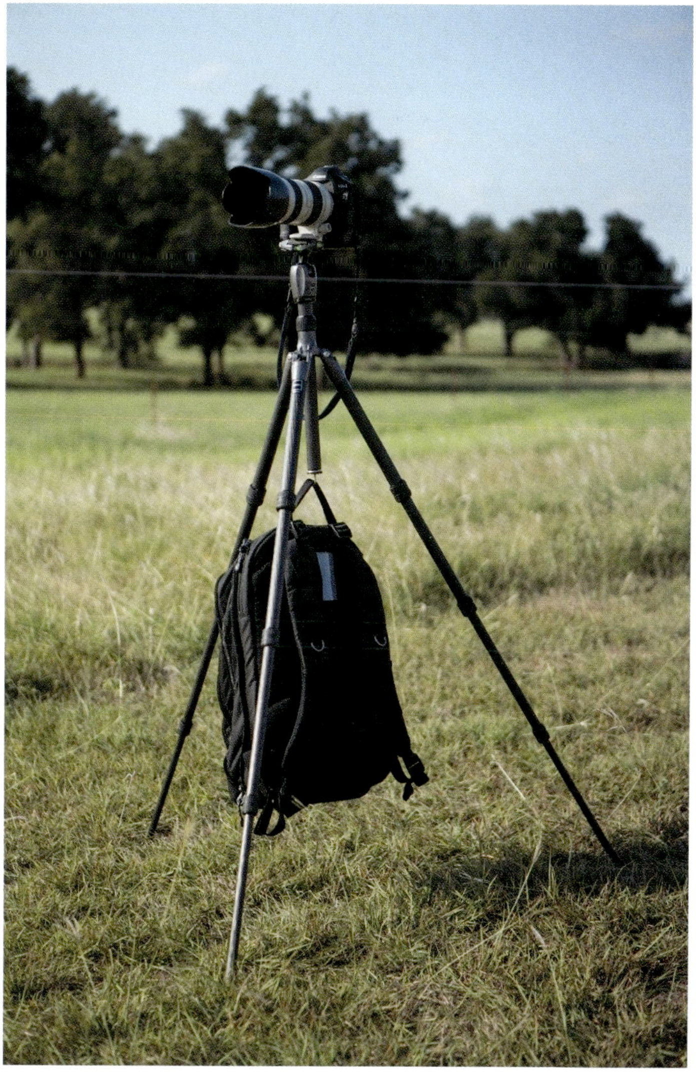

Figure 5.50 **Hanging a bag from the middle column of a tripod is a great way to add weight for stability.**

Monopods

Let's be honest here. Tripods can sometimes be a royal pain to lug around. Sometimes shooting doesn't call for that much baggage and it needs to happen much quicker than setting up a tripod allows. Enter the monopod. With only one column of support, the monopod is more like an extension of your hand and arm, just more stable. Monopods really come in handy when you need to carry around a long lens for a long time—like an entire college football game—and avoid fatigue on the human platform. Certainly, they come in handy when the minimum sustaining shutter speed is breached, but their real purpose is for the long haul. We can certainly handhold a few shots with a big EF 500mm f/4L IS, but we would get real tired of holding it up.

Some folks like to use a monopod in place of a tripod. Make no mistake, they serve two different purposes, and they are not necessarily interchangeable. A tripod, in my opinion, is a photographic necessity. A monopod is necessary in certain types of photography (like sports and some wildlife) when the purpose of using one—endurance and efficiency—is paramount.

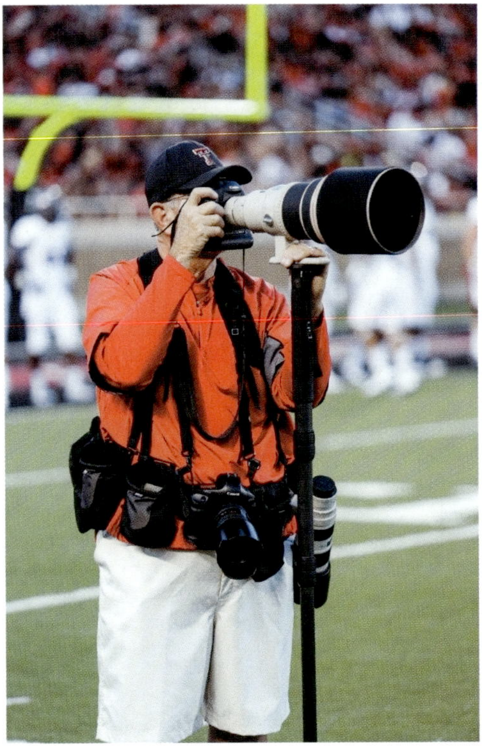

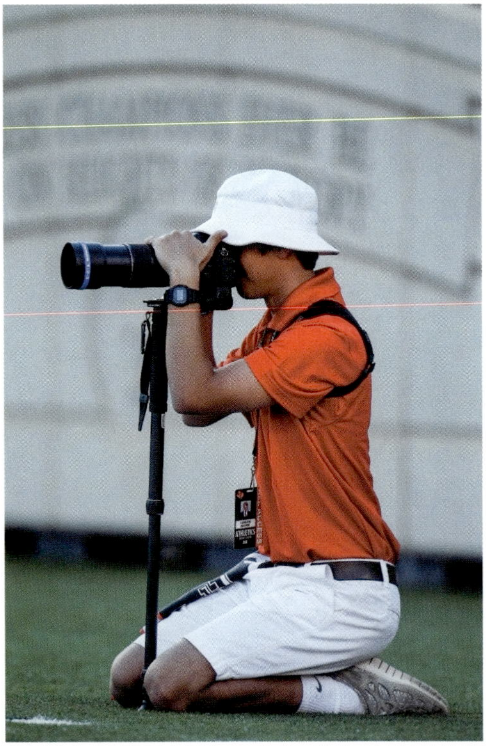

Chapter 5 Assignments

Telephoto focal lengths take the most effort to use effectively. It is not all about simply zooming into the action. They are also a bit touchy to handhold. Work through the following assignments to help you with both seeing through a telephoto lens and shooting without a monopod or tripod.

Go long!

Like I did in Chapter 3, I encourage you to take a photo walk with only one focal length. This time, rack your lens out to 200mm (if you have a lens that goes to 135mm instead, lock it there). This is a nice standard telephoto focal length that will force you to see the world around you in terms of compression and composition at a distance. Make images only at this focal length to become comfortable with the lens as well as to become more capable of previsualizing images at this focal length. If you have a zoom lens, it might be easy to just zoom in and out depending on your composition, but I encourage you to leave it where you started to train your eye. If you would like, take another photowalk using only 300mm, and another with 400mm if you have it. Unless you're using telephoto focal lengths all of the time, it is difficult to see or imagine the shots you can make with them. This exercise, although simplistic, helps do just that.

Pick out patterns

While on that photowalk discussed above, look for repetitive patterns, rows, and layers to tighten in on and create images that attract the eye but do not necessarily give away the subject outright. If you are downtown, concentrate on the sides of buildings, windows that are lit well or reflect an interesting sky, manhole covers, or layers of people walking during rush hour. If in the wilderness, consider layers of plant leaves, trunks of trees, or boulders in a stream, and always be cognizant of the cloud structure in the sky.

Practice tracking

One of the hardest techniques to do without practicing is tracking a moving subject with a long lens, especially if said subject is moving fast. Work with another person—perhaps a runner or cyclist—and practice tracking her movement with a telephoto focal length of at least 200mm (go longer for a more challenging exercise). Switch the autofocus mode on the camera to one that constantly engages the autofocus system for movement (AI Servo). Have your subject move across your field of vision as well as toward and away from you at angles. Practice handholding the lens while you make shots of her, keeping only one autofocus point locked on her as much as possible. The closer the subject matter, the more challenging tracking becomes.

Share your results with the book's Flickr group!
Join the group here: www.flickr.com/groups/canonlenses_fromsnapshotstogreatshots

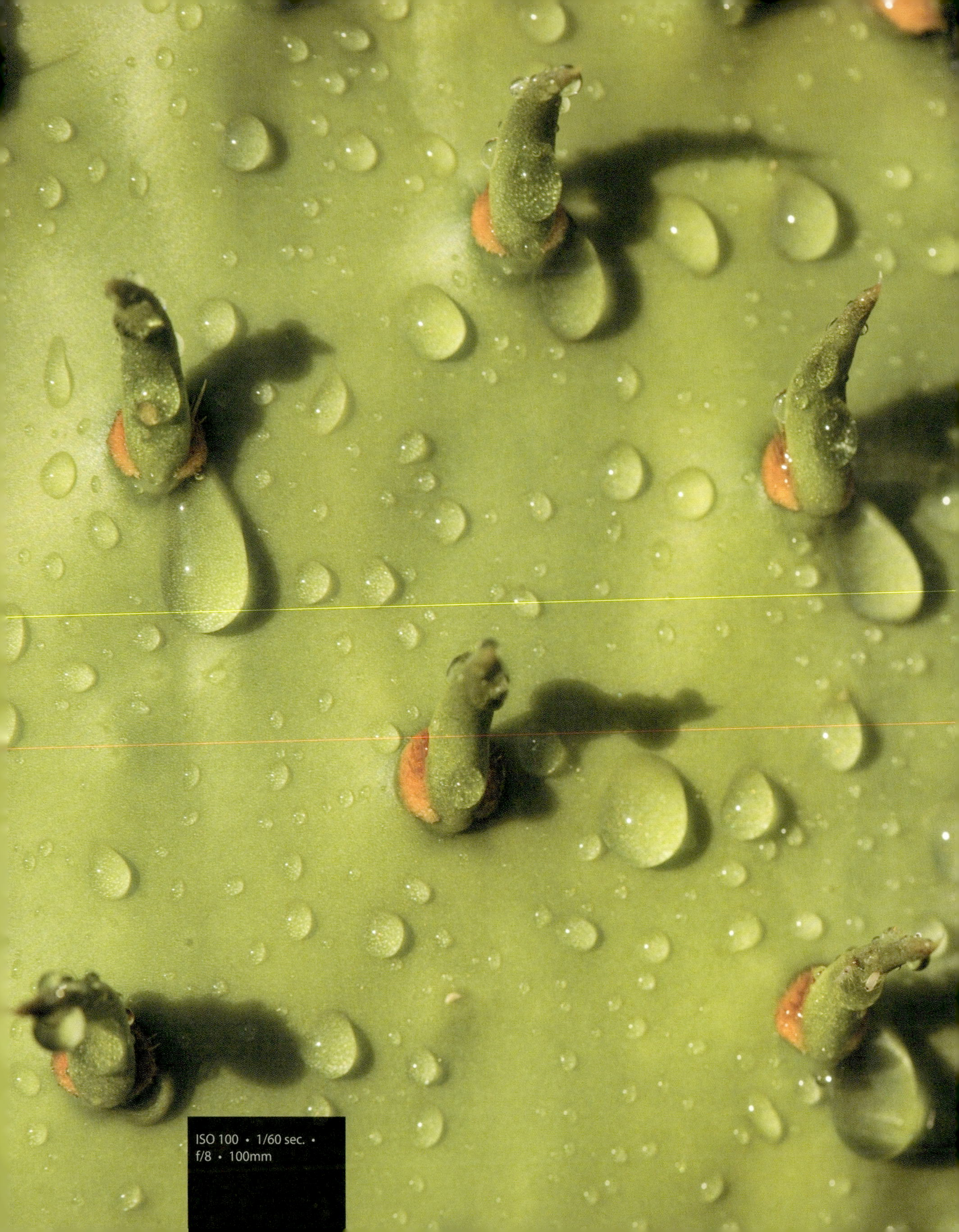

ISO 100 • 1/60 sec. •
f/8 • 100mm

6 Specialty Lenses

Macros and tilt-shifts

I don't often practice macro photography (which requires a lens that is essentially a low-powered microscope), but for two consecutive weeks each year I lead a photography field course in a diverse area of Texas rich in greenery and natural color. During that time, shooting the expanse of flowers is just not enough. I also need to get low and close to my subject matter—so close that a trusty telephoto lens is useless due to its long minimum focusing distance. To get extremely close, I need a dedicated macro lens, designed to have a short minimum focusing distance, allowing me to push close enough in on a flower that I can count the veins in the petals. Every spring, I'm thankful that these lenses are available.

Every lens could be considered a specialty lens. Each has its typical area of use—wide-angles for landscapes, medium telephotos for portraits, super telephotos for wildlife, and so on. However, Canon manufactures some lenses that fit within the previous designations but are also capable of much more. Enter macro and tilt-shift lenses, two different types of lenses with two very different and creative functions.

Poring Over the Picture

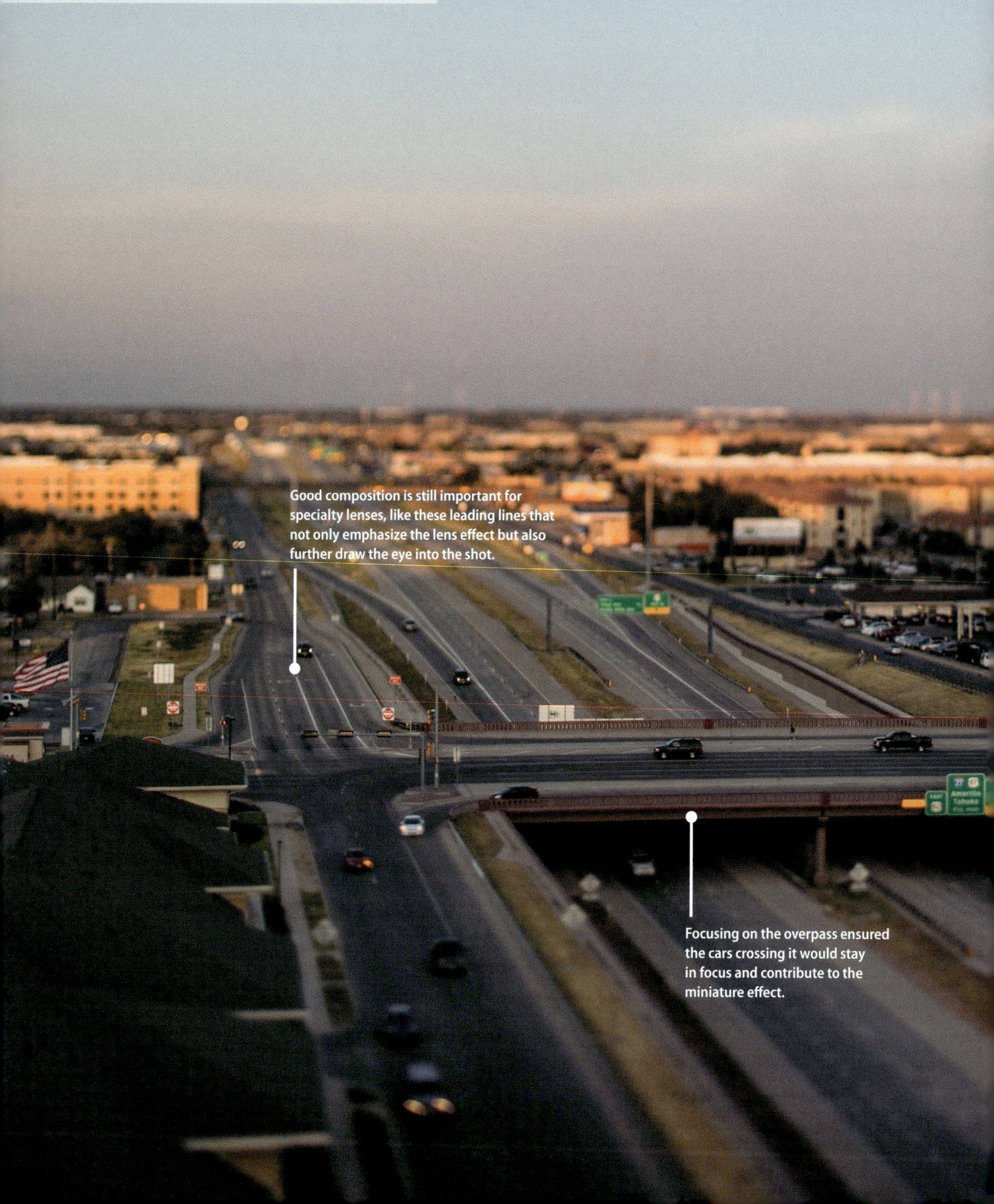

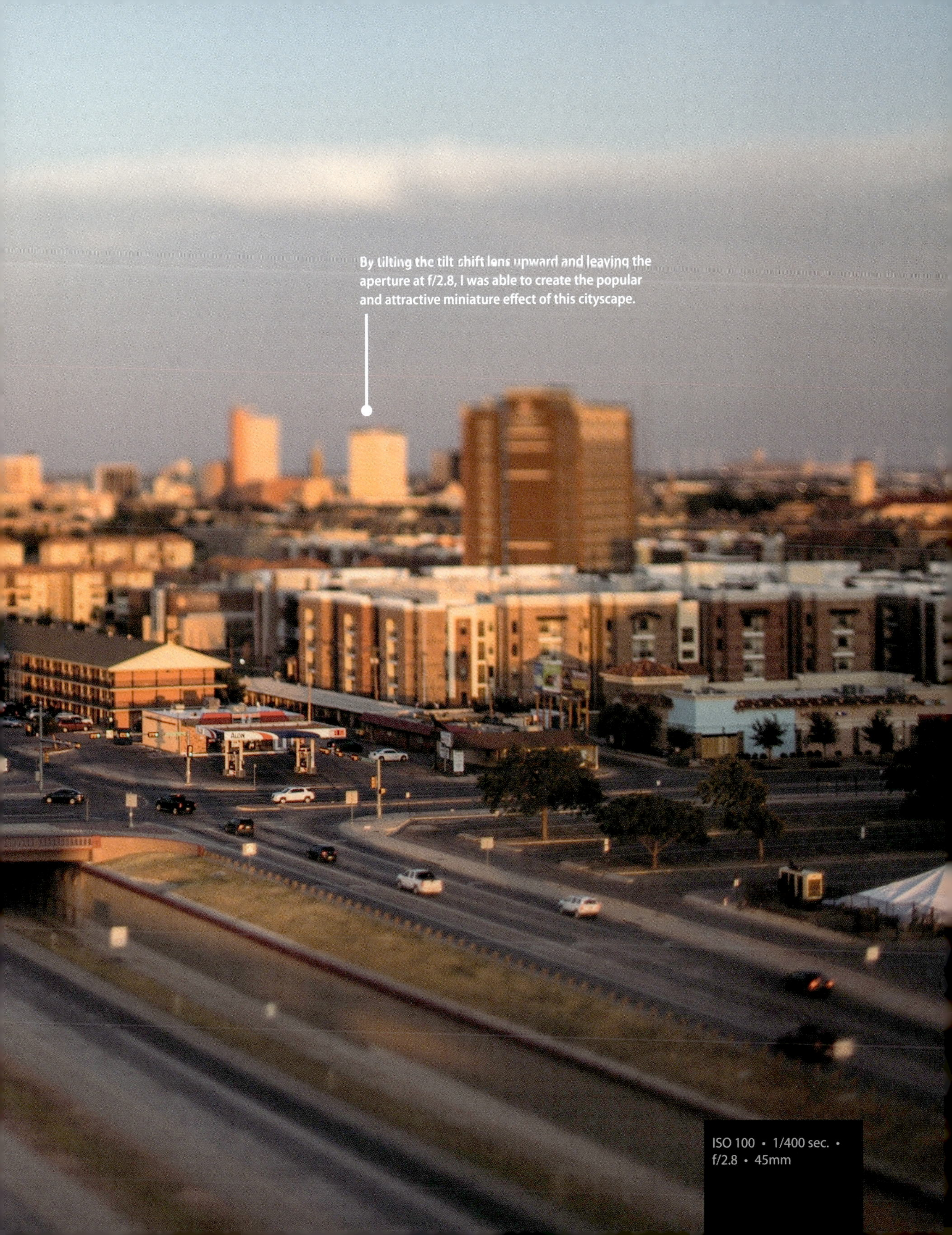

By tilting the tilt shift lens upward and leaving the aperture at f/2.8, I was able to create the popular and attractive miniature effect of this cityscape.

ISO 100 • 1/400 sec. • f/2.8 • 45mm

Macro Lenses

"Macro" is not usually associated with "small." However, in the case of photography, macro lenses are what it takes to shoot the ultimate close-ups. I'm a sucker for great flower photography, and in order to capture the delicate nature of the flower's structure, the minimum focusing distance—the closest one can focus on a subject—of many lenses is simply too long. That's not to say you can't crop an image to make it a closer shot of the subject, but then you sacrifice printability and image real estate. Some folks also use their telephotos to zoom in tight on a subject, but this risks motion blur and a lower level of compositional control. Macro lenses are just the thing to get in close on a subject without sacrificing quality and aesthetics.

The Lineup

Macro lenses are built with short minimum focusing distances for their overall focal length. Canon makes six dedicated macro lenses: the EF 50mm f/2.5 Compact Macro, the EF-S 60mm f/2.8 Macro, the MP-E 65mm f/2.8 1–5x Macro, the EF 100mm f/2.8 Macro, the EF 100mm f/2.8L Macro IS (**Figure 6.1**), and the EF 180mm f/3.5L Macro. The longest lens in the lot, the EF 180mm f/3.5L Macro can focus as close as 1.6 feet away from the subject, with the other lenses able to focus even closer. Don't think that sounds impressive? The closest focusing distance of an EF 70–200mm f/2.8L, a lens that encompasses 180mm, is 4.9 feet.

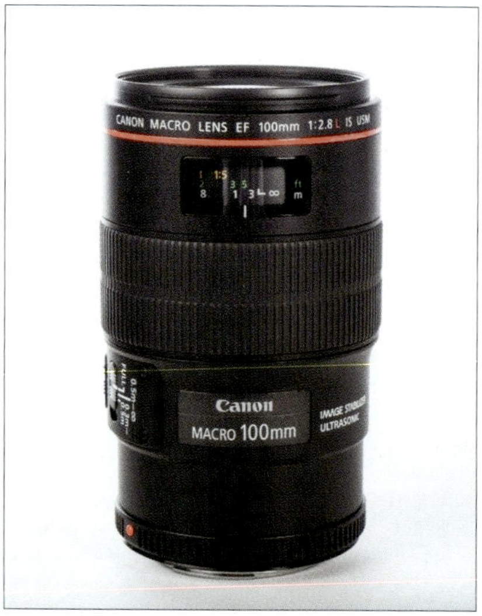

Figure 6.1
My personal favorite macro lens, the EF 100mm f/2.8L Macro IS

Thinking Smaller

The first time you use a macro lens is fun, letting you see a very different, almost magical world our eyes cannot see. However, making nice images with macro lenses can be daunting. In many cases, it forces photographers to explore the frame and its content in a very different way than they would a wider, backed-out shot of a larger context, such as a landscape.

We have to put ourselves into the macro mindset. This means instead of looking at a large area for composition, you look for it in several square inches of space, or less! Macro photography requires a great deal of patience. Folks who consider themselves macro photographers can spend an hour in a spot no larger than a sedan if it is rife with subject matter. Working on a much closer scale amplifies both the subject and the precise technique required (covered later in the chapter). Macro work can often be therapeutic, especially outdoors with the right light.

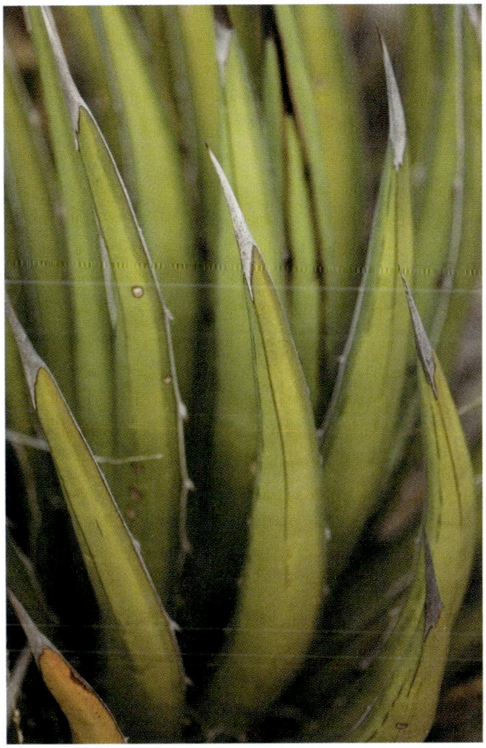

Figure 6.2
Soft front lighting does little to produce dramatic shadows since they are mostly behind the subjects of interest.

ISO 400 • 1/200 sec. • f/4.5 • 180mm

Light

As with other areas of photography, where the lens is pointed in relationship to the direction of light hitting the subject is of great importance. Light from over the shoulder (**Figure 6.2**) is not as dramatic as light coming from the side (**Figure 6.3**) or behind the subject. In fact, front light can sometimes be downright boring for macro work.

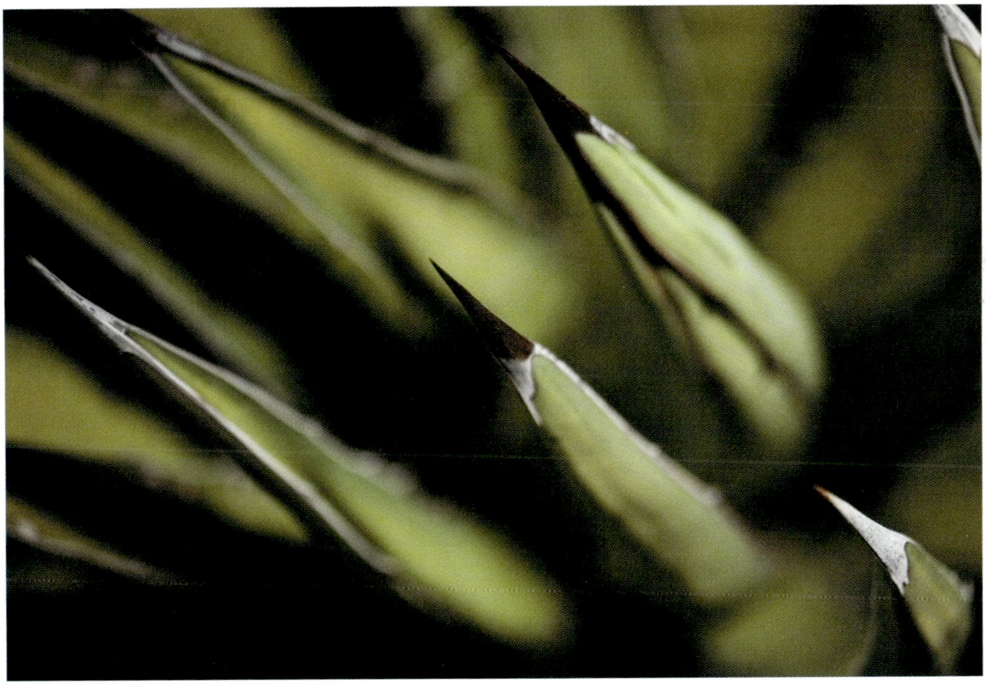

Figure 6.3
Shooting the same subject with artificial light hitting it from slightly off-axis increases the visual intensity of the shot and makes the lechuguilla look more mean.

ISO 50 • 1/2000 sec. • f/3.5 • 180mm

Diffused light is the softest, most relieving type of light for natural subject matter like flowers (**Figure 6.4**). When I'm in a park, my ideal day for photography includes strong, dramatic light in the early morning and late evening, and overcast skies in between. In overcast conditions, sunlight is dispersed in all directions as it exits the clouds toward Earth, dissipating any strong shadows on subjects of interest.

Ultimately, light will react the same way on a smaller scale as it does on a larger one. Working the light in macro photography just means you have to adjust your idea of what large and small lights do for a particular subject. While a relatively large light source, such as a floor-to-ceiling window, may provide soft shadows for a portrait, the same light source used with something much smaller can completely remove shadow.

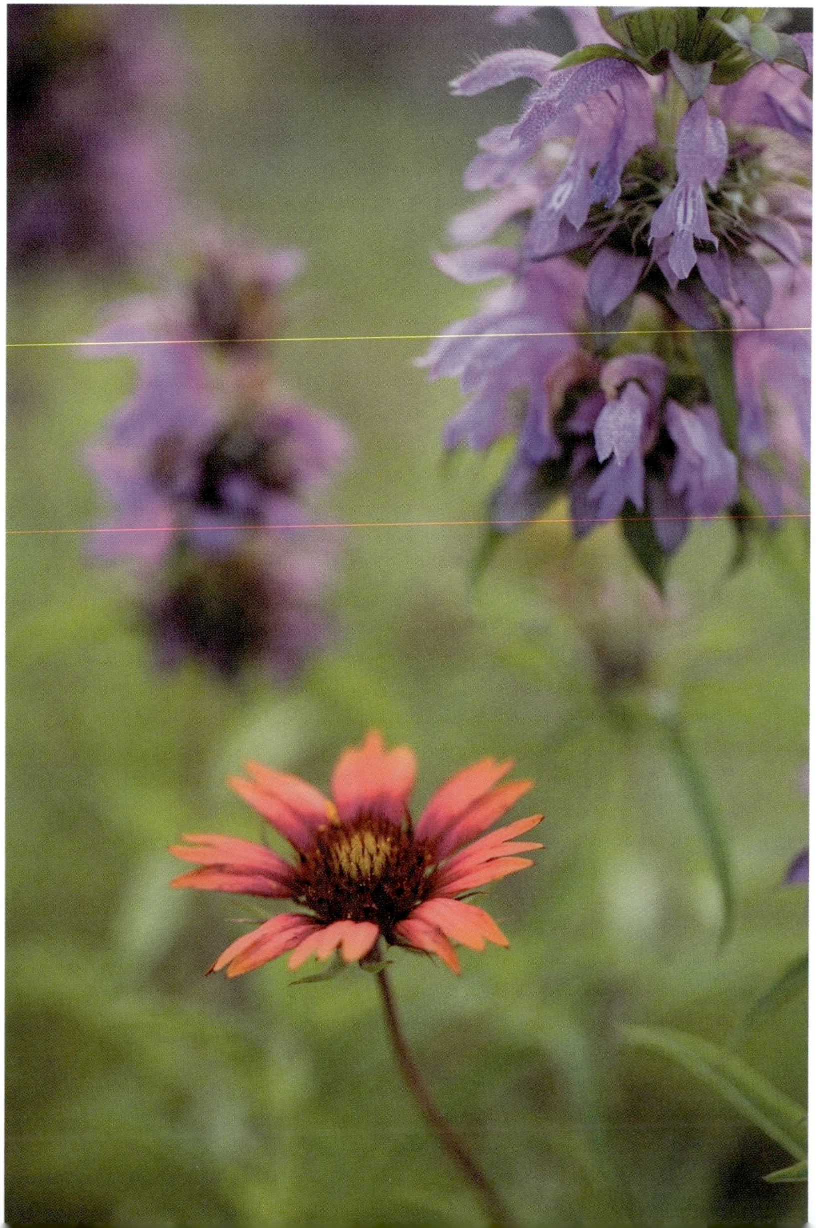

Figure 6.4
Diffused light, like that produced by overcast skies, reveals great color detail.

ISO 100 • 1/125 sec. • f/2.8 • 100mm

Composing with macro lenses

You need patience when composing with macro lenses. You cannot just walk up to a macro subject, quickly compose, and fire off a shot. It takes time and minute adjustments to the placement of the lens in order to find just the right composition. Principles like the rule of thirds still have their value, but macro shots often involve one subject that really stands out, so your composition will revolve around that primary point.

I usually consider design when I'm composing, especially with macro images. Since I shoot quite a bit for magazines, I want shots to engage a viewer with great leading lines (even if they are part of the shot's bokeh), to have visual real estate so the eyes move freely around, and allow for a designer to use that space (**Figure 6.5**). For many of my macro shots, the depth of field is very shallow, and the bokeh is a void space that counterbalances the subject. I want such a space to complement the subject instead of provide another visual attraction (**Figure 6.6**). Taking the time to find this balance of void versus content is valuable. I love close-up shots where the visual direction of the image is pushed primarily by out-of-focus nothingness!

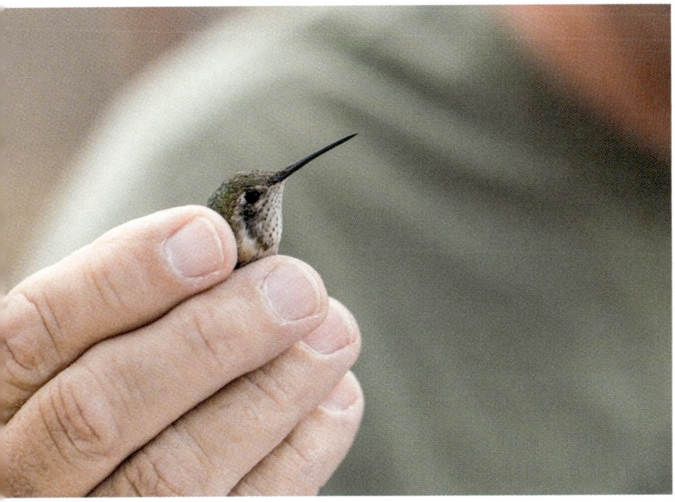

Figure 6.5 (above) Because a large area to the right of the hummingbird is out of focus, a magazine designer can include type for a story about these small flyers.

ISO 100 • 1/320 sec. • f/4 • 100mm

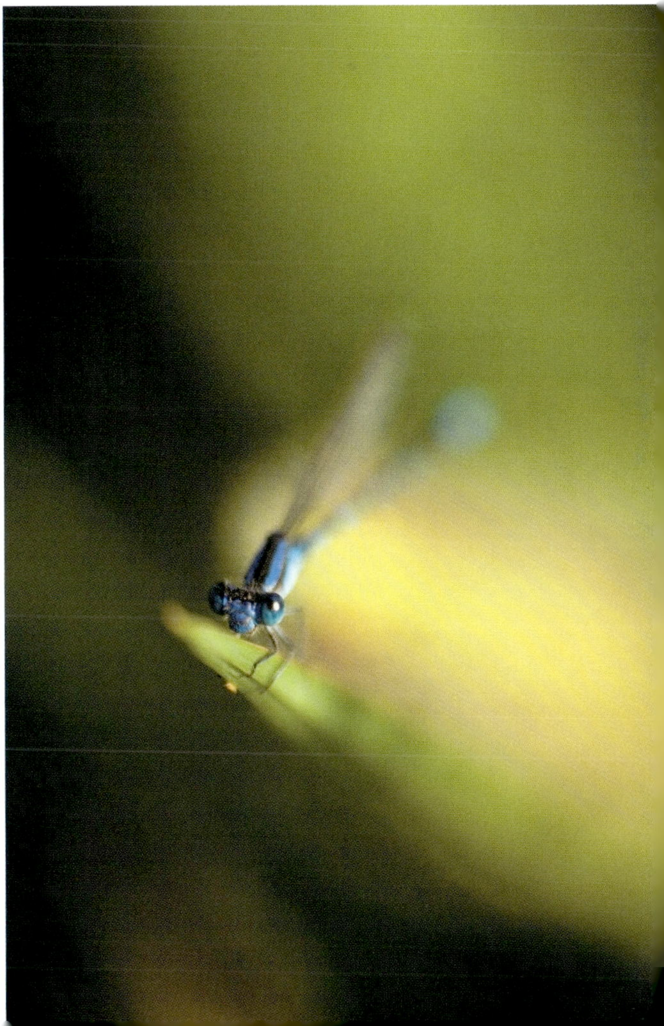

Figure 6.6 (right) There's not much other than the dragonfly's eyes to draw the eye compositionally in this shot of it resting atop a blade of grass.

ISO 200 • 1/320 sec. • f/3.5 • 180mm

Also consider the angle at which the lens is pointed at a subject. My first hundred or so macro shots of flowers were from straight above, splays of colorful petals. I would move in on one flower, throw the background completely out of focus with a large aperture, and shoot. Great, right? For some shots, yes (**Figure 6.7**). There are fantastic ways of composing shots like this, with one flower taking up most of the frame and a couple more reaching into the image.

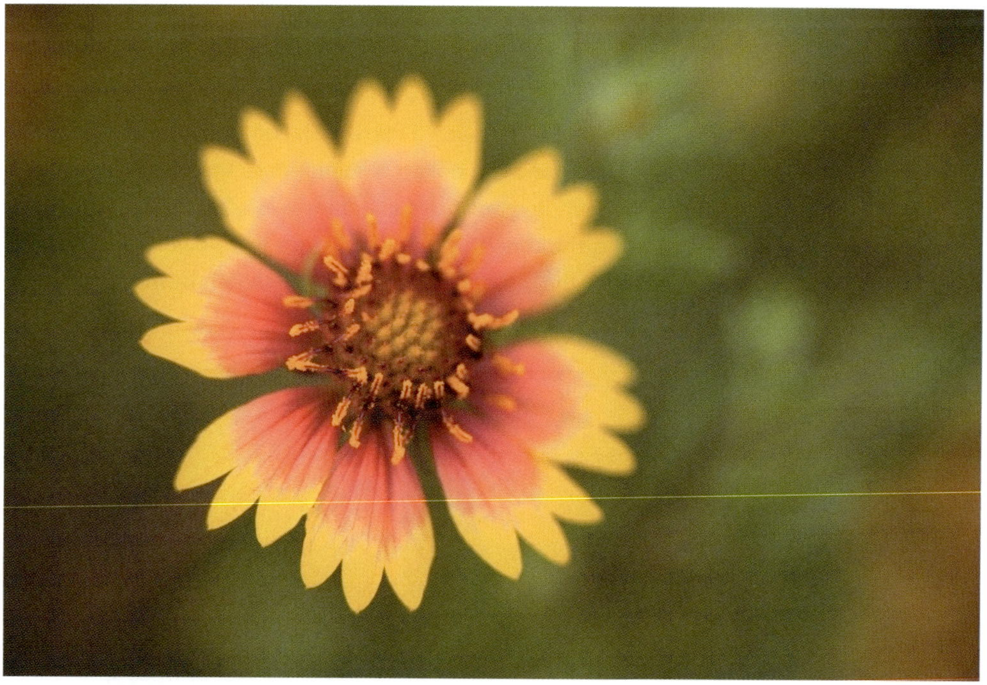

Figure 6.7
Shooting straight down on macro subject matter works, but it can result in a less-than-dynamic visual, such as this flower that seems to be floating on top of a bed of green.
ISO 400 • 1/400 sec. • f/2.8 • 100mm

For other shots, shooting straight down on a subject like this can result in images lacking dimension and personality. One way to resolve this is to simply angle the lens—and in doing so, the plane of critical focus—away from being parallel to the subject. Even if you are shooting with very shallow depth of field, angling the lens just the slightest adds visual depth to macro shots. In fact, a very soft bokeh is sometimes necessary to stress this depth. For flowers, I like to use the stem as a strong leading line to the main subject matter, the petals (**Figure 6.8**). You can only find the flower's stem by angling the lens. The stem will more than likely be out of focus, but it will appear as if it is emerging from far below to bring a colorful gift (**Figure 6.9**).

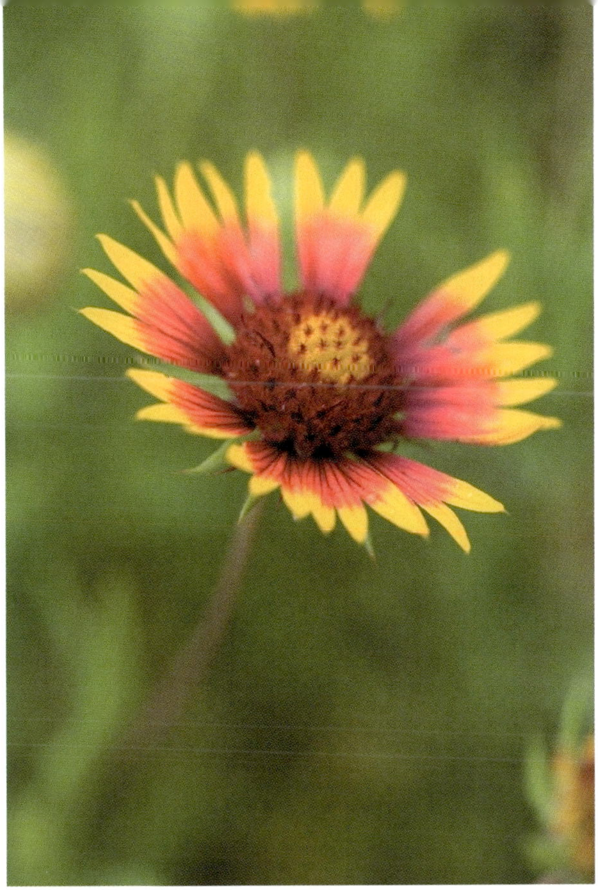

Figure 6.8

Moving the lens to where it is at a more extreme angle to the flower reveals the stem as a leading line to the primary subject.

ISO 200 • 1/160 sec. • f/4 • 100mm

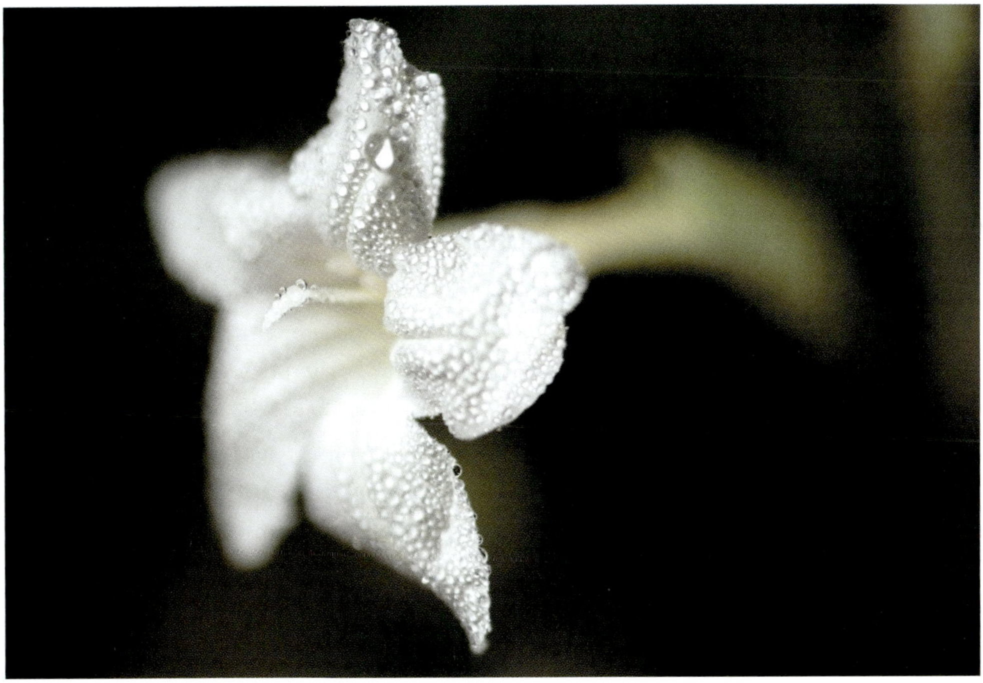

Figure 6.9

Stems and other leading lines do not necessarily need to be in focus for them to draw the eye.

ISO 50 • 1/8000 sec. • f/3.5 • 180mm

Depth of field and shutter speed

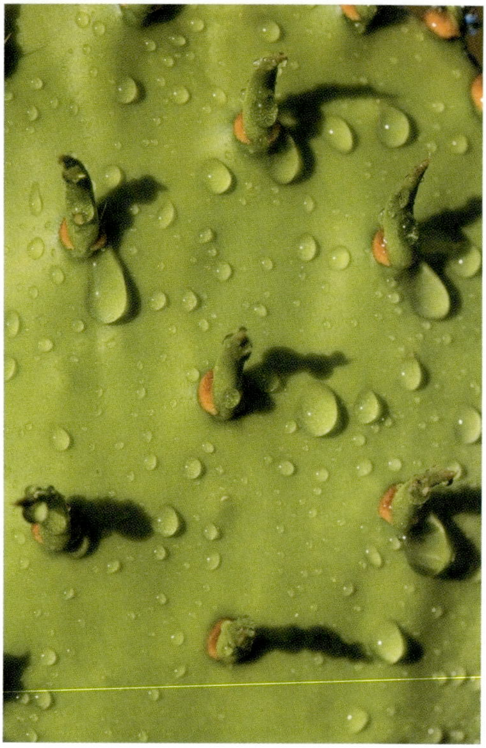

Figure 6.10 **I shot the prickly-pear cactus pad straight on using an aperture of f/8 to ensure the small spines would be in focus as well.**

ISO 100 • 1/60 sec. • f/8 • 100mm

Something you should know about depth of field with macro images: It's a bit more shallow than you think. Relative to the focal length and its macro capability, the selected aperture setting will provide you the proper amount of depth of field, but since the area being photographed is much smaller and the lens is much closer to the subject, the depth of field seems much more shallow than if the shot was a portrait from ten feet away (**Figure 6.10**).

Why is this worth talking about? For one, at extremely shallow depth of field, any movement of the camera and/or subject will knock the image out of focus. Even if the shutter speed is fast enough for both types of movement, the subject can easily be moved away from the focal plane and the shallow depth of field. This is true for all lenses with fast apertures, but it is amplified at macro distances (**Figure 6.11**). If you encounter this issue, consider stopping the aperture down a full stop, or maybe more (**Figure 6.12**). The effect on the soft bokeh behind and in front of the subject will be minimal, and the smallest parts of the subject that were out of focus will become clear with the depth-of-field expansion.

It is also wise to work with a tripod when shooting macro. A tripod might feel like it slows you down, but it will mitigate the amount of movement in your shot. It will also keep you from creating a blurry shot from using too slow a shutter speed. Like super-telephoto lenses, macro lenses—when pushed in extremely close to the subject—are essentially telescopes to handhold steadily on a subject. What might be a fast-enough minimum shutter speed to shoot a portrait will more than likely be too slow for a macro shot. Use a tripod or try to shoot with at least a one-stop-faster shutter speed and save yourself frustration at the computer later. If you're using a tripod, be sure to use a shutter-release cable.

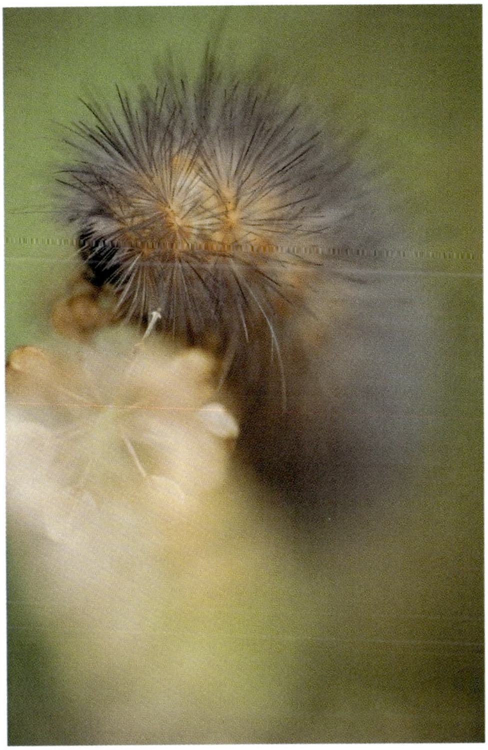 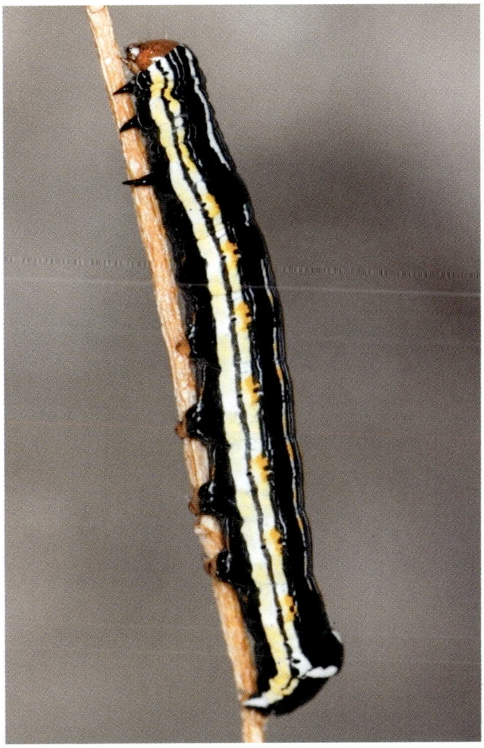

Figure 6.11 (left)
Using a maximum aperture on some macro subjects shot at an angle may not provide the necessary depth of field for strong subject identification.

ISO 200 • 1/60 sec. • f/3.5 • 180mm

Figure 6.12 (right)
Shooting a profile of the caterpillar at f/11 captures the creature mostly in focus.

ISO 100 • 1/200 sec. • f/11 • 180mm

If I Had to Choose: EF 100mm f/2.8L Macro IS

I have used several macro lenses, but the one that takes the cake for me is the EF 100mm f/2.8L Macro IS. Simply put, it is a great focal length for macro work. The lens is sharp as a tack, extremely light for the focal length and maximum aperture, and it has a great Optical Image Stabilization system. Although its construction is mostly plastic, it still has the heft of an L-series lens, yet it is much lighter and more mobile than its big brother, the EF 180mm f/3.5L Macro. It also is one of just two lenses that incorporate Canon's Hybrid Image Stabilization system, which compensates for both shaking the camera parallel to the subject as well as moving the camera at angles from a center axis. It is quite easy to handhold this lens, even when you are shooting close to a subject.

The lens does not include a tripod collar, but you can purchase one. I enjoy using a tripod collar with macro lenses just so the weight of the lens does not shift the image's composition after I let go.

Note that the EF 100mm f/2.8L Macro IS is expensive (albeit much less so than the 180mm), but it's a great value. For someone wanting to get into macro photography while also wanting a versatile lens (also great for portraits), this is the one I recommend.

Tilt-Shift Lenses

Most people will never use a tilt-shift lens, not even most professional photographers. Why? For one, they just look complicated (**Figure 6.13**), what with all the knobs and the strange-looking barrel construction. Two, they *are* kind of complicated—at least at first. There's a learned technical and creative approach to using them. Three, they are very specialized. Sure, you can use any of Canon's four tilt-shifts as prime lenses, but you don't buy or rent them for that. Most people use tilt-shifts for perspective control, and in doing so, create a unique look in their images (some smartphone apps mimic this look in their presets). The fourth reason: They're pricey. Even the non-L-series lenses run over US$1,000 brand new.

Why even have a section on these lenses when the majority of this book's readers may never use them? This type of lens serves a purpose for a number of us, and offers a creative outlet for others. Traditional landscape, commercial architecture, food, and portrait photographers use tilt-shifts in many ways. And the lenses are easy to rent (this is what I do).

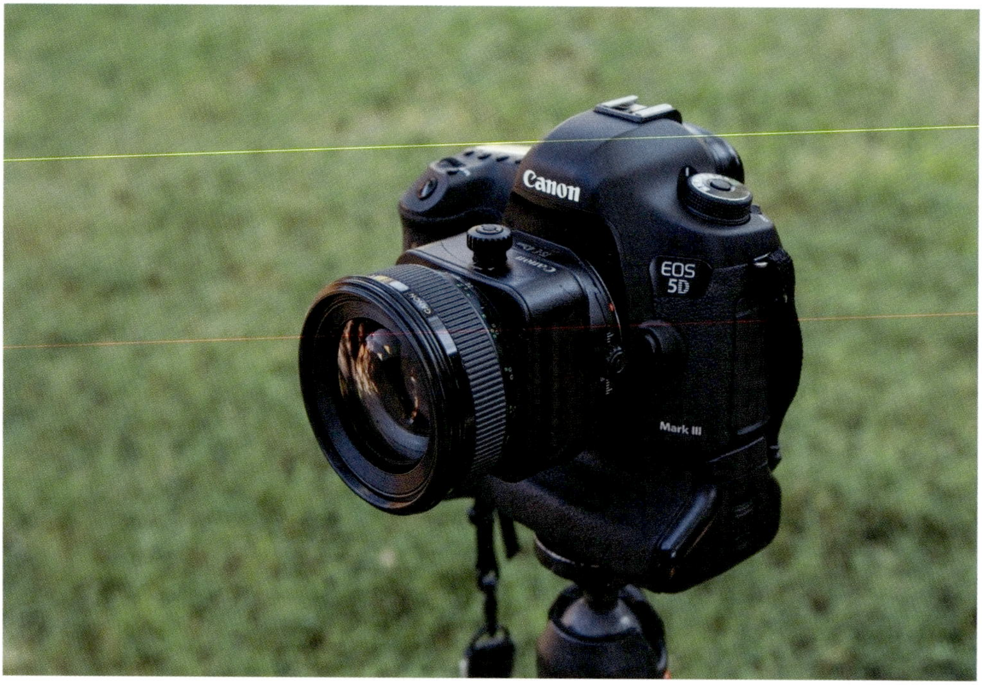

Figure 6.13
It is easy to avoid or be intimidated by tilt-shift lenses, like this TS-E 45mm f/2.8, with its strange knobs and absence of autofocus!

How Tilt-Shift Lenses Work

All four Canon tilt-shift lenses—the TS-E 17mm f/4L, the TS-E 24mm f/3.5L, the TS-E 45mm f/2.8, and the TS-E 90mm f/2.8—are about control over perspective and depth. They are constructed in a way that the user can manipulate not only a lens's focus but also the angle of the focal plane and the position of the lens's optics parallel to the camera's sensor. Sound confusing yet? Let's break down the lens's technological capabilities.

Shift

The Shift function of the lens allows the user to move the optics of the lens up/down or left/right while keeping them parallel to the camera's sensor. When you turn the Shift knob, marked by an S (**Figure 6.14**), you will notice the bulk of the lens move, or shift, parallel to the camera itself. Shifting vertically (up or down) is a great way to correct for optical distortion, particularly the wide-angle variety (**Figures 6.15** and **6.16**).

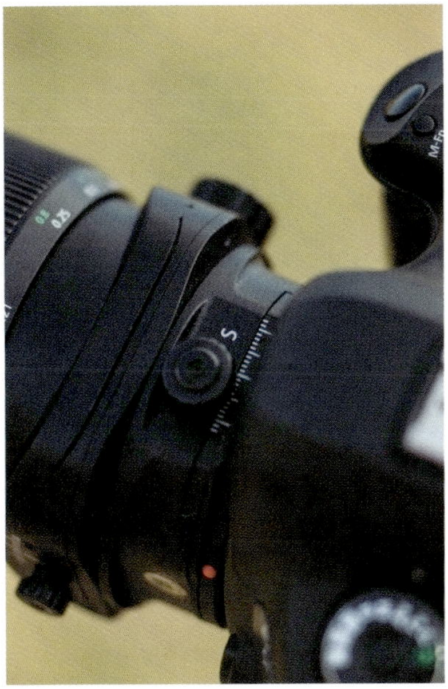

Figure 6.14
The Shift function offers maneuverability to correct for optical distortion, usually made more dramatic by wide-angle focal lengths.

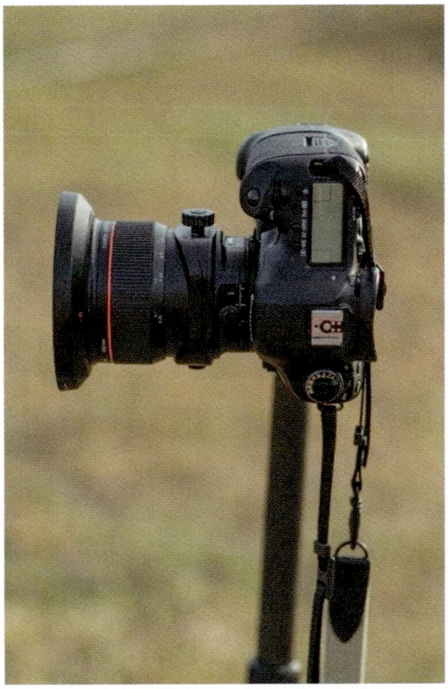

Figure 6.15
An unshifted TS-E 24mm f/3.5L set to shoot vertically on a tall subject.

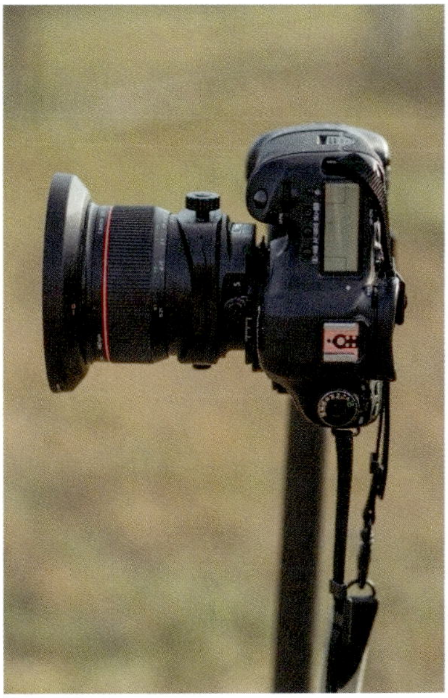

Figure 6.16
Shifting a tilt-shift lens moves the entire lens up/down (or right/left) parallel to the camera's sensor.

Keystoning, an issue we discussed in Chapter 3, can be corrected using the Shift function (**Figures 6.17** and **6.18**). For example, when you have to point a wide focal length (let's say 24mm) upward to photograph something very tall, like a building, the vertical lines of everything in the shot begin to converge toward the middle of the frame. Keystoning might be tolerated in many areas of photography, but in commercial or architectural photography, it is a faux pas. Enter the tilt-shift lens.

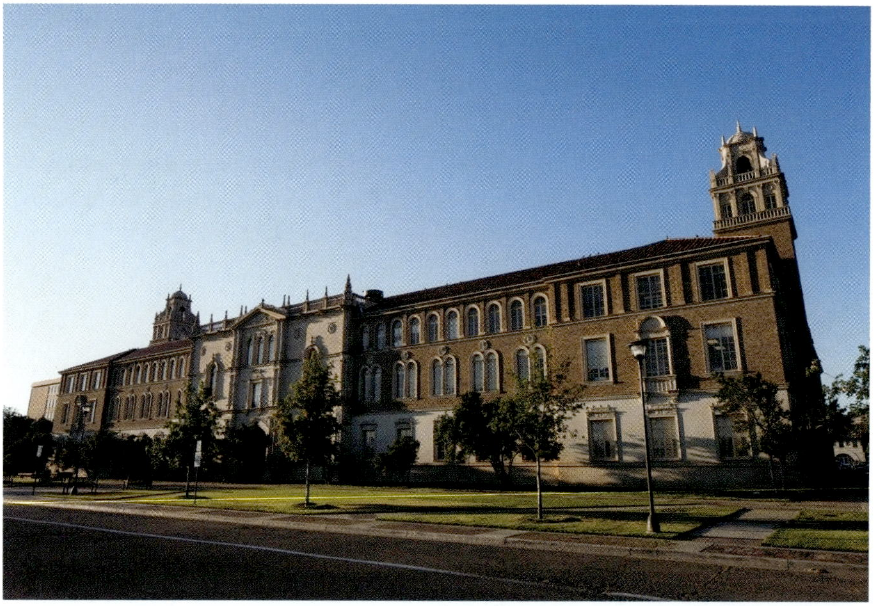

Figure 6.17
Shooting upward on a building at 24mm will result in dramatic keystoning, where the vertical lines of the subject angle inward toward an optical center. For many photographers, this is an issue worth fixing.

ISO 100 • 1/100 sec. • f/11 • 24mm

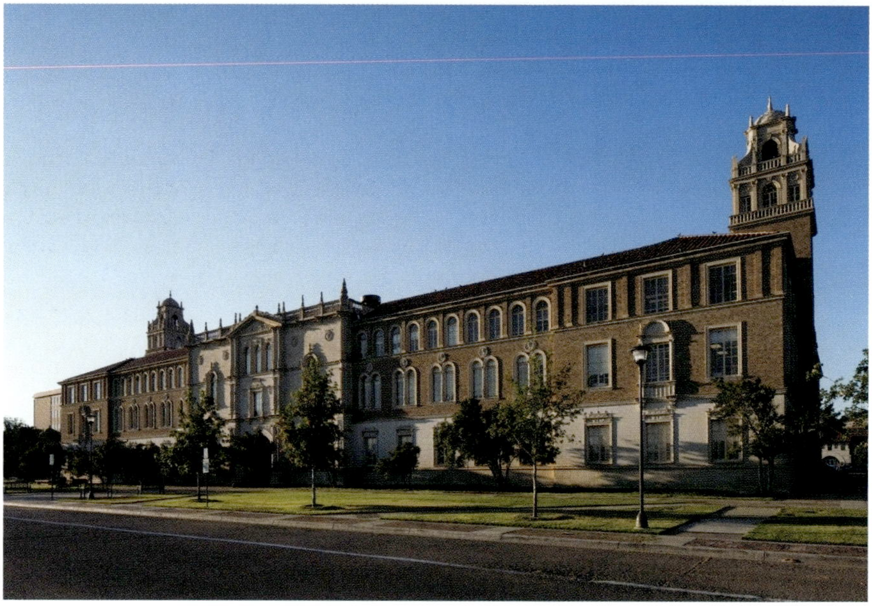

Figure 6.18
Simply shifting the lens up after leveling the camera to the subject straightens out the walls of the building and corrects the distortion.

ISO 100 • 1/100 sec. • f/11 • 24mm

To correct for keystoning (**Figure 6.19**), place the lens on a tripod (tripods work well for these types of lenses) and with the subject of interest composed where you want it, level your camera out. Level it vertically and horizontally. What happened? More than likely, the horizon is in the middle of the frame, and the building's top is cut off (**Figure 6.20**). Not to worry. Using the Shift knob, shift the lens up vertically until the top of the building is where you want it in the frame (**Figure 6.21**). Turn on your camera's Live View to help you see this in action. As a result of shifting the perspective of the lens's optics, you are able to keep vertical lines straight while still working at wide (and all) angles. Likewise, you can also operate this lens vertically by the simple flick of a small locking switch near the lens mount, on the right side of a tilt-shift lens.

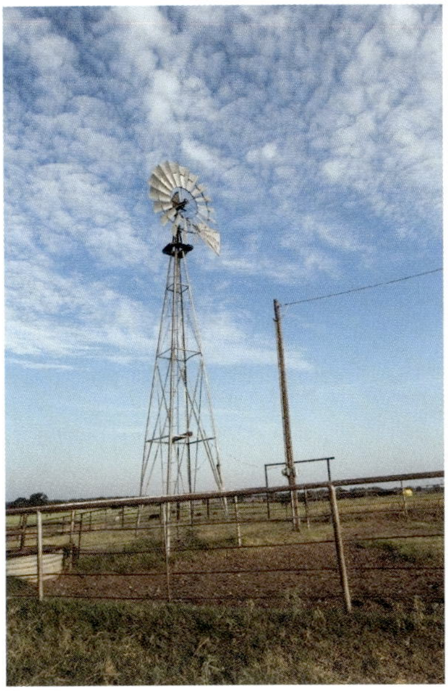

Figure 6.19 Keystoning appears in all vertical lines in the frame, even the structure of the windmill itself.

ISO 100 • 1/400 sec. • f/8 • 24mm

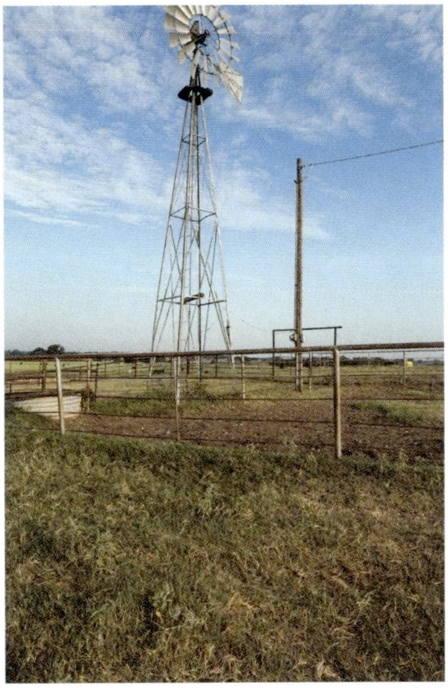

Figure 6.20 The first step in correcting keystoning with a tilt-shift lens is to level the camera to the point that all vertical lines are parallel with the vertical sides of the image frame.

ISO 100 • 1/400 sec. • f/8 • 24mm

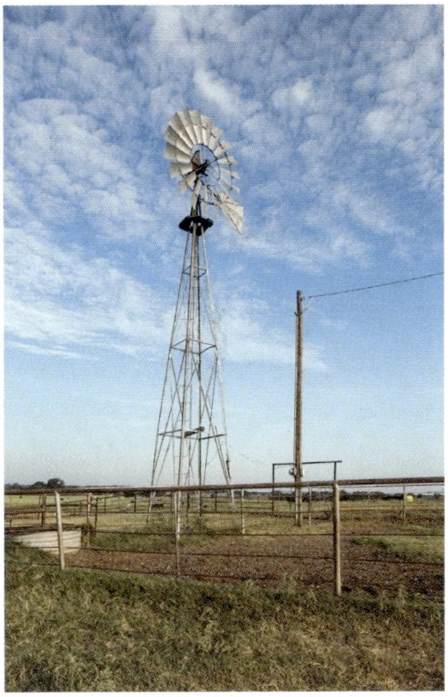

Figure 6.21 After you level the camera, a simple shift up will lower the horizon and bring the subject completely in the frame as well as maintain the straight vertical lines.

ISO 100 • 1/400 sec. • f/8 • 24mm

Tilt

The Tilt function of the lens lets the user take control over the focal plane. Normally, the focal plane is parallel to the camera's sensor, just like the lens's optics. The Tilt mechanism allows the user to swing the focal plane, on a horizontal or vertical axis, away from being parallel.

This function can be used to obtain extreme depth of field in cases where f/22 is not enough or when such a small aperture slows the shutter down too much. When you tilt the lens downward—using the knob marked T (**Figure 6.22**)—the focal plane, and the subsequent depth of field, are laid over the frame instead of moving into the frame (**Figures 6.23** and **6.24**). This means that the infinite theoretical plane that makes up the plane of critical focus can now be simply placed on top of the content in the shot, and you can use a larger aperture to obtain maximum depth of field. This is more complicated than shifting a lens, but the technique is now easier than ever with digital cameras. Turn on Live View again to aid in seeing what happens when you tilt the lens down or up and then stop the aperture open or down. To obtain maximum depth of field after tilting the lens on the subject, start with a middle aperture, maybe around f/8. Theoretically, with the focal plane tilted onto the subject, a middle aperture value will provide you enough depth of field to ensure everything is in focus. If you do not see it as so, stop down the aperture more and/or tilt the lens onto the subject more.

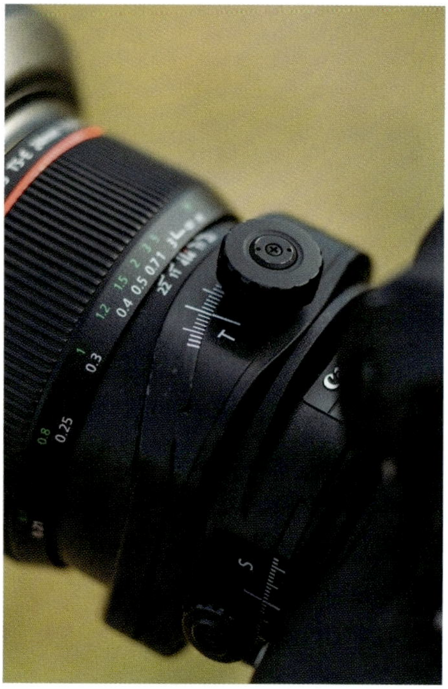

Figure 6.22 **The Tilt function of tilt-shift lenses allows the user to swing the focal plane horizontally or vertically, making for some interesting manipulations of an image.**

If I Had to Choose: TS-E 45mm f/2.8

I don't own any tilt-shift lenses simply because I don't use them enough to justify the expense (I rent instead), but if I were to go out and buy one today, it would be the TS-E 45mm f/2.8.

The TS-E 45mm f/2.8 is sharp, built like a tank but fairly lightweight for a tilt-shift, and it is versatile. It is a great lens for architecture as well as a nice lens for shooting panoramas and portraits. Even though it is not considered an L-series lens, it is a well-built piece of gear, and the f/2.8 maximum aperture works well for night photography and handheld shots. It also doubles as a prime lens that is close to sporting normal perspective. The lens is great for just about any type of photography (bearing in mind that the lens requires manual focus). If I photographed food more often, I might consider the TS-E 90mm f/2.8, but my money is on the TS-E 45mm f/2.8 for the broad spectrum to which it applies.

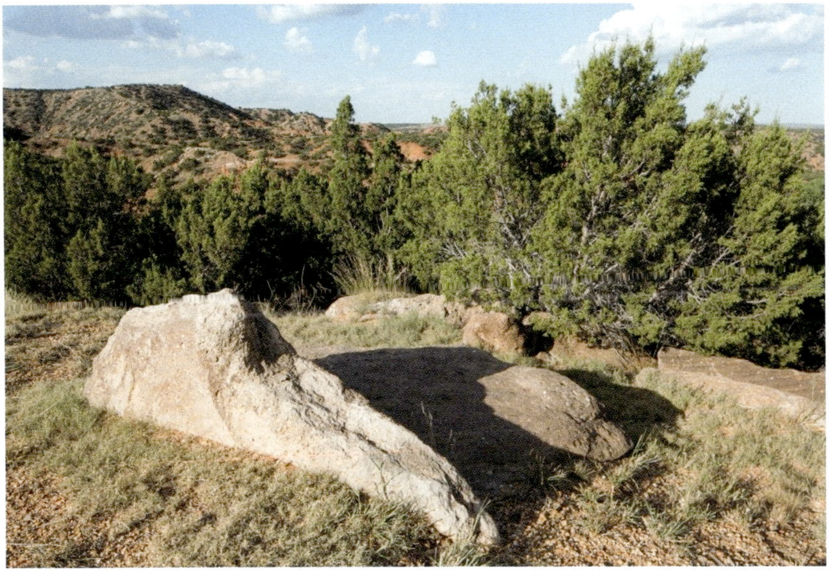

Figure 6.23

At f/11 and with the plane of critical focus placed on the top of the rock in the foreground, there is not enough depth of field to pull the hillside into focus.

ISO 100 • 1/100 sec. • f/11 • 24mm

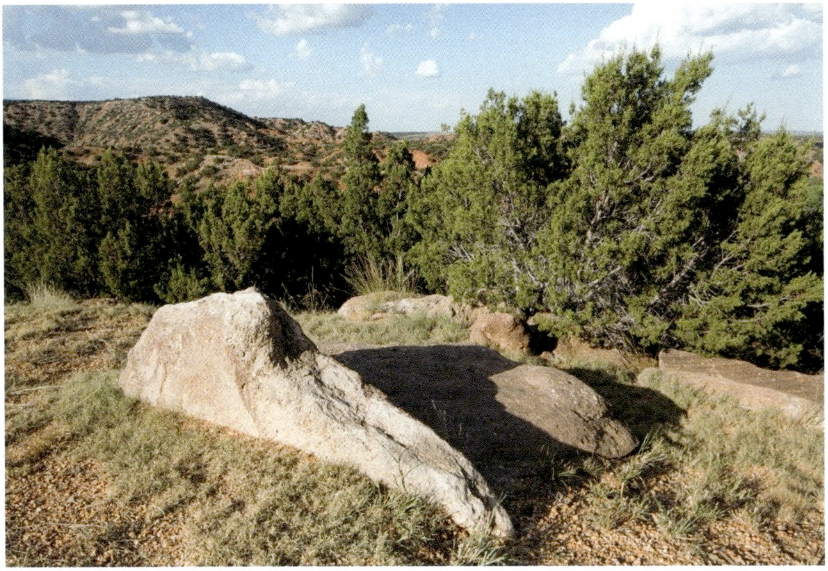

Figure 6.24

When you tilt the focal plane downward ever so slightly, f/11 pulls everything into focus, from foreground to background.

ISO 100 • 1/100 sec. • f/11 • 24mm

You can use the Tilt function to maximize focus into an area of the frame without adding depth of field. This works especially well when you are photographing a row of similar objects that are not parallel to the camera. Leaving the aperture fairly open and the lens untilted, depth of field falls off just like it normally would with any lens (**Figures 6.25** and **6.26**). However, you can tilt the focal plane horizontally (or vertically, depending on your original orientation) to where it lines up with the row of subjects. The result is a row of subject matter that is in focus but with areas outside the row blurred (**Figures 6.27** and **6.28**). This is a popular technique for commercial-product photographers.

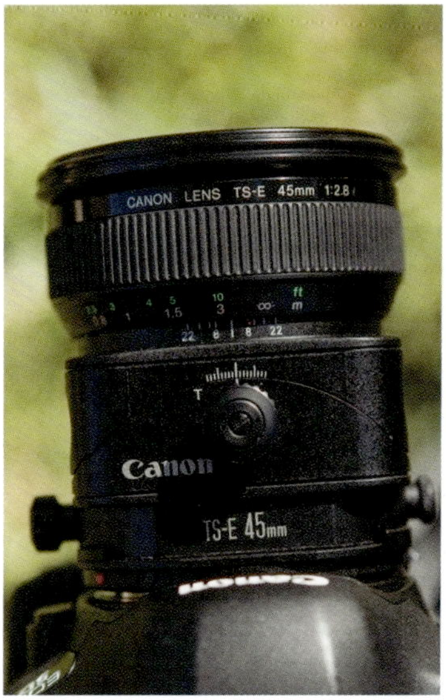

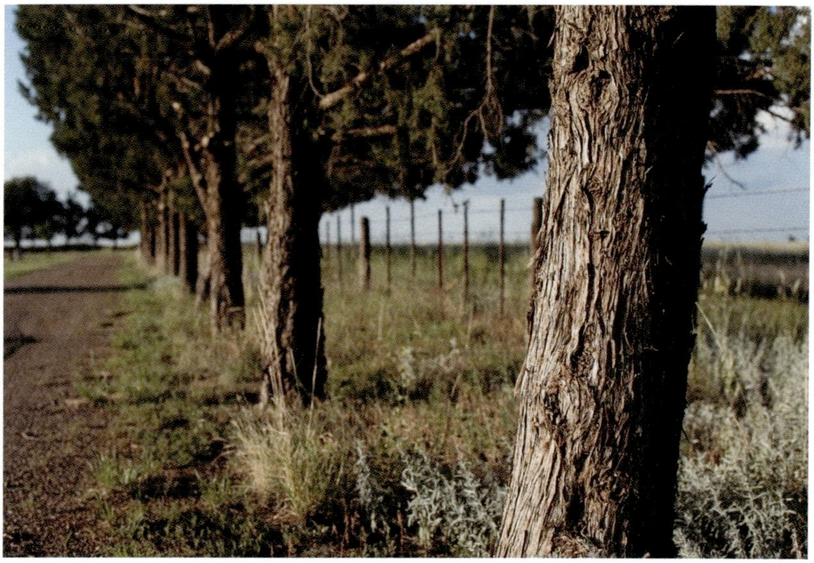

Figure 6.25 Left "zeroed" out, a tilt-shift lens, such as this TS-E 45mm f/2.8, will act just like any prime lens.

Figure 6.26 The depth-of-field drop-off is the result of the focal plane being parallel to the camera's sensor; the out-of-focus area starts directly after the tree on which the focus is placed.

ISO 100 • 1/800 sec. • f/4 • 45mm

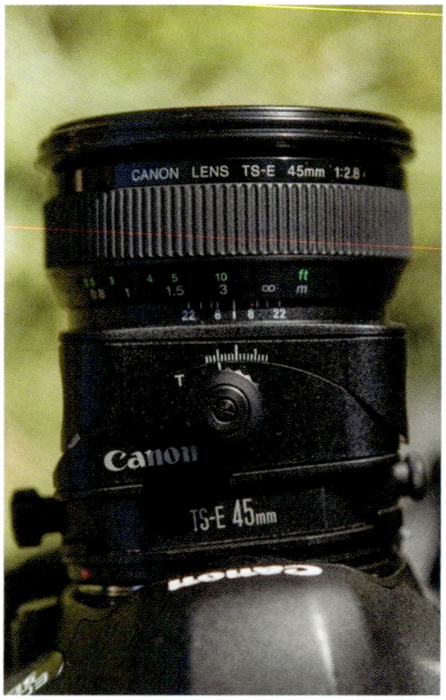

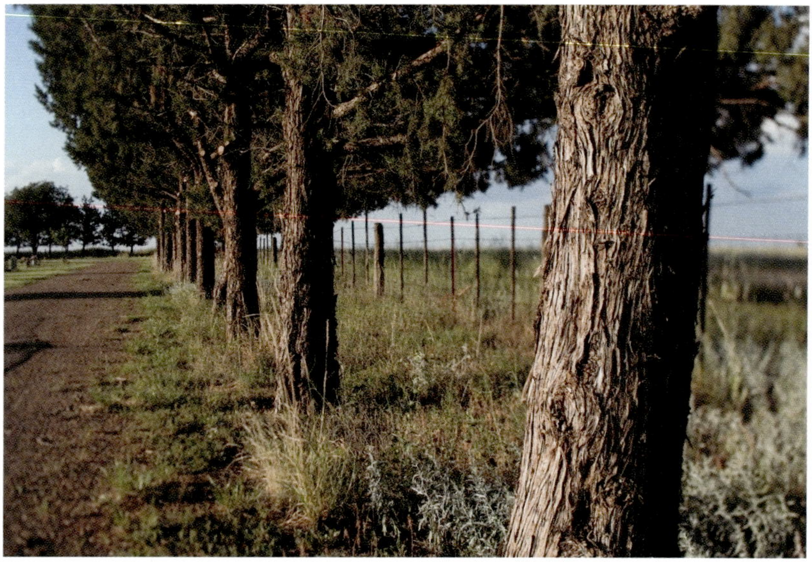

Figure 6.27 Tilting the lens swings the focal plane so it is diagonal to the camera's sensor.

Figure 6.28 The lens is tilted enough to place the focal plane along the row of trees, but the fairly open aperture keeps the depth of field that extends from that plane to a minimum.

ISO 100 • 1/800 sec. • f/4 • 45mm

Tilt-Shift Creative Applications

Tilt-shift lenses offer similar capabilities to those of old view cameras (still used by some photographers). The accordion-like construction of view cameras lets the user shift and tilt the optics at the front of the camera easily. This not only enables you to control perspective and optical issues, but it also allows for quite a bit of creative flexibility. With modern-day tilt-shift lenses, these creative applications are put into practice with the Tilt function.

The miniature effect

Probably the most popular tilt-shift look in the past decade, the miniature effect has done quite a bit to bring tilt-shift lenses into the mainstream (**Figure 6.29**). Simply put, tilt-shift lenses can be used to make an otherwise normal-looking world seem as though it was a toy. This is a fun and interesting way to showcase an environment as well as a unique way to grab the viewer's eyes.

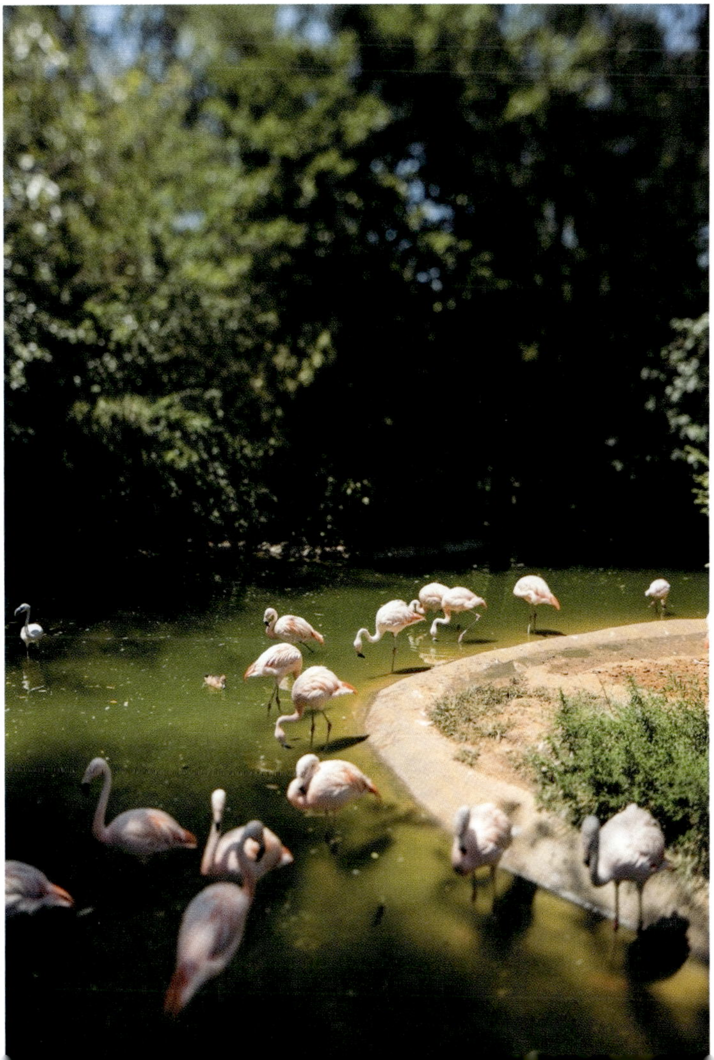

Figure 6.29
Tilting a tilt-shift lens upward while using shallow depth of field can quickly create a miniature effect. The effect is exaggerated when there are many similar subjects within the frame.

ISO 100 • 1/640 sec. • f/3.5 • 24mm

Invoking the miniature effect is quite simple. Find a worthy looking land- or cityscape, and find a place where you can position yourself a bit higher than ground level. A bridge, hill, or ladder will work. Once you are in position, you can choose to shoot vertically or horizontally (**Figure 6.30**).

Get the miniature effect in three steps: (1) Point the lens down while composing the shot. (2) Tilt the lens upward, away from the relative position of the subject matter in your shot. (3) Use a large aperture, such as f/2.8 or f/4. As a result, the only thing(s) in focus will be content through which the focal plane passes, and everything below and above the plane will go out of focus (**Figure 6.31**). This special tilt of the optics is synonymous with the miniature effect. Remember, though, that if you increase the aperture too much, you will quickly increase depth of field. The miniature effect relies on shallow depth of field. Use cars, planes, and other modes of transportation (or people) in your shot to help convey the toy look.

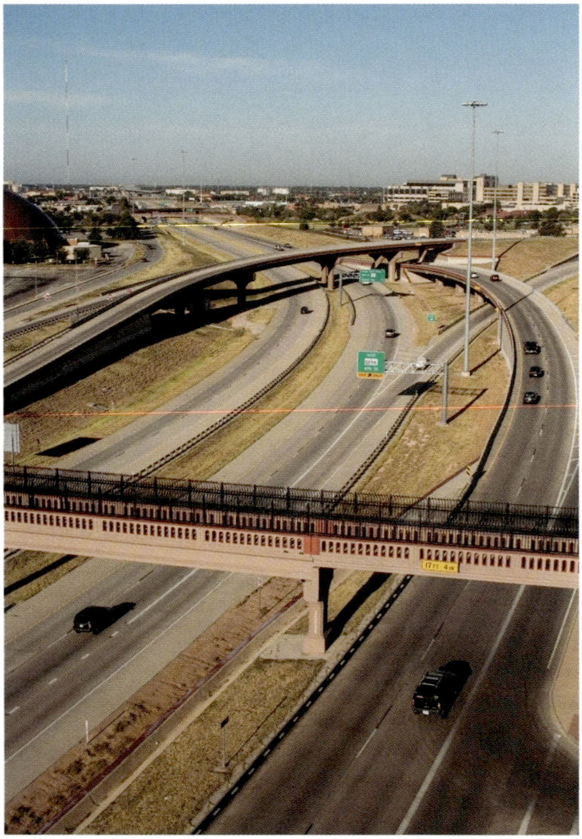

Figure 6.30 **An untilted (normal) look down a freeway.**

ISO 100 • 1/2000 sec. • f/3.5 • 45mm

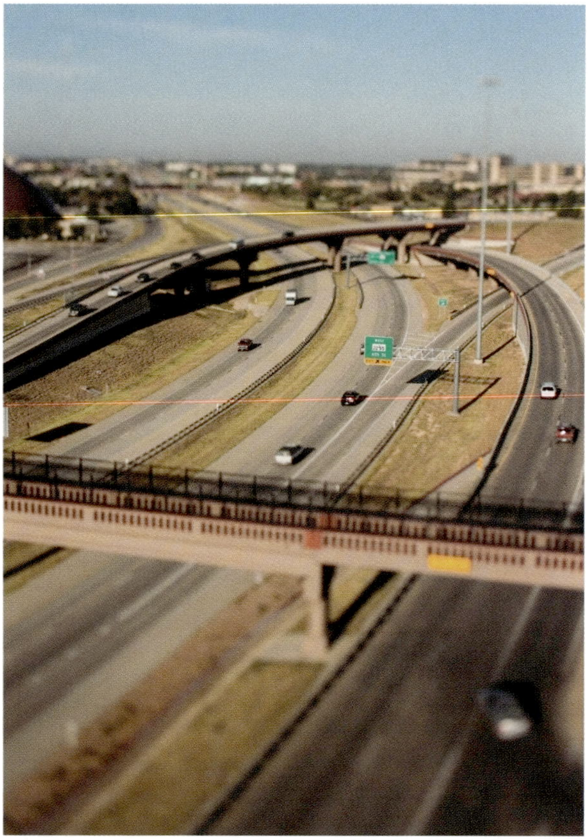

Figure 6.31 **The same freeway with the lens tilted upward and set to f/2.8. Increase the miniature effect by photographing from an elevated position, such as this nine story parking garage.**

ISO 100 • 1/2000 sec. • f/2.8 • 45mm

The miniature effect is based on a vertical tilting of the lens. However, nothing is stopping you from tilting the lens horizontally. Simply use the lock near the lens mount to rotate the lens on the camera, and your tilting capabilities move horizontally. Although tilting the lens horizontally, even with a shallow depth of field, does not result in a miniature effect, it creates a great way to showcase important subject matter (**Figure 6.32**).

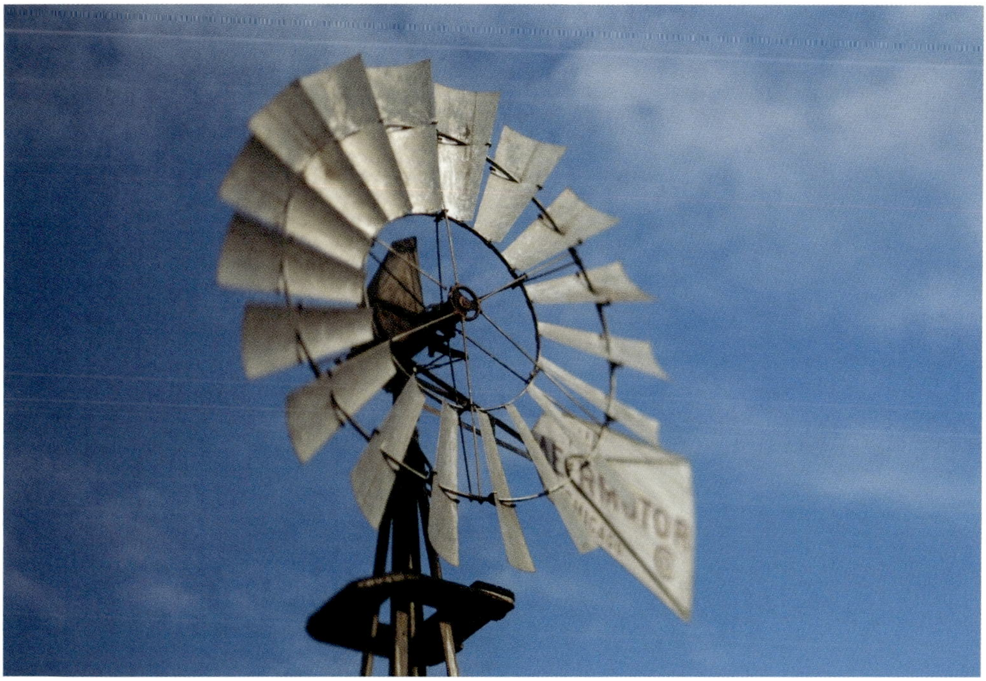

Figure 6.32
Tilting the lens horizontally results in a creative, view-camera-type look.

ISO 100 • 1/1600 sec. • f/2.8 • 90mm

Portraits

We are all drawn to portraits with a soft background and foreground and tack-sharp focus on the subject. But what if you wanted the background and foreground out of focus as well as everything else except the subject's head? No worries. You can do that with a simple tilt of the lens and some precise focusing.

Creating unique portraits with the Tilt function is similar to creating the miniature effect, except you do not need to be above your subject. For example, this portrait of my brother, Seth, was shot from slightly under him (he is much taller than me) with the lens tilted all the way to the left (**Figure 6.33**). I set the aperture at f/2.8. Be aware that using the maximum aperture for portraits may result in a harder time focusing on the subject's eyes or face. The effect you are going for is possible using a stop or two down from maximum. You can also rotate the lens (using the aforementioned lock switch) on 30-degree angles to create even more focusing possibilities for your portraits (**Figure 6.34**).

Figure 6.33

With the focus on the subject's left (camera-right) eye, a tilted portrait offers another creative perspective.

ISO 100 • 1/1250 sec. • f/2.8 • 45mm

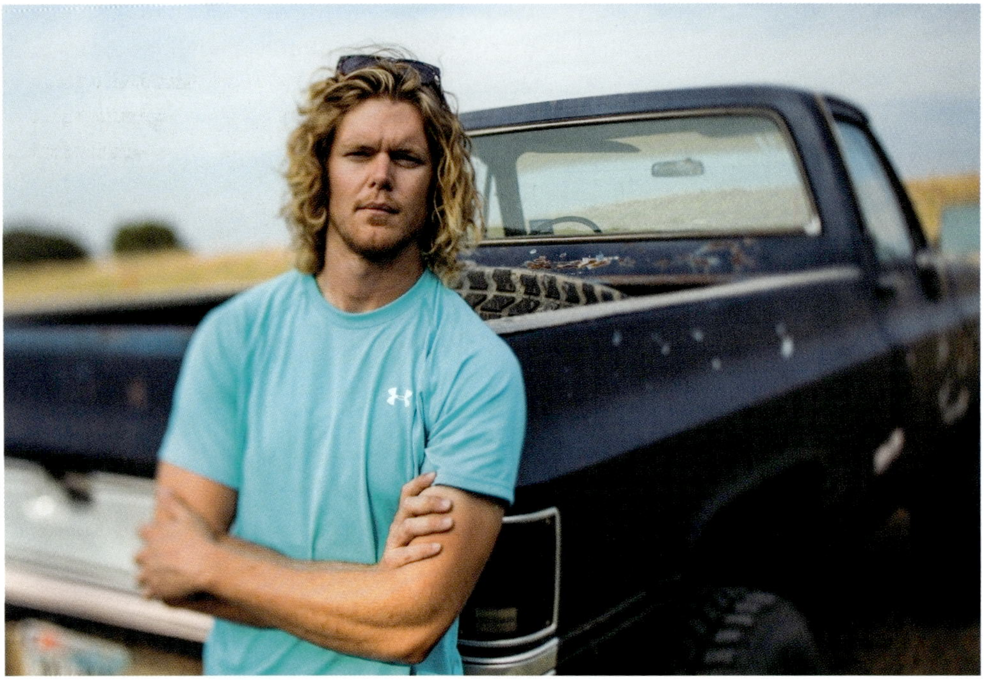

Figure 6.34

Whether horizontal or vertical, portraits made with tilt-shift lenses can be fun to make. It's easier to keep both eyes in focus if the tilt is vertical.

ISO 400 • 1/200 sec. • f/2.8 • 90mm

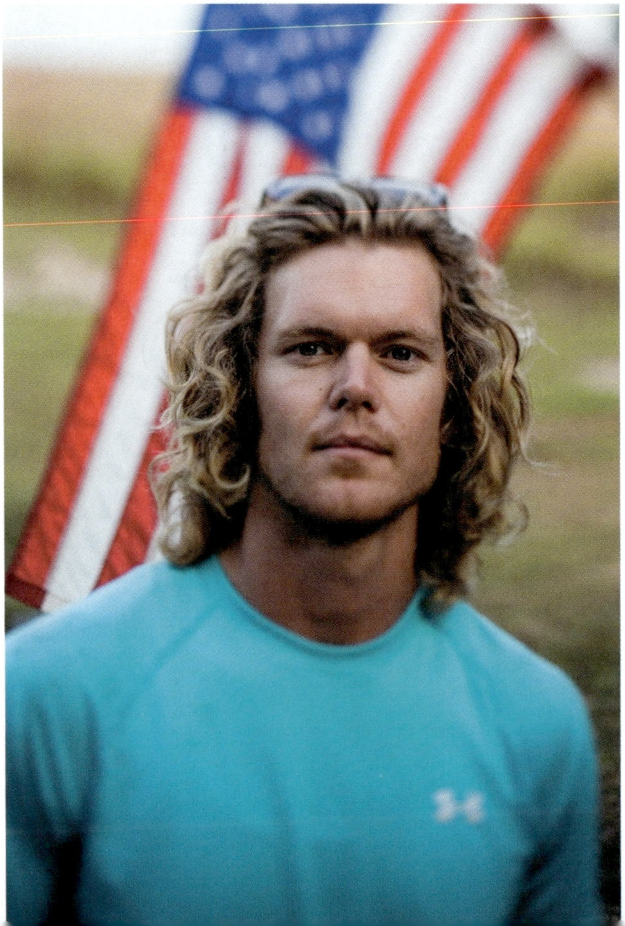

Panoramas

Tilt-shift lenses are also great for creating images that stitch together in a panorama. The first, and probably the easiest, way to shoot a panoramic image with a tilt-shift is to simply shoot multiple images along a Shift range. You need to set up the camera on a tripod the same way you would when correcting distortion: Level it out so the horizon is in the middle and the vertical lines are straight up and down. Now, with the Shift knob, shift the lens along its horizontal range (you can also do this vertically), shooting an overlapping image at each full mark highlighted on the lens. You will create five images that can then be stitched together in post with software such as Adobe Photoshop (**Figure 6.35**). This technique can be used with any of the tilt-shift lenses available, even the wide-angles. The optical distortion of such lenses is corrected before the shooting begins, so there is no need to worry about the wide angle being an issue.

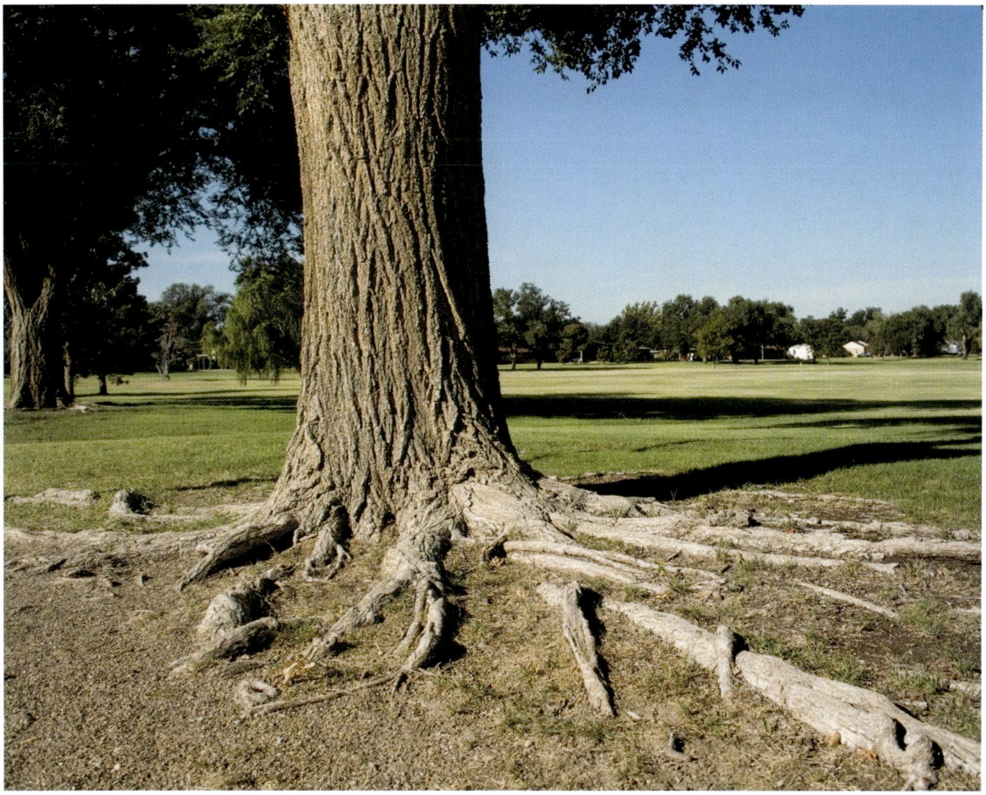

Figure 6.35 A panorama comprised of five vertical images shot by shifting the lens horizontally. Although not particularly long, the pano showcases a wide perspective without the optical distortion associated with wider focal lengths.

ISO 100 • 1/200 sec. • f/9 • 45mm

The second way to create a pano with a tilt-shift is more traditional. Again, a tripod is necessary, as well as a tripod head designed for panoramic photography (**Figure 6.36**). This type of head is designed so you can rotate the camera without having to loosen the entire structure, risking moving the camera out of line. In this scenario, a tilt-shift lens atop the tripod (shifted for perspective control) is rotated in set increments to create multiple overlapping images. This setup is more for those instances when the Shift range of a lens is not long enough for the very long panoramas we're used to seeing in galleries. However, this technique of creating panos is losing steam due to the advancements in stitching software and high-resolution cameras. Many folks are now handholding their panos (**Figure 6.37**). As a side note, it is best to shoot these types of panos with the camera turned to a vertical orientation.

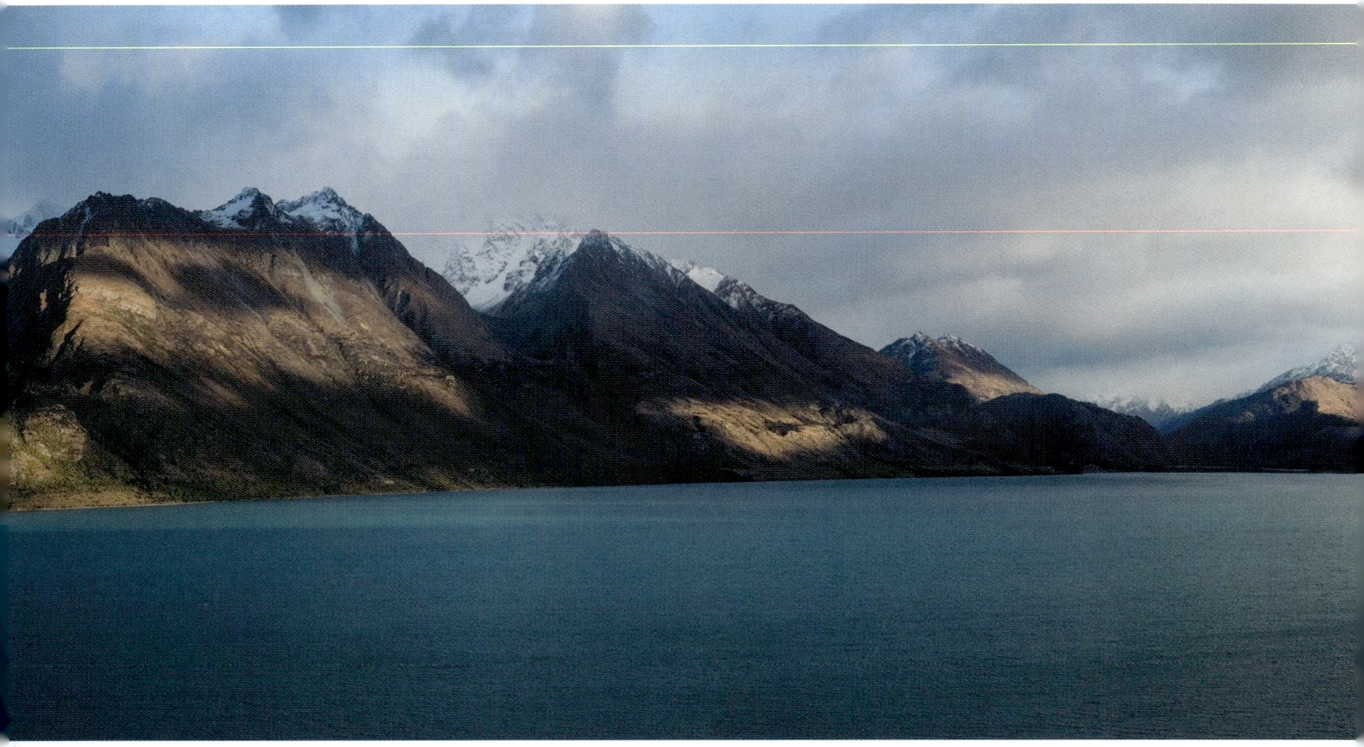

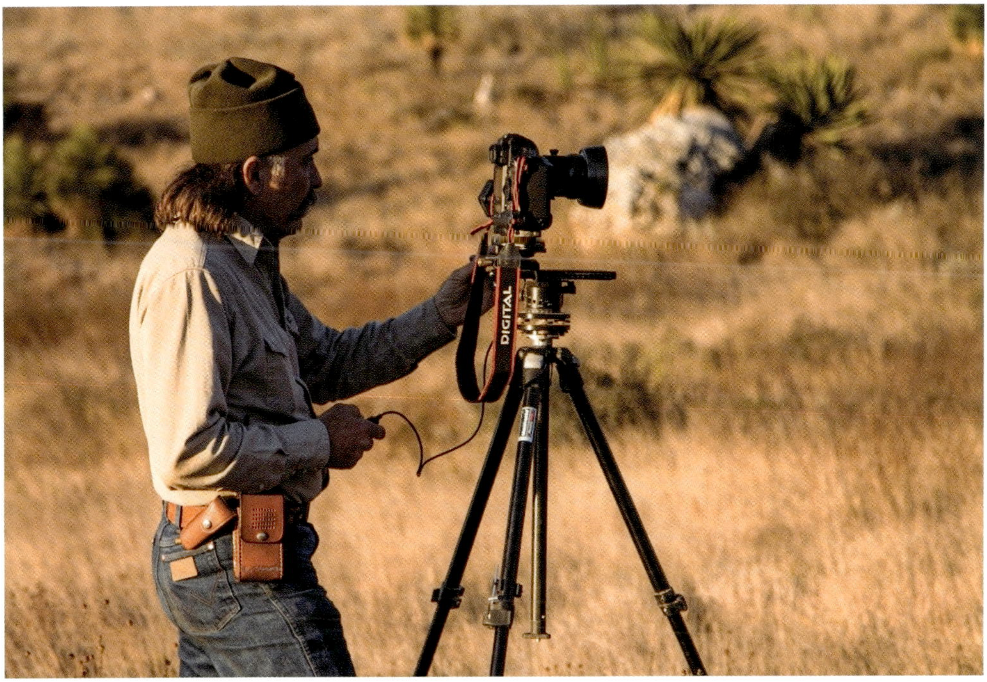

Figure 6.36
Photographer Wyman Meinzer uses a Manfrotto Virtual Reality and Pan Pro Head on top of a set of Manfrotto tripod legs to shoot a panoramic of a north Mexican mountainscape.

ISO 100 • 1/200 sec. • f/4 • 105mm

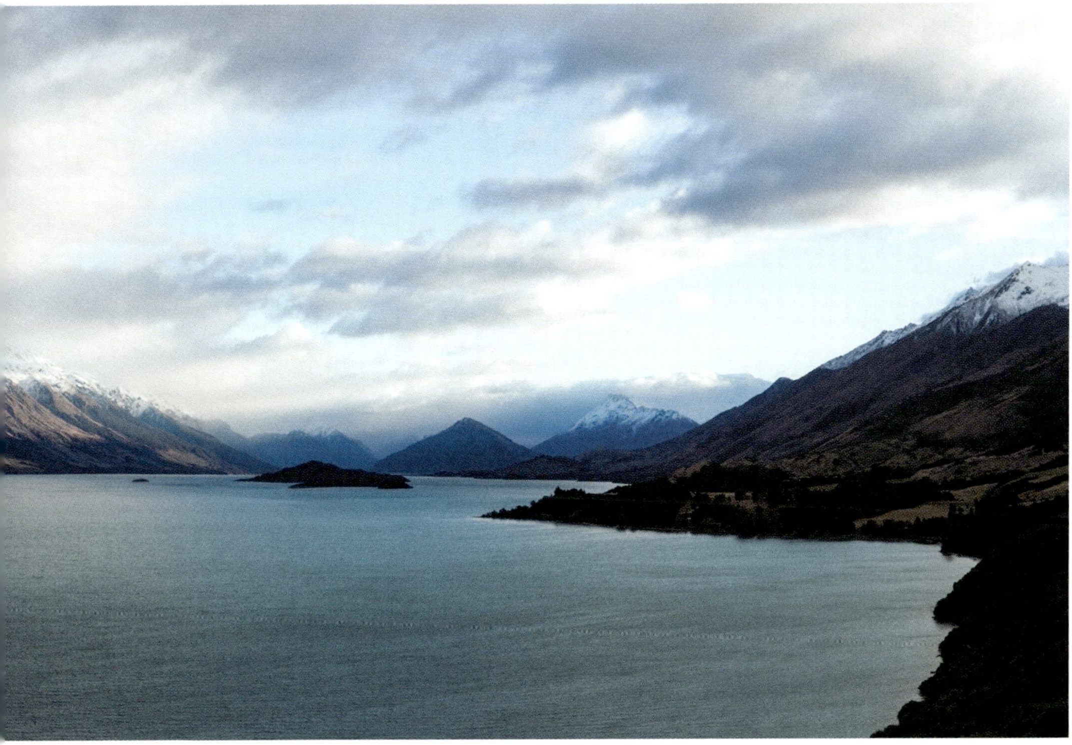

Figure 6.37
I handheld this nine-shot pano of Lake Wakatipu near Queenstown, New Zealand. The images were overlapped enough for Photoshop CC to easily stitch them together in post.

ISO 200 • 1/200 sec. • f/8 • 70mm

Tilt-Shift Considerations

Along with the tilt-shift's special properties and unique look comes a learning curve. Once you use these lenses for some time, the tilt-shift mindset becomes second nature, but there are a few things to keep in mind when starting out.

First, there is no autofocus. There's nothing you can do about it other than learn to love manual focus. Fortunately, the focus rings on these lenses are sensitive and nice turners.

Second, the focus shifts a little when you use the Tilt function. When you tilt the lens to one extreme or the other, you should notice either in Live View or in the viewfinder that the focus moves. Keeping this in mind will force you to tweak the focus back to where you want it and save you the frustration of seeing the image out of focus later on the computer screen. This movement does not occur when you *shift* the lens, but it is always wise to focus before tilting or shifting.

Third, it is best practice to shoot from a tripod. In many situations, especially portraits, you may not need to shoot from a tripod. However, when you need to shift the lens quite a bit—particularly for panoramas—the tripod is worth its weight in gold. For example, I have tried to handhold shots that corrected for keystoning, and I usually pointed the camera either up or down during that split second of exposure, reintroducing the distortion I wanted to mitigate. Don't consider the tripod a hindrance when using tilt-shifts. Consider it part of the package.

Fourth, experiment. This is not an issue but rather an encouragement to let yourself explore using these interesting pieces of glass. There are a lot of so-called rules about using tilt-shifts. Feel free to break the rules. Turn knobs, flick switches, and photograph anything to get a sense of the lens and its visual possibilities for your work.

Chapter 6 Assignments

Although specialty lenses can be used as prime lenses, they excel in those niche areas for which they are manufactured. Whether you own one, are looking to buy one, or are renting one for a weekend photo walk, take some time to work the lens the way it was intended. Use the following assignments to improve your technical and creative skills.

Push in tight

Using macro lenses is all about seeing the possibilities in a very small space. One of the best areas to explore with a macro lens is a small garden. Look for interesting subject matter to shoot, and find out how far you can push the lens in and maintain focus. Open the aperture up all the way and create mystical dreamscapes of color, but also pay attention to how low amounts of depth of field can be potentially distracting. Compose at all angles, giving special consideration to creating abstract leading lines to the primary subjects. Learn how to be patient by spending time with each subject (to start off, try working each small subject for at least ten minutes).

Adjust for keystoning

Take a wide-angle tilt-shift lens, such as the TS-E 17mm f/4L or the TS-E 24mm f/3.5L, and go hunting for structures that would normally keystone a great deal if shot with these focal lengths. Consider photographing a large church or just about any building that is over two stories high. The taller the building, the more extreme the keystoning. Shoot the building from a nice angle (or several), and correct for distortion. It's best to use a tripod. First, shoot the building at the desired angle, keystoning and all. Second, level the camera to where all vertical lines are exactly that: vertical. More than likely, this will cut the top of the building out of the frame. Third, use the lens's Shift function to shift the optics up, bringing the structure fully into the frame at the angle you originally desired without the keystoning. Keep in mind that if you are too close to the structure, you may not be able to shift up enough to include the top of the building in the frame (so back up). Do this for both horizontal and vertical shots of the structure.

Create small worlds

Master the miniature effect. From an elevated position, such as a pedestrian bridge, building rooftop, parking structure, or even a ladder, identify subject matter and composition that would make for a great miniature-effect shot. I like to shoot traffic along city roads. Using a tilt-shift lens (I suggest a 24mm or 45mm), make a shot or two of the scene sans miniature effect to give you an idea of the composition. Then, simply tilt the lens upward and open the aperture up all the way. You will more than likely need to refocus after tilting. See the miniature effect come alive in the viewfinder. You can increase the depth of field if desired, but don't do it too much or the effect will dissipate. Remember to be careful while shooting from an elevated position! Few shots are worth falling and breaking bones.

Share your results with the book's Flickr group!
Join the group here: www.flickr.com/groups/canonlenses_fromsnapshotstogreatshots

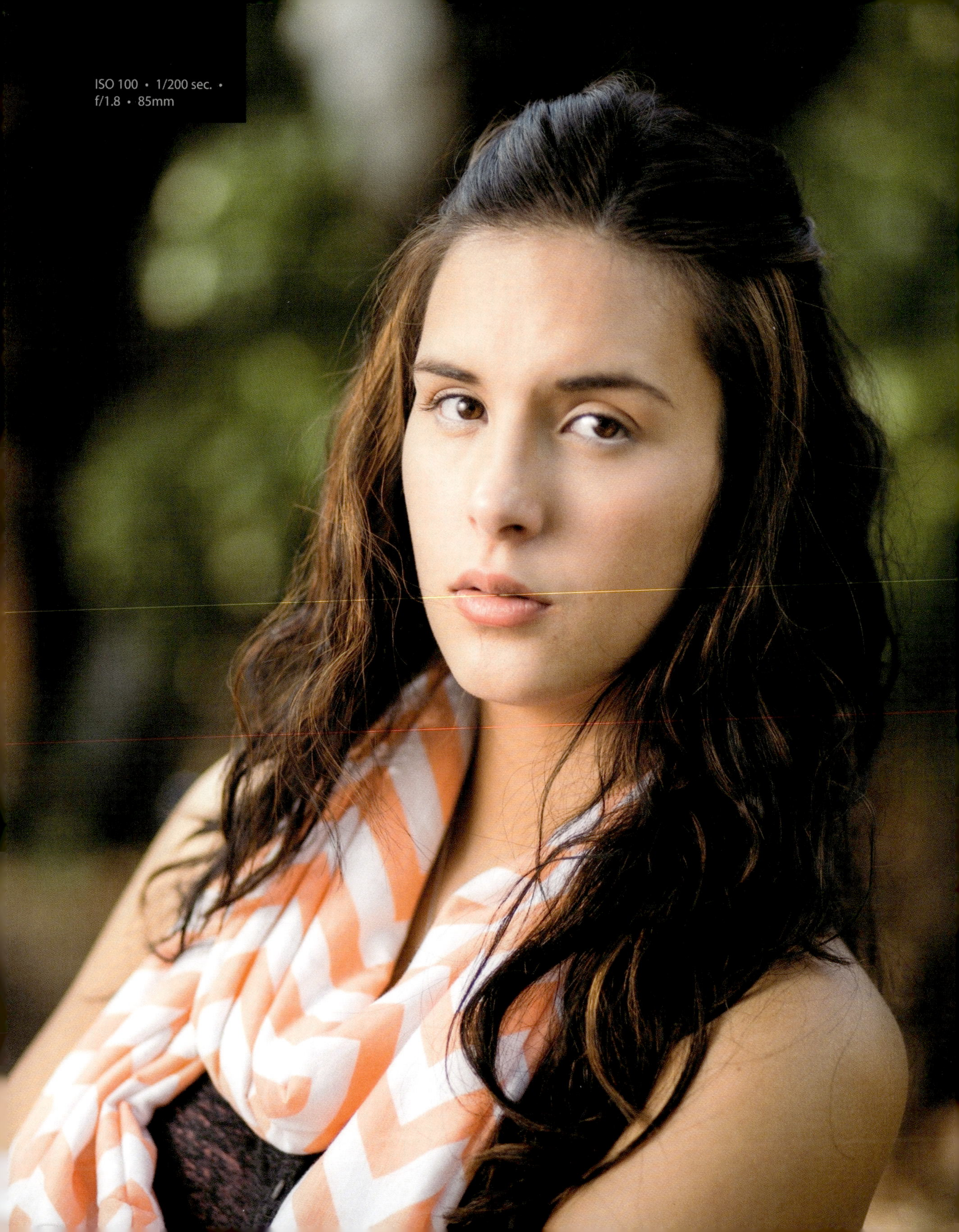

ISO 100 • 1/200 sec. • f/1.8 • 85mm

7

Accessorizing

Lens add-ons that work

When you purchased your camera and lens, whether online or in a store, you were likely asked if you wanted to add some extras to your shopping cart—a gear bag, perhaps a memory card or two, and for the lens, maybe a UV and/or polarizing filter.

Accessories are the ancillary tools that work in concert with your new gear. There's an entire industry built on proprietary and third-party accessories. Do you need them? Maybe, maybe not. It's inevitable that we'll pick up certain gadgets that help us make pictures along the way, and some of these gadgets are made specifically for your lens(es).

This chapter highlights some of the most popular lens accessories. There is a world of niche accessories not explored here; you can find more-obscure and lesser-used tools for your lenses in any camera store or online retailer. What are perhaps the most important accessories of all—hoods, lens caps, and cleaning supplies—are covered in the next chapter.

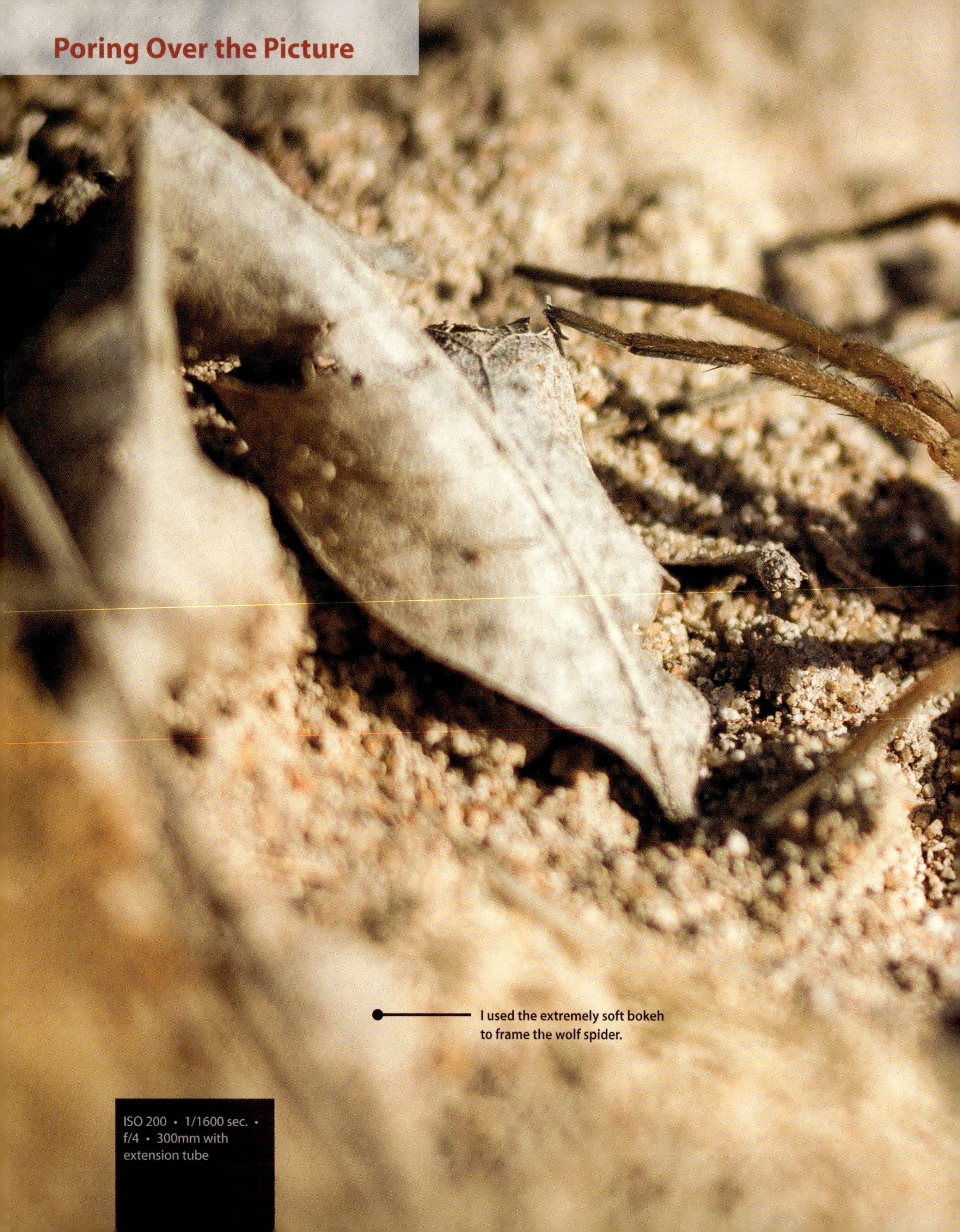

I used the extremely soft bokeh to frame the wolf spider.

ISO 200 • 1/1600 sec. • f/4 • 300mm with extension tube

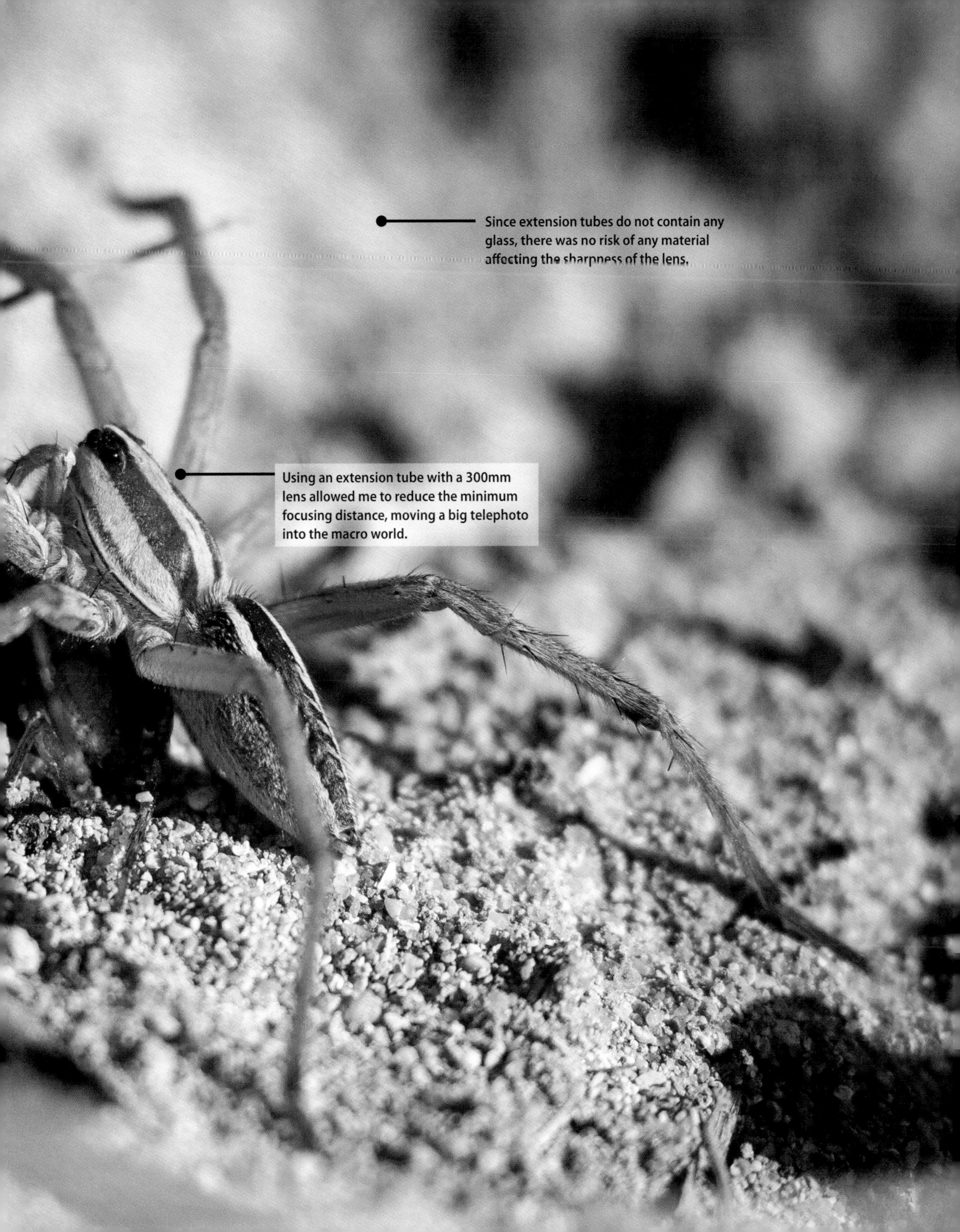
Since extension tubes do not contain any glass, there was no risk of any material affecting the sharpness of the lens.
Using an extension tube with a 300mm lens allowed me to reduce the minimum focusing distance, moving a big telephoto into the macro world.

Teleconverters (Extenders)

When you survey the field of Canon telephoto lenses, you'll notice that going longer means digging deeper into your pocket. It also means carrying some more weight on your shoulder. The solution to both of these issues lies in Canon's two *teleconverters* (also known as *extenders*), devices that extend the focal length of the lens to which they are attached (**Figure 7.1**).

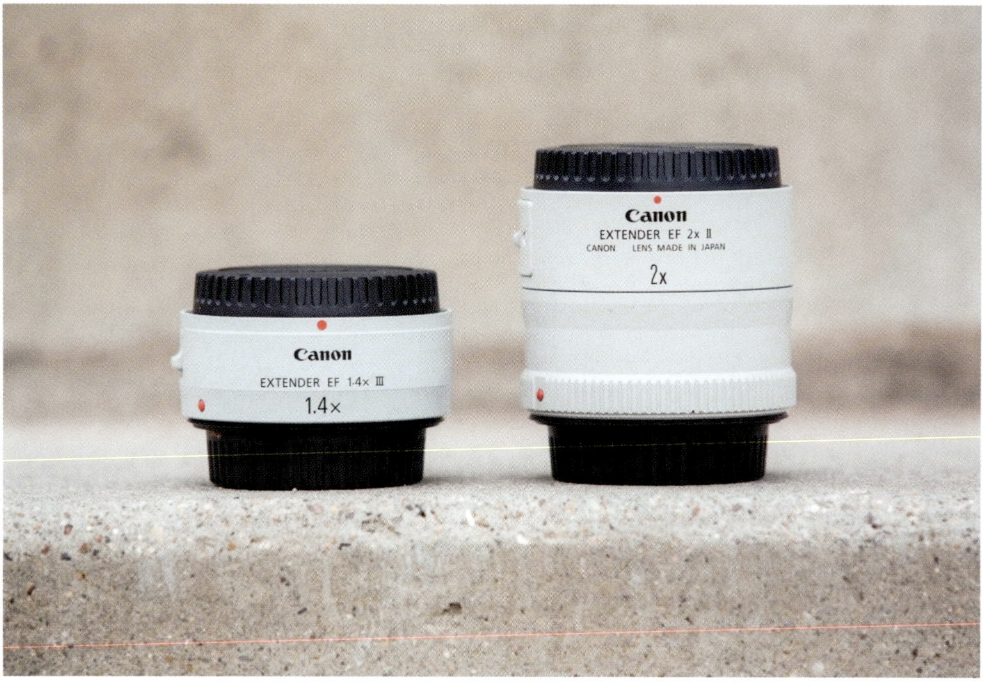

Figure 7.1
Canon's two teleconverters, the Extender EF 1.4X III (left) and the Extender EF 2X II (right), are good for reaching out in genres such as wildlife and sports.

How They Work

Canon's two models are the Extender EF 1.4X III (commonly referred to as the *one-four*) and the Extender EF 2X III (the *two-X*). The focal length of any lens used in conjunction with either of the converters is simply multiplied by the factor in the accessory's name. For example, a one-four extender used with a 200mm focal length (1.4 x 200mm) will produce a focal length of 280mm. A two-X extender used with the same focal length (2.0 x 200mm) will provide an effective 400mm focal length. The extenders, which are built with similar construction to most L- series telephoto lenses, use optic-grade glass to perform the focal length magnification. The setup is pretty simple—just attach the extender to the camera body like you would any other lens, and then attach the lens to the extender.

Using an extender is an excellent way to go long without needing to acquire another lens. I often carry a one-four or two-X with me when I travel and need to keep the amount of lenses I pack to a minimum. However, they are also popular with wildlife and sports photographers who already use extremely long focal lengths. A 400mm lens quickly becomes a 560mm lens with the one-four, and 800mm with the two-X. Talk about versatility in a small package (**Figures 7.2, 7.3,** and **7.4**)! Bird and other wildlife photographers love converters since controlling their subject matter's distance from the lens is often impossible or comes at great risk (think grizzly bears).

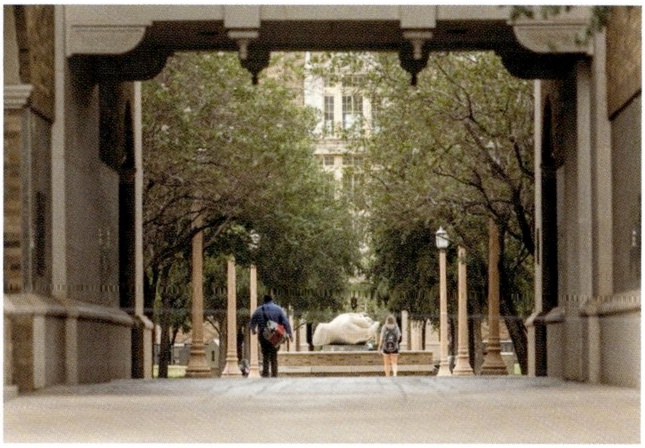

Figure 7.2 **Taken without a teleconverter, this shot has merit given the framing and interesting background subject matter.**

ISO 400 • 1/800 sec. • f/4 • 200mm

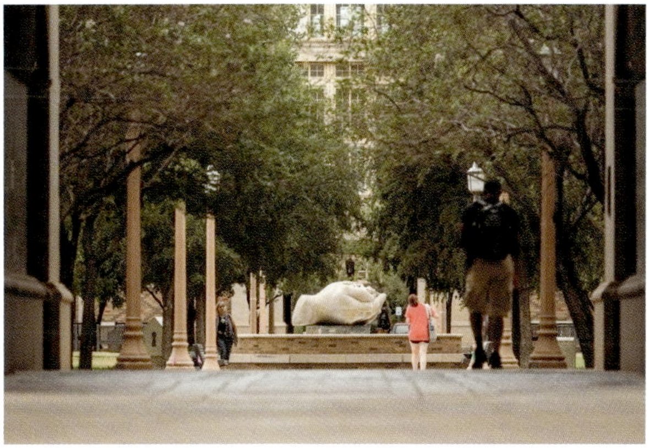

Figure 7.3 **A one-four extender pushes the 200mm focal length to 280mm, doing away with the frame in the first shot.**

ISO 400 • 1/400 sec. • f/5.6 • 280mm (200mm with 1.4X teleconverter)

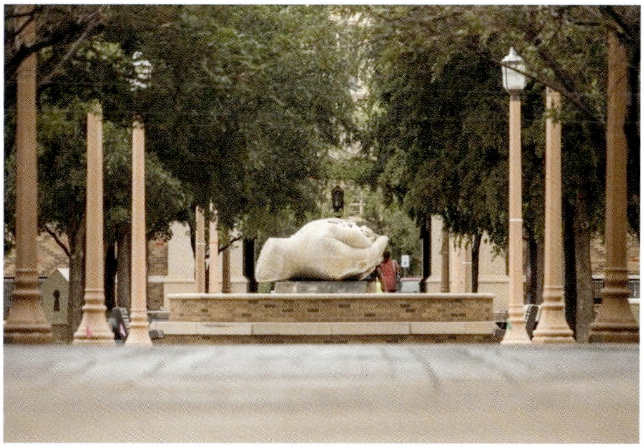

Figure 7.4 **From the same position, a two-X extender produces yet another look, this time using the light poles as framing devices for the fountain.**

ISO 400 • 1/200 sec. • f/8 • 400mm (200mm with 2X teleconverter)

Extender Caveats

Extenders sound great, right? For the most part, they *are* great. However, there are a few things to ponder before purchasing.

First, both the one-four and the two-X only work with certain Canon lenses. According to the manufacturer, they work only with prime L-series lenses at and longer-than-135mm, as well as the L-series 70–200mm models (both f/2.8 and f/4) and the EF 100–400 f/4.5–5.6L. These lenses have rear elements that are deep enough within their construction that the converting optics in the extender can fit snuggly inside (**Figure 7.5**).

The second issue to consider is the effect extenders have on maximum aperture. Using a one-four extender will cost you one stop of aperture, and the two-X will cost you two. For example, if you are using a lens that opens up to f/2.8 and you slap a one-four on it, you can only open the aperture to f/4. With a two-X, the maximum aperture would be f/5.6. This issue alone might keep some folks from investing in an extender. I love using my EF 300mm f/4L IS, but after attaching it to a two-X extender, I can only open up to f/8. This isn't necessarily an issue when it comes to depth of field, but in losing two stops of aperture, I lose two stops of light and am forced to shoot with a much slower shutter speed (two stops slower) or bump my ISO up two stops (which increases the noise in the image).

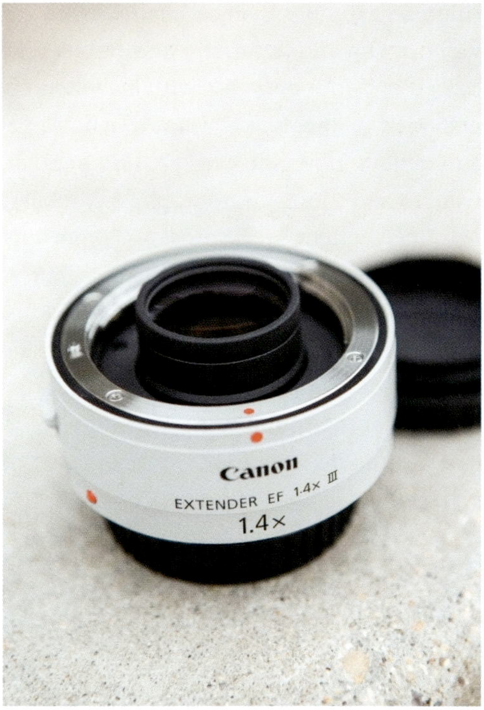

Figure 7.5 Optics contained within an extender and the way extenders are constructed to work with Canon lenses limit the lenses with which they can be used.

Third, extenders can slow down or eliminate autofocus capabilities. A camera's autofocus system needs light for it to detect contrast and find focus. By putting an extender between the camera and lens, and reducing the maximum aperture of said lens, you are essentially reducing the amount of light let in through the lens and detected by the autofocus sensor. The greater the reduction in maximum aperture, the slower the autofocus becomes. Imagine shooting a fast-paced sports game with a sluggish autofocus system. But where does it fail completely? Anywhere past f/8. At f/8 (a combination of an f/5.6 lens and a one-four extender, or an f/4 lens and a two-X extender), autofocus is typically sluggish. Combine a two-X converter with an f/5.6 lens (f/11 maximum aperture) and say goodbye to autofocus.

Re-emphasizing a point made in Chapter 5, the fourth issue to consider is what extending the focal length means for your minimum sustaining shutter speed. Using an extender may necessitate putting the camera on a tripod or monopod to accommodate the longer focal length and the increase in sensitivity to any lens movement.

Fifth, some photographers claim that extenders degrade image quality. It's true that putting another piece(s) of glass between your lens and camera might introduce certain deficiencies. It's hard to detect, but extenders can magnify the effect of a lens's chromatic aberration and some vignetting. Canon's newly designed extenders work hard to mitigate the negative effects. Older versions of the Canon two-X had a softening effect, but the most current iteration is much improved. I have heard nothing but praise for the one-four extender; I've yet to see any visible degradation.

Finally, even though extenders are cheaper than new telephoto lenses, they're still not cheap. Even with rebates, both extenders are somewhere north of US$400.

Extension Tubes

In the previous chapter, I highlighted how great Canon's macro lenses are for getting in tight on small subject matter. What if there was a way to do the same thing—minimize the focusing distance of your lens—without forking over the cash for a new piece of glass and without sacrificing image quality? You'd probably say, "Sign me up!" Enter extension tubes.

How They Work

Extension tubes look and feel like extenders, but there is no glass inside their barrel construction (**Figure 7.6**). They are simply tubes—placed between your lens and the camera—that decrease the minimum focusing distance by moving the lens's optics away from the camera's sensor, and in some cases, allowing you to push the lens much closer to the subject than any macro lens allows. A telephoto zoom lens, such as an EF 70–200mm f/2.8L, is my favorite lens to combine with one or more extension tubes. (The tubes work equally well with a shorter lens, such as an EF 24–105mm f/4L IS.) I like using zoom lenses with extension tubes because the zoom ring becomes more of a focus ring. With a bit of experience, you can become comfortable using extension tubes by moving in tightly on a subject and using the zoom ring to manipulate focus. The focus ring will also fine-tune where the image is sharp, but it serves a lesser role in these circumstances.

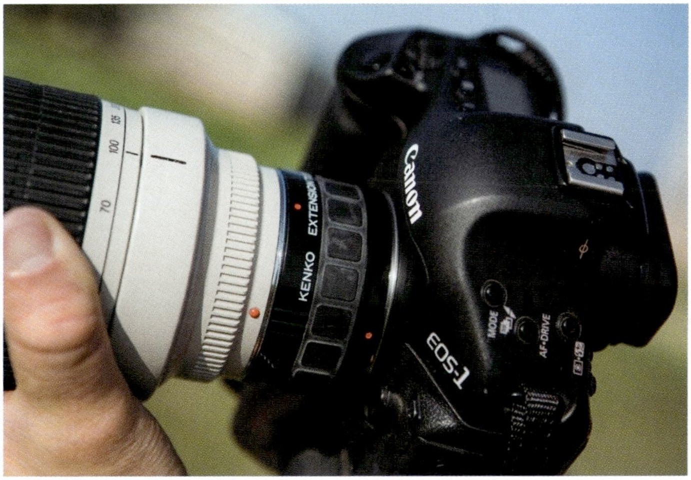

Figure 7.6 **Like teleconverters, extension tubes fit between the body of the camera and the lens.**

You can purchase extension tubes individually or as a package of three. They come in various sizes; the longer the tube, the tighter you can push in on a subject. I usually advise purchasing proprietary gear when you choose a camera system, but I use Kenko extension tubes (**Figure 7.7**). For just over the price of one Canon tube, you can purchase a set of three Kenko tubes that retain autofocus, transmit data electronically from the lens to the camera, and fit both EF and EF-S lens mounts. For around US$180, you can convert just about any lens you own into a close-focusing macro lens. Since the tubes don't include glass, you don't need to worry about them degrading the optical quality of a lens. Some vignetting may occur, and if all three tubes are used in conjunction with your lens, some light may drop off, but sharpness is not a concern.

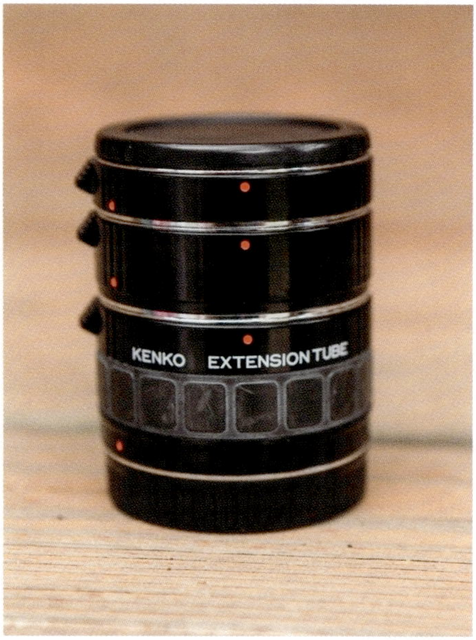

Figure 7.7 **For less than US$200, a set of three Kenko extension tubes can turn any of your Canon lenses into a close-focusing macro machine.**

Using Extension Tubes

Extension tubes share many of the same rules and techniques as traditional macro lenses. It is best and most stable to put a camera-extension tube(s)-lens combination on a tripod. The lens is more sensitive to movement in the macro world, and the tripod adds more stability than the human body. Using a shutter release also helps prevent movement in an image (**Figure 7.8**).

Also, become comfortable with manual focus. Even though Canon and Kenko extension tubes allow you to use autofocus, in many macro settings autofocus can get in the way. Using the lens's zoom ring as a focus pull gives you much more nuanced control over the focal plane, especially when you have your composition just right and need to tweak focus just a bit (**Figure 7.9**).

Last, have fun and experiment. As I said in the last chapter, I enjoy the stress- relieving qualities of shooting macro. Be patient and methodically try out different compositions, using one, two, or three of the extension tubes in tandem. Becoming comfortable with how the tubes work will result in some interesting images (**Figure 7.10**).

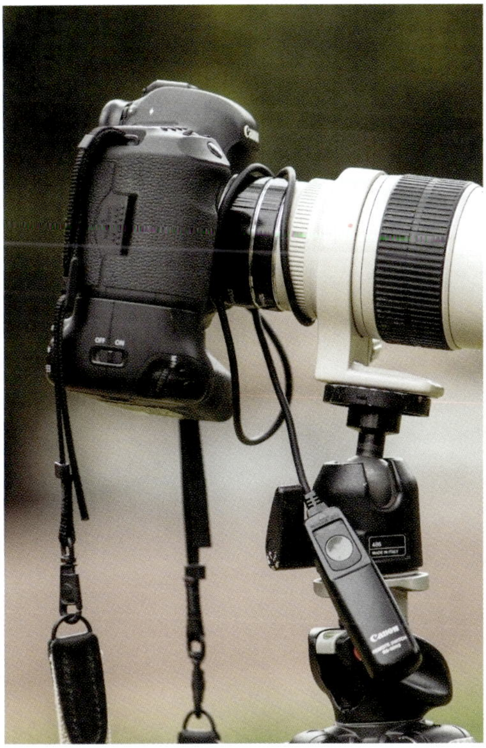

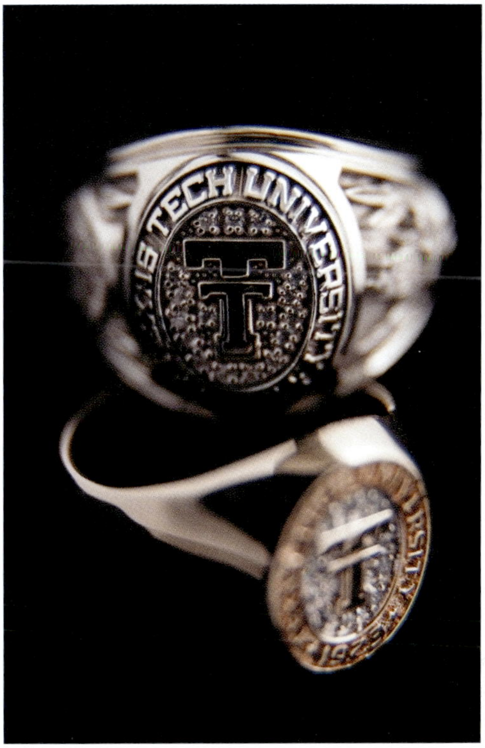

Figure 7.8 (left)

I often wrap my shutter release cable around the lens barrel and extension tubes when shooting macro to keep it close at hand while carefully composing images in the little world.

Figure 7.9 (right)

I shot this magazine cover in my office with nothing more than a standard zoom lens, a small piece of white fabric, a couple of lights, and one extension tube.

ISO 200 • 1/80 sec. • f/4.5 • 105mm with extension tube

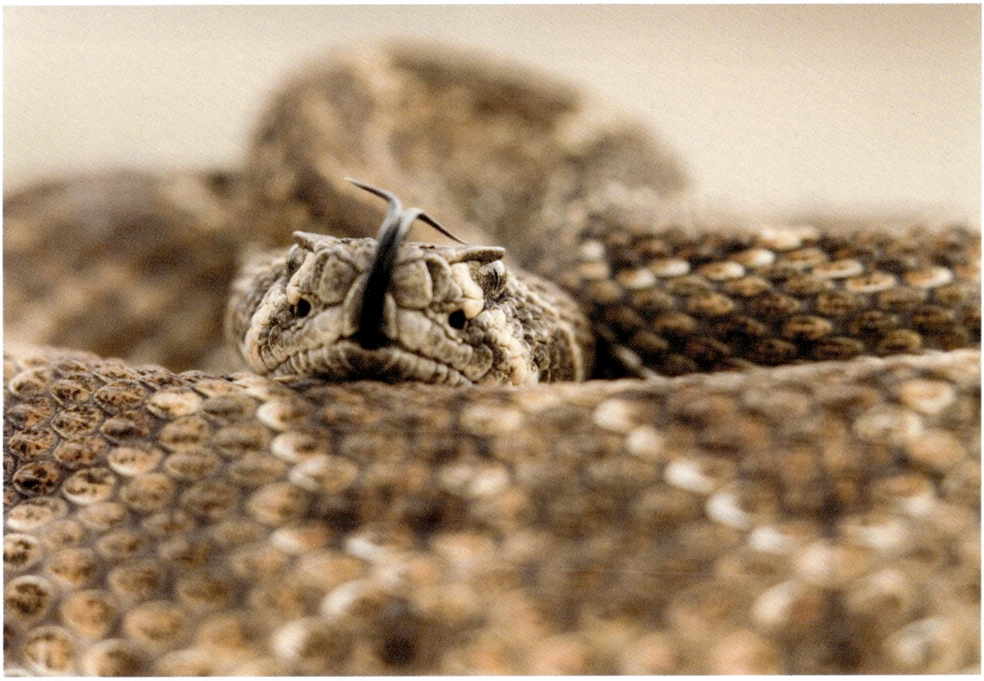

Figure 7.10

A small extension tube on a telephoto lens can help you push in just a bit more for a dramatic image.

ISO 50 • 1/160 sec. • f/4 • 115mm with extension tube

Keep in mind that, like with macro lenses, using a shallow depth of field may result in an image that either misses focus on the primary subject or one that renders the subject "unreadable" (**Figure 7.11**).

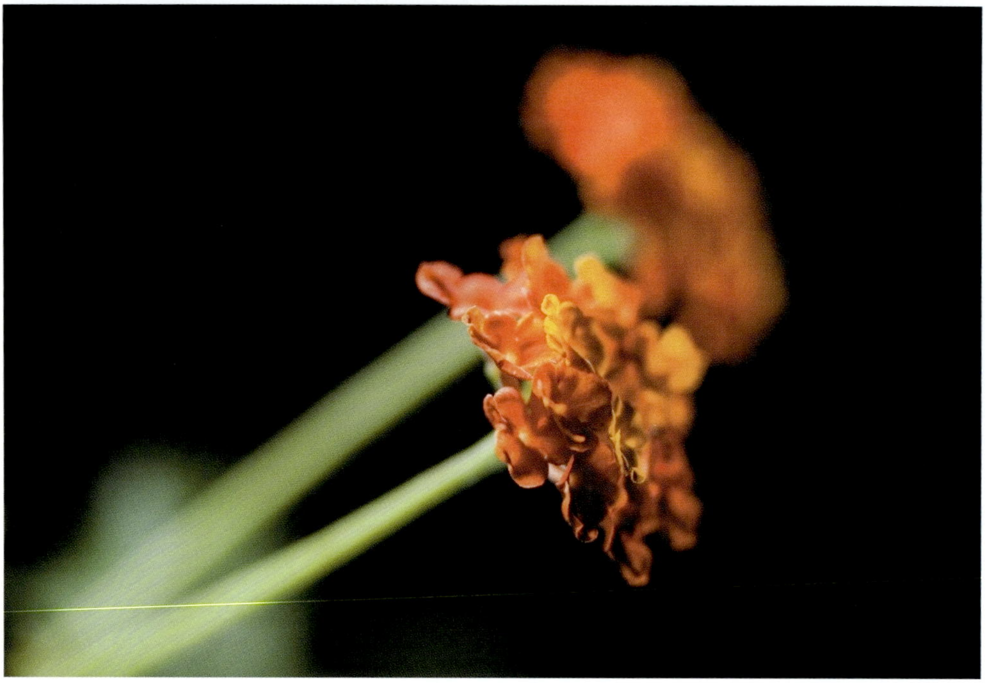

Figure 7.11
I nailed the focus on the front of the flower, but the first flower doesn't stand out from the one in the background. Using extension tubes on an already fast lens resulted in a short, soft depth of field.

ISO 50 • 1/8000 sec. • f/2.8 • 93mm with extension tube

Filters

The ultimate lens accessory is a filter. Or perhaps several filters. Filters are valuable to photography and they can be employed strategically and creatively in your work. Yet, filters are probably the accessories that cause the most consternation among photographers. I don't use them much, except for the occasional neutral density filter.

There is a large variety of filters out there. The following sections highlight three of the most popular types. Like most camera gear, filters come at several different price points via several manufacturers. They are also manufactured out of different materials, such as glass, plastic, and a high-quality resin. While filters do get expensive, it is in the buyer's best interest to not go cheap. That doesn't mean you must buy the priciest filters available, but it does mean do your research. I try to avoid plastic filters altogether.

UV Filters

Perhaps the most popular filter is one that greatly reduces or completely blocks ultraviolet (UV) rays from passing through the lens (**Figure 7.12**). UV filters have been around for a while. Film was especially prone to the effects of UV rays, which are invisible to our eyes. UV filters were an essential addition to many film photographers' lenses, helping to mitigate loss of contrast and an anemic haziness sometimes seen on film.

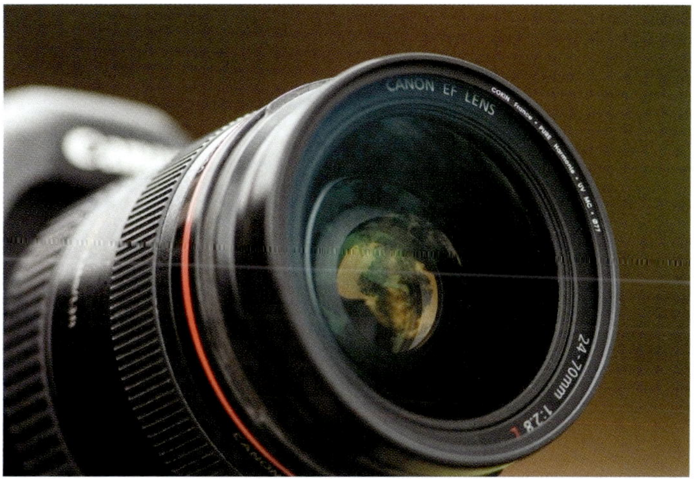

Figure 7.12 **It would be easy to mistake a good UV filter as simply another clear piece of glass in front of a lens.**

UV filters still do what they have always done, but since digital sensors are not affected by UV rays, these filters are less relevant now. It's hard to detect the lens's effect (**Figures 7.13** and **7.14**). They do come in handy where UV rays are prevalent, such as at higher altitudes. However, these days many folks simply fix any issues in postprocessing.

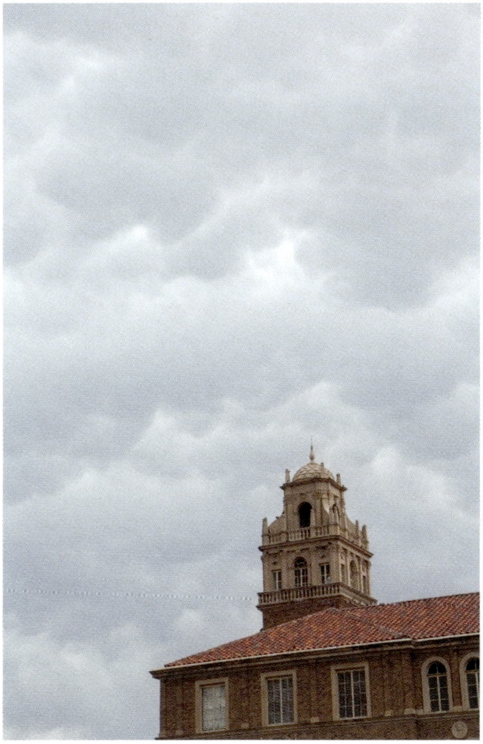

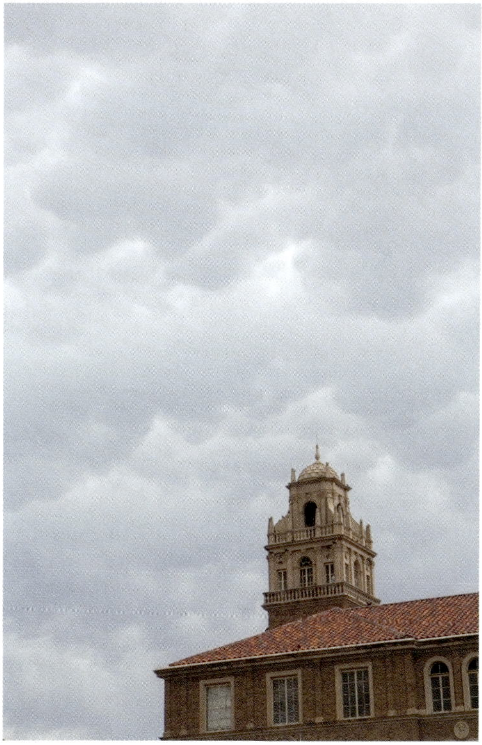

Figure 7.13 (left) **Without a UV filter**

ISO 100 • 1/320 sec. • f/5.6 • 70mm

Figure 7.14 (right) **With a UV filter in front of the lens, it is hard to detect whether it has any effect on the image.**

ISO 100 • 1/320 sec. • f/5.6 • 70mm

Why even consider buying a UV filter? One very important reason: to protect the front element (**Figure 7.15**). Imagine dropping your lens and the front element hits something jagged or hard. Having a good UV filter in front of that element is like having an extra insurance policy on it as you go banging through the streets. And, if it prevents any negative effects of UV rays along the way, all the better. This is also why I always use my lens hood—to reduce the chance that my front element ever comes in contact with anything.

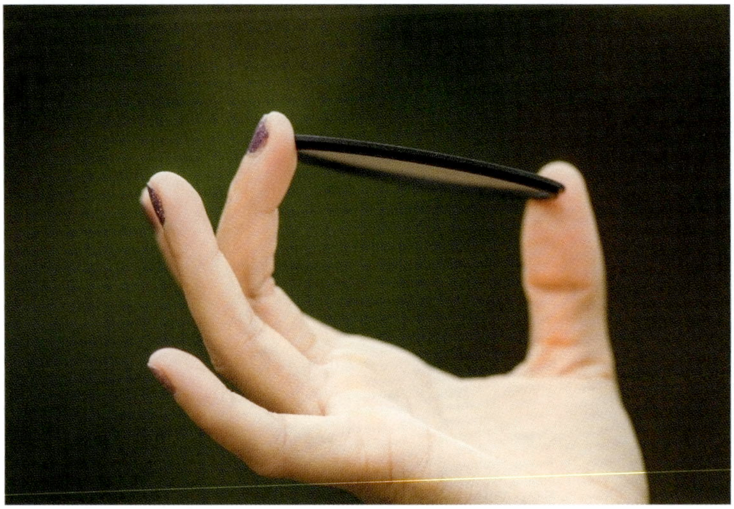

Figure 7.15 UV filters offer great protection for your lens's precious front element, and they are being manufactured by some companies, like Cokin, in a thinner form than in previous years.

With this protection comes a risk of decreased image fidelity, which is why I don't use a UV filter often. (It is worth pointing out that any filter will degrade the quality of the image.) That being said, many photographers claim that good UV filters don't negatively impact image quality.

Compared to other types of filters, UV filters are relatively inexpensive. And they are the type of filter you can leave on your lens all the time. Make sure you purchase a multicoated glass filter that is less prone to greasy smudges and scratches.

Polarizing Filters

Unless you've taken a physics or engineering course, polarization may be a tough subject to swallow. My head still spins when someone tries to explain vertical and horizontal (both linear) and circular polarized light, as well as unpolarized light. Essentially, photographers use a polarizing filter to manipulate light. Certain light waves in a field of vision that are not polarized the same way as others can simply be blocked from entering the lens via a polarizing filter.

Circular polarizers and position

For photographers, the most popular type of polarizing filter is the one called a circular polarizer (**Figure 7.16**), a rotating filter that allows the user to block different light waves based on their polarization. For example, when the filter is rotated to allow only vertically polarized light to pass through, horizontally polarized light is barred entrance. All other light waves that are neither vertical nor completely horizontal are only partially allowed through depending on their angle to those two axes.

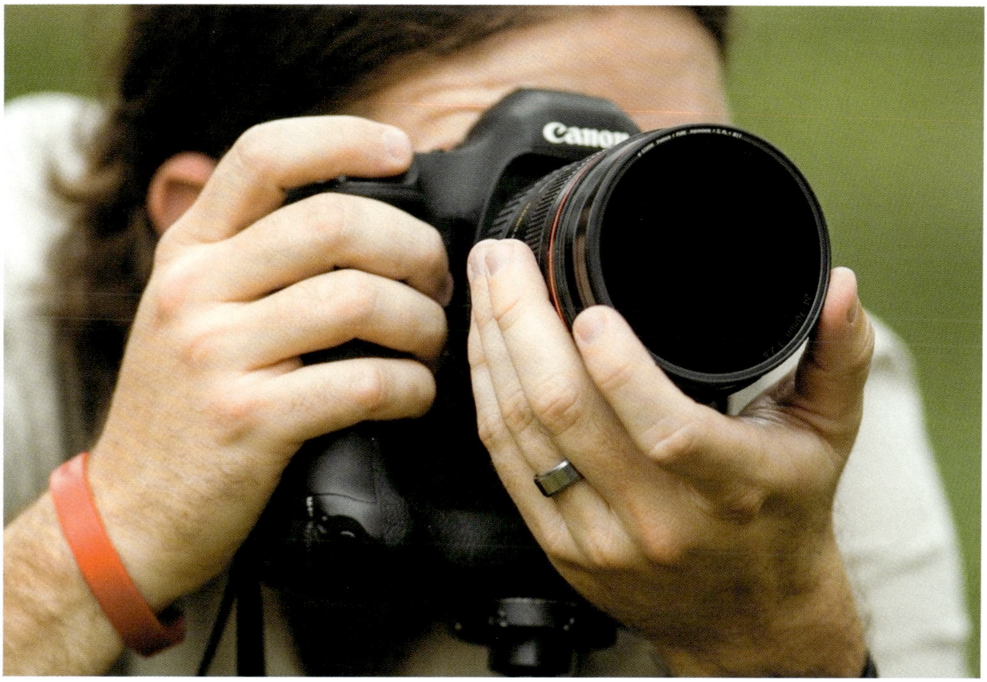

Figure 7.16
A circular polarizing filter allows the photographer to dial in the appropriate angle of polarization by spinning the outer ring.

Practically speaking, colors become more saturated and reflections disappear when you bar some light with a polarizing filter. As you rotate the filter, the angle of light allowed through changes, enabling you to take advantage of polarized light waves entering the lens at many different angles (**Figures 7.17**, **7.18**, **7.19**, and **7.20**). You can see this change take place through the viewfinder or Live View display as you rotate the filter. It is very difficult, if all but impossible, to replicate this type of physical effect through postprocessing.

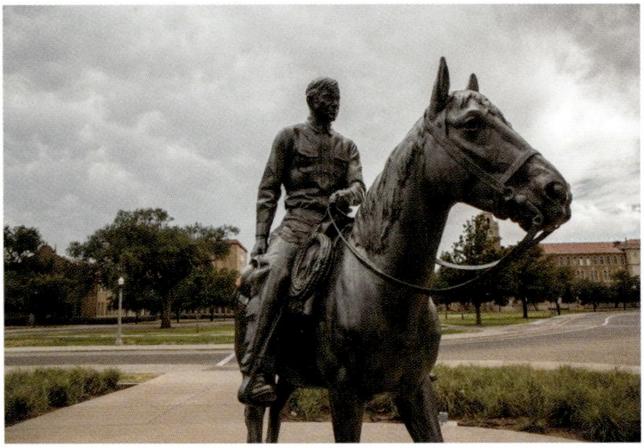

Figure 7.17 Even on an overcast day, a bronze statue can reflect a large amount of light.

ISO 100 • 1/100 sec. • f/5.6 • 24mm

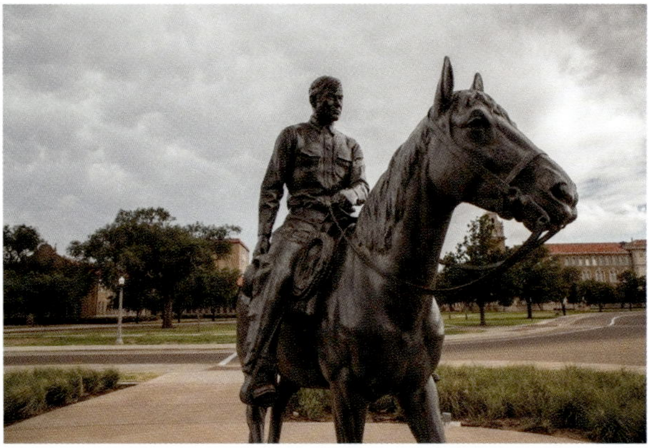

Figure 7.18 By turning the outer element on a circular polarizer, certain light waves are barred from passing through the lens, resulting in a different reflection in the statue.

ISO 100 • 1/100 sec. • f/5.6 • 24mm

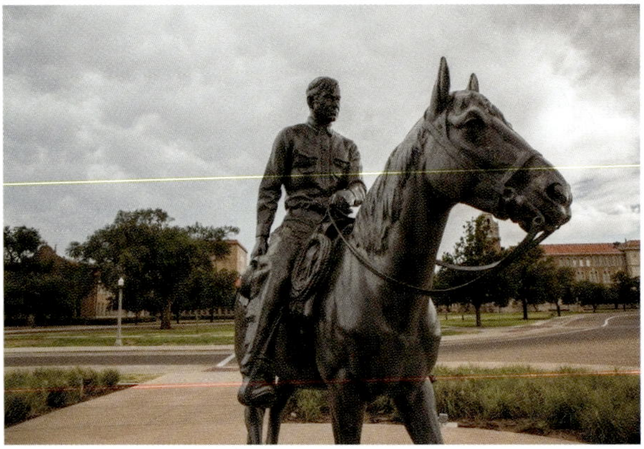

Figure 7.19 Turning the polarizing filter even more continues the change in reflection.

ISO 100 • 1/100 sec. • f/5.6 • 24mm

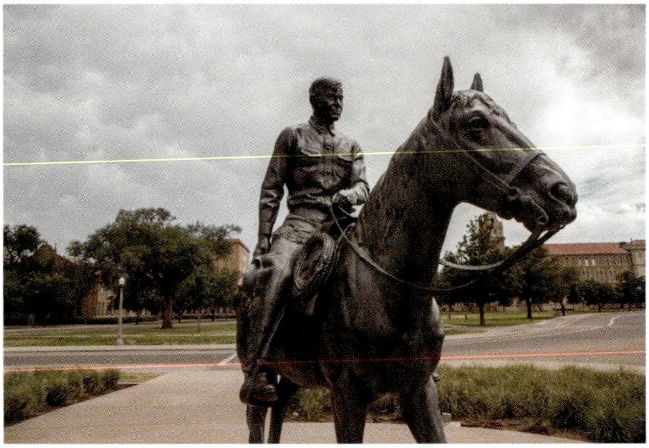

Figure 7.20 While you turn a polarizing filter, the change in effect is continuous and visible through the viewfinder, letting you fine-tune the amount of polarization for any particular light-wave orientation.

ISO 100 • 1/100 sec. • f/5.6 • 24mm

Note that the effect of the filter is strongest at 90-degree angles from the direction of the sun, and it lessens the more you point toward the sun or directly away from it. For example, since the sun rises in the east, you would need to point your camera either north or south to see the effect of the filter, as opposed to due west.

Saturation

During the middle of the day, light and color can be weak, especially in a digitally captured image. Time for a polarizing filter. At an appropriate position to the sun, rotate the filter against a weak blue sky to get a saturated blue that contrasts nicely with white clouds (**Figures 7.21** and **7.22**). At its most saturating, the filter is barring the prevailing angle of polarized light and essentially underexposing the sky as a result of this reduction in light passing through the filter.

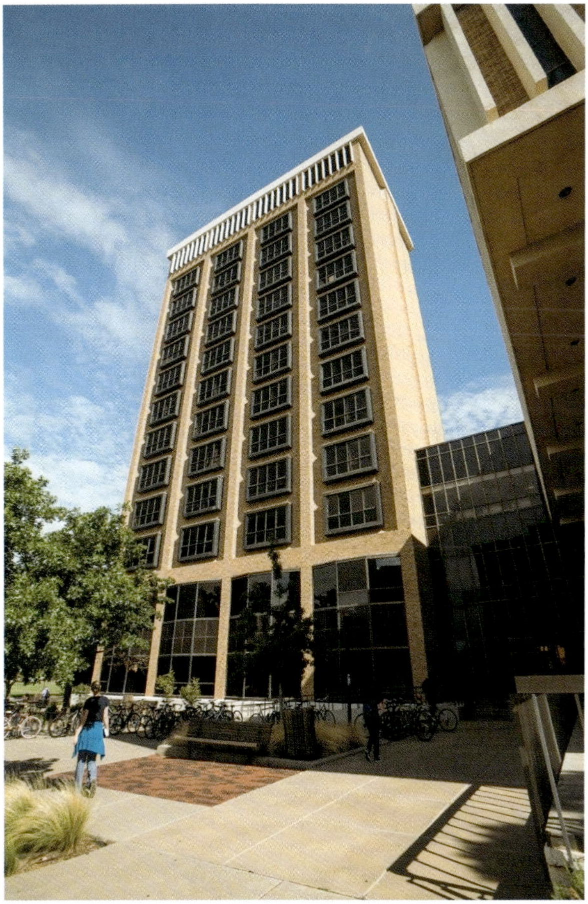

Figure 7.21 **Late-morning light can dull an otherwise interesting sky with good cloud structure.**

ISO 100 • 1/200 sec. • f/5.6 • 17mm

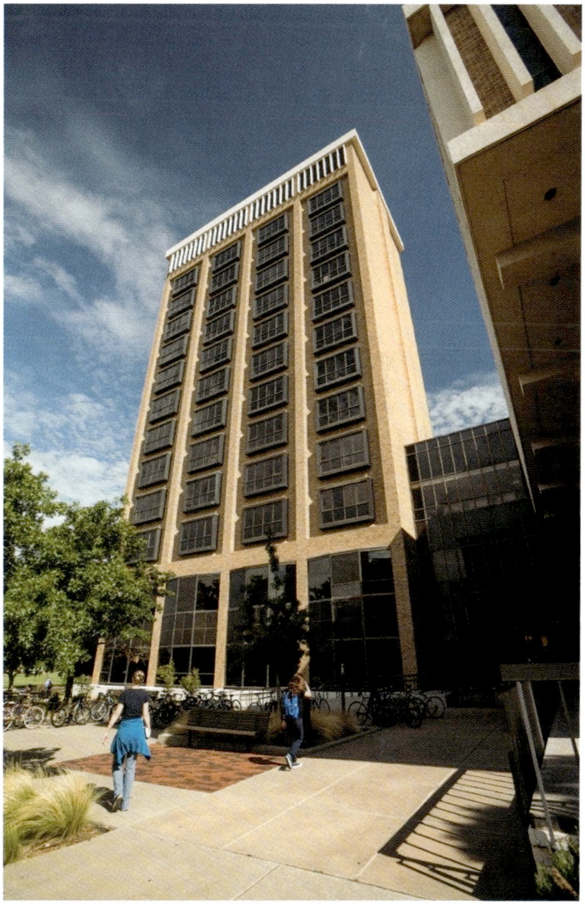

Figure 7.22 **A circular polarizer can saturate the blue in the sky and boost the contrast between the blue and the white clouds.**

ISO 100 • 1/200 sec. • f/5.6 • 17mm

Be careful not to oversaturate. If the sky appears very dark (note that the higher in elevation you go, the darker the sky), it might not fit with the foreground exposure or content, producing an unrealistic-looking image (**Figure 7.23**). After making a few images of a sky at what seems like the correct level of color, rotate the filter back just to be sure you haven't gone too far (**Figure 7.24**).

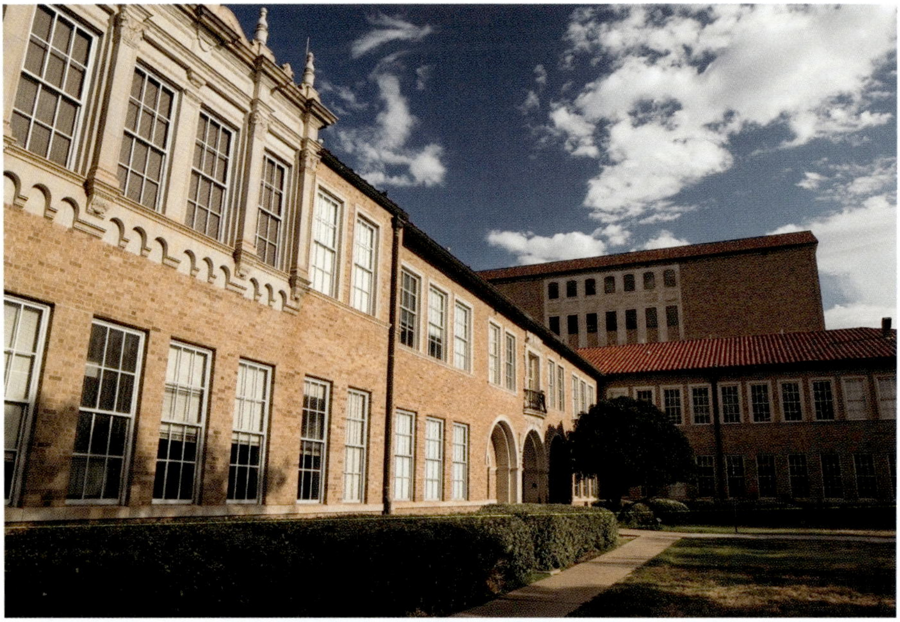

Figure 7.23
Even though the result is dramatic, a polarizing filter's saturation can go a bit too far, as shown in the sky above the lit building.

ISO 100 • 1/400 sec. • f/5.6 • 24mm

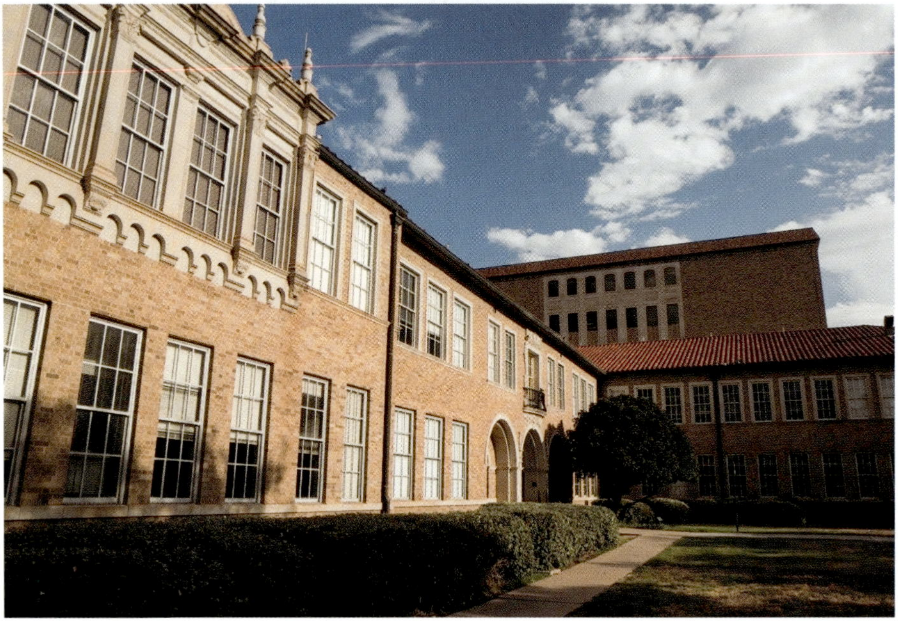

Figure 7.24
Recognizing that the saturation is too much for the content, rotate the filter back to lighten the sky.

ISO 100 • 1/400 sec. • f/5.6 • 24mm

Polarizers sometimes stand out when used in conjunction with wide-angle focal lengths. Since such focal lengths have wide angles of view, the field of view captured in the frame may include areas of the sky that are not at 90-degree angles from the sun. The result is a band of saturation that will appear close to that 90-degree mark but nowhere else (**Figure 7.25**). It is awkward to have this band of color move through the frame with two areas of nonsaturated color on both sides of it in the sky.

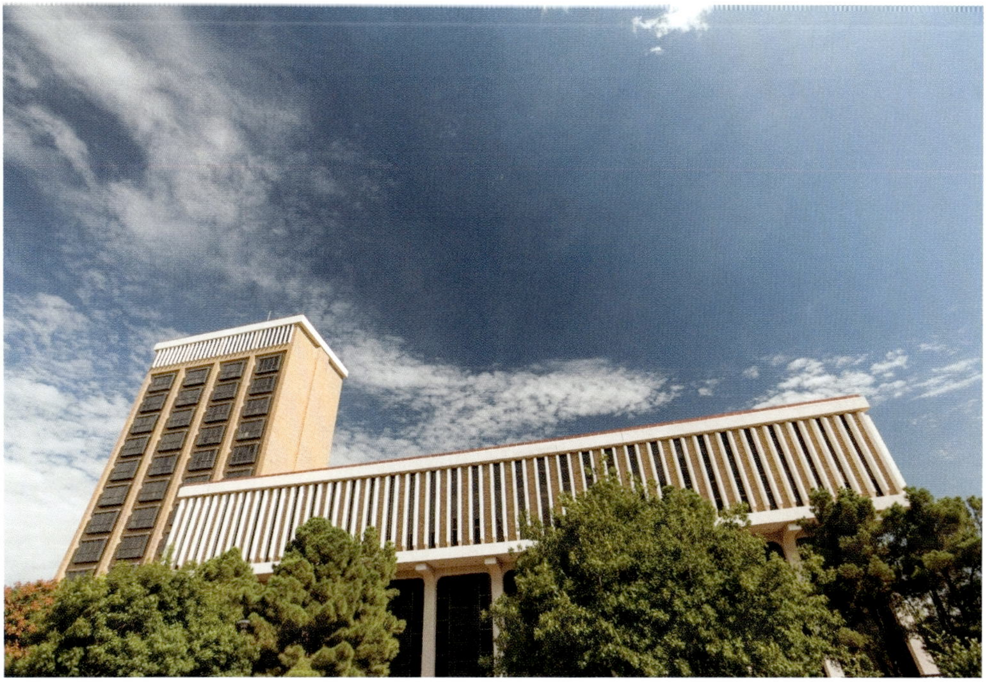

Figure 7.25
Even at a 90-degree angle to the sun, an ultra-wide focal length with a polarizer can produce an obvious saturated band in the sky.

ISO 100 • 1/250 sec. • f/5.6 • 17mm

Reflections

Polarizers are also great for cutting through reflections. Imagine shooting through a window from a city sidewalk. More than likely, you will capture a reflection of the building across the street or something else outside the window. You can use a circular polarizer to reduce the light waves that create this reflection, allowing you to make a picture of what is inside the window (**Figures 7.26** and **7.27**).

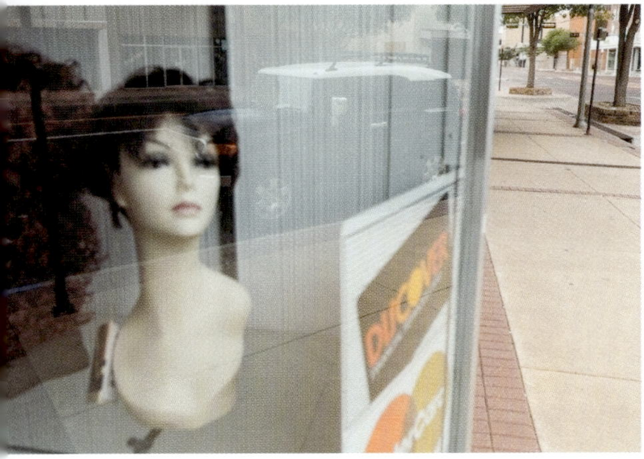

Figure 7.26 **Without a polarizing filter, the reflection of the vehicle in the window is quite distracting.**

ISO 100 • 1/60 sec. • f/4 • 30mm

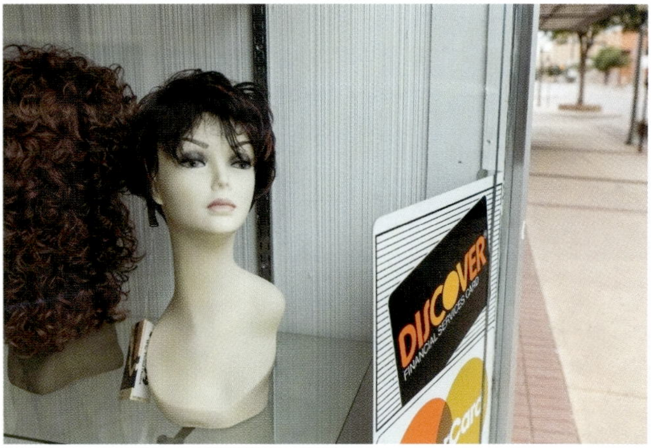

Figure 7.27 **A polarizer blocks the light waves responsible for the vehicle's reflection.**

ISO 100 • 1/60 sec. • f/4 • 30mm

The same technique applies to reflections on highly specular surfaces, such as water, oily roads, and just about any shiny surface that is mostly horizontal to your position. Instead of being blinded by the light reflecting off water (**Figures 7.28** and **7.29**), use a circular polarizer to cut through such reflections. If the water is clear enough, you can see what lies below its surface (**Figure 7.30**).

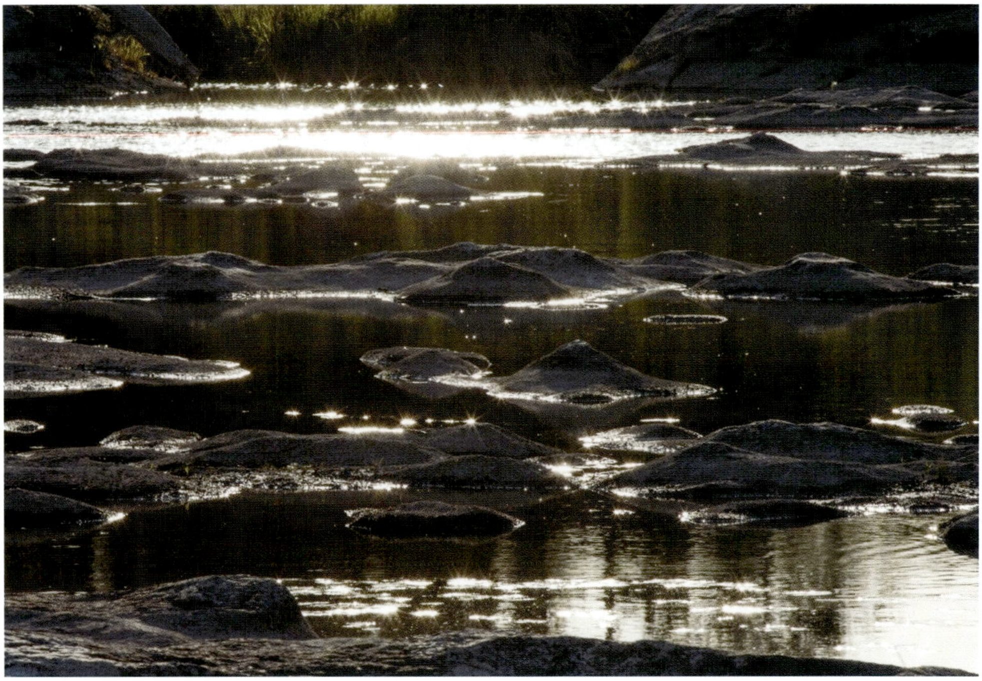

Figure 7.28 **Bright, distracting specular highlights dot the surface of the Llano River.**

ISO 100 • 1/25 sec. • f/32 • 300mm

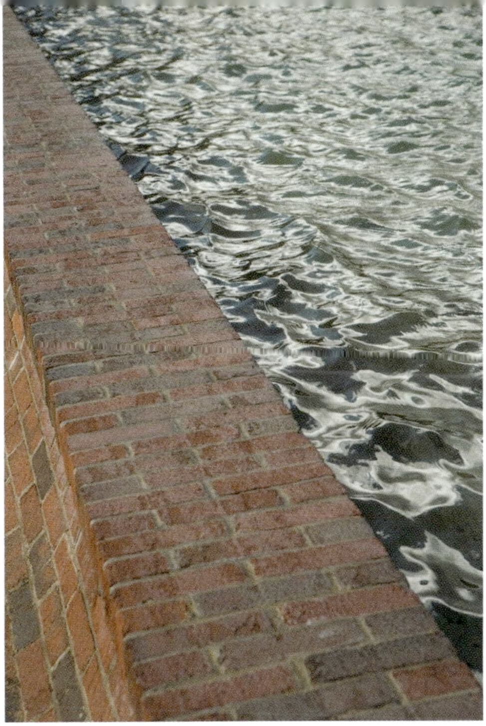

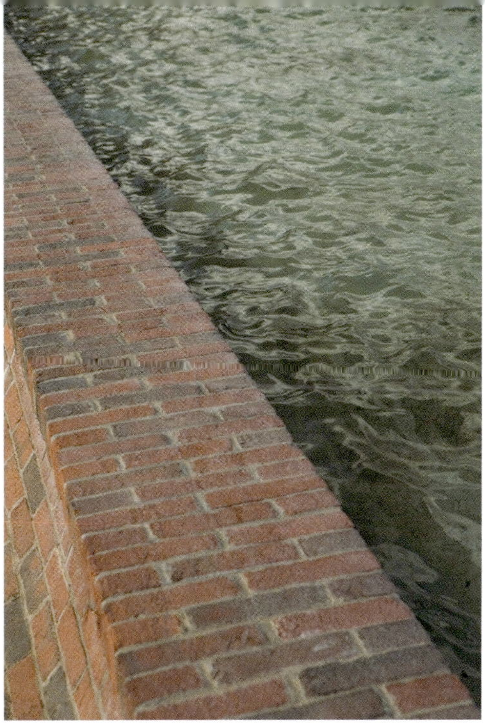

Figure 7.29 (left)
Even with overcast skies, reflections in the water can shine fairly bright.

ISO 100 • 1/125 sec. • f/5.6 • 70mm

Figure 7.30 (right)
A polarizer can mitigate the presence of that reflection, and with calm waters, allow you to see past the surface.

ISO 100 • 1/125 sec. • f/5.6 • 70mm

Finally, polarizers are great in reducing the light reflections on some vegetation. I like overcast days for shooting plant life, but a sunny day is not necessarily reason to quit shooting as long as you have a polarizing filter. For a lot of green vegetation with reflective leaves, you can reduce the brightness and reveal detail in the leaves and plant surfaces in the image (**Figures 7.31** and **7.32**). The polarizer reduces contrast (much like the overcast sky does) and helps bring out colors in the vegetation.

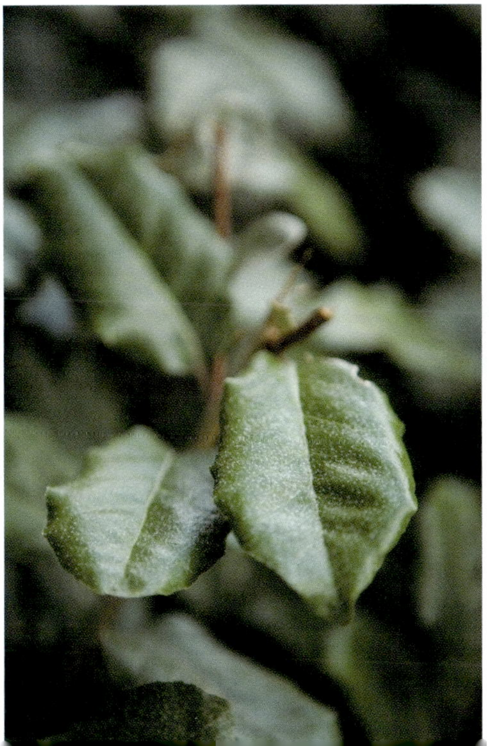

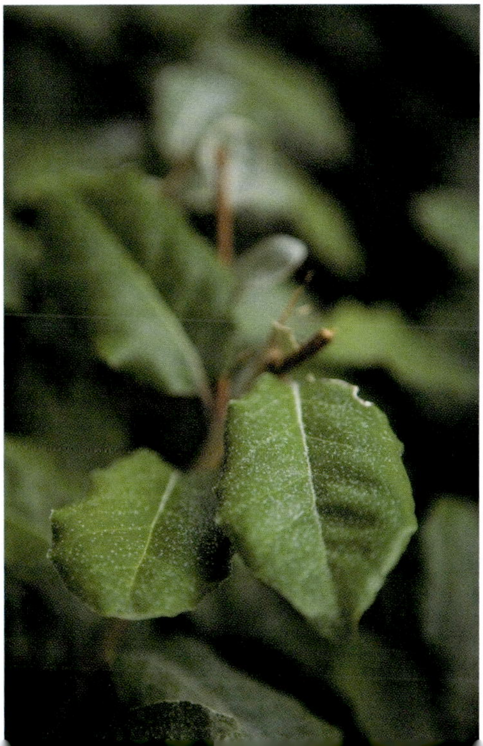

Figure 7.31 (left)
Glossy green leaves can often be highly reflective, resulting in a loss of detail in the specular areas.

ISO 100 • 1/160 sec. • f/2.8 • 70mm

Figure 7.32 (right)
Use a circular polarizing filter to reduce the reflections, bring back detail to the leaves, and saturate the greens.

ISO 100 • 1/160 sec. • f/2.8 • 70mm

Polarizer best practices

Aside from keeping a polarizer at a right angle to the direction of sunlight, here are three best practices for working this kind of filter.

First, you must take into account the drop in exposure caused by a polarizer. When a polarizer blocks certain light waves from passing through, it also reduces the amount of exposure by up to two stops. Be sure to compensate for this drop in exposure by slowing down your shutter speed. But note that if you open up your aperture to make this compensation, you also change the image's depth of field.

Second, be aware of what is called *birefringence* when pointing a polarizing filter toward surfaces like LCD monitors, tinted windows, and certain translucent plastics such as those that cover some smartphones (**Figure 7.33**). If you wear polarized sunglasses, you know exactly what this is. Birefringence shows itself as a rainbow effect on some surfaces. Although this psychedelic effect can be interesting, many people frown upon it. Note that if you rotate the circular polarizer enough, you can block all light emitted from these types of surfaces, especially computer LCDs.

Third, it's not a good idea to use a polarizer at night or in dark interiors. It's hard to see through them when there is not much light. Remember that, depending on its rotation, a polarizer can reduce the light coming through by two stops. And since an abundance of light is what makes the polarizer sing, it's just not worth keeping it on when it gets dark.

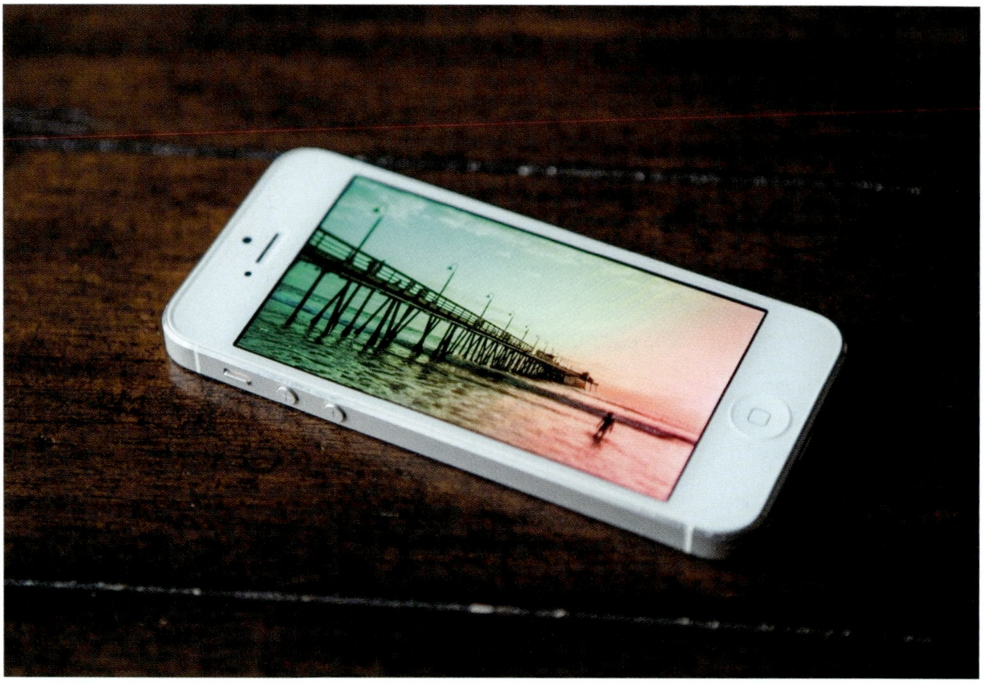

Figure 7.33
Although birefringence adds an interesting, psychedelic effect when you photograph surfaces like a smartphone screen, it's a distracting element in a shot.

ISO 400 • 1/60 sec. • f/2.8 • 70mm

Neutral Density Filters

The type of filter I use most often is a variation on the popular neutral density (ND) filter. An ND filter is just a dark yet transparent piece of glass, resin, or plastic you put in front of your lens. It does not affect anything except exposure, hence the name *neutral*. ND filters come in several versions based on darkness, from less than one stop of light reduction up to ten stops. You can load up on several ND filters, or you can opt for a variable ND filter (**Figure 7.34**), which rotates through levels of exposure reduction. For those who want the most flexibility out of an ND filter, the variable ND is the way to go. They are more expensive than individual ND filters, but over time they are a money saver if you would otherwise buy multiple filters.

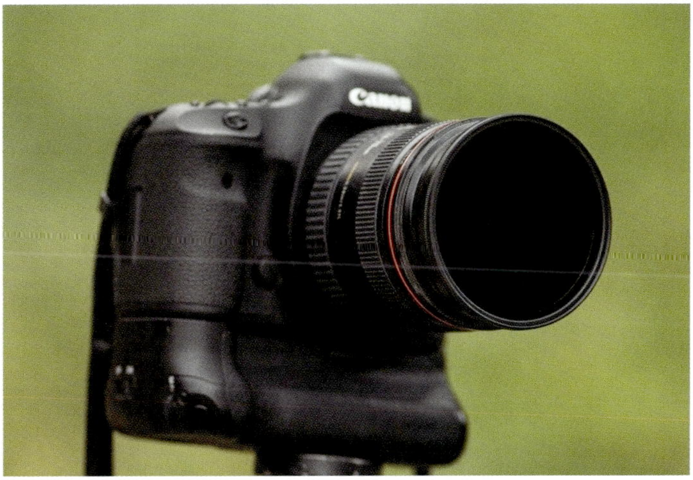

Figure 7.34 **It's easy to spot a variable ND filter—the end of the lens looks as dark as an abyss!**

Creative applications

So what's the big deal? It's amazing what can be achieved by having less light for the camera's meter to measure. You have seen those images of piers in lakes surrounded by what seems like swirling smoke or those waterfalls that were obviously shot with extremely long shutter speeds. Although some of these shots were made when the light was conducive to longer shutter speeds (**Figure 7.35**), others were made with the light-blocking assistance of an ND filter.

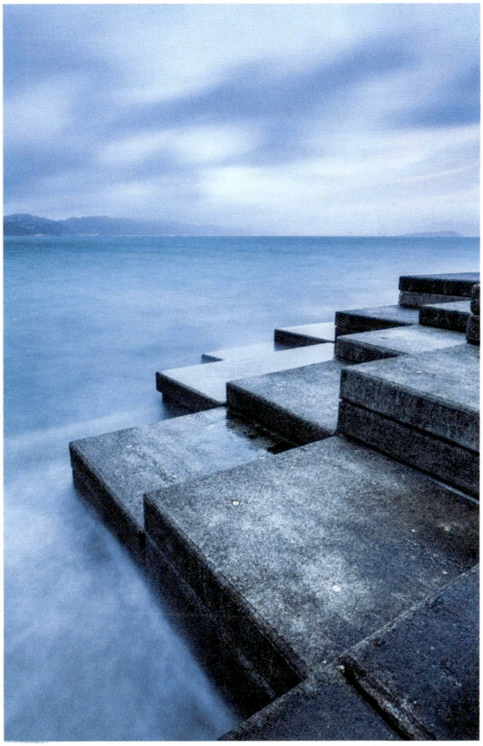

Figure 7.35 **Pre-sunrise light is low enough to get extremely long shutter speeds. However, not all situations are alike, and obtaining the same effect for the water at any other time might call for a dark ND filter.**

ISO 50 • 20 sec. • f/22 • 24mm

By reducing the amount of light passing through the filter, the camera must expose much longer to compensate for that drop. This means using slower shutter speeds, and the resulting effect of such speeds on dynamic subject matter like water can be drastic (**Figures 7.36**, **7.37**, and **7.38**). We all enjoy using long shutter speeds on waterfalls, but with the help of an ND filter, the smoothing effect becomes that much stronger.

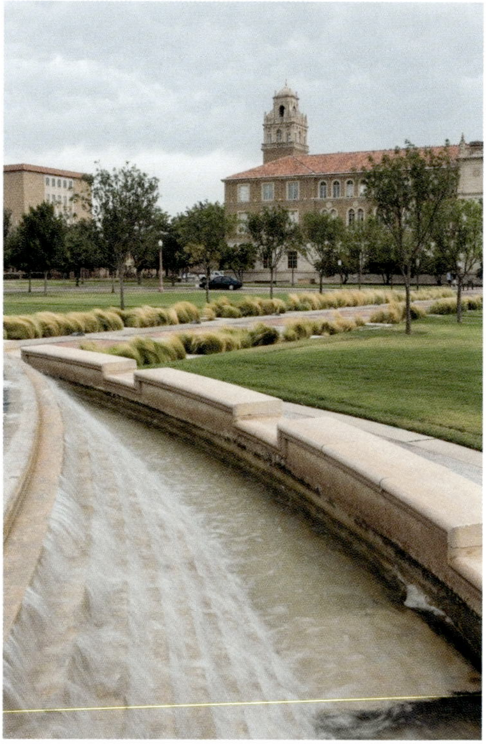

Figure 7.36 One-eighth of a second was as slow as I could get the shutter speed on this overcast day. It made some motion blur in the water, but the speed was too fast for a dramatic effect.

ISO 100 • 1/8 sec. • f/22 • 42mm

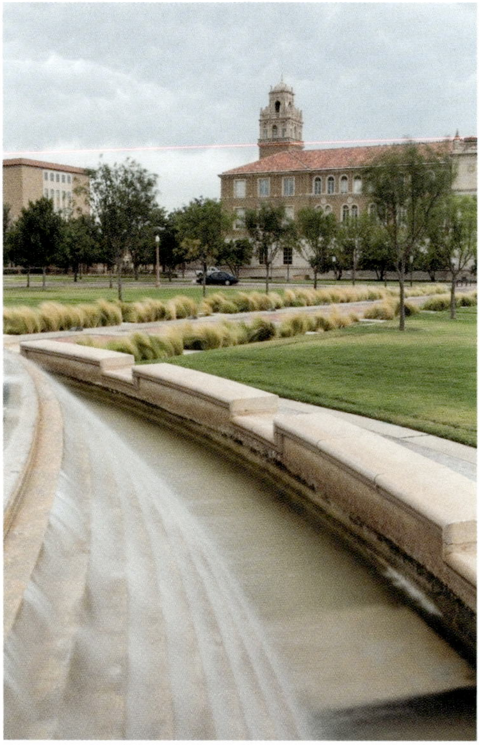

Figure 7.37 (left) With a variable ND filter on the lens, I lowered the incoming light's intensity by four stops, resulting in a misty fountain.

ISO 100 • 2 sec. • f/22 • 42mm

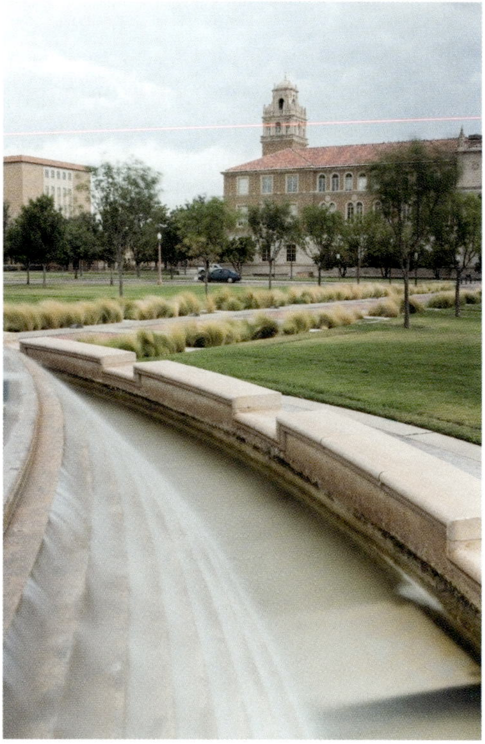

Figure 7.38 (right) With the ambient light dialed down seven stops, I was able to get a 15-second exposure and an even smoother waterfall and pool. Notice that at such a long exposure, the trees are less in focus due to the wind.

ISO 100 • 15 sec. • f/22 • 42mm

Lighting issues

ND filters also help photographers combat intense light during the middle of the day. Although high noon may not have the best or most flattering light to shoot with, it's sometimes the most convenient time. An ND filter can help take a bit of intensity out of the bright light, and as a result, the photographer can use wider apertures and achieve shallower depth of field than if she had no filter.

Many cameras have a maximum shutter speed of 1/4000 of a second. While this is fairly fast, opening a fast prime lens's aperture up to, say, f/1.4, even while using a very low ISO, may necessitate a faster shutter speed usually reserved for higher-end cameras. It will force you to close down your aperture and gain depth of field. If this is not the look you are going for, throw on a one- or two-stop ND filter, and you can then open your aperture back up (**Figures 7.39** and **7.40**).

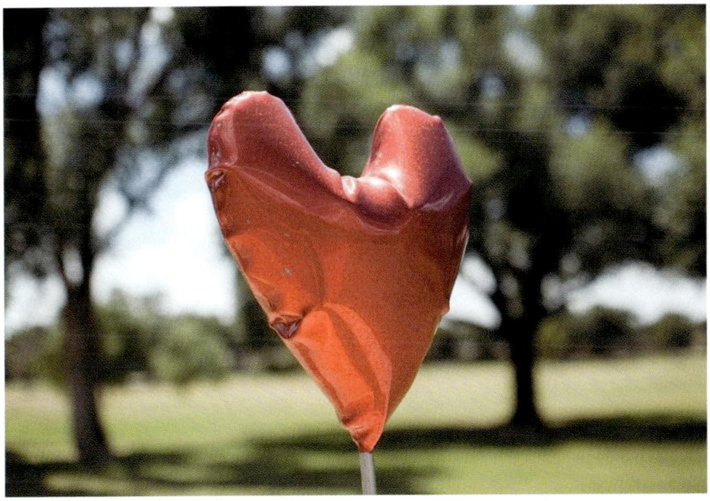

Figure 7.39
At high noon, some cameras would top out at 1/4000 of a second, forcing the photographer to stop down a fast lens and sacrifice a bit of what the lens is about—extra-soft bokeh.

ISO 100 • 1/4000 sec. • f/2 • 50mm

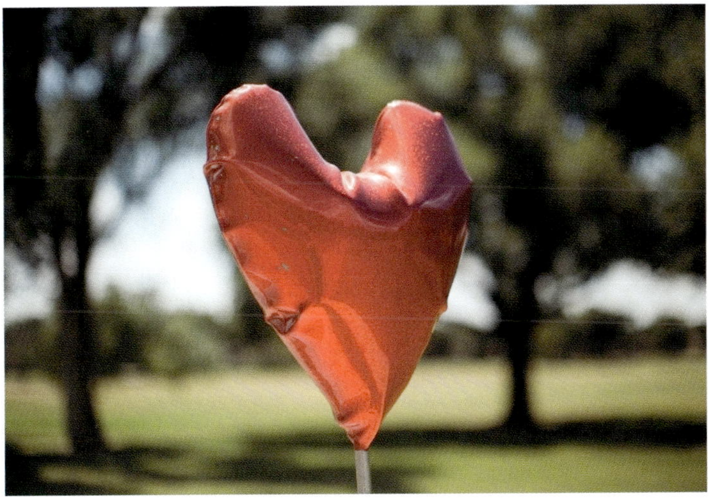

Figure 7.40 **A one-stop ND filter allowed me to recoup one stop of depth of field, and I didn't have to touch the shutter speed.**

ISO 100 • 1/4000 sec. • f/1.4 • 50mm

ND filters are especially useful for portrait photographers using artificial light. Many cameras paired with speed lights or studio flash systems sync with the lights at 1/200, 1/250, or 1/300 of a second, which are not fast shutter speeds when you want to open up an aperture to f/1.8 (**Figures 7.41** and **7.42**). Using an ND filter will knock the ambient light down enough in many cases that you can slow your shutter speed to an adequate sync speed and achieve the look you want.

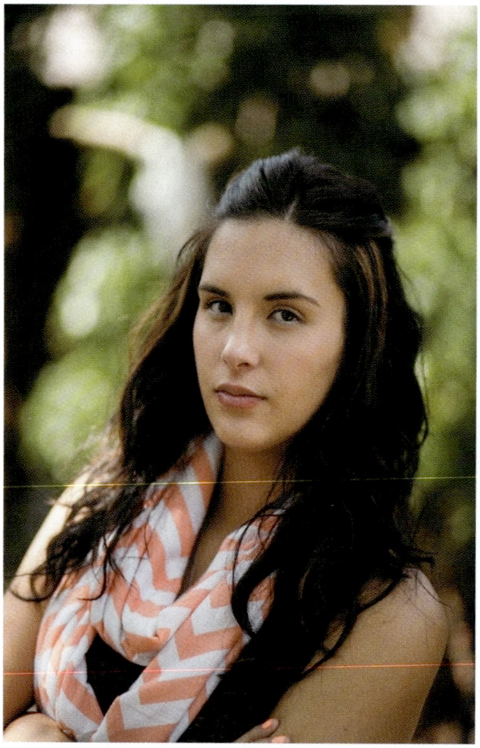

Figure 7.41 **Although the light on Naomi is pleasant enough, the shutter speed I'm forced to use with my aperture open all the way will not sync with my lights.**

ISO 100 • 1/640 sec. • f/1.8 • 85mm

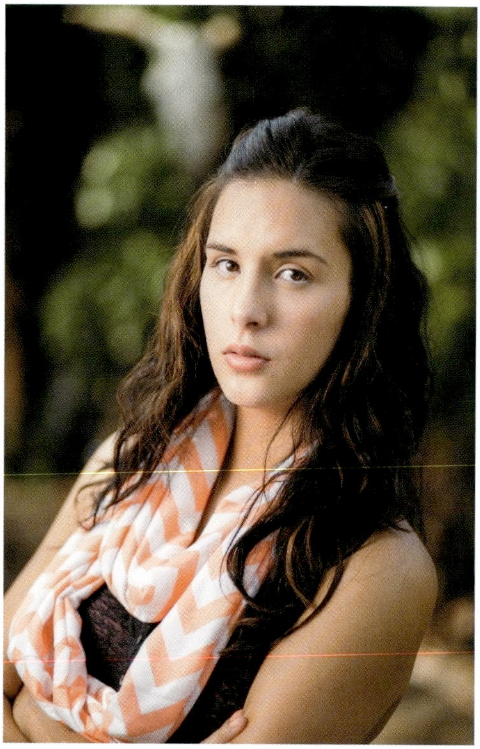

Figure 7.42 **By dialing in nearly two stops of darkening filtration, I used a variable ND filter to reduce the ambient light and allow my shutter speed to sync with artificial light units, even with the aperture opened up all the way. The drop in ambient light muted the background and let Naomi stand out.**

ISO 100 • 1/200 sec. • f/1.8 • 85mm

Likewise, ND filters work in a studio setting, especially when a drop in depth of field is necessary but difficult to achieve given the intensity of many standard studio flash systems (**Figures 7.43**, **7.44**, and **7.45**).

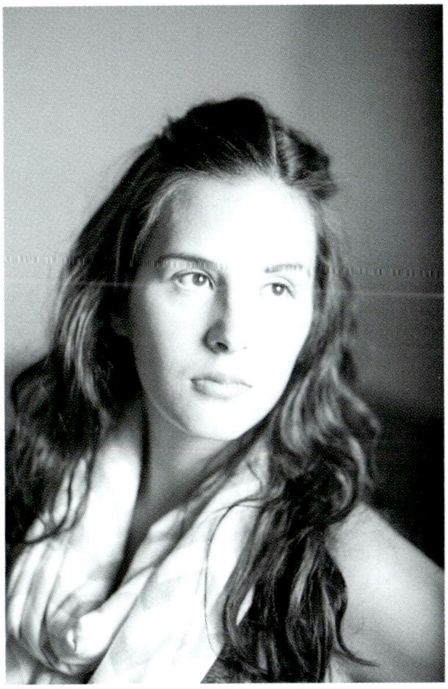

Figure 7.43 When you want to create a portrait at extremely wide apertures, like f/1.8, some studio lighting units are simply too powerful, even at their lowest setting.

ISO 100 • 1/200 sec. • f/1.8 • 85mm

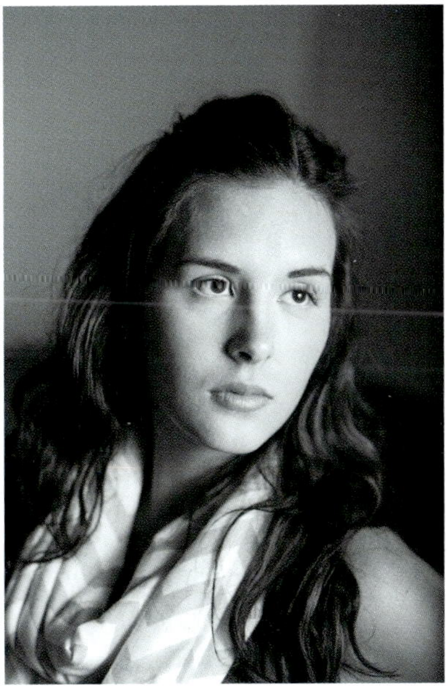

Figure 7.44 One way to offset overpowering studio lighting units is to simply stop the aperture down. However, this comes with a gain in depth of field—an effect I did not wish to have in this portrait.

ISO 100 • 1/200 sec. • f/2.8 • 85mm

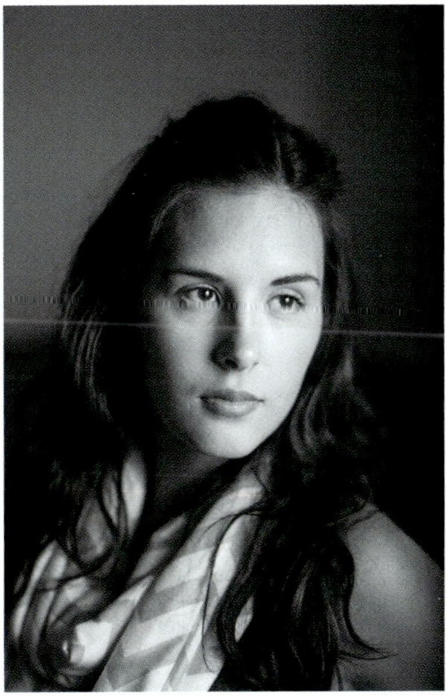

Figure 7.45 Using a variable ND filter to reduce the light by a little over a full stop, I was able to open the aperture back to f/1.8 while keeping the studio lighting unit's output the same and the shallow depth of field where I wanted it.

ISO 100 • 1/200 sec. • f/1.8 • 85mm

Graduated ND filters

A variation on the traditional ND filter is a graduated ND filter—a clear filter that gradually transitions to a darker area (**Figure 7.46**). Graduated ND filters are especially popular among landscape photographers who want to darken a bright sky above relatively dark terrestrial subject matter (**Figures 7.47** and **7.48**). For example, shooting among mountains or tall hillsides usually poses exposure issues. If you meter on the ground, the brighter sky will more than likely overexpose. Metering on the sky will render the ground too dark.

Figure 7.46 A graduated ND filter darkens a portion of the frame while gradually transitioning to complete transparency.

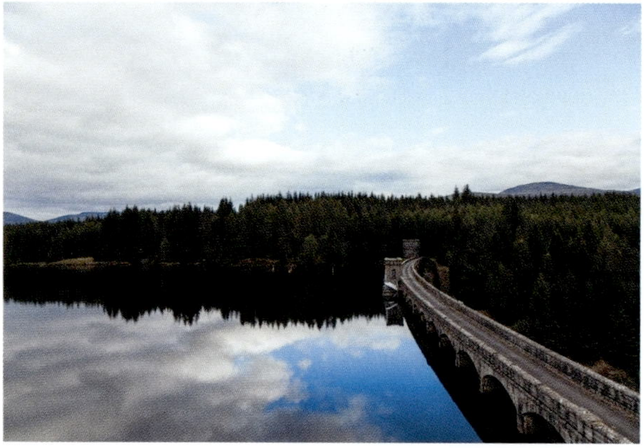

Figure 7.47 **The sky above the darkened foreground of this Scottish forest and reservoir is just above one stop overexposed.**

ISO 200 • 1/125 sec. • f/8 • 24mm

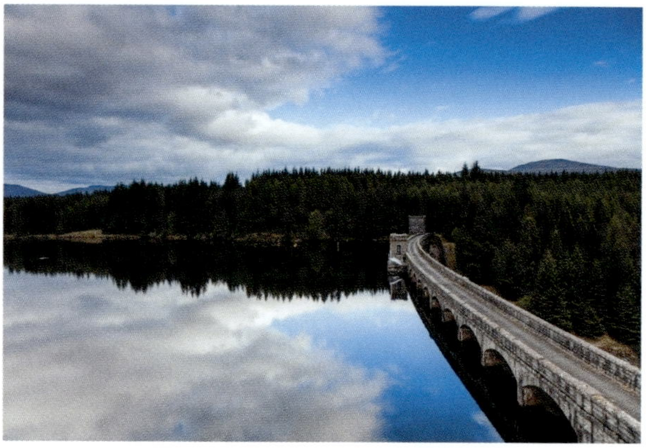

Figure 7.48 **Using a two-stop graduated filter to darken the sky above the horizon makes for a colorful and more compelling image, and the sky matches its reflection in the water.**

ISO 200 • 1/125 sec. • f/8 • 24mm

A graduated filter set to where the areas transition or close to the horizon in the frame will allow the photographer to meter on the ground yet subdue the bright sky and maintain detail in both areas (**Figures 7.49** and **7.50**).

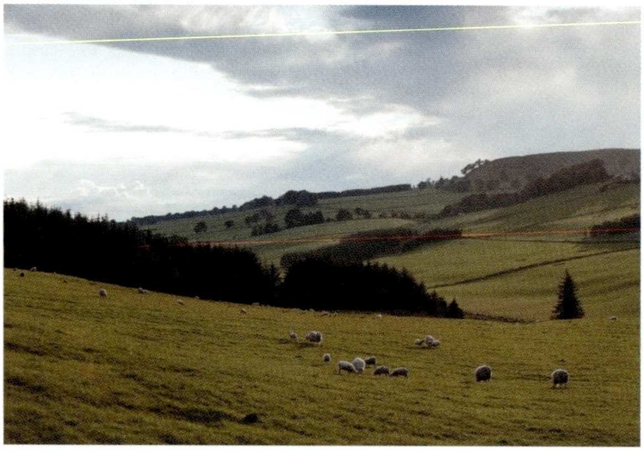

Figure 7.49 **The overexposed areas of the sky take away from the lovely roll of the Scottish farm hills.**

ISO 100 • 1/500 sec. • f/2.8 • 70mm

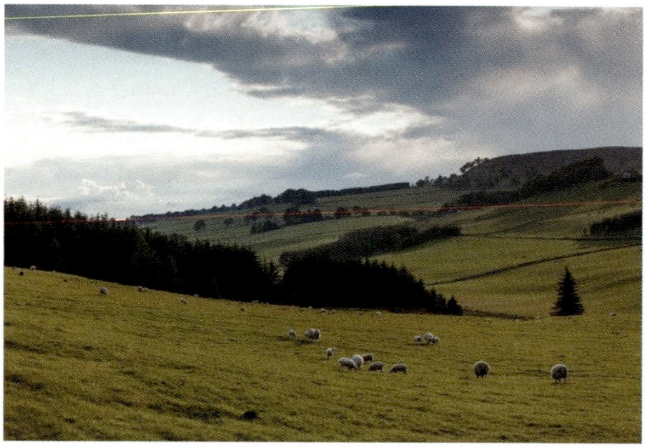

Figure 7.50 **A graduated filter with the transition point positioned on the upper-third horizon line helped tame the sky and save the shot.**

ISO 100 • 1/500 sec. • f/2.8 • 70mm

Graduated ND filters, like their nongraduated brethren, come in various levels of darkening strength. The most popular graduated ND filters are those you can simply drop into a filter holder attached to the end of the lens (**Figure 7.51**), as opposed to screwing the filter itself to the lens. A filter-holder system like this makes using graduated ND filters an efficient process (you can use several filters together), and it also allows the photographer more precision on where the filter's graduation appears in the frame. Other types of filters, including polarizers, are often manufactured as rectangle or square drop-in filters and can be used with such a system. The entire toolset may look complicated, but it really is quite simple and useful.

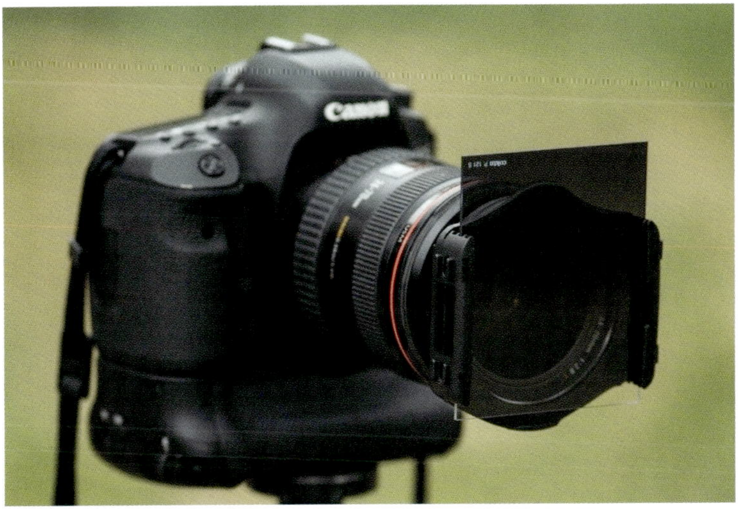

Figure 7.51
A square filter holder like this Cokin system is the most efficient mechanism for working with individual or combined graduated ND filters as well as other filters in square format.

The effect graduated ND filters create can be replicated in postprocessing with software like Adobe Lightroom and Photoshop (**Figure 7.52**), and some photographers choose to bypass purchasing ND filters. However, using graduated ND filters in the field can often save you time on the computer later. Even though software programs have strong processing engines, I still haven't seen one bring back completely overexposed highlights like a graduated ND filter can.

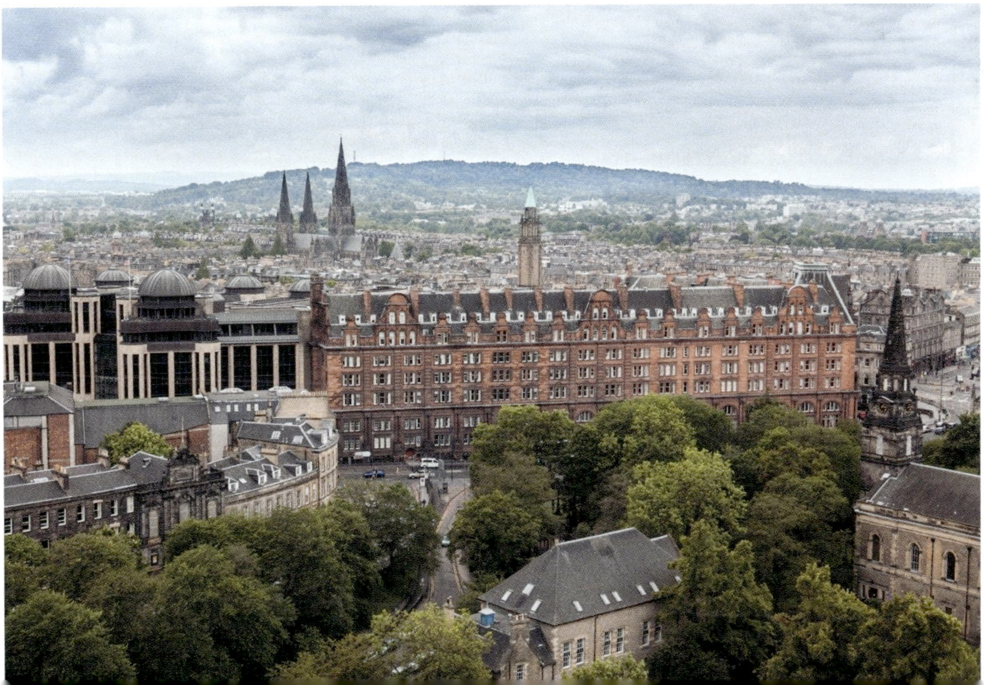

Figure 7.52
I brought the exposure of the bright sky above Edinburgh down one stop using Adobe Lightroom, one of many software applications that can be used instead of graduated ND filters.

ISO 100 • 1/400 sec. • f/4 • 50mm

Take Care of Your Filters

Filters can be pricey. A Cokin variable ND filter is upwards of US$180. It goes without saying that it is important to take care of them. Like lenses, filters get dirty, but luckily you can clean them like you would lenses (discussed in the next chapter). More importantly, they are more likely to fall because they're more delicate.

Much of filter care is how you handle filters when they're not on a lens. Most, if not all, filters come in some sort of case when you purchase them. Hold on to this case and always keep the filter stored in it when not in use. Some companies, like Ruggard, make filter pouches that are designed not to scratch or mar filters while in storage. Avoid transporting filters without any protection in your camera bag, and forget stuffing them in your pockets. I once loaned a graduated ND filter to a student for a day, and after carrying it around in his shirt and back pants pocket, he returned a heavily scratched (and fairly useless) ND that I threw in the nearest trash bin. Avoid touching the actual filter; handle it by its edges and frame structure.

Lens Covers

Photographers have been covering up their lenses with different materials, for different purposes, for as long as lenses have been used outdoors. The following sections highlight lens covers that can be used for transportation, blending in, and protection from the elements.

Neoprene Casings

Neoprene is a fantastic material. It is lightweight, thin, easily conformed, and impact absorbent. Neoprene makes for a great transportation and storage material for camera gear, especially for lenses. Many camera-bag manufacturers incorporate neoprene into their products, some of which are bags designed specifically for individual lenses. LensCoat is a company that specializes in neoprene wraps that can be installed around telephoto lenses that are used in rowdy environments, such as sports events and landscape and wildlife photography.

Are individual neoprene cases and covers necessary? Maybe not. It depends on the level of security you wish your lenses to have. I don't use them. When I don't need a lens in hand, mine goes right back to its bag (some of which have neoprene components). However, LensCoat's neoprene covers are worth considering for protecting expensive telephoto lenses. They also help reduce the public visibility of such lenses, allowing you to remain more inconspicuous.

Camouflage

Speaking of visibility, wildlife photographers will certainly benefit from encasing their lenses in camouflage. Many of Canon's long lenses are white (for heat-dispersing reasons), and they can be alarming to some species of wildlife. Imagine setting up to photograph white-tailed deer, unknowing that you won't see one because they notice that big white blob in front of your camouflaged body. Get that lens covered up as well!

LensCoat makes several neoprene covers that are camouflaged with popular patterns, and for around US$100, you can get a lens cover that protects and blends into the environment. Not a bad deal. However, there are other options. My favorite is simply wrapping my lens with a camouflage fabric stretch wrap (**Figure 7.53**). You can pick up a 4-yard roll at a sporting-goods store for around US$8. It is thin, easily wrapped around a lens, and it stays put (**Figure 7.54**). Be sure to get a type of stretch wrap that does not leave any adhesive residue on your lens. More than likely, it is reusable in case you need to remove it and put it back on.

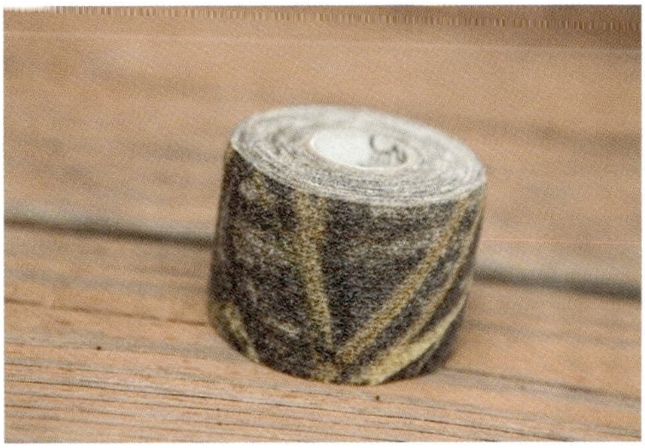

Figure 7.53
Pick up a roll of camouflage wrap for just a few dollars at a sporting-goods store.

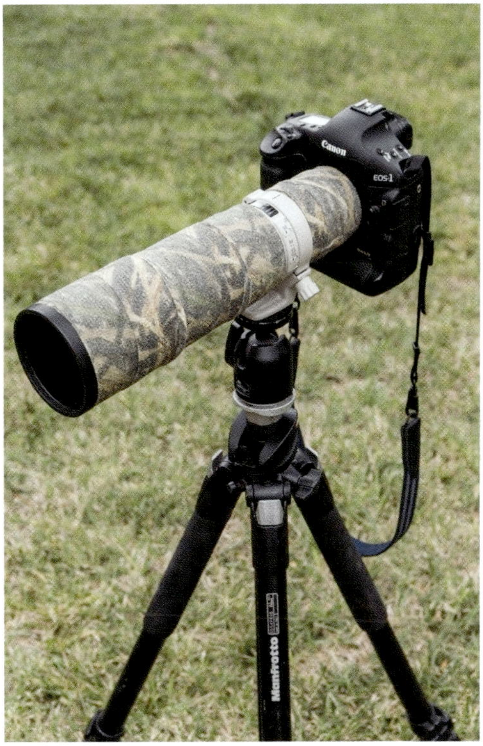

Figure 7.54
In about 2 minutes, you can change an EF 400mm f/5.6L from a white-barreled spectacle to an easily concealed wildlife lens.

Rain/Weather Covers

Quite possibly the most useful lens covers are those that protect your glass from inclement weather. There have been several times on the field during football season when I needed to protect my lenses from a rain or dust storm (I live in west Texas). These are great moments to employ a cover like the Think Tank Hydrophobia or the OP/TECH Rainsleeve (**Figure 7.55**).

These covers fit securely around a lens's hood, and the cover encloses the camera body as well, with an opening in the rear for you to see through the viewfinder while protected from the elements. Many of the more expensive rain covers are tailored for a particular range of lenses, but other affordable options are made for general use.

To save money, grab a plastic trash bag and a rubber band large enough to fit snuggly around a lens hood. After unfolding the bag, use scissors to cut the bottom out. Place the camera and lens in the bag, using the rubber band to fit one opening around the lens hood. The other opening is an entrance for you to access the camera (**Figure 7.56**). You can customize the bag to fit more securely or to fit around a monopod or tripod. I usually carry a few large plastic trash bags in my camera bag for this reason. Here's a tip: Spend the extra US$2 for good-quality Hefty bags for increased protection.

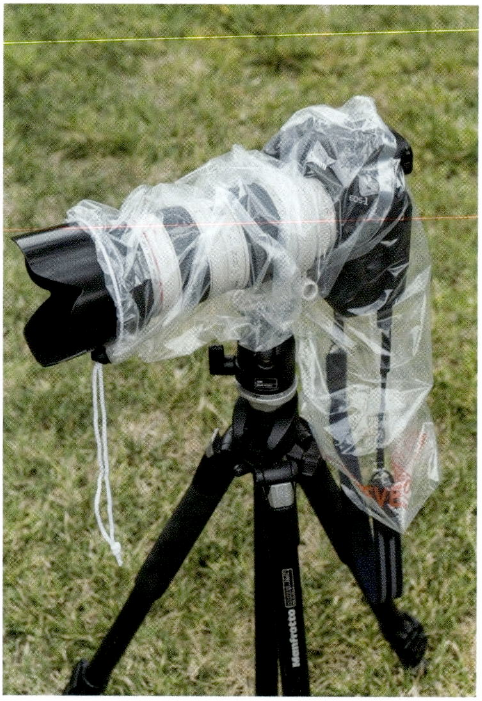

Figure 7.55 The OP/TECH Rainsleeve is a very affordable and easy-to-use guard against the elements.

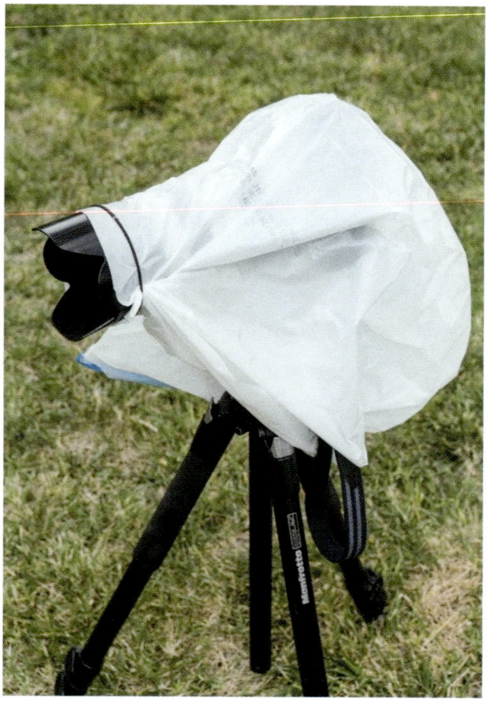

Figure 7.56 In a pinch, a large trash bag and a rubber band or hair band can serve as a rain cover.

Chapter 7 Assignments

Lens accessories, such as filters and extenders, are optional equipment, but when the shot counts, they are invaluable. The following assignments help familiarize you with some of the more popular lens accessories.

Go macro with extensions

If you're into macro photography, extension tubes offer a very affordable way to get in close without breaking the bank. Most extension-tube manufacturers, like Kenko, offer an option to buy three together, and they can be used individually or in conjunction. Start with the thinnest tube between the camera and lens (make sure it is a lens that will reach past 85mm to get the best macro effect). See how close you can focus, paying attention to how you can fine-tune focus with the lens's zoom ring.

Make a few pictures of your subject, changing your composition as you get used to how the tubes affect the frame's content. Add an additional tube. Repeat the process, but just a bit tighter, exploring in more detail. Add the last tube to see how the ambient light drops a bit and how getting in even closer affects your composition. Notice how the depth of field decreases with every extension tube you add.

Polarize the world

A polarizing filter's effect is the only effect that postprocessing-software applications cannot replicate. Spend a morning shooting with just your circular polarizer on a standard zoom lens. Get a feel for how it works in a number of scenarios, keeping in mind that the filter's effect is most prominent when you point the lens 90 degrees from the sun's rays. Shoot wide, including the sky, to see how saturated you can make the blues, noting how the changes convey different moods.

Go window shopping on a commercial street and learn how you can eliminate reflections in shop windows by turning the polarizer. Near a lake instead of a downtown? Shoot long exposures of the lake with the polarizer to minimize distracting reflections and see through the top of the water.

Share your results with the book's Flickr group!
Join the group here: www.flickr.com/groups/canonlenses_fromsnapshotstogreatshots

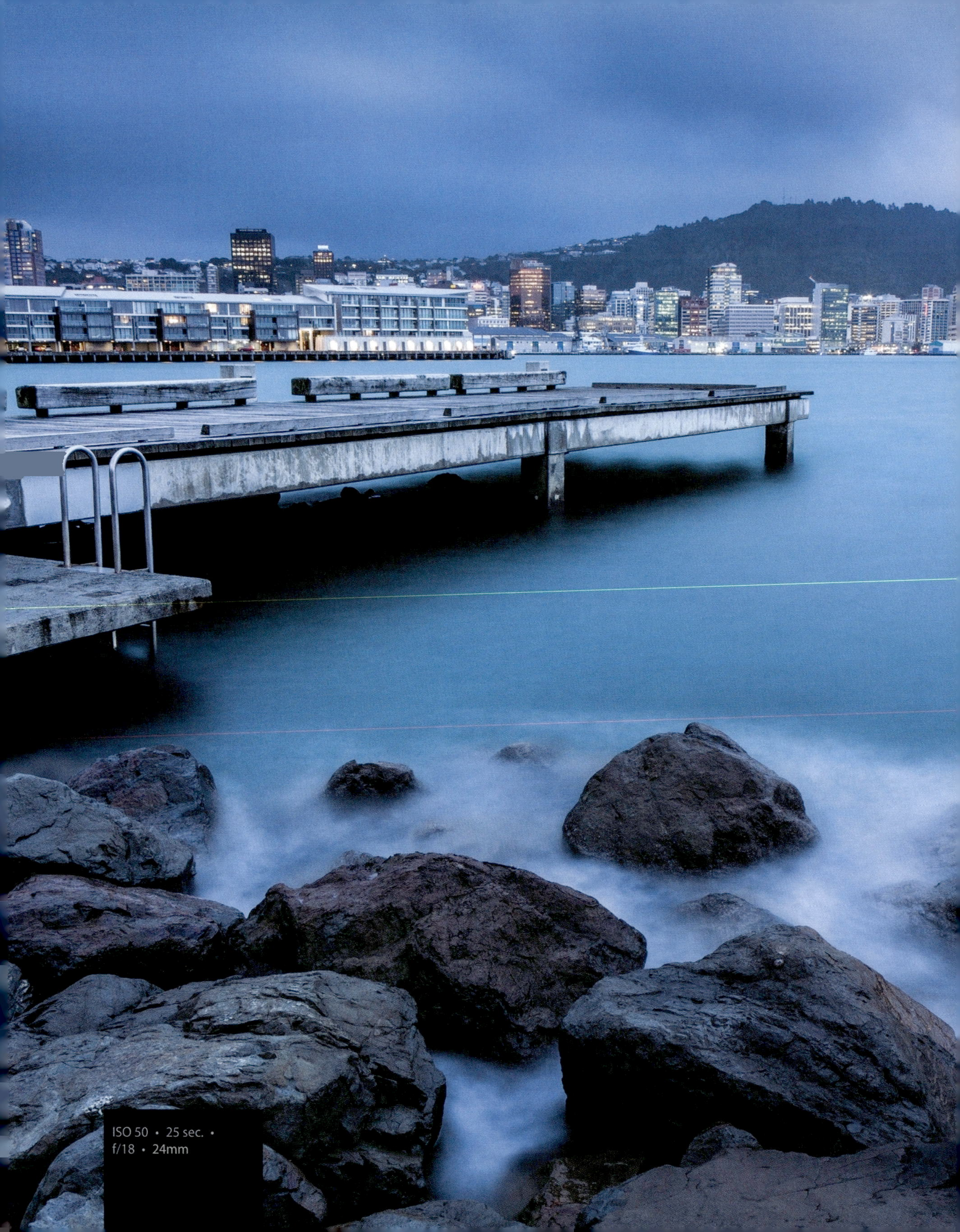

ISO 50 • 25 sec. •
f/18 • 24mm

8

Best Practices

Lens care and tips for making better pictures

Imagine you are standing on the dock of a marina before sunrise, camera atop a tripod, and you've just lined up the perfect shot of boats. You want them to sway, so you plan a long exposure. You begin to shoot, using a shutter release. The first shot indicates a good exposure, an intentional blur of the boats, and the reflection of the sky is glorious. However, the shot is out of focus. A 30 mph wind is whipping straight at the camera, and the camera strap is knocking the camera around on the tripod. You wrap the strap around the tripod head's base. The next shot is also out of focus. You put weight on the tripod but get another out-of-focus shot. You then realize the lens hood is catching the oncoming wind. Noticing no threat of lens flare, you remove it, and the resulting shot is a keeper.

The above scenario represents a number of best practices you can employ while working with an assortment of lenses in different shooting environments. This chapter runs through a few of these best practices, from maintenance to photographing different subject matter to techniques that are unique to the lenses (as opposed to the camera).

Poring Over the Picture

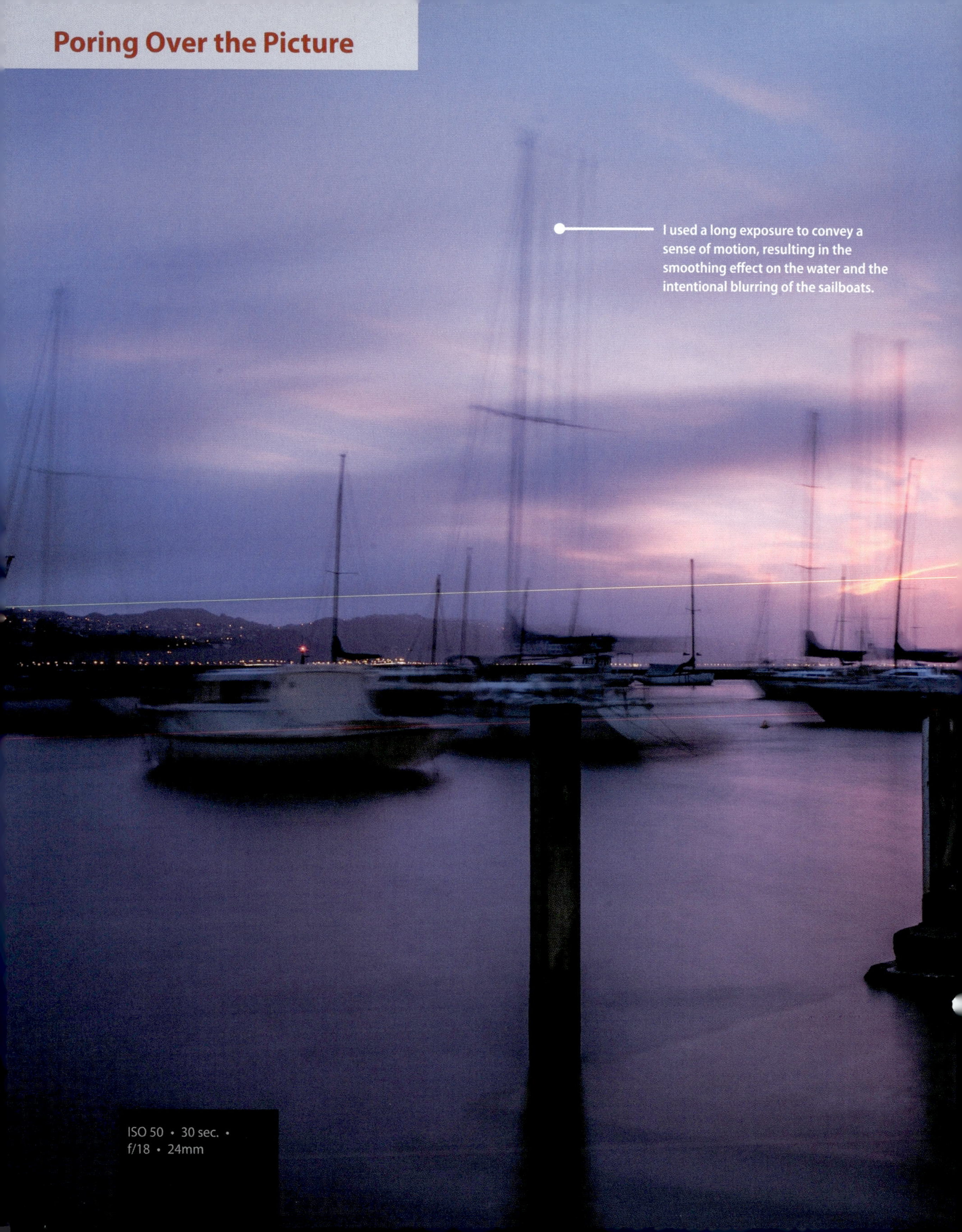

I used a long exposure to convey a sense of motion, resulting in the smoothing effect on the water and the intentional blurring of the sailboats.

ISO 50 • 30 sec. • f/18 • 24mm

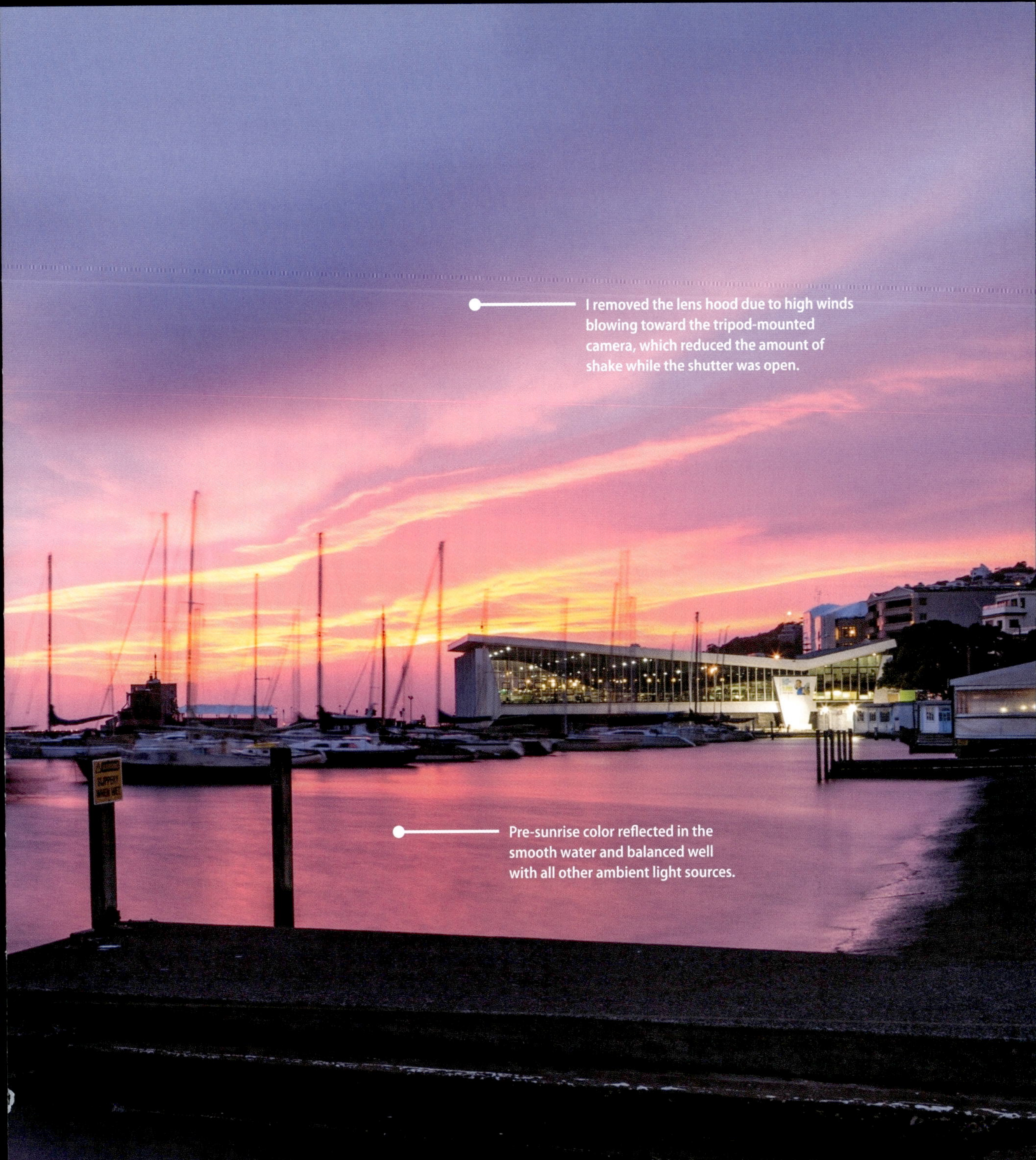
I removed the lens hood due to high winds blowing toward the tripod-mounted camera, which reduced the amount of shake while the shutter was open.
Pre-sunrise color reflected in the smooth water and balanced well with all other ambient light sources.

Maintenance and Good Habits

It pays to take care of your gear. Lenses are investments and deserve to be treated as such. From the photography student to the seasoned professional, those who take care of their lenses get the most mileage out of them.

Cleaning

Lenses get dirty. Keep them clean. It's as simple as that. Lenses collect dust, and even mud when you stumble down a 12-foot-deep pipeline ditch (**Figure 8.1**). Do you have a lens that grinds a bit when you turn the zoom or focusing rings? If so, there is dust or sand inside those particular mechanisms.

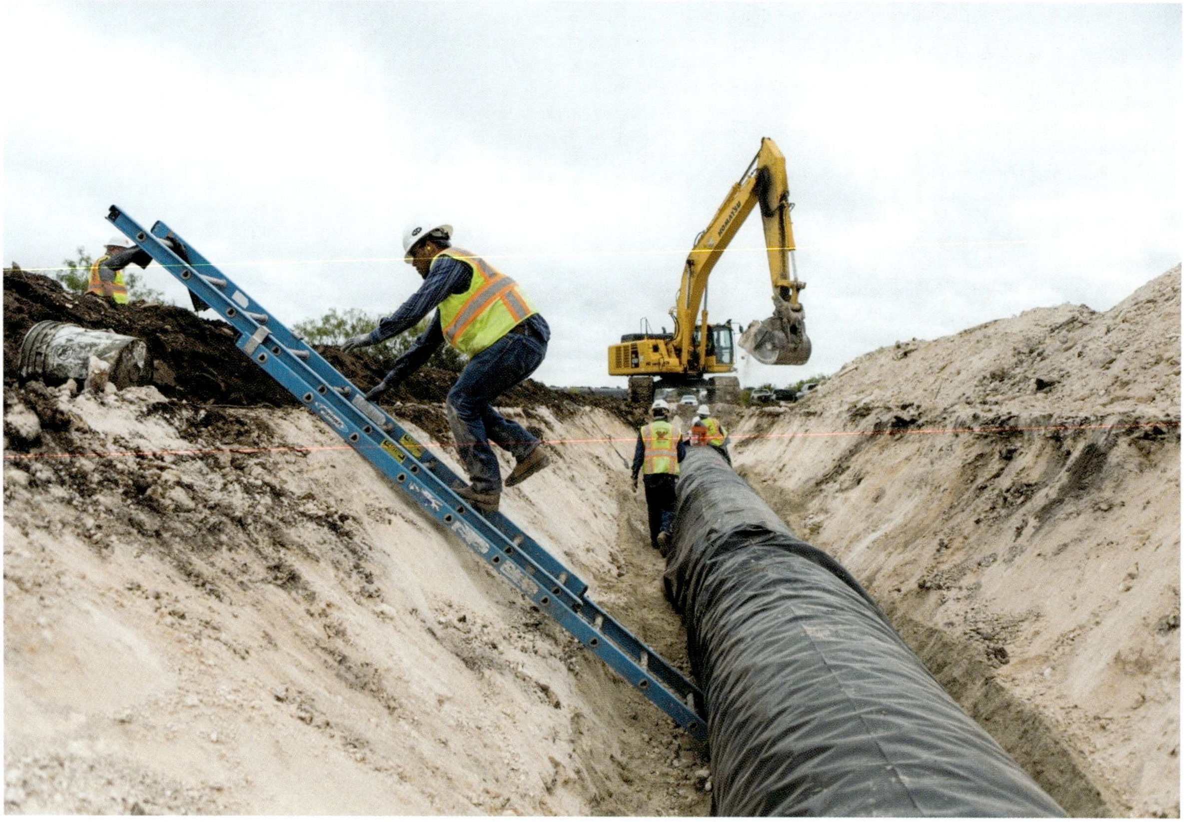

Figure 8.1 **To get this shot, I slid down the embankment on my backside, dragging cameras and lenses in the dirt with me, necessitating a thorough cleaning after the shoot!**

ISO 400 • 1/6400 sec. • f/2.8 • 24mm

Cleaning cloths

A proper cleaning cloth for any lens is made of microfiber and large enough to cover more than just the lens element. You can pick one up at every camera or electronics store. Just make sure it is indeed for camera lenses. Microfiber (**Figure 8.2**) is incredibly soft, does not scratch the glass or important coatings on the outside of the elements, and is a magnet for dust. I recommend getting one at least the size of your hand so you don't leave a thumbprint on the glass. Your fingers are especially oily, and when they come in contact with lens elements, try to clean the lens as soon as you can. A soft cotton T-shirt will also work. *Never* use anything polyester based, or tissues or paper towels.

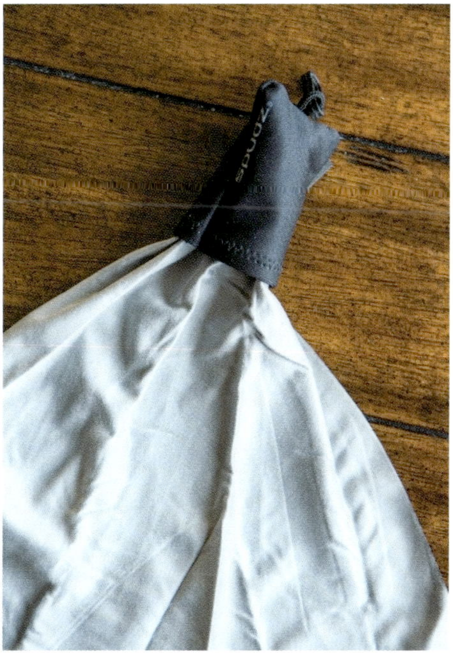

Figure 8.2
Microfiber cloths are extremely lightweight and not abrasive to lens glass. I like to keep a few Spudz cloths attached to my camera bags.

Before wiping with a cloth, be sure the glass is free of any sand or other abrasive elements that can scratch the glass. Use a fine lens brush or air blower. With your cloth, wipe your lens's glass in a circular motion, paying extra attention to the area where glass meets the lens construction (the edge of the element). Wipe both outer elements, being extremely careful not to touch either with your fingers, especially the rear element nearest the camera (this one gets tough to clean if it needs any more than just a blow of air and a wipe).

If you need to clean a dusty lens barrel, a lens cloth will work. However, if there are large chunks of dirt or mud (or any sticky material) on the barrel, dampen a normal cleaning cloth and use it to lightly loosen all of the grime. Make sure to wring the cloth out very well before using, lest you get water in the seams and seals around the zoom and/or focus rings and buttons. Keep in mind that this is just for the barrel. If you want to apply a cleaning solution to the front and rear elements, I suggest you use an optic-grade product.

Solutions

At times, using a cleaning solution to wipe up grimier spots on lens elements is essential. Use a methyl alcohol solution when cleaning your lens elements. It is best to dampen your lens cloth with a few drops of it and then wipe instead of applying the solution directly to your glass. This reduces the risk of liquid seeping in through the seam of the lens barrel and glass construction. Take your time and wipe gently. Applying too much pressure may cause some unseen obstruction to scratch the glass, or at the very least the coatings necessary for great color and contrast rendering. If you do not have any solution at the time you notice grime on your lens, you can also breathe softly on the glass, fogging it up, and then wipe gently.

Air blowers

It seems I have an air blower in every camera bag. I believe an air blower should never be too far out of reach for both camera bodies and lenses. There are several brands of air blowers, but I lean toward the Giottos Rocket Air Blaster because of its durable, rubberized construction and force (**Figure 8.3**). Although they seem more useful for cleaning camera sensors, air blowers are nice for blowing large pieces of dust off of lens elements, as well as blowing grime away from seams and buttons. As if you were cleaning the digital sensor on your camera, hold the surface you are blowing upside down so debris clinging to your lens will fall away from it (**Figure 8.4**).

When I do a thorough cleaning of all my gear, I use the air blower to knock the first layer of dust off. I often use the air blower in place of a soft lens brush. I never—and nor should you—use canned air to clean any of my gear, especially my lenses and camera sensors. Canned, or compressed, air often spits and spurts fluorocarbons onto your gear, and the last thing you want is some of this leaking into your lenses. You may never be able to get it out.

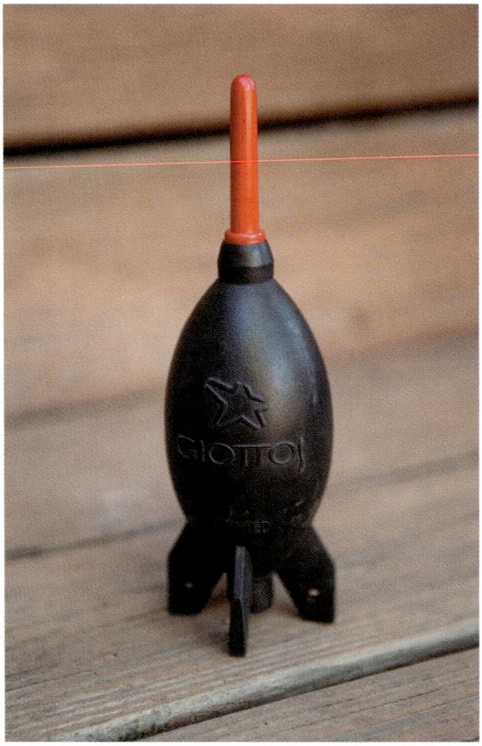

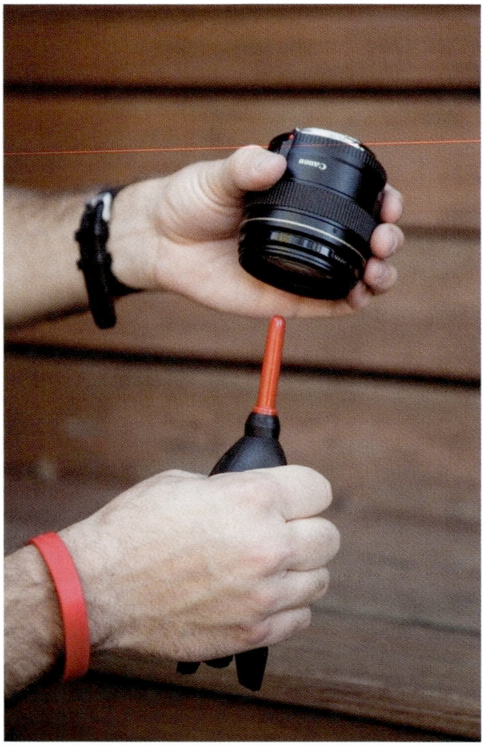

Figure 8.3 (left)
A rubber air blower, such as the Giottos Rocket Air Blaster, is an indispensable accessory.

Figure 8.4 (right)
When using an air blower on your lenses, turn the surface upside down and blow upward, ensuring any debris on the glass or barrel falls to the ground.

Storage

I cringe at how some of my students store their camera gear, haphazardly thrown into backpacks or slung low and loose around the body. I need to stress the importance of storage. There are always going to be instances when you don't treat your gear with the utmost care, but hopefully this is when you're in pursuit of making great images instead of just transporting the gear around town.

Choose the right bag

Bags are a touchy subject among photographers. Many of us have our favorite brands (mine is Think Tank Photo), we have different functional requirements, and we want bags to have just a little style. Regardless of your brand preference, I suggest that you really examine the structure of a bag before you purchase. If you are lucky enough to have a camera store in your city, pay it a visit and compare bags of different makes and price points.

Although lightweight, bags with thin, almost paperlike, internal dividers are not very protective. Nearly all camera bags these days come with moveable dividers, and some even come with extra dividers. It is nice to have a bag that can be configured to your needs yet keeps your gear secure in case of a fall (**Figure 8.5**).

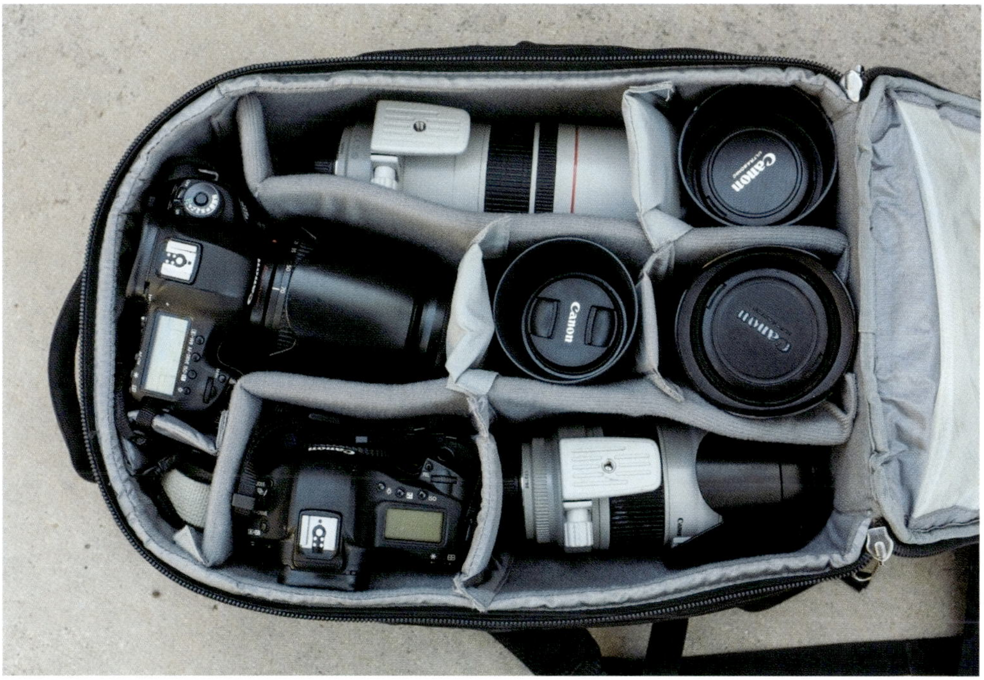

Figure 8.5
Ensure your camera bag has sufficient padding for transporting your lenses. This Think Tank StreetWalker Hard-Drive has thick but lightweight dividers. (I "Frankensteined" it with a couple Lowepro dividers as well.)

Also compare the bags' zippers. One of the reasons I use Think Tank Photo is that they use sturdy zippers (**Figure 8.6**). The last thing I need is a zipper busting loose on my backpack, especially when it's full of equipment and on my back.

If you are an outdoors photographer, consider getting a bag that has water-resistant or waterproof exterior features, such as special cloth materials, zippers, and covers (**Figure 8.7**). I often use a Lowepro Pro Trekker when taking long hikes with a lot of gear due to its superior internal padding and water-resistant zipper for the main compartment (**Figure 8.8**). Take it from someone who has dunked a camera bag full of gear in a river: This is a feature you want.

Some lenses, usually the higher-end L-series pieces, come in their own bags. These are nice for transport when you need to pack a lens in luggage, insulating it from other non-camera gear. However, they are not all that practical when you also own a good camera bag with internal dividers. (I never use the bags that come with my lenses.) The large telephotos come packaged in their own hard-shell cases, but most photographers will acquire bags to transport these lenses more efficiently. The bottom line is there are many camera-gear bags out there. Shop for durability, protection, and comfort (in that order).

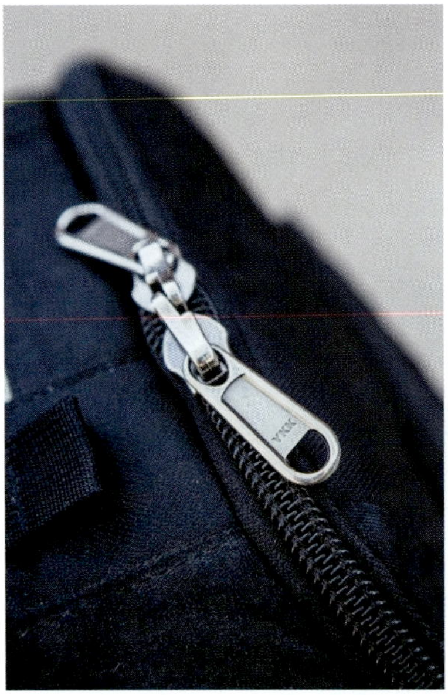

Figure 8.6 They might seem unimportant, but stout, big zippers are one of my first considerations when shopping for new bags. You do not want your zippers failing when you are transporting your bag or accessing the gear inside.

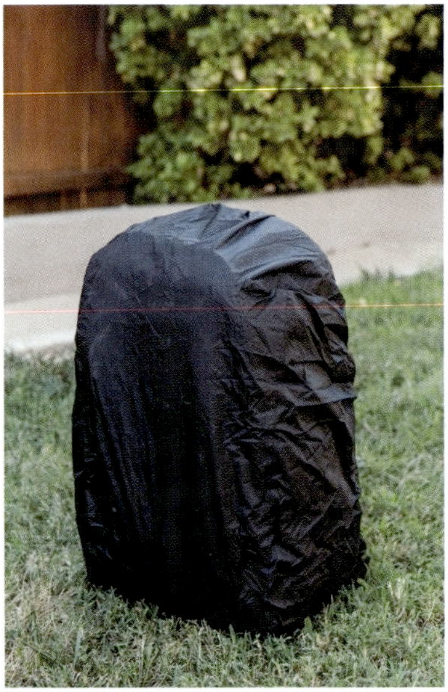

Figure 8.7 When shopping for a bag to transport your gear, make sure it comes with a rain cover.

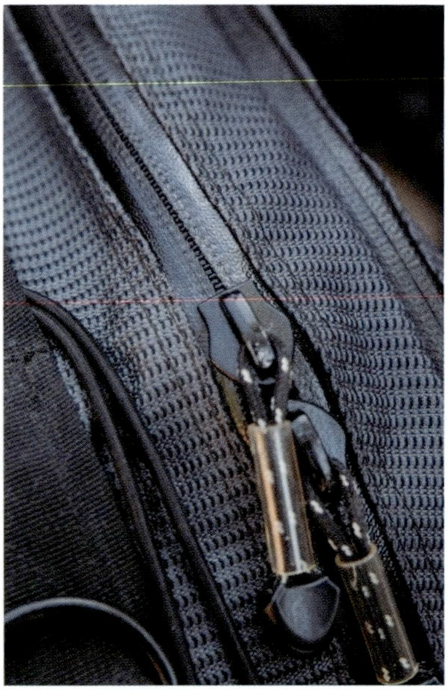

Figure 8.8 Many bags, including this Lowepro Pro Trekker, have water-resistant zippers. If you are photographing near or on water quite a bit, this is a valuable asset.

Leave the lens on

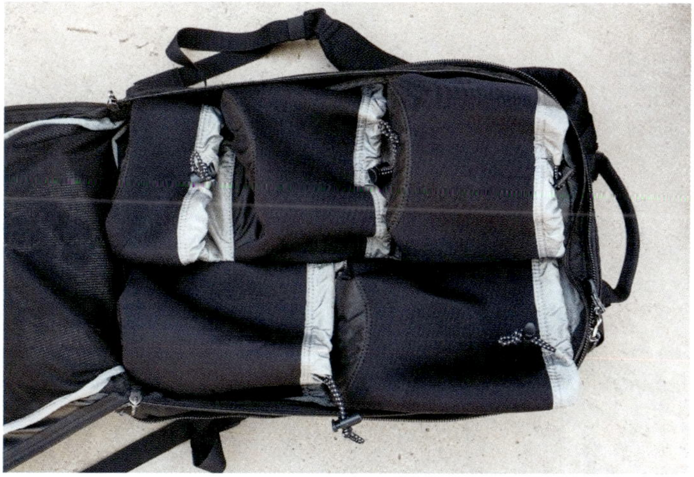

Figure 8.9 **The Think Tank Photo Shape Shifter is a wonderful bag, but it doesn't allow the camera and lens to stay connected during transportation.**

I often see beginning photographers finish a shoot and then take their lens off their camera, put the body cap on the camera and the rear lens cap on the lens, and then put both in their bag separately. Some bags are designed to carry your gear like this, minimizing space needed for the bag itself (like the Think Tank Photo Shape Shifter in **Figure 8.9**). For the most part, I recommend keeping a lens on a camera. Why? Simply to keep the inside of the camera and the rear element of the lens cleaner. Every time you remove your lens from the camera, you invite dust to collect inside both pieces of gear. Clearly, you'll need to change lenses, but limiting the number of times you do it reduces the chances of debris collecting on the camera's sensor or rear lens element.

As a side, it is also important to turn off your camera when changing lenses or taking one off to store the equipment. Leaving the camera on attracts static-friendly dust. Along the same lines, it is best practice to keep the camera facing downward when changing lenses.

Keep the lens cap on

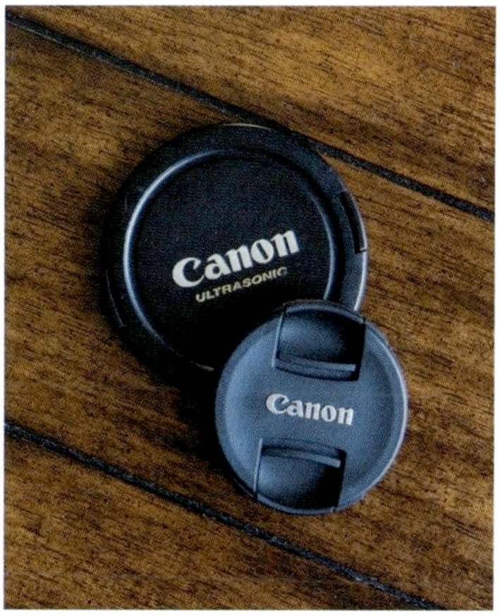

Figure 8.10 **Keep your lens caps close. They are the first defense against nicks, scratches, and grimy fingers.**

One of the worst things you can do is lose a lens cap, a simple necessity (**Figure 8.10**). The lens cap is the number-one defense against fingerprint smears and small scratches. You might not need it when just photowalking around the city or out in the countryside, especially if you are using a lens hood, but it never hurts to put the cap on when you are hiking around rocky areas or stopping at the local pub for a pint.

Be sure to store your lens with the cap on. Most camera bags are constructed with internal materials that will not hurt your outer lens elements, but that doesn't keep you from putting in things (such as loose change) that might. Also, always remember where you put your lens cap. Every time I take off a lens cap, I put it in a pocket, usually my back pocket. I know that when it's time to return the lens back to the bag, the lens cap is somewhere on my body.

Reverse Your Carrying Position

My buddy Alan Hess gave me a good tip about carrying cameras. Alan is a fantastic live-event photographer, and he works in a variety of fast-paced environments, usually with one camera in hand and the other hanging on his shoulder. He slings his camera and lens on his shoulder with the lens pointed in toward his body. Most people sling their cameras with the lens pointed out and the camera's LCD screen against the body (**Figure 8.11**). However, reversing this position reduces how much the camera protrudes from the photographer's side. The lens will point down the photographer's leg instead of out (**Figure 8.12**). This position decreases the chance of the lens banging into objects.

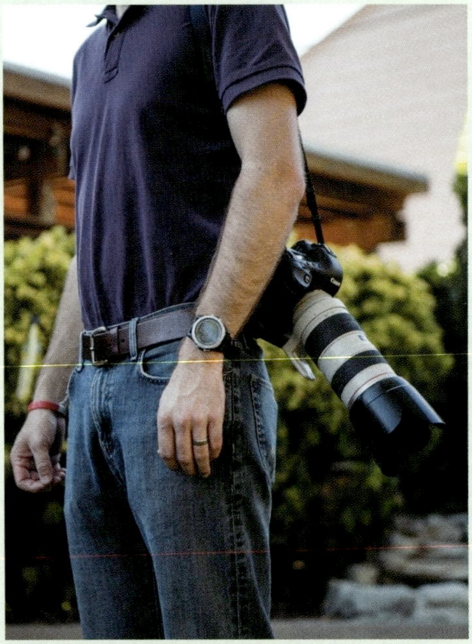

Figure 8.11 Slinging a camera on your shoulder with the LCD facing your body leaves the lens protruding from your side, making it prone to knocks.

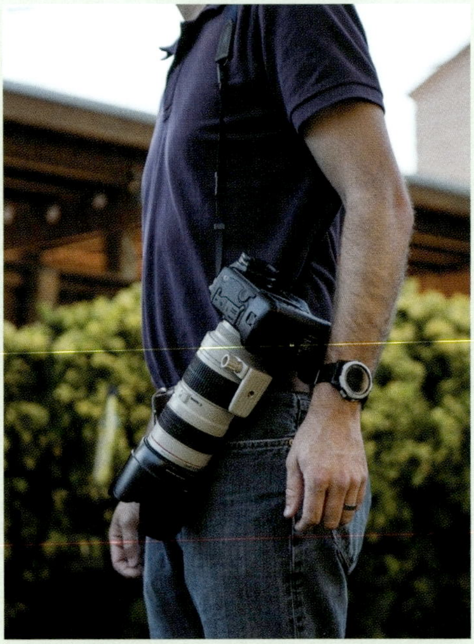

Figure 8.12 Reversing the sling position keeps the lens (and LCD) close to the body.

Say no to the car

I'm going to be very blunt: Do not store your camera equipment in the car. Unfortunately, I know several people who have had their gear stolen. Vehicles are just too easy to break into, and it's difficult to hide camera gear. If you live in a hot area, cars can become ovens as well. Although I don't know of any instances when the heat of a parked car damaged gear, I can't stand the idea of gear composed of silicon, glass, plastic, and glue sweltering in a hot vehicle.

So, what is the alternative if you have to leave your vehicle somewhere for a while? Carry your gear with you. Practice good judgment about your surroundings, but for the most part, you should just schlep your gear around.

Shooting Equipment and Techniques

When it comes to actually shooting with your lenses, the process seems pretty simple: Point the lens at what you want to capture, compose the shot, and snap. However, there is more to it, particularly in regard to maintaining focus and moving it with your subject matter (when shooting active subjects). Previous chapters discussed strategies and accessories for capturing great images with various types of lenses. The following section includes additional tips and suggestions for all lenses.

The Lens Hood

Part protector, part shooting necessity, the lens hood is the sister to the lens cap. Whereas all lenses come with lens caps, not all are packaged with a lens hood. I suggest getting a hood for every lens, for a number of reasons (**Figure 8.13**).

Lens flare

Most people associate a lens hood with reducing lens flare. Lens flare is caused by direct light—mostly sunlight, but anything with a high-intensity spot characteristic—hitting the lens elements at extreme angles. Photographers whose work involves turning their lenses in the direction of the sun deal with flare most often. Flare creates visible spots or artifacts or a global haze in a shot. A lens hood helps reduce flare simply because it provides a shade to block the sunlight. Lens hoods range in size. Make sure you get one manufactured specifically for the lens on which you wish to use it; otherwise, the hood may show up in the frame!

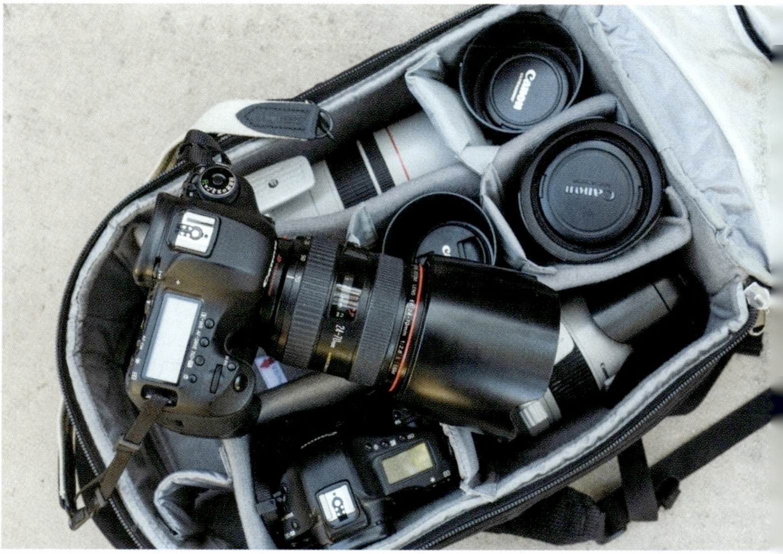

Figure 8.13
As bulky as some lens hoods are, like this one for the EF 24–70mm f/2.8L, a hood does more than just reduce the potential for flare. It is also a great shock absorber and lens guard.

Shock absorber

I use a lens hood every time I shoot mostly because it provides the lens (and camera) with a great shock absorber. A lens hood is round, protrudes from the end of the lens, has a wider circumference than the lens itself, and is made of strong plastic with a little bounce in it. I once dropped a camera and lens from the seat of an 18-wheeler truck, and because it landed first on the lens hood, the only damage was a scuff on the side of the lens hood. Don't worry if the hood gets a few scratches or dings.

Shooting in the wind

As much as I love its simple functions, the lens hood is relatively worthless in high winds, especially when you need to shoot into those winds. The hood is basically a cup at the end of your lens, and it catches direct and cross winds like a sail. Whether you are hand-holding a shot or making one from a tripod, wind blowing hard against a lens hood can vibrate and destabilize a shot. Certainly, the faster the shutter speed, the more able you are to make a focused shot, but it may not be possible.

When shooting long exposures, the effect of the wind is amplified (**Figure 8.14**). During these times, simply take the hood off. The lens may still catch a little wind but not nearly as much. A hood for L-series lenses is often big enough that you can place it around your hand and wear it as a bracelet—just in case you might lose it.

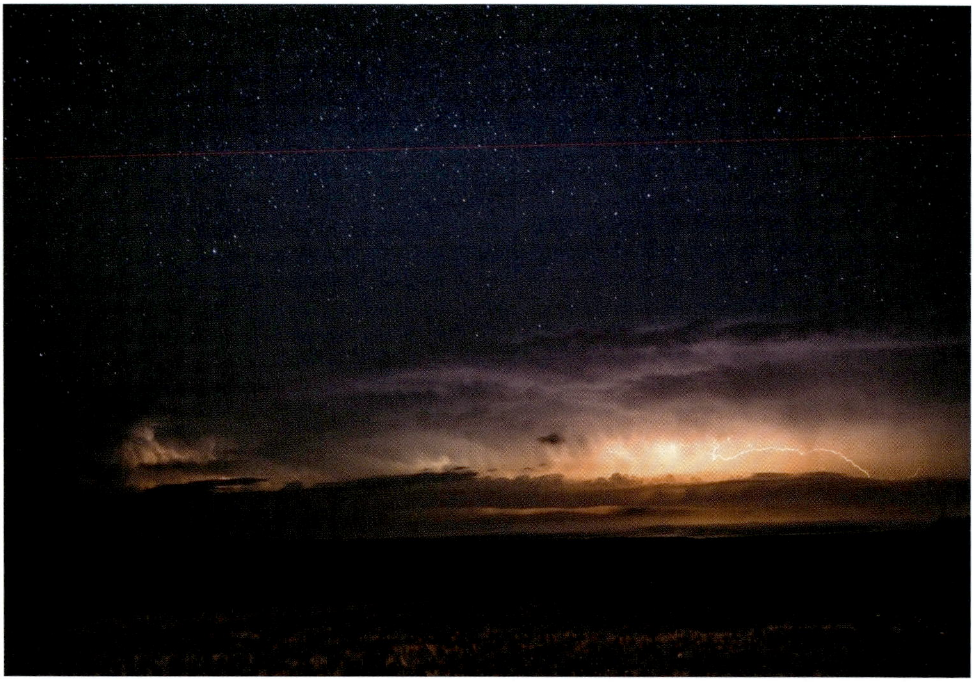

Figure 8.14
The wind was blowing so hard that the lens hood was like a small wind sail that shook the camera during the long exposure and knocked previous shots out of focus.

ISO 800 • 15 sec. • f/2.8 • 52mm

Image Stabilization

Image Stabilization (IS) is usually found on long prime lenses or zoom lenses that reach out past 100mm. However, the technology has trickled down into more standard zoom lenses as well. (You won't see too many wide-angle lenses with Image Stabilization.) As mentioned in Chapter 1, Canon's Image Stabilization can offer up to four stops of stabilization (**Figure 8.15**).

Sports and wildlife photographers, event photographers, and many others who shoot in dimly lit environments find Image Stabilization a lifesaver when using slow shutter speeds without a tripod or monopod. Landscape photographers, on the other hand, might have image-stabilized lenses but rarely engage the technology. Image Stabilization is best used when there is a threat of your body's movement causing blur in your shots. IS excels when you shoot slower than your minimum sustaining shutter speed (**Figure 8.16**).

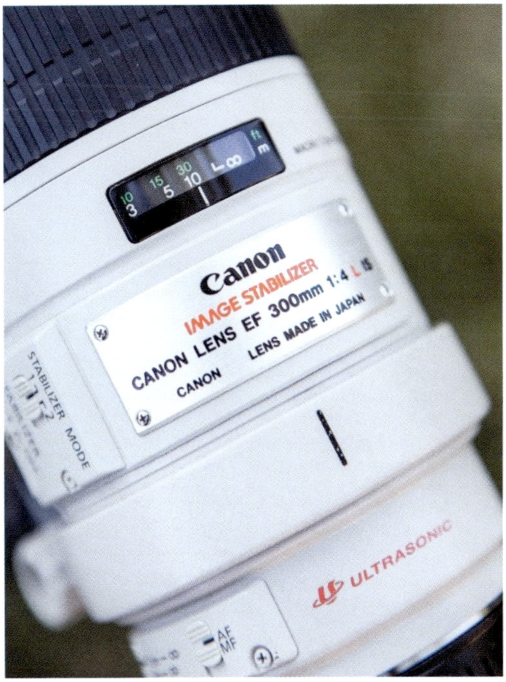

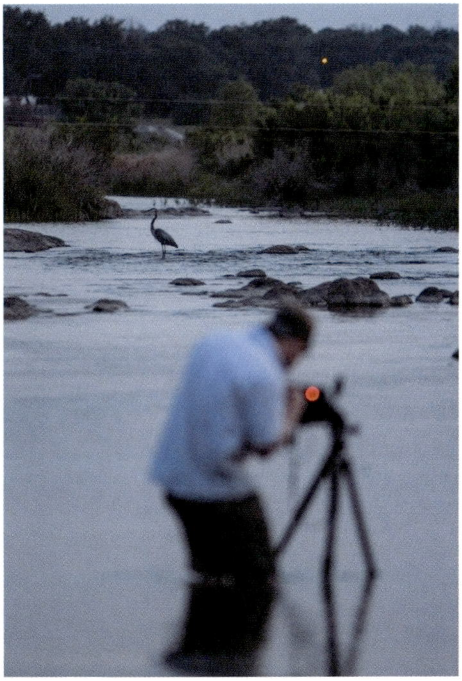

Figure 8.15 (left) Canon lenses that feature Image Stabilization offer up to four stops of motion-caused blur reduction.

Figure 8.16 (right) For this image of photographer Jacob Copple and his subject, Image Stabilization allowed me to shoot much slower than my minimum sustaining shutter speed for a 300mm lens.

ISO 1600 • 1/60 sec. • f/4 • 300mm

Image Stabilization also comes in handy when you are photographing in dark environments, with apertures closed down past maximum (**Figure 8.17**). Keep in mind, IS only helps you handhold slower shutter speeds. It has nothing to do with freezing the movement of your subject.

When shooting with fast shutter speeds for the lens you are holding, it might be best to disengage Image Stabilization (**Figure 8.18**). For example, let's say you are handholding a 300mm focal length and shooting with a shutter speed of 1/640 of a second. More than likely, this is fast enough to handhold without using Image Stabilization. If engaged, IS may shift your composition a bit, and it can even drain your battery.

Likewise, if you are shooting from a tripod, Image Stabilization can often do more damage than good. IS can slightly recompose a shot that was meticulously set up on a tripod. The optics may shift from where you originally intended the frame to be. With longer exposures on a tripod, the IS function may even cause blur based on the amount of movement it makes. The solution? Turn Image Stabilization off when you put the camera on a tripod.

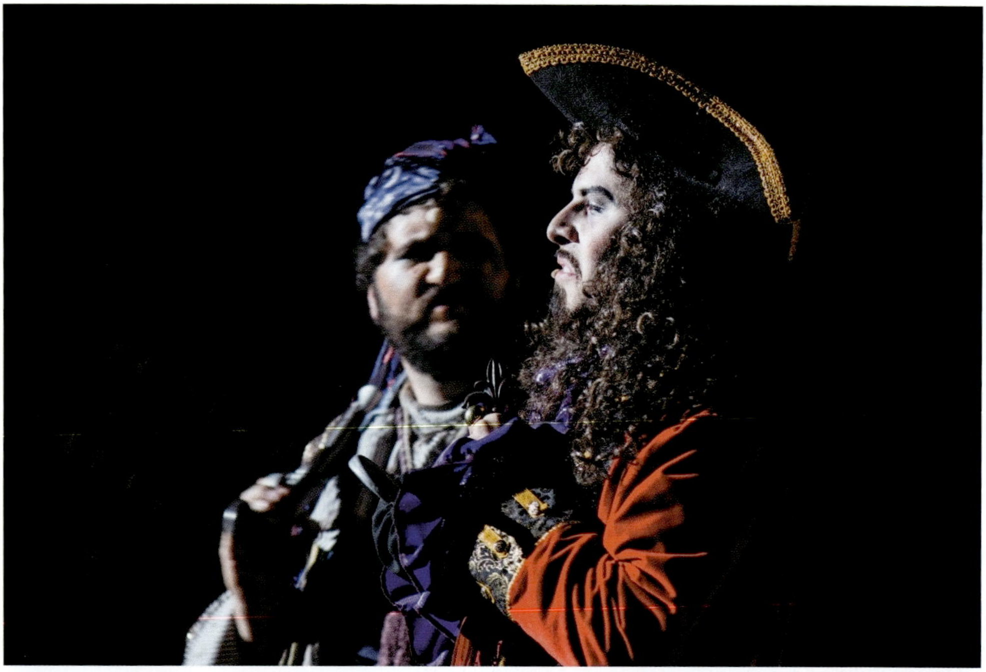

Figure 8.17
Live theatrical and music performances with dim lighting are perfect subjects for activating Image Stabilization.
ISO 3200 • 1/50 sec. • f/4 • 300mm

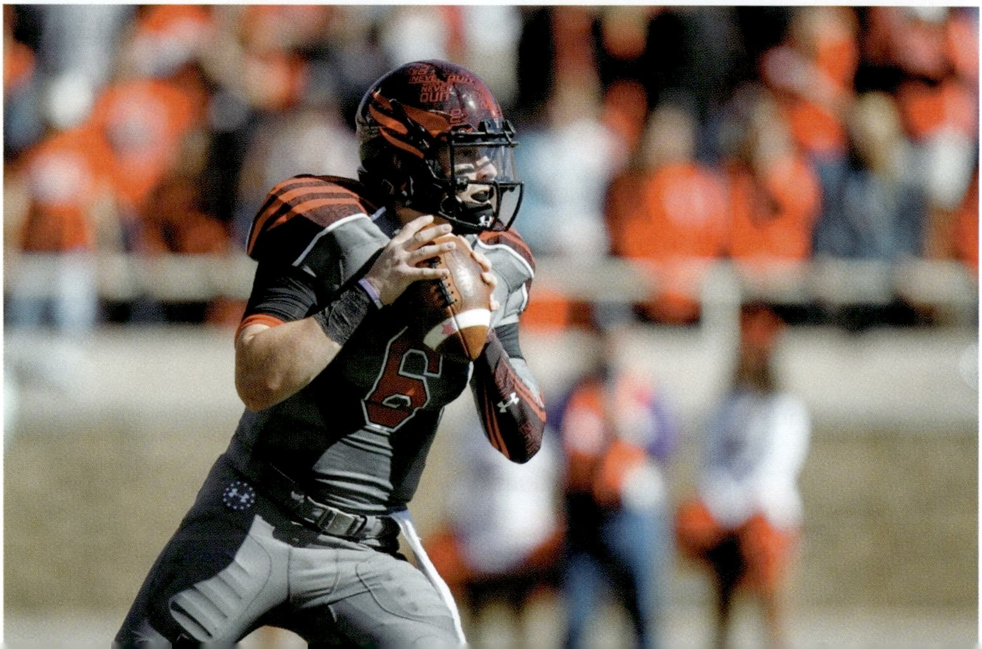

Figure 8.18
Sports events often take place in bright light, allowing shutter speeds fast enough to negate Image Stabilization. In fact, IS may shift the image's composition.
ISO 100 • 1/1600 sec. • f/2.8 • 400mm

Image Stabilization Modes

Lenses that feature Image Stabilization incorporate Canon's Optical Image Stabilizer system of reactive motion sensors, which feel the movement of a lens and attempt to counteract it to ensure a sharp photograph at slower-than-normal shutter speeds. Most lenses with the Optical Image Stabilizer system have only one standard mode of stabilization, which is adapted for shooting static (nonmoving) subject matter. This type of stabilization accounts for minute vertical and horizontal movements of the lens and is ideal for shooting in low-light situations.

Some lenses incorporate a second Optical Image Stabilizer mode (Mode 2) that is ideal for stabilizing shots of moving, or dynamic, subject matter (**Figure 8.19**). For example, when a photographer is shooting a football player running across a field, the movement is a pan from one side to the other. The first stabilizer mode mentioned above would detect this panning and activate stabilization for horizontal movement, possibly affecting the framing of the image. Mode 2 instead takes into account such movement and only stabilizes along the opposite axis—the vertical axis. So, when the lens is panned from left to right, Mode 2 stabilization accounts for shifts in vertical movement. The opposite is true if the panning movement is along the vertical axis, or up and down. Mode 2 is an ideal mode for high-action sports and wildlife photography. This is why you see Mode 2 stabilization incorporated in longer telephoto lenses and the high-end super-telephotos.

Optical Image Stabilizer Mode 3 takes Mode 2 one step further. Found in only five lenses—the most exclusive super-telephotos such as the EF200–400mm f/4L IS, the EF 400mm f/2.8L IS (second version), and longer—Mode 3 stabilization is only activated at the full press of the shutter button. Mode 1 and 2 stabilization are both activated when the shutter button is depressed halfway. In holding off activation until exposure, Mode 3 reduces the opportunity for the stabilization system to affect the composition of the image. This is truly the epitome of stabilization for sports-photography lenses, and it is one of the reasons such glass is so expensive.

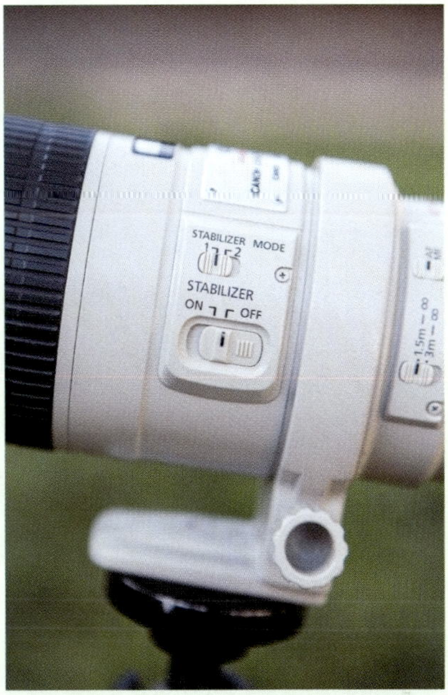

Figure 8.19 **Switching between Image Stabilizer modes (on select Canon lens models) is easy, especially while shooting.**

Two lenses, the EF 24–70mm f/4L IS and the EF 100mm f/2.8L Macro IS, incorporate what Canon calls Hybrid Image Stabilization. This stabilization mode not only counteracts camera shake, but it also compensates for any shake that moves the camera parallel to the subject. The macro lens benefits greatly from this technology since much of the human-incurred movement of the lens is done so close to the subject that the slightest shift can knock the image out of focus.

One more DSLR lens, the EF-S 18–135 f/3.5–5.6 IS STM, features Dynamic Image Stabilization. Dynamic IS is ideally suited for mitigating shifts while shooting video. In the past, photographers shooting video were encouraged to turn off Image Stabilization. However, Dynamic IS is like having your own little Steadicam. Look for this technology to move into other lenses in the future.

Tripods

The tripod—every photographer's best friend and worst enemy. Best friend because there's no better way to stabilize a camera and lens for a wide range of photographs. Worst enemy because it is such a pain in the posterior to carry around. Undoubtedly, the tripod is a worthy tool. There are a couple of lens-related considerations to keep in mind when shopping for and using tripods.

Construction

Whenever I'm asked for tripod suggestions, I always give the same advice: Look for sturdy legs and a sturdy head. Unfortunately, there are a lot of bad tripods out there. For example, the drugstore variety of tripods—made of lower-grade aluminum with a plastic head and mount that is moved up and down with a small plastic crank—are inexpensive for a reason. They are not sturdy platforms, and I have seen more than one break in a river and float downstream.

Tripods should not be an afterthought. By shopping around and spending just a few more dollars, a photographer can get an extremely stable tripod that will last. There are a number of tripod brands. I recommend Manfrotto for aluminum and Gitzo for carbon fiber, but you should compare different models. A nice set of aluminum legs and a strong head can cost as little as US$200. Aluminum is heavier than carbon fiber but less expensive (although carbon fiber is coming down in price).

I also advise shopping for legs and heads separately (but looking at the combos or kits in case there is one that contains the legs and head you want). This forces you to analyze the legs separately from the head, making sure both will hold up to the weight of heavy lenses.

There are two ways to mount your camera or lens onto a tripod: by screwing the gear directly onto a ball head—my preference (**Figures 8.20** and **8.21**)—or using some version of a quick-release (QR) plate that is first attached to the camera or lens and then attached or detached from the tripod head (**Figures 8.22**, **8.23**, and **8.24**). Regardless of which type of mount you use, make sure it is metal. Plastic mounts are flimsy and break easily. This is especially true of plastic quick-release plates that mount into plastic heads. Metal mounts can stand under pressure as you tighten your gear to them, resulting in a much more stable platform for heavier lenses.

The mounts that allow you to screw the head directly into the camera or lens are arguably the sturdiest. Although it takes longer to mount the camera and lens to the tripod, once it is there, it is essentially a part of the entire platform. Landscape photographers value this type of mount since they are on a tripod a large percentage of the time. I appreciate the efficiency of the quick-release plate—and often use one with one of my tripods—but the QR mount tends to wobble more than a direct mount to a ball head after some use.

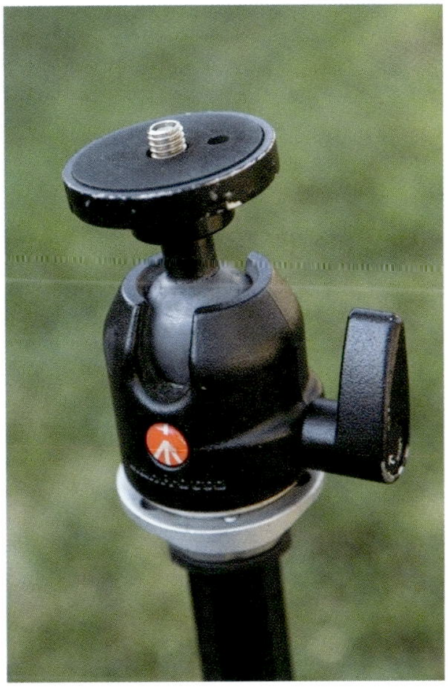

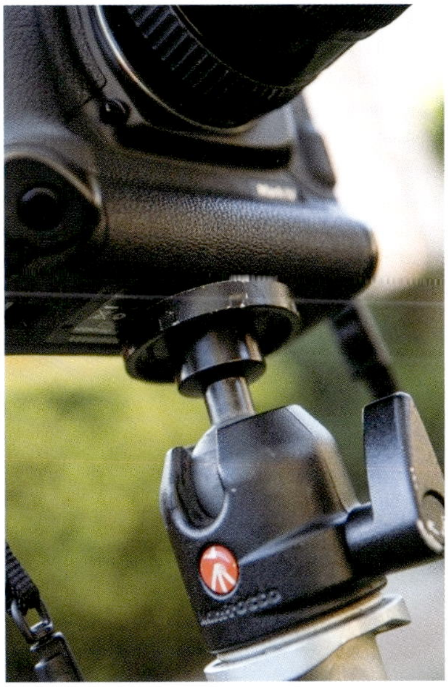

Figure 8.20 (left) A Manfrotto 486 Compact Ball Head is a simple but sturdy head, known for its ease of use and reliability.

Figure 8.21 (right) Traditional ball heads screw right into the bottom of the camera or lens tripod collar, making for a secure, albeit somewhat inefficient platform on which to mount your gear.

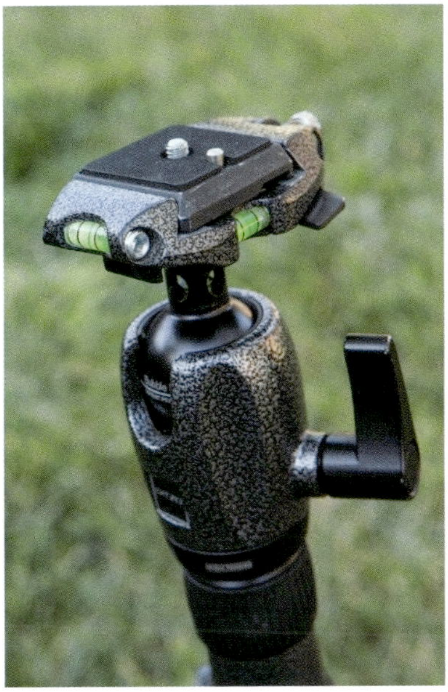

Figure 8.22 A quick-release (QR) tripod head, like this Gitzo Traveler version, is a popular style of head for photographers who need to work quickly.

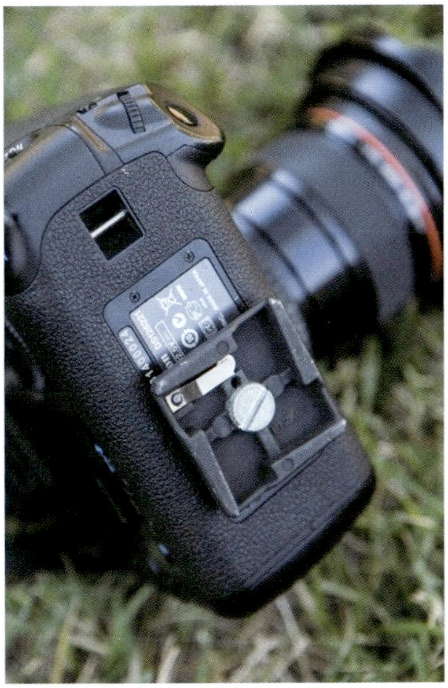

Figure 8.23 The QR plate screws into the tripod mount on any camera or lens collar.

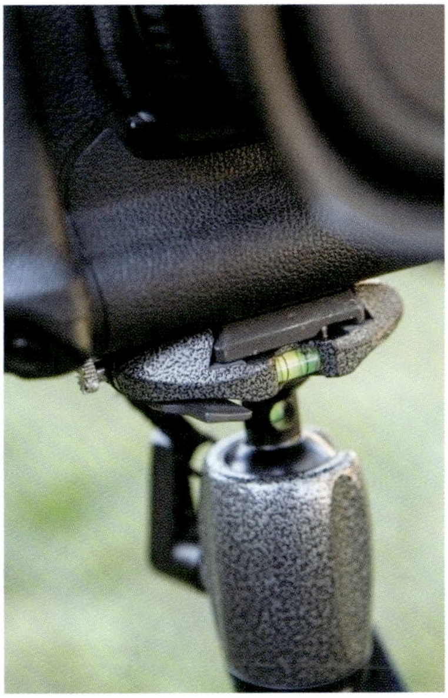

Figure 8.24 Make sure to test the sturdiness of the QR plate's connection to the head on any tripod for which you are shopping. QR plates have a habit of becoming loose over time.

The longer-lens shake

To reiterate a point from Chapter 5, the longer the lens (physical length), the less stable it is on a tripod. When using a telephoto lens, it is best if you mount it by its own tripod collar as opposed to mounting the camera to the tripod. Most L-series telephoto lenses come with a tripod mount collar that can be used just like the mount on the bottom of the camera body (**Figure 8.25**). This results in a more balanced distribution of weight on the tripod.

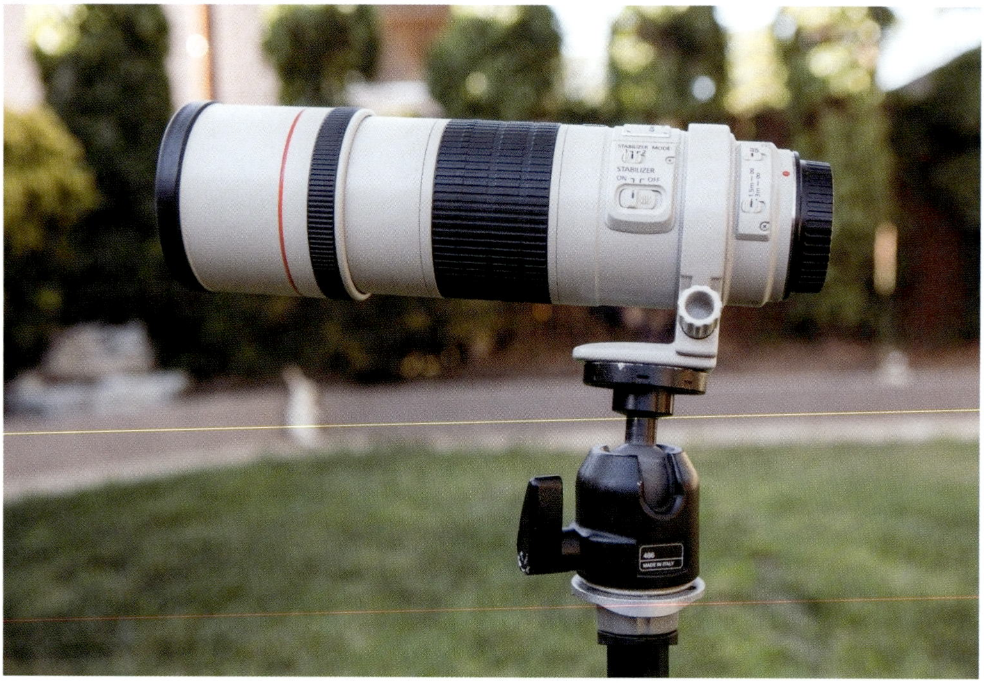

Figure 8.25
If your heavy telephoto lens includes a tripod collar, use it to secure the lens to the tripod. Don't leave the weight of the lens hanging off the camera's much-weaker lens mount.

A tripod mount collar also helps prevent the bounce that may occur when you mount a camera body attached to a long lens at the camera. The uneven, out-front weight of such a combo makes the head and camera body flex up and down, potentially bouncing a shot out of focus. Lenses that are not manufactured to mount with a collar, like the EF 70–300mm f/4–5.6 IS, are not considered heavy enough to create such a drastic bounce or flex of the camera and tripod head. However, I have seen these relatively lightweight lenses become more unstable on cheap, drugstore-variety tripods—one more reason to consider a heavier set of legs and head.

For extremely long and heavy lenses—such as the EF 400mm f/2.8L IS, the EF 500mm f/4L IS, and longer—special gimbal heads are often necessary to take on the extreme weight as well as offer superior stabilization and mobilization (**Figure 8.26**). Wildlife and bird photographers are attracted to these types of heads for their fluid motion, ease of use with heavier lenses, and quality construction. Some tripod and gimbal head setups do come at a price (they can cost into the thousands), but if you can afford to purchase a US$10,000+ lens, you will want to place it on the best platform possible.

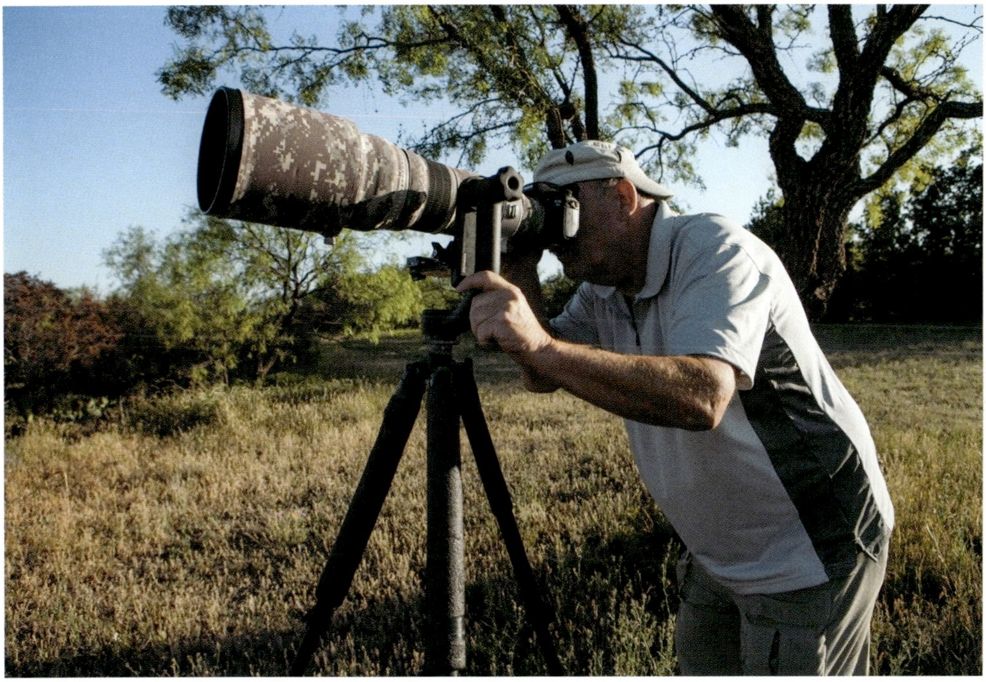

Figure 8.26
Gimbal heads are able to support and efficiently move a very heavy, tripod-mounted telephoto lens, and they are popular with many wildlife photographers.

Going Solar

Who says not to include the sun in your shots? Well, me, for the most part. However, there are a few creative ways of making such a bright, overbearing light source work inside your frame.

Flare

Lens flare comes in two basic varieties: visible artifacts and haze. Flare is caused by pushing a lens's ability to focus light through its various lens elements. Many photographers are reluctant to include flare—especially artifacts—in their shots because of the potential negative impact on an image (**Figure 8.27**). Over the years, flare has become a bit cliché as well. However, sometimes it does have its purpose.

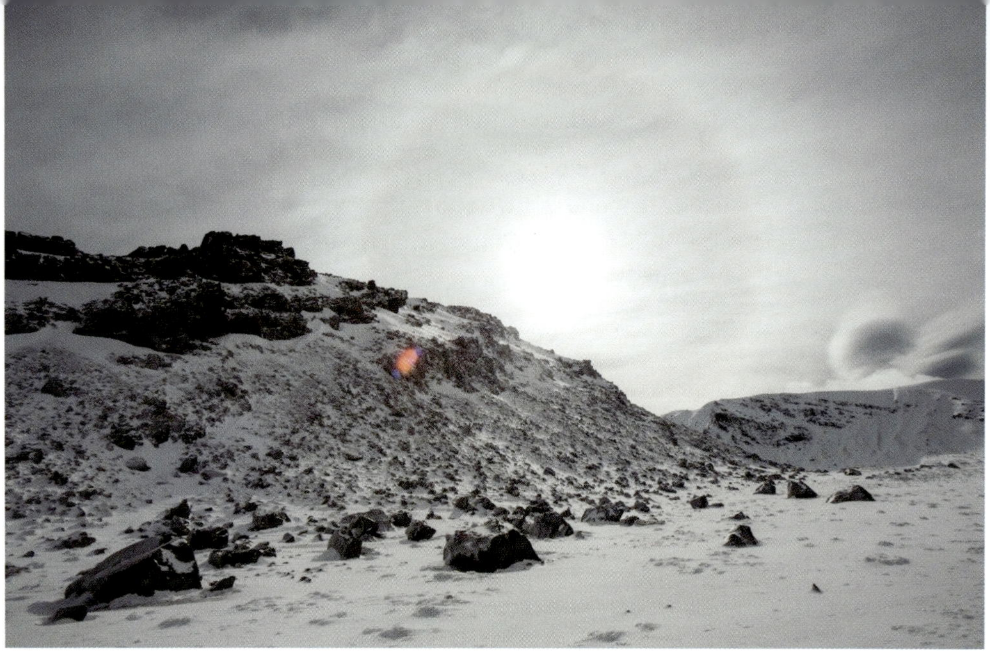

Figure 8.27
While attempting to capture a solar ring on an alpine hike in Tongariro National Park, New Zealand, I included a colorful yet annoying flare as a result of shooting directly into a cloud-covered sun.

ISO 200 • 1/400 sec. • f/22 • 17mm

Artifact flare can be used to stress extreme personality in a shot, as well as direct the eye to, or away from, something significant. Flare is sometimes used in sports shots and those expressing a characteristic of an environment, such as an oppressive desert climate or barren snowscape (**Figure 8.28**).

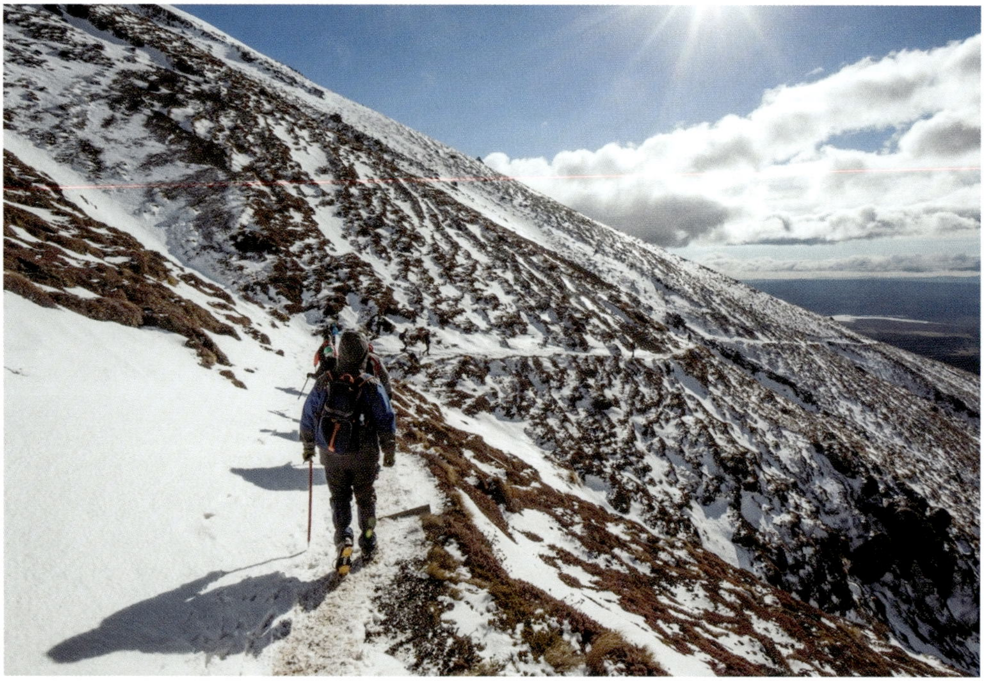

Figure 8.28
The flare in this shot, more of a starburst, coincides with the adventurous spirit of the hikers.

ISO 100 • 1/250 sec. • f/16 • 17mm

A haze effect is essentially one large flare artifact that covers an entire frame. A haze flare can often be an advantage, warming up an otherwise cool scene, and it is useful in toning a compressed, layered scene. Using flares is an aesthetic choice, but in my opinion, they work well in landscape photography (**Figure 8.29**). I have also seen them put to good use in portraiture (**Figure 8.30**).

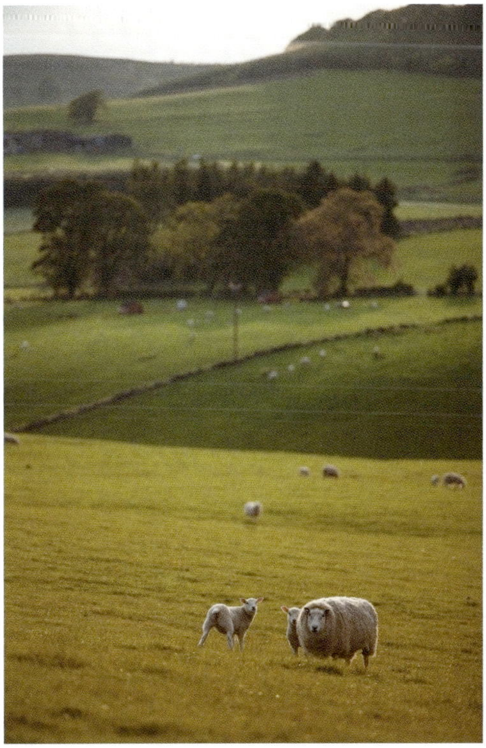

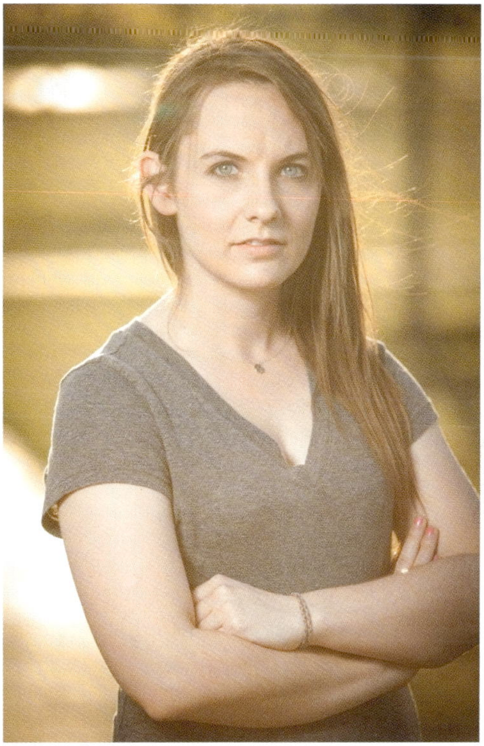

Figure 8.29 (left)
The subtle warmth of this Scottish countryside is due greatly in part to the late-evening flare covering the lens's entire angle of view.

ISO 100 • 1/400 sec. • f/2.8 • 175mm

Figure 8.30 (right)
Although the subject is artificially lit, the warm haze that provides ambience to the shot is actually an encompassing flare caught late in the evening.

ISO 50 • 1/200 sec. • f/2.8 • 140mm

Starburst technique

There are starburst (or star, for short) filters that make every specular light in a frame shine like a star, but you can also create a starburst with the sun, a subject, and a lens (**Figure 8.31**).

The process is fairly simple. Find a subject and composition in which you would like to have a starburst accent the scene. The sun must be in the shot, so you will likely be shooting directly into it. The catch is to block much of the sun with the subject matter, such as a tree. Place the sun where branches meet the trunk of the tree or where they branch out even more, among the canopy. Let a bit of sun shine through to the lens right at the point where a branch meets another part of the tree at an angle.

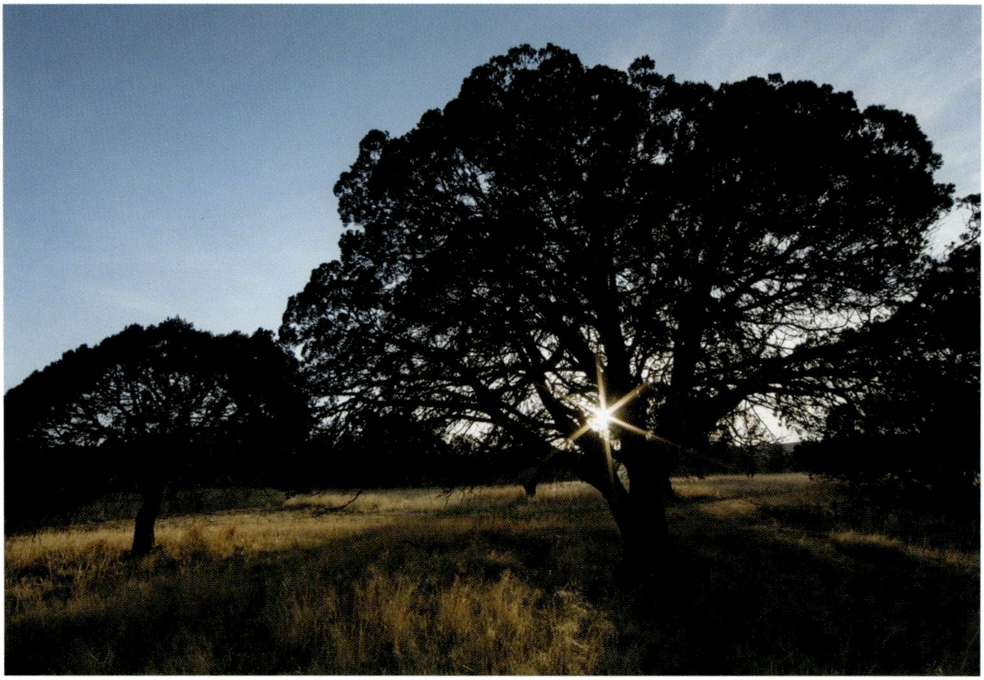

Figure 8.31
With a stopped-down aperture and subject matter obstructing the sun, a pristine starburst is but a shutter-click away.

ISO 200 • 1/100 sec. • f/18 • 14mm

This is where the lens comes into play. Set your aperture to f/8 or higher. This will help focus the sunlight and shape it into what looks like a multipoint starburst. The more closed down the aperture, the more focused the starburst; if the aperture is set wide open, the burst may be indistinguishable. It might take you a few shots to get it the way you want. Be careful not to employ this technique too much if you are shooting editorial work, for risk of being repetitious.

Shooting at Night

At night, light is a major consideration, especially how the light from sources not "on" during the day, such as stars, will look in your frame. You will need to expose for longer periods of time and/or turn up the ISO to capture light more quickly.

One important tip for using lenses at night: Get the shot set up before the light is gone. For example, you might have a great night shot set up among the stars with a bit of the horizon in it and some structure on the ground that you want the small amount of light to expose while the shutter is open. If it gets too dark before you set up, focusing where you want will be very difficult, given that focus works by detecting contrast in light values. If the focus sensor cannot detect an edge of a subject or the horizon, it makes an educated guess.

The following are a couple more tips for when you're working the lens at night. Note that these have more to do with long exposures than anything else, and some of these issues have already been covered.

Which aperture?

Light at night is obviously dim compared to light during the day. Therefore, it is typical to leave the aperture more open than closed when shooting at night, especially if the night sky is your subject.

Stars are extremely dim to the camera's sensor, simply because they are so far away. They may be very powerful, but the distance knocks their intensity out. I start my night sky exposures using an aperture of f/4 or f/5.6. This is particularly fitting for when I want to do extremely long exposures of over 5 minutes (**Figure 8.32**). At an ISO of 100, f/5.6 is open enough to let in a nice amount of starlight but closed down enough that over a long exposure the stars do not burn too long in one spot. However, it is worth knowing that the more closed down the aperture, the dimmer the overall exposure will be, especially the star trails.

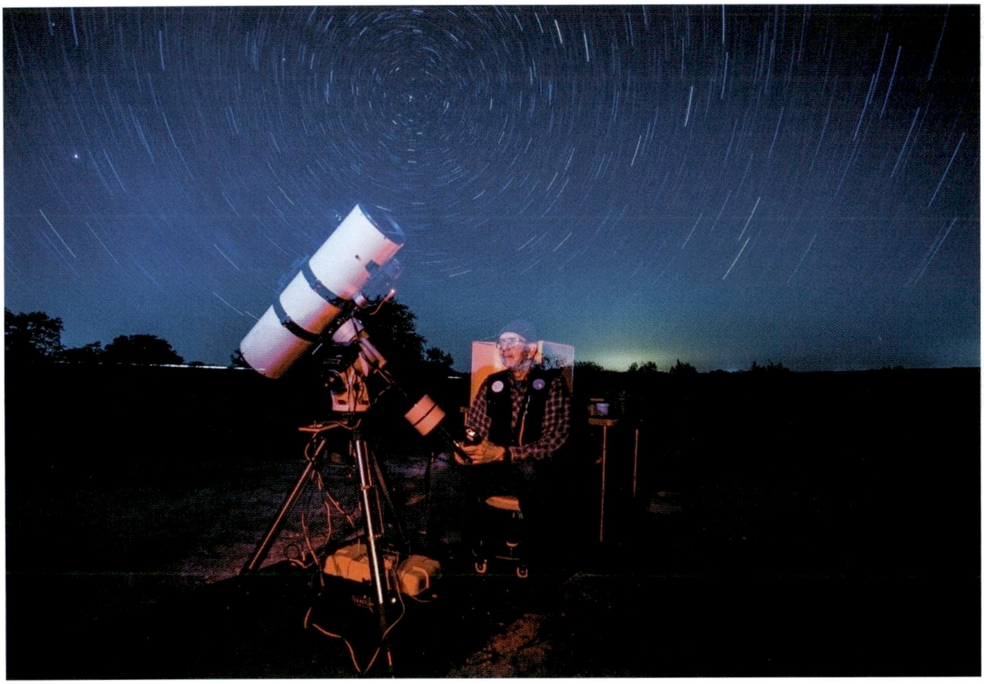

Figure 8.32
Star trails are usually accomplished with a low ISO, a very long exposure (in excess of 5 minutes for long trails), and an aperture that is not completely wide open. Don't forget a tripod!

ISO 100 • 31 min. • f/4 • 17mm

If you want to go for those shots that expose the stars exactly where they are in the sky, instead of star trails, open up your aperture all the way, crank your ISO up, and shoot for around 30 seconds. I really enjoy lenses that open up to f/2.8 for this application, but f/3.5 is great as well. The key is to let in as much light as possible during that 30 seconds and burn the stars on the sensor before the earth rotates enough for trails to be created. That's why the ISO is cranked high and the aperture wide open (**Figure 8.33**). Keep in mind that if there is any light near the horizon on which you are pointing, like the residue of a sunset or a city off in the distance, it will register more quickly using this technique.

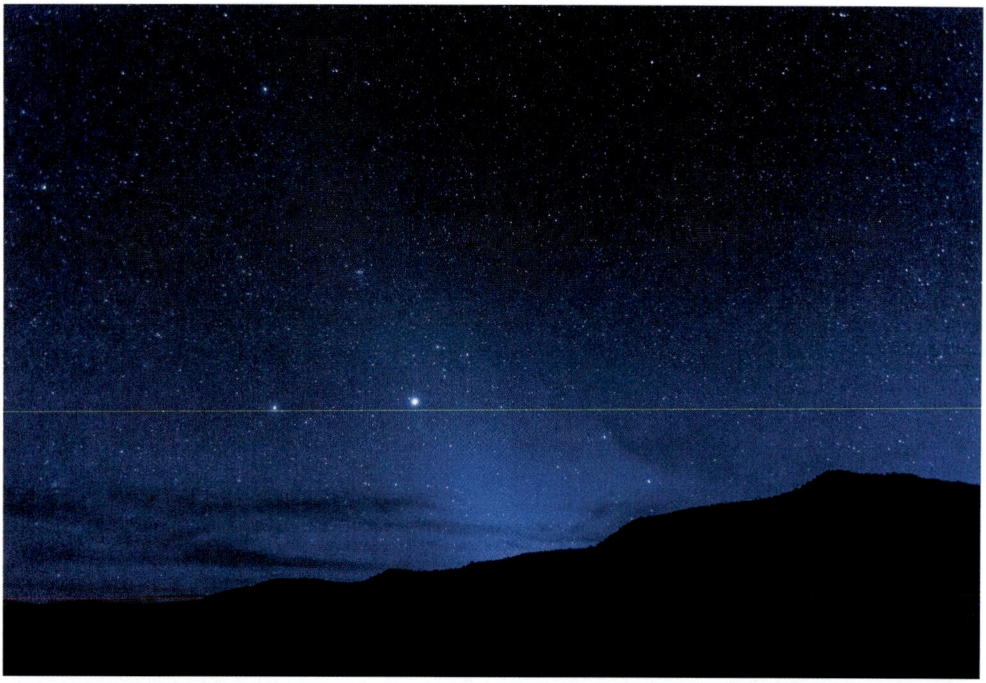

Figure 8.33
Capture the abundant night sky with a high ISO and an open aperture. Make sure to get out of town into dark-sky country, and set up before the sun goes down to avoid fumbling around for composition in the dark.

ISO 1600 • 20 sec. • f/4 • 14mm

Distortion and the night sky

If you're like me, you enjoy those wide-angle, expansive shots of the night sky. When just shooting the stars as they stand with high ISO and wide-open aperture, the distortion the lens creates is rarely recognizable, aside from any subject matter you might have composed in the foreground, such as a mountain or tower.

However, something very interesting happens when you point a wide-angle lens high into the night sky and shoot a long exposure (something long enough to render star trails, like 5 to 10 minutes). This setup may result in trails that arc like a rainbow and *another* set of trails that arc in a reverse rainbow above the aforementioned trails (**Figure 8.34**). This usually occurs with ultra-wide-angle focal lengths, such as 14mm. The double arc of trails is the result of the extreme curvature of the lens, where one set of trails curves away from the midpoint toward the horizon and one curves the other way. If the second arc of trails bothers you, angle the lens farther down toward the horizon, reducing the presence of this second arc.

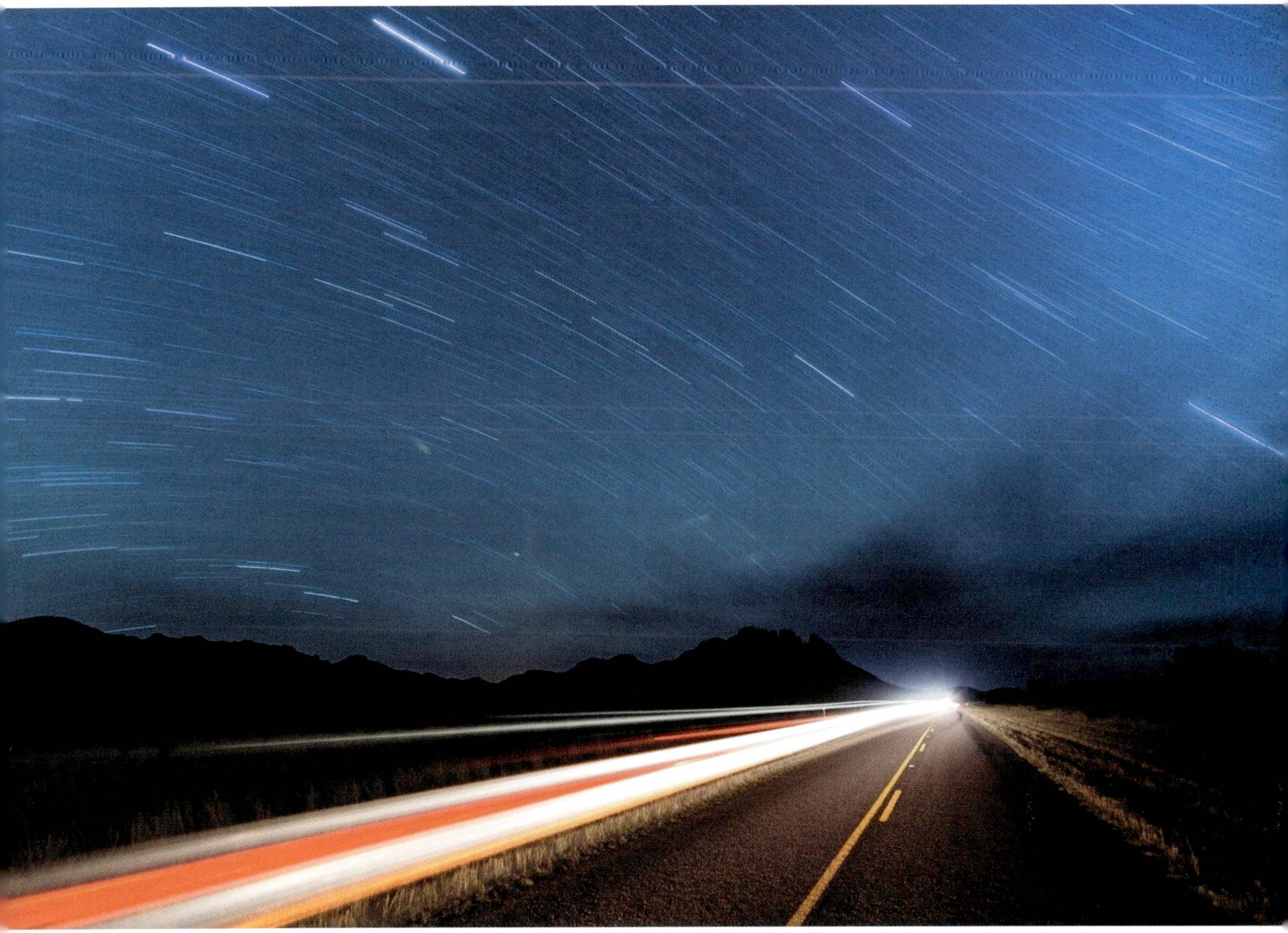

Figure 8.34 **With an ultra-wide-angle lens pointed far enough up on a night sky, a long exposure will produce two arcs of star trails.**

ISO 100 • 28.5 min. • f/4 • 14mm

Pay Attention to Those Before You

It is important to keep our eyes and ears open to practices that will help us create better images and make sure our gear lasts for the long haul (like my tip from Alan Hess about how to carry your camera and lens when they're slung across your shoulder). A great deal of information exists on the Internet in regard to maintaining and operating your equipment, but I advise you to also find someone local who has been shooting for some time (maybe a professional, maybe an experienced amateur or teacher) and form a relationship. Not only will you be creating community around your craft and passion, but you will also be gaining a resource for questions you have along the way.

Be open to discussion about some of the issues posed in this book. Everyone operates a bit differently, and you never know what you are going to learn. I know a wildlife photographer who adds ankle weights to lighter-weight telephoto lenses to stabilize them when he is handholding a shot. I never would have thought of that, but it makes sense. Through a relationship with an experienced photographer, you will always be able to glean best practices that might help you in your own image making.

Chapter 8 Assignments

Taking care of your lenses is essential. So is using them in ways that make for the best photographs. The first assignment highlights the importance of keeping your gear clean and operable. The second is a useful but often intimidating technique to perform when shooting with any lens.

Treat your lenses with care

Assess how you handle your lenses (and all of your gear, for that matter). Is it with care, or are you lax about wear and tear? Do you have the standard accessories for keeping your gear clean? This is a good time to take inventory. If you do not already own them, acquire a lens microfiber cloth, a reputable lens-cleaning solution, and an air blower (not compressed air).

Learn how to use them all. Ask your local camera-store representative to show you how to use each of the items, or lean on online resources, like B&H Photo, for proper care of your glass. Institute a regularly scheduled cleaning (either after every shoot or once a week if the shooting has been light or in clean environments).

Create a starburst

Making starbursts is fun, creative, and easy to accomplish. If you have never performed this technique, start on something small, like a backyard tree. Wait until late evening (or get up early) when the sun is closer to the horizon. Position the tree between you and the sun, and focus on its branches. Put the entire tree in the frame, or select a portion of its branches for your composition. Expose for the sky behind the tree, forcing you to silhouette the tree. Stop your aperture down to somewhere around f/11 or f/16.

The tricky part is placing the sun slightly behind a branch and slightly exposed to the lens. Use your Depth of Field Preview button to stop down your aperture while looking through the viewfinder, and as you position the sun behind parts of the tree, you should be able to see it burst as a star in your frame. Where it bursts is where you want it positioned. Typically, the more you stop down your aperture, the more focused the star becomes. Practice this at home, and then use walls of buildings in cities, water towers, mountains, even flowers! I can't say starburst shots are in high demand, but they are certainly fun to make.

Share your results with the book's Flickr group!
Join the group here: www.flickr.com/groups/canonlenses_fromsnapshotstogreatshots

Index

D

E

U

V

W

Z